Lecture Notes in Computer Science

Lecture Notes in Artificial Intelligence 16202

Founding Editor

Jörg Siekmann

Series Editors

Randy Goebel, *University of Alberta, Edmonton, Canada*
Wolfgang Wahlster, *DFKI, Berlin, Germany*
Zhi-Hua Zhou, *Nanjing University, Nanjing, China*

The series Lecture Notes in Artificial Intelligence (LNAI) was established in 1988 as a topical subseries of LNCS devoted to artificial intelligence.

The series publishes state-of-the-art research results at a high level. As with the LNCS mother series, the mission of the series is to serve the international R & D community by providing an invaluable service, mainly focused on the publication of conference and workshop proceedings and postproceedings.

Emilio Corchado · Héctor Quintián ·
Alicia Troncoso Lora · Hilde Pérez García ·
Esteban Jove Pérez · José Luis Calvo Rolle ·
Francisco Javier Martínez de Pisón ·
Pablo García Bringas ·
Francisco Martínez Álvarez · Álvaro Herrero ·
Paolo Fosci · Ramos Sérgio Filipe
Editors

Hybrid Artificial Intelligent Systems

20th International Conference, HAIS 2025
Salamanca, Spain, October 16–17, 2025
Proceedings, Part I

Editors
Emilio Corchado
University of Salamanca
Salamanca, Spain

Alicia Troncoso Lora
Pablo de Olavide University
Seville, Spain

Esteban Jove Pérez
University of A Coruña
Ferrol, La Coruña, Spain

Francisco Javier Martínez de Pisón
University of La Rioja
Logroño, Spain

Francisco Martínez Álvarez
Pablo de Olavide University
Seville, Spain

Paolo Fosci
University Of Bergamo
Dalmine, Italy

Héctor Quintián
University of A Coruña
Ferrol, La Coruña, Spain

Hilde Pérez García
University of León
León, Spain

José Luis Calvo Rolle
University of A Coruña
Ferrol, La Coruña, Spain

Pablo García Bringas
University of Deusto
Bilbao, Spain

Álvaro Herrero
University of Burgos
Burgos, Spain

Ramos Sérgio Filipe
School of Engineering at the Polytechnic
Institute of Porto
Porto, Portugal

ISSN 0302-9743　　　　　　　ISSN 1611-3349　(electronic)
Lecture Notes in Artificial Intelligence
ISBN 978-3-032-08464-4　　　ISBN 978-3-032-08465-1　(eBook)
https://doi.org/10.1007/978-3-032-08465-1

LNCS Sublibrary: SL7 – Artificial Intelligence

© The Editor(s) (if applicable) and The Author(s), under exclusive license
to Springer Nature Switzerland AG 2026

This work is subject to copyright. All rights are solely and exclusively licensed by the Publisher, whether the whole or part of the material is concerned, specifically the rights of translation, reprinting, reuse of illustrations, recitation, broadcasting, reproduction on microfilms or in any other physical way, and transmission or information storage and retrieval, electronic adaptation, computer software, or by similar or dissimilar methodology now known or hereafter developed.
The use of general descriptive names, registered names, trademarks, service marks, etc. in this publication does not imply, even in the absence of a specific statement, that such names are exempt from the relevant protective laws and regulations and therefore free for general use.
The publisher, the authors and the editors are safe to assume that the advice and information in this book are believed to be true and accurate at the date of publication. Neither the publisher nor the authors or the editors give a warranty, expressed or implied, with respect to the material contained herein or for any errors or omissions that may have been made. The publisher remains neutral with regard to jurisdictional claims in published maps and institutional affiliations.

This Springer imprint is published by the registered company Springer Nature Switzerland AG
The registered company address is: Gewerbestrasse 11, 6330 Cham, Switzerland

If disposing of this product, please recycle the paper.

Preface

These two volumes of *Lecture Notes in Artificial Intelligence (LNAI)* include accepted papers presented at the *20th International Conference on Hybrid Artificial Intelligence Systems (HAIS 2025)*, held in the beautiful city of Salamanca, Spain, in October 2025.

HAIS has become a unique, established, and broad interdisciplinary forum for researchers and practitioners who are involved in developing and applying symbolic and sub-symbolic techniques aimed at the construction of highly robust and reliable problem-solving techniques and bringing the most relevant achievements in this field.

The hybridisation of intelligent techniques, originating from various computational intelligence areas, has gained popularity due to the growing awareness that such combinations often outperform individual techniques, such as neurocomputing, fuzzy systems, rough sets, evolutionary algorithms, agents, and multi-agent systems, among others.

Practical experience has indicated that hybrid intelligence techniques might help solve some challenging real-world problems. In a hybrid intelligence system, a synergistic combination of multiple techniques is used to build an efficient solution to deal with a particular problem. This is, thus, the setting of the HAIS conference series, and its increasing success is proof of the vitality of this exciting field.

From 120 submissions, the HAIS 2025 International Program Committee selected 53 papers, which are published in these conference proceedings after a single-blind reviewing process with an average of three reviews per submission, yielding an acceptance ratio of about 44%.

The selection of papers was extremely rigorous to maintain the high quality of the conference, and we would like to thank the Program Committee for their hard work in the reviewing process. This process is very important in creating a conference of a high standard, and the HAIS conference would not exist without their help.

The large number of submissions is certainly not only a testimony to the vitality and attractiveness of the field but also an indicator of the interest in the HAIS conference itself.

HAIS 2025 enjoyed outstanding keynote speeches by distinguished guest speakers: Prof. Ajith Abraham at Bennett University (India) and Prof. Sung-Bae Cho at Yonsei University (South Korea).

HAIS 2025 has teamed up with "Neurocomputing" (Elsevier) and "Logic Journal of the IGPL" (Oxford University Press) for a suite of special issues, including selected papers from HAIS 2025.

Particular thanks go as well to the conference's main sponsors, Startup Olé, the CIBER-OLÉ project (within the National Cybersecurity Industry Promotion Program, framed within the INCIBE Emprende program and financed by INCIBE and the University of Salamanca-USAL), the BISITE research group at the University of Salamanca, the CTC research group at the University of A Coruña, and the University of Salamanca. They jointly contributed actively and constructively to the success of this initiative.

This activity was carried out in execution of the Strategic Project "Critical infrastructures cybersecure through intelligent modelling of attacks, vulnerabilities and increased security of their IoT devices for the water supply sector" (C061_/23), the result of a collaboration agreement signed between the National Institute of Cybersecurity (INCIBE) and the University of A Coruña. This initiative was carried out within the framework of the funds of the Recovery, Transformation and Resilience Plan, financed by the European Union (Next Generation), a project of the Government of Spain that outlines the roadmap for the modernization of the Spanish economy, the recovery of economic growth and job creation, for solid, inclusive and resilient economic reconstruction after the COVID-19 crisis, and to respond to the challenges of the next decade. This activity was also promoted by PID2022-137152NB-I00 funded by MICIU/AEI/10.13039/501100011033 and by ERDF/EU. We want to thank all the contributing authors, members of the Program Committee, and the Local Organising Committee for their hard and highly valuable work. Their work has helped contribute to the success of the HAIS 2025 event.

We thank the staff of Springer for their help and collaboration during this demanding publication project.

October 2025

Emilio Corchado
Héctor Quintián
Alicia Troncoso Lora
Hilde Pérez García
Esteban Jove Pérez
José Luis Calvo Rolle
Francisco Javier Martínez de Pisón
Pablo García Bringas
Francisco Martínez Álvarez
Álvaro Herrero
Paolo Fosci
Ramos Sérgio Filipe

Organization

General Chair

Emilio Corchado University of Salamanca, Spain

International Advisory Committee

Ajith Abraham Sai University, India
Antonio Bahamonde University of Oviedo, Spain
Andre de Carvalho University of São Paulo, Brazil
Sung-Bae Cho Yonsei University, South Korea
Juan M. Corchado University of Salamanca, Spain
José R. Dorronsoro Autonomous University of Madrid, Spain
Michael Gabbay King's College London, UK
Ali A. Ghorbani University of New Brunswick, Canada
Mark A. Girolami University of Glasgow, UK
Manuel Graña University of the Basque Country, Spain
Petro Gopych Universal Power Systems USA-Ukraine LLC, Ukraine
Jon G. Hall Open University, UK
Francisco Herrera University of Granada, Spain
César Hervás-Martínez University of Córdoba, Spain
Tom Heskes Radboud University Nijmegen, Holland
Dusan Husek Academy of Sciences of the Czech Republic, Czech Republic
Lakhmi Jain University of South Australia, Australia
Samuel Kaski Helsinki University of Technology, Finland
Daniel A. Keim University of Konstanz, Germany
Marios Polycarpou University of Cyprus, Cyprus
Witold Pedrycz University of Alberta, Canada
Xin Yao University of Birmingham, UK
Hujun Yin University of Manchester, UK
Michał Woźniak Wrocław University of Technology, Poland
Aditya Ghose University of Wollongong, Australia
Ashraf Saad Georgia Southern University – Armstrong Campus, USA

Fanny Klett	German Workforce Advanced Distributed Learning Partnership Laboratory, Germany
Paulo Novais	Universidade do Minho, Portugal
Rajkumar Roy	EPSRC Centre for Innovative Manufacturing in Through-Life Engineering Services, UK
Amy Neustein	Linguistic Technology Systems, USA
Jaydip Sen	Tata Consultancy Services Ltd., India

Program Committee Chairs

Emilio Corchado	University of Salamanca, Spain
Héctor Quintián	University of A Coruña, Spain
Alicia Troncoso Lora	Pablo de Olavide University, Spain
Hilde Pérez García	University of León, Spain
Esteban Jove	University of A Coruña, Spain
José Luis Calvo Rolle	University of A Coruña, Spain
Francisco Javier Martínez de Pisón	University of La Rioja, Spain
Pablo García Bringas	University of Deusto, Spain
Francisco Martínez Álvarez	Pablo de Olavide University, Spain
Álvaro Herrero Cosío	University of Burgos, Spain
Paolo Fosci	University of Bergamo, Italy
Sérgio Filipe Ramos	Polytechnic Institute of Porto, Portugal

Program Committee

Adrian Petrovan	Technical University of Cluj-Napoca, Romania
Agustín García Fischer	University of A Coruña, Spain
Alfredo Cuzzocrea	University of Calabria, Italy
Álvaro Michelena	University of A Coruña, Spain
Alejandro Vidal Bralo	University of A Coruña, Spain
Anca Andreica	Babeş-Bolyai University, Romania
Ángel Arroyo	University of Burgos, Spain
Antonio Díaz-Longueira	University of A Coruña, Spain
Antonio Jesús Díaz Honrubia	Polytechnic University of Madrid, Spain
Arkadiusz Kowalski	Wrocław University of Technology, Poland
Carlos Pereira	ISEC, Portugal
Cleber Zanchetti	Federal University of Pernambuco, Brazil
Damian Krenczyk	Silesian University of Technology, Poland
Darius Galis	West University of Timisoara, Romania
David Iclanzan	Sapientia University, Romania

Diego Granados Lopez	University of Burgos, Spain
Diego P. Ruiz	University of Granada, Spain
Dragan Simic	University of Novi Sad, Serbia
Eiji Uchino	Yamaguchi University, Japan
Eneko Osaba	TECNALIA Research & Innovation, Spain
Enol García González	University of Oviedo, Spain
Enrique De La Cal Marín	University of Oviedo, Spain
Enrique Onieva	University of Deusto, Spain
Esteban Jove	University of A Coruña, Spain
Federico Divina	Pablo de Olavide University, Spain
Fermin Segovia	University of Granada, Spain
Fernando Martins	University of Oviedo, Spain
Francisco Javier Martínez de Pisón Ascacíbar	University of La Rioja, Spain
Francisco Martínez-Álvarez	Universidad Pablo de Olavide, Spain
Francisco Zayas-Gato	University of A Coruña, Spain
Georgios Dounias	University of the Aegean, Greece
Giorgio Fumera	University of Cagliari, Italy
Giuseppe Psaila	University of Bergamo, Italy
Gloria Cerasela Crisan	"Vasile Alecsandri" University of Bacău, Romania
Héctor Quintián	University of A Coruña, Spain
Hugo Sanjurjo-González	University of Deusto, Spain
Ignacio Turias	University of Cádiz, Spain
Iker Pastor-López	University of Deusto, Spain
Javier De Lope	Polytechnic University of Madrid, Spain
Jose Divasón	University of La Rioja, Spain
Jose Dorronsoro	Autonomous University of Madrid, Spain
Jose Garcia Rodriguez	University of Alicante, Spain
Jose Luis Calvo-Rolle	University of A Coruña, Spain
José Luis Verdegay	University of Granada, Spain
Jose M. Molina	University Carlos III of Madrid, Spain
Jose Manuel Lopez-Guede	University of the Basque Country, Spain
José Ramón Villar	University of Oviedo, Spain
José-Luis Casteleiro-Roca	University of A Coruña, Spain
Juan Humberto Sossa Azuela	CIC-IPN, Mexico
Juan J. Gude	University of Deusto, Spain
Juan Pavón	Complutense University of Madrid, Spain
Lidia Sánchez-González	University of León, Spain
Mailyn Moreno-Espino	Complutense University of Madrid, Spain
Manuel Graña	University of the Basque Country, Spain
Manuel Rubiños	University of A Coruña, Spain

Mara Hajdu Macelaru	Technical University of Cluj-Napoca, Romania
Mario Villar	University of Oviedo, Spain
Míriam Timiraos	University of A Coruña, Spain
Ovidiu Cosma	Technical University of Cluj-Napoca, Romania
Pablo García Bringas	University of Deusto, Spain
Paula M. Castro	University of A Coruña, Spain
Paula Patricia Arcano Bea	University of A Coruña, Spain
Paulo Novais	University of Minho, Portugal
Peter Rockett	University of Sheffield, UK
Petrica Pop	Technical University of Cluj-Napoca, Romania
Qing Tan	Athabasca University, Canada
Ruben Fuentes-Fernandez	Complutense University of Madrid, Spain
Sean Holden	University of Cambridge, UK
Urszula Stanczyk	Silesian University of Technology, Poland

HAIS 2025 Organising Committee Chairs

Emilio Corchado	University of Salamanca, Spain
Héctor Quintián	University of A Coruña, Spain

HAIS 2025 Organising Committee

José Luis Calvo Rolle	University of A Coruña, Spain
Esteban Jove	University of A Coruña, Spain
José Luis Casteleiro Roca	University of A Coruña, Spain
Francisco Zayas Gato	University of A Coruña, Spain
Álvaro Michelena	University of A Coruña, Spain
Míriam Timiraos Díaz	University of A Coruña, Spain
Antonio Javier Díaz Longueira	University of A Coruña, Spain
Paula Patricia Arcano Bea	University of A Coruña, Spain
Manuel Rubiños Trelles	University of A Coruña, Spain
Marta María Álvarez Crespo	University of A Coruña, Spain
Alejandro Vidal Bralo	University of A Coruña, Spain
Agustín García Fisher	University of A Coruña, Spain
Iker Pastor López	University of Deusto, Spain

Contents – Part I

Agricultural and Environmental Monitoring

Comparative Analysis of Cattle Behavior Across Intensive Dairy Farms
Through Dimensional Reduction Techniques 3
  *Manuel Rubiños, Álvaro Michelena, Agustín García-Fischer,
  Anabel Díaz-Labrador, Gonzalo Xoel Otero-González,
  and José-Luis Casteleiro-Roca*

Environmental Sound Recognition for Human-Robot Interaction in Social
Robots 15
  *Irene González Fernández, David Sobrín-Hidalgo,
  Juan Diego Peña-Narvaez, Francisco J. Rodríguez Lera,
  Camino Fernández Llamas, and Francisco Martín*

A New Transformer-Based Hybrid Model to Forecast Olive Fruit Fly
Using Multimodal Data 27
  *A. M. Chacón-Maldonado, N. Martínez Van der Looven,
  G. Asencio-Cortés, and A. Troncoso*

Infrared Driver Monitoring Systems – A Review, New Opportunities
and Trends 39
  Bogusław Cyganek and Mateusz Knapik

Ambient Intelligence Integration in Vocational Education: Evaluating
Smart Learning Environments for Digital Skills Development 52
  Ana Costa and Dalila Durães

Zero-Shot and Few-Shot Learning with Vision-Language Models
for Post-disaster Structural Damage Assessment 64
  Oriol Chacón-Albero, Jaume Jordán, Vicent Botti, and Vicente Julian

Biomedical Applications

Analyzing the Impact of Data Augmentation on Tumor Detection
and Classification in Mammograms 79
  Mădălina Dicu, Enol García González, Camelia Chira, and José R. Villar

An Enhanced Hybrid Machine Learning Model for Plant Disease
Detection and Classification 91
  Mara Măcelaru, Petrică C. Pop, Rareş Chiuzbăian, and Norbert Kovacs

Interpretable ML for Stress Detection from Vital Signs Using SHAP 103
    Samson Mihirette, Enrique Antonio De la Cal Martin, and Qing Tan

Learning from Normal Brain Activity for Automatic Detection
of Photoparoxysmal Responses as Electroencephalogram Anomalies 115
    *Fernando Moncada Martins, Víctor M. González, José R. Villar,
María Antonia Gutiérrez, Pablo Calvo Calleja, Sara Urdiales Sánchez,
Ricardo Díaz Pérez, and Alinne Dalla-Porta Acosta*

Subsymbolic and Symbolic Pipeline for an Explainable EEG
Authentication System 127
    Marcos Rodriguez-Vega and Pino Caballero-Gil

Cybersecurity and Network Protection

Analyzing DoS Attacks on CoAP Networks Using Low-Dimensional
Latent Representations 143
    *Álvaro Michelena, Jose Aveleira-Mata, Marta-María Álvarez-Crespo,
Emilio Lima-Bullones, Agustín García-Fischer, Carmen Benavides,
and José Luis Calvo-Rolle*

An Approach to Anomaly Detection with Dynamic Threshold Definition
for Real-World Environments 154
    *Gabriel Souza Marques, Maynara Souza,
Flávio Arthur Oliveira Santos, Cleber Zanchettin, and Paulo Novais*

Loss Functions for Time Series Forecasting in Network Security Situation
Awareness 166
    Richard Staňa, Pavol Sokol, and Jakub Nižník

A Hybrid Feature Selection Approach Using Filter-Wrapped Evaluation
(FWE) for Attack Detection in SDN 180
    Chin Jia Wen and Tan Saw Chin

RAG Embeddings Storage Optimization Through Quantization
and Dimensionality Reduction 198
    *Naamán Huerga-Pérez, Rubén Álvarez, Álvaro Sánchez-Fernández,
and Javier Díez-González*

Exploratory Visualization of IoT Attacks on the NF-CSE-CIC-IDS2018
Dataset 210
    *Álvaro Villar-Val, Diego Granados-Lopez, Angel Arroyo,
and Álvaro Herrero*

Data Mining and Decision Support Systems

A Microservice System Architecture for Receiving ETL System Patterns 225
    Rui Monteiro, Bruno Oliveira, and Orlando Belo

A Novel General Hybrid System for Data Feature Selection 237
    Dragan Simić, Zorana Banković, José R. Villar, José Luis Calvo-Rolle,
    Svetislav D. Simić, and Svetlana Simić

Profiling Public Instagram Accounts with a Multimodal Vector for Hate
Exposure Analysis 250
    Asier Gonzalez-Santocildes, Iker Pastor López,
    Marta Gorraiz-Bengoechea, and P. Garcia Bringas

Symbolic Regressor: An Interpretability Tool for Non-intrusive Load
Monitoring 260
    Danel Rey-Arnal, Pablo G. Bringas, and Ibai Laña

IoT Device Fingerprinting: Optimized with Data Diversity and Feature
Selection for Computational Efficiency 272
    Chan Yeng Hui and Tan Saw Chin

Improvement of Multi-Label Self-Adjusting Memory kNN Classifier
for Sparse and Class-Imbalanced Data Streams 284
    Thinzar Tun and Yuichi Goto

HYBPARSIMONY-IDT: Hybrid Parsimonious Search for Interpretable
Decision Trees 296
    Francisco Javier Martinez-de-Pison, Alpha Pernia-Espinoza,
    and Jose Divasón

Analysis of Kernel Thinning for Scalable Support Vector Machines 309
    Blanca Cano, Ángela Fernández, and José R. Dorronsoro

Author Index 323

Contents – Part II

Deep Learning and Representation Learning

Knowledge Distillation of Class Activation Maps from Two Teachers for Continual Learning 3
    Minkai Sheng, Hyung-Jun Moon, and Sung-Bae Cho

RAPID: Robust Adaptive Probabilistic Inference with DINO Features 16
    Vladimir Frolov, Vitaliy Vorobyov, Leonid Ugadiarov, and Aleksandr Panov

MapFM: Foundation Model-Driven HD Mapping with Multi-task Contextual Learning 28
    Leonid Ivanov, Vasily Yuryev, and Dmitry Yudin

Revisiting Automatic Essay Assessment: A Relative Approach 41
    Anda Leşeanu, İbrahim Rıza Hallaç, Burçin Buket Oğul, and Hasan Oğul

Evaluating the Usefulness of Large Language Models for Human Activity Recognition Data Augmentation via Few-Shot Samples 53
    Maynara Souza, Flávio Arthur Oliveira Santos, Paulo Novais, and Cleber Zanchettin

Determination of Galaxy Photometric Redshifts Using Conditional Generative Adversarial Networks (CGANs) 66
    M. Garcia-Fernandez

Hybrid Vision System for Minor Pre-assembly Identification in a Robotic Welding Cell 79
    Paula Arcano-Bea, Francisco Zayas-Gato, Héctor Quintián, Santiago José Tutor Roca, and Adolfo Lamas

An Energy Efficient Model Based on the Feature Pseudo-embedding 91
    Lingfeng Chen and Iker Pastor López

HAIS Energy Applications

Forecasting Thermal Demand in Citizen Energy Communities Using
Machine Learning: Application to the Urberoa Case Study 107
    Raul Saenz-Herreros, Alejandro Muro-Belloso,
    Ignacio Guisasola-Iparraguirre, Ignacio Lázaro-Llorente,
    and J. David Nuñez-Gonzalez

A Hybrid Modelling Approach for Forecasting the Acquired Electrical
Power from Photovoltaic Panels 119
    Anabel Díaz-Labrador, Ángel Delgado, Héctor J. Pérez-Iglesias,
    Óscar Fontenla-Romero, and José Luis Calvo-Rolle

KARMA: KAN Meets ARIMA 131
    Arnau Garcia-Cucó, Javier Palanca Cámara, and Vicente Juan Botti

IIoT-Driven Time Series Imputation for Sustainable Metalworking Fluid
Monitoring 143
    Félix De Miguel, Nuria Velasco, Félix Movilla, Daniel Urda,
    Carlos Cambra, and Álvaro Herrero

Evolutionary Computation and Optimization

An Adaptive Memetic Algorithm for Solving the Multiple Knapsack
Assignment Problem 157
    Adrian Petrovan, Petrică C. Pop, and Cosmin Sabo

Advanced Decomposition-Based Bioinspired Algorithms
for Multiobjective Phylogenetics 169
    Sergio Santander-Jiménez and Miguel A. Vega-Rodríguez

An Ant Colony Optimization Approach for Safest Path Pair Computation
Under Correlated Failures 183
    Zoltán Tasnádi, Balázs Vass, and Noémi Gaskó

DRL-Driven Batch-Oriented SDN Migration with Weighted Traffic
Matrix Clustering for Dynamic Networks 197
    Kai Yuan Tan and Saw Chin Tan

Reinforcement Learning and AI Planning

Emotional Value-Aware Agents: A Viewpoint Paper 215
    Carmengelys Cordova, Elena Del Val, Joaquin Taverner,
    and Vicente Botti

Neuro-Symbolic Reasoning with Multiple Large Language Models
Combined by First-Order Logic 227
    Jieun Kim and Sung-Bae Cho

SimplyQRL: A Modular Benchmarking Library for Hybrid Quantum
Reinforcement Learning 239
    Javier Lazaro, Juan-Ignacio Vazquez, and Pablo García Bringas

Enhancing World Models with Specialized Prediction Networks
for Reinforcement Learning 251
    Alvaro Mellado-Ibanez, Nestor Arana-Arexolaleiba,
    and Juan-Ignacio Vazquez

Smart Mobility and Transportation Optimization

Clustering-Based Route Optimization for Mixed Ride-Sharing Under
Time Constraints 265
    Mercedes Ccesa-Quincho, Jenny Fajardo-Calderin, Xabier Cantero,
    Antonio D. Masegosa, and Leire Serrano

Origin-Destination Frequency Tensors and Their Application in Machine
Learning Modelling 277
    Dani Marchuet, Javi Palanca, and Vicent Botti

Fast-TRACLUS: An Optimized Trajectory Clustering Algorithm
for Large-Scale Datasets 290
    Álvaro González Delgado, Santiago Porras Alfonso,
    Bruno Baruque Zanón, and Hector Cogollos Adrian

Action Space Size Effects in Reinforcement Learning for the Vehicle
Routing Problem 301
    Jon Díaz-Aparicio, Gabriel Duflo, Jenny Fajardo-Calderin,
    and Enrique Onieva

Time Series and Forecasting Methods

Perplexity, Uncertainty, and the Limits of Active Learning 315
    Pablo Turón and Montse Cuadros

Channel Selection and Creation Algorithms for Electroencephalography
Classification with HIVE-COTE 328
    Aiden Rushbrooke, Matthew Middlehurst, Saber Sami,
    and Anthony Bagnall

Multivariate Regime Identification and Prediction in Financial Markets
via Gaussian Mixture and Gradient Boosting Methods 340
　　Álvaro Sánchez-Fernández, Javier Díez-González,
　　Naamán Huerga-Pérez, and Hilde Perez

On-Edge Task Planning with Large Language Models for Service Robotics 354
　　Alejandro González-Cantón, Miguel A. González-Santamarta,
　　Francisco J. Rodriguez Lera, Ángel M. Guerrero-Higueras,
　　Irene González-Fernández, and Francisco Martín-Rico

Author Index 367

Agricultural and Environmental Monitoring

Comparative Analysis of Cattle Behavior Across Intensive Dairy Farms Through Dimensional Reduction Techniques

Manuel Rubiños[1](✉), Álvaro Michelena[1], Agustín García-Fischer[1], Anabel Díaz-Labrador[1,2], Gonzalo Xoel Otero-González[1], and José-Luis Casteleiro-Roca[1]

[1] CTC, CITIC, Department of Industrial Engineering, University of A Coruña, Avda. 19 de febrero s/n, Ferrol, A Coruña 15405, Spain
{manuel.rubinos,alvaro.michelena,agustin.garciaf,anabel.dlabrador,x.otero, jose.luis.casteleiro}@udc.es
[2] Fundación Instituto Tecnológico de Galicia, A Coruña, Spain

Abstract. Driven by accelerated population growth and increasing globalization, the demand for food, particularly dairy and meat products, has risen to unsustainable levels, placing pressure on the livestock sector to adopt more efficient management strategies. Precision Livestock Farming (PLF) has emerged as a key response to this demand, developing tools based on individualized animal monitoring data. Among these, activity-monitoring collars have proven to be very promising, enabling a detailed tracking of each cow's behavior in real time. This study explores the use of three dimensionality reduction techniques, t-SNE, UMAP and k-PCA, to characterize and classify the daily behavioral patterns of dairy cows that are part of an intensive farming system. Based on activity-monitoring collars data, it has been studied how each method captures the underlying structure of animal activity. Among the techniques assessed, UMAP proved to be particularly effective as a visual tool for identifying behavioral discrepancies between animals that are part of different farms. This characterization and classification capabilities are essential for the future development of predictive models improving herd management efficiency and supporting the sustainability of the livestock industry.

Keywords: Smart collars · Precision Livestock Farming · Dimensionality reduction

1 Introduction

Spain is one of the leading livestock producers in the European Union, with a strong emphasis on the development of high-quality animal products. This production model is aligned with European policies that promote rigorous standards in food safety, environmental protection, and animal welfare.

In recent years, the sector has received significant support for innovation and technological development, with the goal of improving sustainability, efficiency, and productivity while maintaining a commitment to animal welfare [1]. These advances have facilitated the integration of digital technologies and artificial intelligence into livestock management [14].

Currently, the use of machine learning and deep learning is helping to automate decision-making processes in livestock farming, gradually reducing the need for continuous human supervision [9,11,15]. Among the various technological applications in this context, animal behavior analysis stands out for its potential to transform the early detection of physiological and pathological events such as illness, estrus, or calving.

Numerous research works, have demonstrated that behavioral changes can be early indicators of health problems that negatively affect productivity [3,13]. Likewise, monitoring behavioral traits such as posture [4], movement patterns [16], and feeding behavior [6] has proven useful for anticipating the onset of conditions such as mastitis, metritis, and metabolic disorders, often before visible clinical symptoms appear.

Identifying deviations from normal behavior is essential for implementing timely interventions that can limit disease progression and improve treatment outcomes [5,8]. In this regard, wearable monitoring systems, such as smart activity collars combined with advanced data analysis techniques, are emerging as powerful tools for enhancing animal health and farm management.

To achieve this, we focus on dimensionality reduction techniques, which have become increasingly relevant in the field of Precision Livestock Farming due to the high-dimensional nature of behavioral data generated by smart monitoring devices. These methods enable the transformation of complex, multivariate data into lower-dimensional spaces that preserve essential structural information, making it easier to visualize and interpret latent behavioral patterns. In particular, techniques such as t-distributed Stochastic Neighbor Embedding (t-SNE), Uniform Manifold Approximation and Projection (UMAP), and kernel Principal Component Analysis (k-PCA) have shown great promise in revealing hidden relationships and differences that may exist between animals or across different farm environments. In this study, we explore and compare these three dimensional reduction techniques to assess their ability to distinguish behavioral profiles across different intensive dairy farms.

The novelty of this work lies in applying and comparing three dimensionality reduction techniques to detect behavioral differences between farms, rather than focusing solely on individual animals within a single herd.

The remainder of the paper is organized as follows: Sect. 2 describes the monitoring system and the datasets used from multiple farms. Section 3 outlines the dimensional reduction techniques applied. Section 4 presents the experimental design and discusses the results. Finally, Sect. 5 concludes the paper and suggests directions for future work.

2 Materials

2.1 Cattle Activity Monitoring Device

For this research, we employed the RUMI activity monitoring collar (Fig. 1), a commercial device developed by the Galician startup Innogando. This smart collar integrates GPS positioning capabilities and advanced sensors that enable the identification of five distinct behaviors in cattle: resting, walking, ruminating, grazing, and eating or playing. Additionally, it accurately tracks the daily number of steps taken by each animal.

Fig. 1. RUMI smart collar.

Designed for durability and ease of use, the device has a compact and lightweight form factor, measuring $130 \times 90 \times 37$ mm and weighing only 350 grams. It is built to withstand harsh farm conditions thanks to its IP67-rated enclosure, which provides resistance to impact, dust, and water, ensuring reliable operation across diverse environmental settings.

The collar is secured around the animal's neck using an adjustable nylon strap, positioned on the left side at mid-neck height. This placement is key to ensuring both measurement accuracy and animal comfort, as it optimizes the detection of movements and behaviors without interfering with the animal's routine.

In terms of energy efficiency, the device is equipped with a long-lasting battery and a small solar panel, allowing for autonomous operation for over eight months, even in conditions with limited sunlight exposure. For data transmission, the RUMI collar utilizes LoRaWAN technology, enabling long-range communication with a central server via a gateway. This feature ensures continuous and effective data transfer, even in remote farming areas.

2.2 Dataset Description

To analyze and compare the behavioral patterns of dairy cows raised under different intensive farming conditions, this study used data collected from two geographically distinct intensive dairy farms located in Galicia, northern Spain. Although both farms follow similar housing and management systems, where animals are kept indoors, their environmental conditions, operating routines and specific practices vary, providing an ideal context for comparing behavior between farms.

A total of 22 Holstein-Friesian cows were selected for tracking, 13 from Farm 1 and 9 from Farm 2. All animals were uniquely identified and selected based on shared physiological criteria, they were not pregnant and covered a wide age range, from 10 months to 7.5 years, allowing for variability in the dataset.

Behavioral data were recorded using the RUMI smart collar, which captures daily information on six key activities: resting, ruminating, walking, grazing, eating/playing and step count. Each cow's behavior was monitored continuously. Farm 1 provided 85 days of data (March 8 to May 31, 2024) and Farm 2 provided 131 days of data (July 1 to November 8, 2023).

Each record in the dataset represents a single day for a specific animal and includes: animal ID, date, duration in minutes of each monitored activity and daily number of steps. The result is a structured time series dataset suitable for dimensionality reduction and latent space visualization, with the objective of detecting commonalities and differences in behavior not only at the individual level, but also between farms. This comparative framework serves as a basis for assessing whether cows from different farms exhibit different behaviors in intensive production systems.

3 Implemented Dimensionality Reduction Techniques

T-Distributed Stochastic Neighbor Embedding t-SNE is an unsupervised dimensionality reduction technique used for high-dimensional data visualization and exploration in an interpretable embedded space. It was presented by Laurens van der Maaten and Geoffrey Hinton in 2008 [10] as an improved version of its predecessor, the Stochastic Neighbor Embedding (SNE) [7].

This algorithm considers the distances between samples in the original dimensional space as a measure of similarity. A Gaussian distribution is then used to transform those distances among samples into probabilities of similarity. This is done in conjunction with the KullbackLeibler divergence to minimize the difference between the original high-dimensional space and the embedded space.

t-SNE is a non-linear technique, which allows it to capture more complex relationships and implicit patterns between features, resulting in more intuitive and more reliable representations than other linear techniques. Also, it is worth mentioning its ability to preserve both the local and global structure of the data between high-dimensional and projected space. On the other hand, its non-deterministic character must be taking into account, as similar parameter configurations can lead to variable results in different executions. Its higher computational requirements are also a remarkable characteristic.

Uniform Manifold Approximation and Projection

UMAP, is a recent data exploration and visualization technique that bases its functioning on mathematical concepts such as algebraic topology and Riemannian geometry. It was introduced by Leland mcInnes et al. in 2008 [12].

This technique constructs a topological structure called fuzzy simplicial complex, which represents the relationships in the high-dimensional space as a weighed graph, using a variable radius based on the k-nearest neighbors for each point. Within this radius, it makes the connectedness of each point fuzzy by transforming it into a probability. This simplicial complex is embedded in a lower-dimensional space using a cross-entropy minimization function [18].

Kernel Principal Component Analysis

Kernel-PCA [17] is an extension of the popular PCA dimensional reduction technique [2]. PCA is a linear method that transforms the original variables into a new set of uncorrelated variables, called principal components, which capture the maximum variance in the data. However, it is limited in capturing non-linear patterns. To address this, a kernel function is applied in order to capture more complex patterns that cannot be properly represented by linear combinations, as the original algorithm does.

More concretely, kernel functions map the original data from the original space, where linear functions are not able to separate the data effectively, to a higher-dimensional space, where the structure of the data becomes linearly separable. After this step, the classic principal component analysis algorithm can be applied. Therefore, the kernel modification makes PCA able to handle non-linearity, improving its applicability.

The main difficulty in the implementation of this technique lies in selecting the most appropriate kernel function, for which a prior study and knowledge of data structure may be required. Among the most common kernel function there is linear, polynomial, Gaussian/RFB and sigmoid, for example.

4 Experiment Setup and Results

4.1 Experiment Configuration

This section presents the workflow followed to carry out this experiment, as shown in Fig. 2. For the development of the script executed to perform the experiment, Python programming language was used, together with specialized libraries such as *sklearn* for the implementation of the mentioned machine learning techniques, and other general-use libraries like *pandas* and *numpy*, among others.

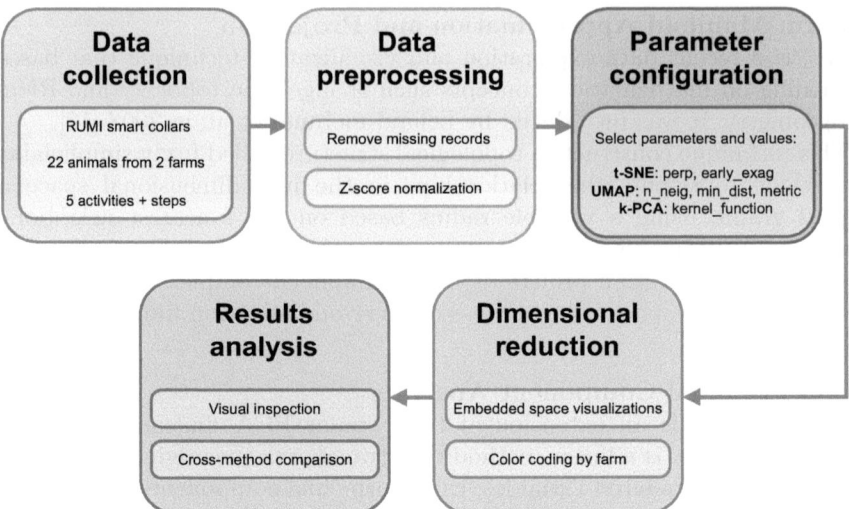

Fig. 2. Experimental setup workflow diagram.

The initial step involved data preprocessing, which consisted of removing daily records with missing values to ensure the integrity of the information under analysis. Next, the dataset was normalized using the z-score method, setting a mean of 0 and a standard deviation of 1. This normalization was crucial for standardizing the data scale and enabling direct comparisons across variables.

The next stage consisted on selecting the most relevant parameters for each dimensional reduction technique, based on its influence over the resulting representation of the embedded space. After selecting the parameters to be tested for each technique, different value configurations were studied:

- **t-SNE:** *perplexity*, which is related to the variance of the Gaussian distribution applied and controls the balance between local and global structure, was tested at 10, 20, 30, 40, 50, 70 and 100 values. Also, *early exaggeration*, which controls the step size of the gradient during the optimization, was set at 10, 20 and 50.
- **UMAP:** the *number of neighbors* is the most influential parameter, as it defines the size of the traced radius which also determines the size of the neighborhood constructed in the high-dimensional plane. Values of 10, 20, 30, 50 and 100 were tested. *Minimum distance* can also help to obtain a more intuitive representation, as it sets how tight data points in the embedded space will be, testing values of 0.01, 0.1 and 0.25. At last, different metrics such as *euclidean*, *cosine* and *manhattan* were studied.
- **k-PCA:** the only parameter that will be taking into account for this technique is the kernel function, which defines how the data is implicitly transformed to capture nonlinear patterns. Five different functions were tested, which are *linear*, *poly*, *rbf*, *sigmoid* and *cosine*.

Each technique results were analyzed separately, selecting the best parameter configuration for each one. Representations that showed better visual differentiation of the implicit groups (separating data by different farms) while minimizing dispersion inside each group were selected.

Finally, an overall analysis was carried out, observing the coincidences and disparities between the three selected embedded space visualizations. A thorough study on the grounds of the observed data structure was also performed.

4.2 Results and Discussion

In this section, the best 2D embedded space representations corresponding to each one of the previously mentioned dimensional reduction techniques are presented and analyzed. Figures 3, 4 and 5 show the results of t-SNE, UMAP and k-PCA, respectively. The corresponding parameter configurations are indicated in the caption of each image.

Before starting commenting on the Figures, it is important to clarify that each point represents a single animal's behavior on a specific day. Therefore, each animal is represented by multiple points. Since the main objective of this work is to compare behavior between animals of different farms rather than analyze behavior at the individual animal level, color coding was used so that each color represents all animals belonging to the same farm.

Starting with Fig. 3, corresponding to the best result achieved with t-SNE, one can be observe how the data is separated into two main regions on the plain. On the left side, there is a clear predomination of red Farm 2 dots, while on the right side the predominant color is blue, corresponding to Farm 1. In the middle region, both colors coexist, showing a gradual transition between farms. Specifically for this technique, there are some blank spaces between the left and right regions that could represent a significant leap between the behavior of both farms. Furthermore, the presence of a pair of cluster of blue dots on the left region is highlighted; the same applies in reverse, since a cluster of red points is present on the right side of the graph.

Continuing with Fig. 4, which represents the best visualization achieved with UMAP, similar characteristics can be observed. The graph is also divided into two main regions, where each is clearly dominated by one color. In this case, the intermediate region takes the form of a bottleneck, emphasizing the difference in behavior between the animals of each farm. However, a transition where both colors coexist can also be identified, although it now shows a much narrower shape in the form of a bottleneck. Again, there are a couple of nucleus of the opposite color present on each of the two regions.

Figure 5 shows the results of k-PCA using the *rbf* kernel. Again, several coincidences with the previous representations can be observed, as the two colors are split in opposite sides of the plane. However, in this case, the transition between groups is not as well-defined, the dispersion is greater and the shape of the data structure is more spherical than in the previous graphs.

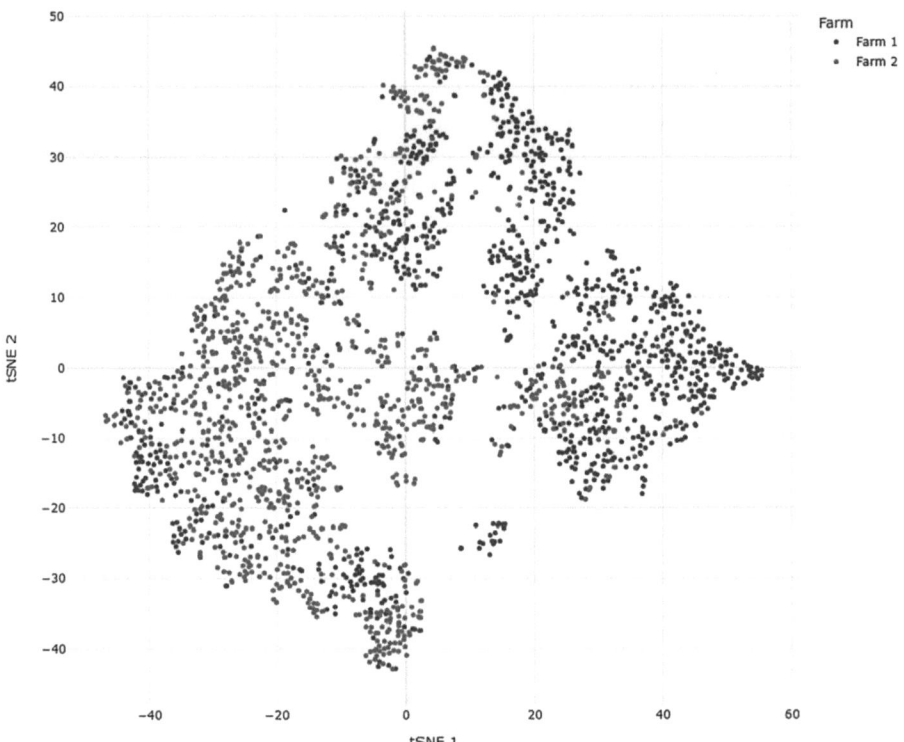

Fig. 3. t-SNE 2D embedded space for *perplexity=50, early_exaggeration= 10*.(Color figure online)

Using t-SNE and UMAP as reference, as they showed to capture patterns more accurately than k-PCA, more in-depth analysis has been made. First, those points belonging to one farm that were located within the part of the plane dominated by the opposite farm were studied, resulting in the fact that there are only a few specific animals that exhibit a behavior closer to the animals of the opposite exploitation. In particular, the cows with references 6777 and 3448, which belong to farm number 1, are completely located on the contrary farm side. The same happens in reverse with the animal referenced as 7997, belonging to farm number 2 but located in the side of farm number 1. Another aspect to highlight is the fact that the structure of the data is well-outlined, as all data points lie within the global shape, without any significant outliers.

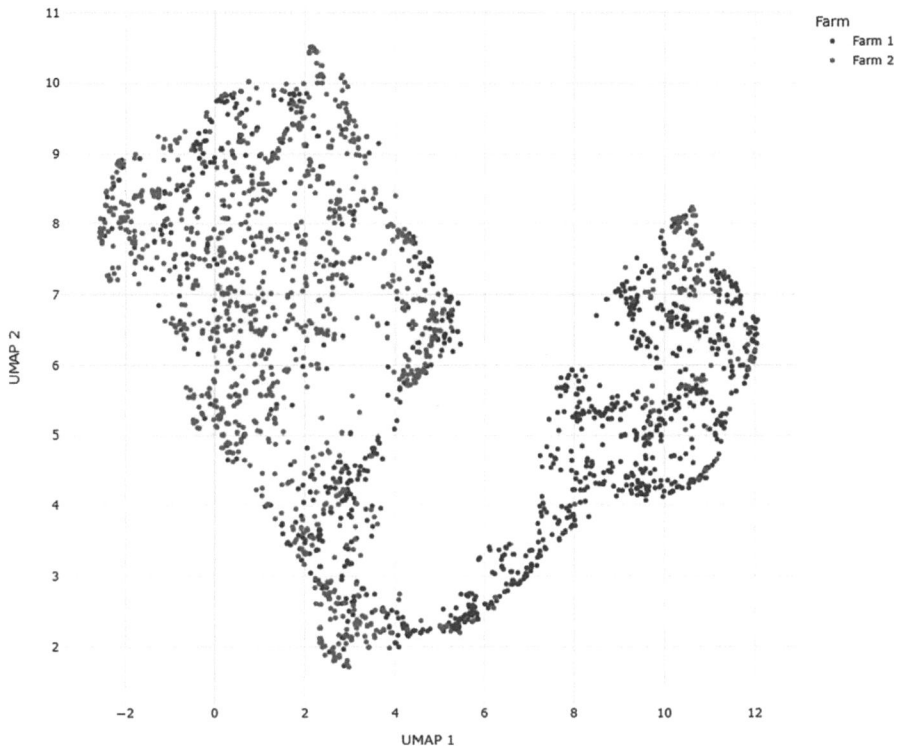

Fig. 4. UMAP 2D embedded space for $n\_neighbors=50$, $min\_dist=0.1$, $metric=cosine$.

The results obtained suggest that the belonging of any animal to one community or another is a fact to be taken into account when trying to characterize and predict their behavior. The first observations showed that the animals that are part of the same farm will, in principle have similar behaviors. This can be explained by the need of each individual to adapt to the dynamics of coexistence with the other animals in close proximity. However, as each animal is a different being, it may be the case that some animals differ from others in the same herd, presenting characteristics closer to animal in other communities. On the other hand, the lack of outliers can be explained through the fact that the standardized, repetitive and more strict routines in intensive farming contribute to a more homogeneous behavior across all animals, as well as inhabiting the same environment.

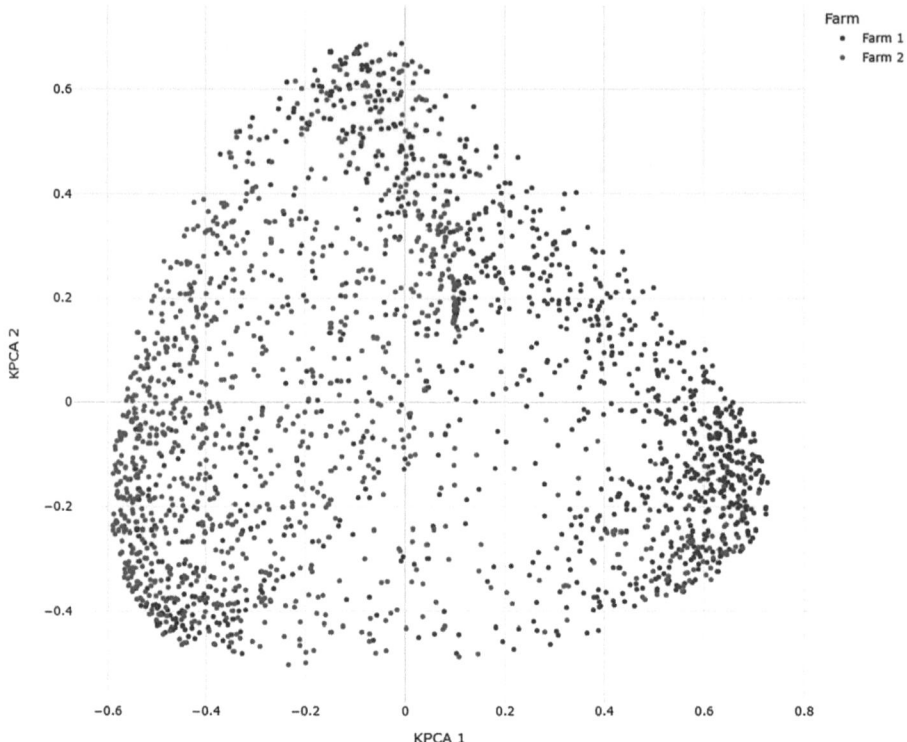

Fig. 5. Kernel-PCA 2D embedded space for *kernel=rbf*.

5 Conclusions and Future Works

In this research, an analysis and comparative of cattle behavior across different intensive livestock farms has been performed. To this end, three unsupervised dimensional reduction techniques, t-SNE, UMAP and k-PCA, were tested, using data about five different activities plus step counting that were monitored by a commercial activity necklace.

Among the dimensional reduction techniques implemented, t-SNE and UMAP showed a better adequacy on capturing the underlying structure of the data than k-PCA. UMAP provided the best visualization, where both farms can be easily separable, but also provides a clear representation of the transition between them, demonstrating its capacity to reveal more complex patterns than other techniques.

Characterizing animal behaviors and routines is a key step for the development of more accurate and robust predictive models, which, in turn, enables the creation of decision-making support systems for livestock management. This would significantly enhance the efficiency of any cattle exploitation, and the animal welfare as well.

Future research will aim to broaden the current study by incorporating a larger and more diverse dataset, including a wider range of cows and herds, and expanding the analysis to farms located in different regions and production systems, both dairy and beef. This expansion will enable a more comprehensive evaluation of the robustness and versatility of dimensionality reduction methods under various farming conditions and management practices.

Additionally, the proposed work includes testing these methodologies in extensive farming systems, where animals are raised in less controlled and more variable environments. This could provide valuable insights into behavioral patterns that may not be observable in intensive production settings.

Acknowledgements. Álvaro Michelena's research was supported by the Spanish Ministry of Universities (https://www.universidades.gob.es/), under the "Formación de Profesorado Universitario" grant with reference: FPU21/00932.

CITIC, as a center accredited for excellence within the Galician University System and a member of the CIGUS Network, receives subsidies from the Department of Education, Science, Universities, and Vocational Training of the Xunta de Galicia. Additionally, it is co-financed by the EU through the FEDER Galicia 2021-27 operational program (Ref. ED431G 2023/01).

Xunta de Galicia. Grants for the consolidation and structuring of competitive research units, GPC (ED431B 2023/49)

Anabel Díaz Labrador's research was supported by the Xunta de Galicia (Regional Government of Galicia in Spain), through grants to industrial PhD (http://gain.xunta.gal/), under the "Doutoramento Industrial 2024" grant with reference: 02_IN606D_2024_3100897.

The dataset has been provided by the Galician startup Innogando.

References

1. Shaping europe's digital future. https://digital-strategy.ec.europa.eu/en/policies/digitalisation-agriculture (2023), Accessed 23 Feb 2025
2. Abdi, H., Williams, L.J.: Principal component analysis. Wiley Interdis. Rev. Comput. Stat. **2**(4), 433–459 (2010)
3. Cocco, R., Canozzi, M.E.A., Fischer, V.: Rumination time as an early predictor of metritis and subclinical ketosis in dairy cows at the beginning of lactation: systematic review-meta-analysis. Prev. Vet. Med. **189**, 105309 (2021)
4. Deming, J., Bergeron, R., Leslie, K., DeVries, T.: Associations of cow-level factors, frequency of feed delivery, and standing and lying behaviour of dairy cows milked in an automatic system. Can. J. Anim. Sci. **93**(4), 427–433 (2013)
5. Dittrich, I., Gertz, M., Krieter, J.: Alterations in sick dairy cows' daily behavioural patterns. Heliyon **5**(11), e02902 (2019)
6. González, L., Tolkamp, B., Coffey, M., Ferret, A., Kyriazakis, I.: Changes in feeding behavior as possible indicators for the automatic monitoring of health disorders in dairy cows. J. Dairy Sci. **91**(3), 1017–1028 (2008)
7. Hinton, G.E., Roweis, S.: Stochastic neighbor embedding. Adv. Neural Inf. Process. Syst. **15** (2002)

8. Liboreiro, D.N., et al.: Characterization of peripartum rumination and activity of cows diagnosed with metabolic and uterine diseases. J. Dairy Sci. **98**(10), 6812–6827 (2015)
9. Lopez Florez, S., González-Briones, A., Chamoso, P., Saberi Mohamad, M.: Automatic detection of faults in industrial production of sandwich panels using deep learning techniques. Logic J. IGPL p. jzae053 (2024)
10. Van der Maaten, L., Hinton, G.: Visualizing data using t-sne. J. Mach. Learn. Res. **9**(11) (2008)
11. Machado, J., et al.: Behaviour of machine learning algorithms in the classification of energy consumption in school buildings. Logic J. IGPL p. jzae058 (2024)
12. McInnes, L., Healy, J., Melville, J.: Umap: uniform manifold approximation and projection for dimension reduction. arXiv preprint arXiv:1802.03426 (2018)
13. Michelena, Á., et al.: Comparative analysis of unsupervised anomaly detection techniques for heat detection in dairy cattle. Neurocomputing **618**, 129088 (2025)
14. Michelena, Á., Fontenla-Romero, Ó., Luis Calvo-Rolle, J.: A review and future trends of precision livestock over dairy and beef cow cattle with artificial intelligence. Logic J. IGPL p. jzae111 (2024)
15. Michelena, Á., Jove, E., Fontenla-Romero, Ó., Calvo-Rolle, J.L.: Evaluation of one-class techniques for early estrus detection on galician intensive dairy cow farm based on behavioral data from activity collars. ADCAIJ: Adv. Distrib. Comput. Artif. Intell. J. **13**, e32508–e32508 (2024)
16. Miguel-Pacheco, G.G., et al.: Behavioural changes in dairy cows with lameness in an automatic milking system. Appl. Anim. Behav. Sci. **150**, 1–8 (2014)
17. Schölkopf, B., Smola, A., Müller, K.-R.: Kernel principal component analysis. In: Gerstner, W., Germond, A., Hasler, M., Nicoud, J.-D. (eds.) ICANN 1997. LNCS, vol. 1327, pp. 583–588. Springer, Heidelberg (1997). https://doi.org/10.1007/BFb0020217
18. Zarzà, I., Curtò, J., Calafate, C.T.: Umap for geospatial data visualization. Procedia Comput. Sci. **225**, 1661–1671 (2023)

Environmental Sound Recognition for Human-Robot Interaction in Social Robots

Irene González Fernández[1](✉), David Sobrín-Hidalgo[2],
Juan Diego Peña-Narvaez[1], Francisco J. Rodríguez Lera[2],
Camino Fernández Llamas[2], and Francisco Martín[1]

[1] Rey Juan Carlos University, Madrid, Spain
{irene.gonzalezf,juan.pena,francisco.rico}@urjc.es
[2] León University, León, Spain
{dsobh,fjrodl,camino.fernandez}@unileon.es

Abstract. This paper presents an auditory perception system for social robots in indoor environments, designed to detect, localize, and categorize environmental sounds in real time, allowing the robot to adapt its behavior according to the situation's relevance. The system uses a transformer-based neural model trained on a publicly available dataset of domestic audio to recognize everyday sound events. The signal is captured by a circular four-microphone array mounted on the robot, which also estimates the direction of sound arrival, enabling the spatial mapping of acoustic events in the environment. Detected sounds are classified into three categories: environmental (ignored), supervised (requiring human attention), and emergency (requiring immediate action). The system has been implemented as a package in ROS 2, a robotic middleware framework, and validated in real domestic scenarios. Results show that integrating auditory perception allows the robot to adapt its behavior more intelligently and safely to unexpected acoustic events.

Keywords: Sound Event Detection · Context-Aware Perception · Human-Robot Interaction · Hybrid Intelligent Systems · Transformer-based Audio Models

1 Introduction

Cognition in robotics is based on the ability to perceive, interpret, and act according to the environment, integrating multimodal information in architectures that enable adaptive decision making. In this context, vision has traditionally been the main perception channel in service robots. However, sound provides useful complementary information in indoor environments, where it can detect relevant events outside the visual field and respond appropriately. This capability improves safety, efficiency, and naturalness in human-robot interaction.

From this perspective, Sound Event Detection (SED) [5] has emerged as a relevant line in auditory processing, driven by the DCASE community [10], which promotes the development of models through competitions with standardized data. One of the most competitive models is ATST-SED [17], a transformer-based neural network fine-tuned on the DESED dataset [16,19]. It classifies short audio segments into predefined household sound classes using attention mechanisms to improve temporal resolution.

However, many of these models prioritize performance over test datasets, without considering their integration into real robotic platforms. In addition, the simultaneous reliance on different audio and video sensors makes it difficult to use them flexibly in situations where not all are available.

To address these limitations, this paper presents an auditory system integrated in a social robot for home environments. The contribution is composed of three key components: (i) acoustic event detection using ATST-SED, (ii) sound source localization with direction of arrival (DOA) estimation, and (iii) semantic categorization that assigns priority of action according to the type of sound. This information allows adapting the robot's behavior in real time according to the detected event, its location, and the task in progress.

The system has been implemented as a package in ROS 2 and has been validated in real scenarios, simulating domestic situations. The remainder of the paper is organized as follows. Section 2 reviews relevant previous work in sound event detection and its application in cognitive robotics. Section 3 describes the proposed architecture. The Sect. 4 presents the experimental design results organized in three demonstrations: an everyday situation, a possible danger, and an emergency. Finally, the discussion Sect 5 and conclusions Sect 6 sections discuss the results and identify future directions.

2 Related Work

In recent years, research in cognitive robotics [11,15] has emphasized the importance of multimodal situational awareness, where auditory perception complements other senses to improve safety and naturalness in human-robot interaction. This aligns with a broader trend in artificial intelligence toward neuro-symbolic approaches, which combine deep learning for perception with symbolic reasoning to balance accuracy, interpretability, and flexibility [9].

Among perceptual capabilities, detecting and classifying acoustic events has become a key task for providing robotic systems with more contextualized perception. This progress has been largely driven by the DCASE (Detection and Classification of Acoustic Scenes and Events) community [10], which has organized annual competitions since 2013 to improve acoustic recognition using standardized datasets.

DCASE Task 4 [13,14] focuses on detecting sound events in domestic environments using real and synthetic recordings with partially labeled data. It uses the DESED (Domestic Environment Sound Event Detection) dataset [16,19], which simulates typical household situations with relevant everyday sounds. DESED combines real audio from AudioSet and YouTube, synthetic events, and background noise from sources like SINS [2] and MUSAN [18]. It includes ten classes of domestic events: alarm, blender, cat, dishes, dog, electric shaver, frying, running water, speech, and vacuum cleaner.

Over the different editions of DCASE, various approaches have been proposed. Early models were based on convolutional networks, such as SE-CRNN or FDY-CRNNN [3], while more recent ones rely on self-supervised transformers like HTS-AT, MAT-SED, or ATST. These transformer-based models improve generalization on unlabeled datasets.

Different metrics are used to compare models. MAT-SED [1] excels in the Polyphonic Sound Detection Score (PSDS), which evaluates robustness under varying thresholds and tolerances, useful in noisy environments. In contrast, ATST-SED [17], a tuned version of the self-supervised ATST-Frame [6], achieves top performance in the event-based F1 score [12], which measures accuracy in real-time detection and suits reactive robotics. For this reason, ATST-SED has been selected in this work, considering both its performance and its integration feasibility in cognitive robotic systems.

Despite the progress of models like ATST-SED and MAT-SED in accuracy and robustness, their integration into real robotic architectures is still limited. Most studies focus on optimizing metrics in offline conditions, overlooking real-time execution, multimodal integration, and adaptability. Robot Operating System 2 (ROS 2) [7,8] has become the standard framework for modular, distributed robotics and supports the integration of complex perception systems. This work addresses that gap by embedding ATST-SED into ROS 2, linking it to a sound localization system, and building a real-time acoustic representation for decision-making in domestic scenarios.

3 Materials and Methods

The proposed system allows a social robot to detect, locate, and categorize acoustic events in real time, adapting its behavior according to the priority of the event in domestic environments. It has been implemented in ROS 2 and is composed of two main packages: a Python node that integrates the ATST-SED model for audio classification, and a C++ perception system that fuses in real time auditory, spatial, and semantic information. This architecture is complemented by a behavioral layer based on decision trees, which changes the robot's response to perceived events.

3.1 Sound Event Detection

The first component performs sound event detection (SED) [5] using the ATST-SED model [17], an adaptation of the ATST-Frame model trained on the DESED domestic dataset [19].

The implementation has been carried out through a ROS 2 node developed in Python, which allows model inference in real time. This node receives the audio signal from the robot's microphone array as a 16-bit integer signal, normalizes it, and converts it into the model's input tensor. The model output identifies the sound class (e.g., *frying*, *dog*, etc.), which is published along with its identifier in a specific topic. This message is retrieved by the perception system for integration with the other information and context-sensitive decision making.

3.2 Sound Source Localization

The second component of the system is the localization of the sound source, which allows estimating the direction and position from which a detected sound comes. For this purpose, a circular microphone array installed on the robot is used, specifically the ReSpeaker 4 Mic Array [4], capable of estimating the DOA in the horizontal plane.

A specific model has been defined in the URDF (Unified Robot Description Format) of the robot that represents the geometry and placement of the microphone array, including the orientation of each microphone that comprises it to the head of the robot, where it is installed. This allows the DOA angle to be interpreted as a relative direction in the microphone coordinate system.

From this direction and the model of the microphone array defined in the robot's URDF, a relative position of the sound source point concerning the microphone coordinate system is calculated. Using the available transformation between this system and the robot's map, the estimated direction is projected in coordinates, thus obtaining an approximate location in the environment. This information, computed in real time, is incorporated into the final message generated by the perception system and is important to contextualize the robot's response to different events depending on their location.

3.3 Sound Perception Integration

The final system (Fig. 1) is in charge of integrating the sound detection and localization results to generate a complete representation of the acoustic event. This representation allows the robot to adapt its behavior depending on the type of event and its context.

This module has been implemented as a C++ node within a package called sound_perception_system. It operates in real time, subscribing continuously to the outputs of the Sound Event Detection node (sound class) and the source location estimation. Once this information is merged, the system categorizes the acoustic event based on its nature and priority level for robot interaction. The system defines three main categories:

- Environmental: environmental sounds that do not require action by the robot (dishes, vacuum cleaner). They are ignored.
- Supervised: events that require the supervision or presence of a human, because they are potentially dangerous sources such as water, fire, or electrical appliances (water running, blender).
- Emergency: critical events such as alarms, which interrupt any task in progress to be attended to immediately.

Finally, the node generates and publishes a message encapsulating the detected class, its associated category, and its location in coordinates based on the map. This representation allows other modules to interpret the event according to its urgency and context, favoring safer and more efficient adaptive decisions in domestic environments.

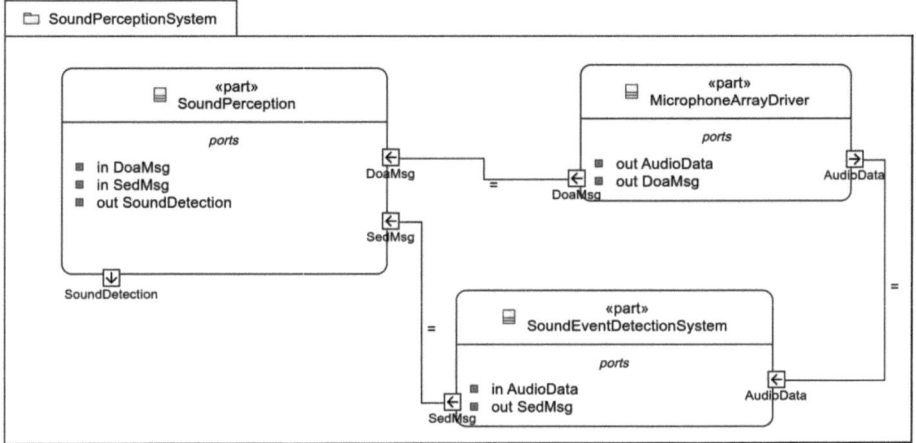

Fig. 1. Representation of the perception system architecture in SysMLv2.

The full source code of the auditory perception system is publicly available at: https://github.com/igonzf/sound_perception_system.

3.4 Behavioral Layer

The auditory perception system described above is integrated into the robot architecture through the behavioral layer, implemented using behavior trees (BTs) that are continuously running, monitoring the occurrence of new acoustic events. Upon receiving a message from the perception system, a decision flow is triggered following the logic shown in the Algorithm 1. Depending on the category of the sound and the current state of the robot, a decision is made whether to ignore the event, verify the context with additional sensors, or interrupt the current task to alert a person.

3.5 Experimental Design

For the evaluation, the TIAGo robot, equipped with a circular ReSpeaker 4 Mic Array located on top of the head, was used. The experiments were performed in the León@Home Testbed [20], a European Robotics League (ERL) certified environment, located at the University of León (Spain). The objective of the

Algorithm 1. Behavior selection based on sound perception

Require: Detected sound event (c, κ)
 1:     $c \in C$, where $C = \{alarm\_bell\_ringing,\ blender,\ cat,\ dishes,\ dog,\ electric\_shaver\_toothbrush,\ frying,\ running\_water,\ speech,\ vacuum\_cleaner\}$
 2:     $\kappa \in \{$environmental, supervised, emergency$\}$ is the semantic category
Require: Estimated sound direction θ, current robot state s_r
Ensure: Executed action
 3: **if** $\kappa =$ environmental **then**
 4:     Ignore the event and continue executing s_r
 5: **else if** $\kappa =$ supervised **then**
 6:     Orient the camera toward direction θ
 7:     $p \leftarrow$ DETECTPERSONPRESENCE(θ)
 8:     **if** $p =$ true **then**
 9:         **if** $s_r =$ idle **then**
10:             Offer assistance to the person
11:         **else**
12:             Continue executing s_r
13:         **end if**
14:     **else**
15:         Interrupt s_r
16:         $p \leftarrow$ SEARCHFORPERSON
17:         **if** $p =$ true **then**
18:             Notify the person about the danger
19:         **end if**
20:     **end if**
21: **else if** $\kappa =$ emergency **then**
22:     Interrupt s_r
23:     $p \leftarrow$ SEARCHFORPERSON
24:     **if** $p =$ true **then**
25:         Alert the person
26:     **end if**
27: **end if**

experiments was to evaluate the robot's behavior to different types of acoustic events in a domestic environment.

For this purpose, three demonstrations were defined. In the first demonstration, the robot detects a common sound in the kitchen, which could be interpreted as someone cooking. Upon finding a person present in the kitchen, the robot assumes that the situation is normal and, if he or she is not performing a priority task, offers to assist in the task. In the second demonstration, the robot recognizes the same sound, but this time, there is no person in the kitchen, leading the robot to interpret the situation as potentially dangerous, such as an unsupervised fire. In this case, the robot looks for a person in the environment and, upon finding them, warns them of the potential risk. Finally, in the third demonstration, the robot detects an emergency alarm, and since this type of sound is categorized as high priority, it immediately interrupts its task and searches for anyone present in the environment to alert them to the emergency.

4 Results

To analyze how sound perception influences decision-making, three demonstrations were performed in domestic environments, each showcasing a different type of event and the system's corresponding behavioral response.

4.1 Demonstration 1: Supervised Sound with Human Presence

This first demonstration (Fig. 2) evaluates how the system reacts to an ambiguous sound, whose interpretation depends on the context in which it occurs. The detected sound corresponds to the class *frying*, which in a domestic environment can have multiple meanings: from a normal cooking activity to a risky situation, such as an unattended burning frying pan or a possible fire.

The robot stands at the entrance to the apartment kitchen, performing a pre-task. Its auditory perception system detects sound classified as *frying*, which is automatically categorized as a supervised sound, indicating that its relevance depends on whether a person is supervising the activity. These types of sounds do not require an immediate reaction, but they do need to be verified before being discarded as irrelevant.

The localization module estimates the direction of the sound source, and the robot orients its camera towards that position, in this case, the kitchen. Through visual perception, it detects that in the kitchen, there is a person standing in front of the counter, apparently manipulating the frying pan.

According to the logic defined in the behavior tree (Fig. 3), a collaborative action is triggered: if the robot is not executing a priority task, it offers help; otherwise, it continues with its previous activity.

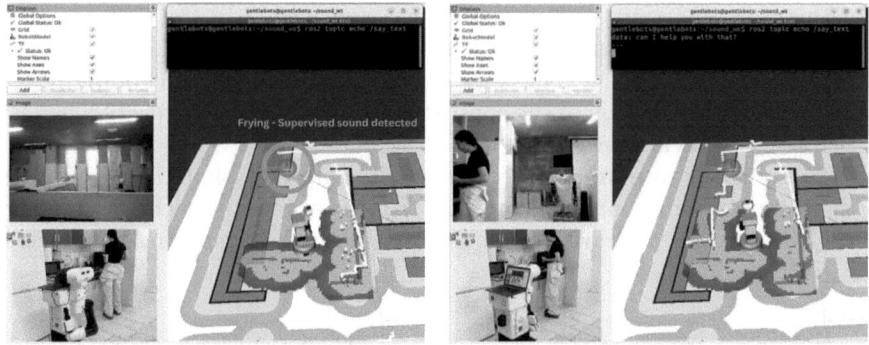

(a) The robot detects a frying sound categorized as "supervised" in the kitchen.   (b) The robot interprets the context, recognizes a person cooking, and, assuming it is a normal situation, offers help.

Fig. 2. Robot behavior during demonstration 1, displayed in RViz (The full video is available at https://drive.google.com/file/d/1TRtrQmlWv4_SAFLh8OXV4q E4BwLylpYQ/view?resourcekeylink).

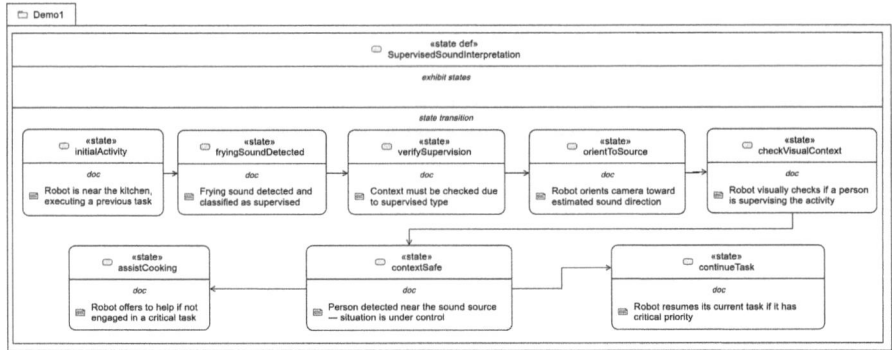

Fig. 3. State transition view of the main steps the robot goes through during demonstration 1, modeled in SysMLv2.

4.2 Demonstration 2: Supervised Sound Without Human Presence

This second demonstration (Fig. 5) evaluates how the system reacts to the same sound (*frying*) as in the previous demonstration, but in a different context, where the situation does represent a danger.

The robot is again at the entrance to the apartment kitchen when it detects the frying sound coming from the kitchen. As in the previous case, the sound is classified under the "supervised" category, indicating that its dangerousness depends on whether there is a person present supervising the action. Following the same procedure, the system estimates the direction of the sound and the robot orients its camera towards the source to visually check the scene.

In this case, the camera does not detect any person in the kitchen. In the absence of visible human supervision, the robot interprets the situation as potentially dangerous: the frying pan is on, but there is no one controlling it. This change in the interpretation of the context triggers a predefined reactive behavior in the robot's behavior tree (Fig 4).

The response is to temporarily abandon its current task and actively search for a person in the environment. Once located, the robot approaches and initiates a verbal interaction to warn about the possible risk, requesting to check the situation in the kitchen.

4.3 Demonstration 3: Emergency Sound

The third demonstration (Fig. 6) evaluates the response of the system to an acoustic event classified as "emergency", specifically a sound of type *alarm_bell _ringing* , which could correspond to a fire alarm. Unlike previous cases, where the robot's action depended on contextual analysis using the camera, in this scenario, the sound category alone determines the need for immediate action.

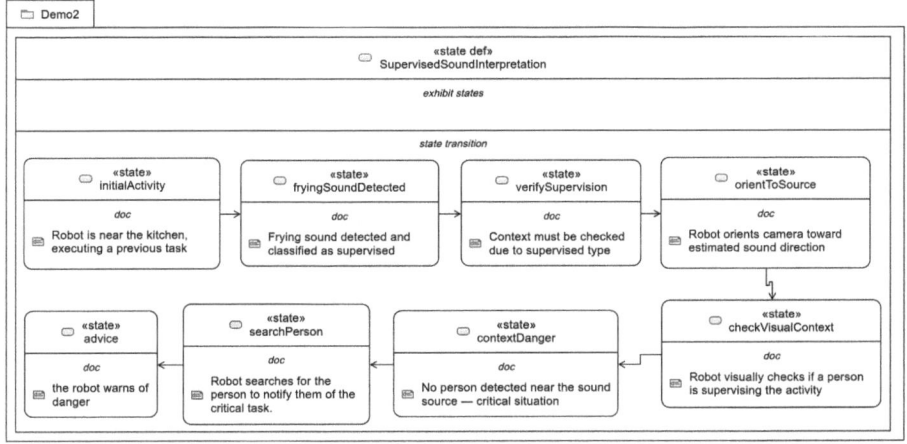

Fig. 4. State transition view of the main steps the robot goes through during demonstration 2, modeled in SysMLv2.

During the execution of a task in the kitchen, the robot detects the sound and, recognizing it as an emergency, interrupts its activity and directly activates the emergency response. The defined behavior consists of locating a person in the environment who, for various reasons, might not have heard the alarm (use of headphones, hearing problems, distraction, etc.), and establishing an interaction to warn them of the danger and request immediate evacuation.

5 Discussion

The experiments presented in Sect. 4 allow for an analysis of the system's ability to perceive, interpret, and act on acoustic events in a domestic environment. Unlike approaches focused exclusively on sound classification, this proposal integrates auditory perception into an architecture that allows context-adapted and real-time executable responses.

The system has shown different responses to identical sound stimuli depending on the context. In the first two demonstrations, the same type of sound (*frying*) triggers different actions: continue with the task or look for a person and warn him or her, depending on whether the situation is potentially dangerous. This demonstrates the importance of incorporating reasoning mechanisms, where the same sound can have multiple interpretations.

The semantic categorization of sounds into three categories (environmental, supervised, emergency) has served as a mechanism for prioritizing events. In the case of the alarm, classified as an emergency, the system reacted immediately without requiring additional interpretation of the context, suggesting its usefulness in critical situations that demand rapid action.

However, the system has certain limitations. The semantic categorization of sounds has been defined manually and may not generalize to other environments.

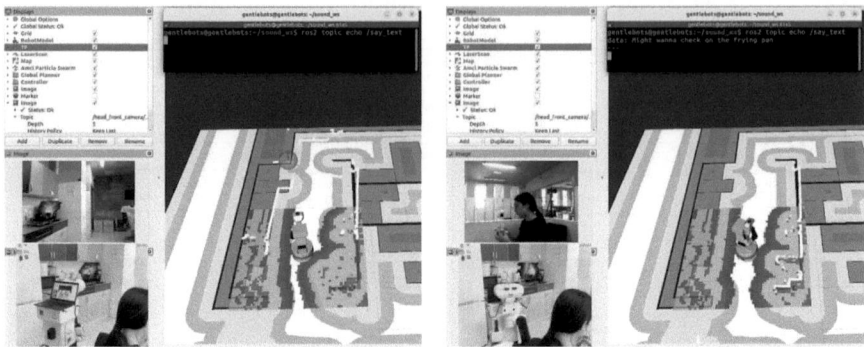

(a) The robot recognizes that the frying sound heard in the kitchen is an unattended fire.

(b) The robot searches for the person in the environment and warns them of danger.

Fig. 5. Robot behavior during demonstration 2, displayed in RViz (The full video is available at https://drive.google.com/file/d/1yEUm6XVsRGQEXDHi-RUoO Hk1JjOlNhlu/view?resourcekey link).

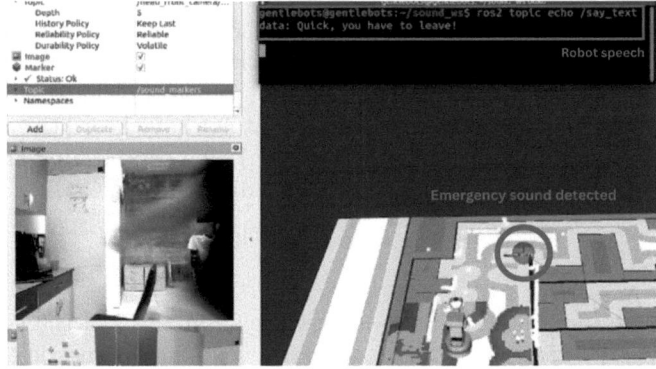

Fig. 6. The robot alerts the person that they have to evacuate after hearing a sound categorized as emergency. The full video is available at https://drive.google.com/file/d/1LzrOtvFc_IqOKAwS8D5m9GJe9nko-U0Z/view?resourcekey link.

In addition, it assumes that all relevant events are audible, which may not be true in more complex scenarios.

Future work will focus on improving the robustness of the classification model to noise and uncontrolled acoustic conditions, while preserving the advantages that led to the selection of the ATST-SED model. Likewise, it is considered relevant to explore symbolic reasoning mechanisms that allow robots not only to recognize sounds, but also to build an understanding of their meaning and implications in the environment and for the people with whom they interact.

6 Conclusions

This work demonstrates that integrating a sound perception system enables a social robot to understand its environment more effectively and adapt its behavior accordingly.

Unlike conventional systems that follow plans without context awareness, our approach allows the robot to respond based on the type of sound and the situation. By combining auditory and visual perception, the robot interprets events before acting, distinguishing between irrelevant, potentially dangerous, and critical situations. This enhances its ability to reorganize priorities, warn of risks, and interact more naturally with people.

Future work will aim to improve robustness under noisy and dynamic conditions, explore symbolic reasoning to infer the meaning of sounds, and evaluate the impact of each component through ablation studies or by comparing against audio-only baselines.

Acknowledgements. This research has been partially funded by the Horizon Europe project CORESENSE (Grant Agreement No. 101070254); by the Recovery, Transformation, and Resilience Plan, financed by the European Union (Next Generation) thanks to the TESCAC project (Traceability and Explainability in Autonomous Systems for improved Cybersecurity), granted by INCIBE to the University of León; and by the EDMAR project: Grant PID2021-126592OB-C21, funded by MICIU/AEI/10.13039/501100011033 and "ERDF/EU". David Sobrín Hidalgo thanks the University of León for the scholarship provided to fund his doctoral studies.

References

1. Boes, W., Van hamme, H.: Multi-source transformer architectures for audiovisual scene classification (2022). https://arxiv.org/abs/2210.10212
2. Dekkers, G., et al.: The SINS database for detection of daily activities in a home environment using an acoustic sensor network. In: Proceedings of the Detection and Classification of Acoustic Scenes and Events 2017 Workshop (DCASE2017), pp. 32–36 (Nov 2017)
3. He, K., Shu, X., Jia, S., He, Y.: Semi-supervised sound event detection system for DCASE 2022 task 4. Technical report, Detection and Classification of Acoustic Scenes and Events 2022 Challenge (2022)
4. Huang, J.: Respeaker 4-mic array for raspberry pi (2023). https://wiki.seeedstudio.com/ReSpeaker_4_Mic_Array_for_Raspberry_Pi/, Accessed 12 May 2025
5. Khandelwal, T., Das, R.K., Chng, E.S.: Sound event detection: a journey through DCASE challenge series. APSIPA Trans. Signal Inf. Proc. **13**(1), e3 (2024). https://doi.org/10.1561/116.00000051
6. Li, X., Shao, N., Li, X.: Self-supervised audio teacher-student transformer for both clip-level and frame-level tasks (2023). https://arxiv.org/abs/2306.04186
7. Macenski, S., Foote, T., Gerkey, B., Lalancette, C., Woodall, W.: Robot operating system 2: design, architecture, and uses in the wild. Sci. Robot. **7**(66), eabm6074 (2022). https://doi.org/10.1126/scirobotics.abm6074

8. Macenski, S., Soragna, A., Carroll, M., Ge, Z.: Impact of ROS 2 node composition in robotic systems. In: IEEE Robotics and Autonomous Letters (RA-L) (2023). https://doi.org/10.48550/arXiv.2305.09933
9. Mayr, S., Weigel, M., Schmid, U.: Cognitive robotics: a survey of the state of the art and future perspectives. Artif. Intell. Rev. (2023). https://doi.org/10.1007/s10462-023-10448-w
10. Mesaros, A., Serizel, R., Heittola, T., Virtanen, T., Plumbley, M.D.: A decade of DCASE: achievements, practices, evaluations and future challenges (2024). https://arxiv.org/abs/2410.04951
11. Pakkala, D., Känsäkoski, N., Heikkilä, T., Backman, J., Pääkkönen, P.: On design of cognitive situation-adaptive autonomous mobile robotic applications. Comput. Ind. **167**, 104263 (2025). https://doi.org/10.1016/j.compind.2025.104263
12. Papers with code: sound event detection on DESED (2025). https://paperswithcode.com/sota/sound-event-detection-on-desed, Accessed 12 May 12 2025
13. Ronchini, F., Cornell, S., Serizel, R., Turpault, N., Fonseca, E., Ellis, D.P.: Description and analysis of novelties introduced in DCASE Task 4 2022 on the baseline system. In: DCASE Workshop (2022)
14. Ronchini, F., Cornell, S., Turpault, N.: DCASE 2021 task 4 challenge. https://dcase.community/challenge2021 (2021), Accessed 11 May 2025
15. Rovida, F., et al.: SkiROS–a skill-based robot control platform on top of ROS. In: Robot Operating System (ROS) The Complete Reference (Volume 2), pp. 121–160. Springer (2017)
16. Serizel, R., Turpault, N., Shah, A., Salamon, J.: Sound event detection in synthetic domestic environments. In: ICASSP 2020 - 45th International Conference on Acoustics, Speech, and Signal Processing. Barcelona, Spain (2020), (hal-02355573v2)
17. Shao, N., Li, X., Li, X.: Fine-tune the pretrained ATST model for sound event detection (2023), https://arxiv.org/abs/2309.08153
18. Snyder, D., Chen, G., Povey, D.: MUSAN: A music, speech, and noise corpus (2015), arXiv:1510.08484v1
19. Turpault, N., Serizel, R., Shah, A.P., Salamon, J.: Sound event detection in domestic environments with weakly labeled data and soundscape synthesis. In: Workshop on Detection and Classification of Acoustic Scenes and Events. New York City, United States (2019)
20. Universidad de León: Leon@Home TestBed. http://robotica.unileon.es/index.php/Testbed, Accessed 11 May 2025

A New Transformer-Based Hybrid Model to Forecast Olive Fruit Fly Using Multimodal Data

A. M. Chacón-Maldonado, N. Martnez Van der Looven, G. Asencio-Cortés, and A. Troncoso[✉]

Data Science and Big Data Lab, Pablo de Olavide University, 41013 Seville, Spain
{amchamal,nmarvan,guaasecor,atrolor}@upo.es

Abstract. Agricultural pest outbreaks pose serious risks to crop productivity, demanding timely and accurate forecasting methods. This work introduces a novel multimodal hybrid framework that fuses spatial features extracted from Sentinel-2 imagery with meteorological time series data to predict olive fruit fly populations one week ahead. A convolutional neural network is employed to capture spatial dependencies from fused satellite images, while different machine learning algorithms including Lag-Llama, Random Forest and XGBoost, are integrated for predictive modeling. Experimental results indicate that the hybrid approach, particularly when using Lag-Llama, outperforms models based solely on individual data modalities. These findings highlight the potential of deep learning and data fusion techniques in enhancing pest management and improving forecasting accuracy in agricultural settings.

Keywords: Multimodal data · foundational transformer model · hybrid deep learning · agricultural pest forecasting

1 Introduction

Agricultural pests pose a major threat to crop productivity, causing substantial economic losses and increasing production costs. Early detection and accurate forecasting of pest outbreaks are essential to implement timely interventions, optimize pest control strategies, and ensure the best sanitary conditions for crops. In particular, the olive fruit fly (Bactrocera oleae) can devastate olive yields, making it imperative to develop reliable tools for anticipating its population dynamics one week in advance.

Deep learning models, particularly convolutional neural networks (CNNs), have demonstrated strong capabilities in learning complex spatial and temporal patterns from high-dimensional data.

Their use of parameter sharing and local connectivity not only enhances computational efficiency but also improves generalization when processing large-scale inputs such as satellite imagery [2,10,16].

Recent advances highlight the value of multimodal integration for pest forecasting. Satellite imagery from Sentinel-2 L2A provides key vegetation and moisture indicators—such as the normalized difference vegetation index (NDVI), the normalized difference water index (NDWI), and atmospheric moisture maps—that reflect plant health, water stress, and microclimatic conditions. When combined with meteorological time series (e.g., temperature, humidity, and precipitation), these data offer complementary perspectives on the environmental drivers of pest activity [1,3].

However, agricultural datasets are often limited in size, posing challenges for deep learning training. To address this, we employ targeted data augmentation techniques—such as random rotations, flips, and spectral shifts—to expand the diversity of image samples and improve CNN generalization on small-to-medium plot-level datasets.

In this work, we propose a multimodal hybrid strategy to forecast olive fruit fly populations one week ahead by fusing spatial features extracted by a CNN with meteorological time series. First, a CNN-based embedding model processes Sentinel-2-derived NDVI, NDWI and moisture images, yielding compact feature representations. These embeddings are then concatenated with aligned weather variables and fed into ensemble tree-based algorithms (Random Forest and XGBoost) as well as a transformer model. We evaluate our approach on data collected from four distinct olive groves in Spain, comparing the fused-model forecasts against standalone baselines that use only imagery or only time series (meteorological data).

2 Related Work

The application of machine learning (ML) and deep learning (DL) techniques in agriculture has gained significant relevance, as they enable scalable solutions to critical problems in pest detection and forecasting. Traditionally, outbreak identification has relied on empirical thresholds and expert knowledge; however, recent DL-based methodologies have demonstrated a greater ability to capture complex spatial and temporal patterns through the use of convolutional neural networks (CNNs) and other advanced architectures [5].

Recent research has explored diverse applications of CNNs and hybrid deep learning models in smart agriculture. The study in [7] offers a comprehensive review of CNN applications in smart agriculture, emphasizing recent developments in areas like weed detection, disease diagnosis, crop classification, water resource management, and yield estimation. In [15], the authors proposed a CNN model that utilizes NDVI data extracted from satellite imagery to forecast drought conditions in India's Kolar district.

Meanwhile, in pest prediction, [14] combined classical ML and DL techniques using crop damage and meteorological data for olives and vineyards, applying SHAP for model interpretability. [8] introduced a hybrid CNN-Transformer model for classifying pests from the IP102 dataset, fusing local and global features via a dual-path aggregation module.

The work present in [11] applied three models–including hybrid ones–to detect olive fruit flies in chromatic trap images, using HOG features with SVM, a LeNet-5-inspired CNN, and PCA with a random forest. Similarly, [17] developed a hybrid model for tomato leaf disease classification, combining region-based CNNs with feature pyramid networks for leaf detection, and a CNN-Transformer fusion for disease recognition.

Data fusion is gaining relevance for enhancing prediction accuracy. [4] reviewed unimodal and multimodal DL architectures for vision tasks, highlighting fusion strategies (early, intermediate, late) and hybrid techniques (e.g., stacking, averaging). Finally, [6] proposed an explainable hybrid model using satellite, meteorological, and field data to predict olive fruit fly counts. It combines an autoencoder with a feed-forward neural network and uses SHAP for explainability.

While many machine learning and deep learning methods exist for detecting current pest infestations, few address the challenge of forecasting their future progression. The literature shows a strong reliance on deep learning for image-based pest detection, but reveals a lack of multimodal hybrid models that integrate satellite imagery and meteorological data–most approaches rely on a single data source. In response to these gaps, the methodology proposed in this work introduces a novel hybrid multimodal framework for pest forecasting, representing a promising and underexplored research direction in agricultural applications.

3 Methodology

This section describes the proposed approach to predict the number of olive fruit flies that will fall into traps one week in advance. In particular, Sect. 3.1 describes the data used to generate the models, as well as their preprocessing and extraction. Section 3.2 provides an overview of the proposed multimodal hybrid method for pest forecasting. Section 3.3 provides a detailed description of training process. Finally, Sect. 3.4 presents the different machine learning algorithms used to test the proposed methodology.

3.1 Input Data

The dataset used covers the period from 2017 to 2023 and integrates information from four olive grove plots located in the autonomous community of Andalusia, Spain. These plots are situated in the municipalities of Algodonales and Olvera (Cádiz), Baena (Córdoba) and Pozo Alcón (Jaén). Each plot is assigned a nearby weather station, selected based on the shortest geographical distance, to provide the corresponding climate data. The years 2017 to 2020 are used for training, while the years 2021 to 2023 are reserved for testing. The data are grouped into three main categories: biological data, meteorological data and satellite imagery. Data have been obtained from Phytosanitary Information and Alert Network (RAIF) of Andalusia [13].

Biological Data. The target variable is the average number of olive fruit flies captured per trap per day. This information is collected weekly by field technicians, who count the captures and calculate the average per plot. The samples include the collection date, the geographical coordinates of the plot, and administrative metadata (province, municipality). Since plot identification codes may change from year to year, a matching process based on geographical coordinates and administrative location is performed to ensure the traceability of each plot over time.

This preprocessing step enables the generation of a uniform structure for the biological dataset, where each instance includes the plot code, collection date, and target value (number of flies), which is later temporally aligned with the corresponding meteorological data and satellite imagery.

Meteorological Data. The climatic data correspond to weather stations associated with each plot. Variables include temperature (minimum, maximum, and average), relative humidity, wind speed (minimum, maximum, and average), solar radiation, and precipitation, recorded daily from 2016 to 2023.

To link each plot with a weather station, their coordinates are compared. If there is no exact match, the closest station is selected based on Euclidean distance. Once the associations are established, a set of weekly statistics is generated for each biological sample: the mean of daily averages, the maximum of daily maxima, and the minimum of daily minima are calculated for temperature, humidity, and wind speed; for radiation and precipitation, the maximum value and the weekly sum are considered.

Additionally, a temporal lag is introduced: the meteorological data used cover both the week prior to the biological sample and the preceding week, in order to capture potential delayed effects of weather conditions on pest activity.

Before computing statistics, missing values (around 0.06%) and outliers are identified. Missing values are removed, and outliers are imputed using a Random Forest model. To do so, anomalous values are marked as missing, and a model is trained to predict these variables based on the remaining features, using the average of all tree predictions to impute the final value.

Satellite Images. Satellite images are obtained through Sentinel Hub, using bands from the Sentinel-2 L2A satellites. Three spectral indices are employed: NDVI (vegetation health and density), NDWI (water content) and Moisture (atmospheric water vapor). Weekly images are generated for each plot based on these indices. For each week, two different dates are selected (within the seven days prior to the biological sample) and images corresponding to the three indices are downloaded for each date.

Subsequently, a fusion process is performed using RGB channels. First, the three images from each day (NDVI, NDWI and Moisture) are combined into a single 9-channel image. Then, the two 9-channel images are merged into a final 18-channel image that incorporates both spectral and temporal variation. These images are normalized by dividing pixel values by 255 and resized to 256×256 pixels to standardize input for the convolutional network.

It is worth noting that the Sentinel-2 satellite has a revisit frequency of 2 to 3 d in regions like Andalusia, allowing for the availability of multiple images per week for most plots, except in specific cases affected by cloud cover or atmospheric interference.

3.2 Hybrid Architecture

The proposed hybrid architecture combines satellite imagery and meteorological time series to predict olive fruit fly infestations one week in advance. The core of the system is a multimodal fusion strategy that leverages a convolutional neural network (CNN) to extract spatial features from fused satellite images, which are subsequently integrated with numerical weather data for final prediction.

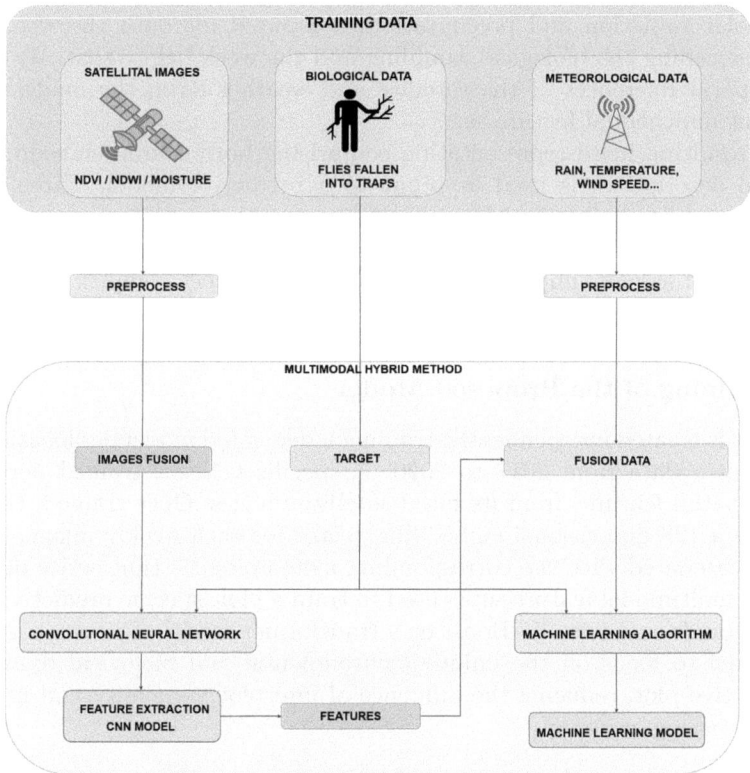

Fig. 1. Framework of the proposed method.

Figure 1 presents a summary of the stages carried out in the methodology, excluding the data acquisition process described previously in Sect. 3.1.

Each week, six satellite images are selected: two for each of the NDVI, NDWI, and Moisture indices, corresponding to different days from the week prior to the biological sampling. For each day, the three images (one per index) are stacked at the RGB channel level to generate a 9 channel composite. Then, the two 9 channel images are fused into a final 18 channel image, encapsulating both temporal and spectral information. These images are normalized and resized to 256×256 pixels to ensure consistency across samples and compatibility with the CNN input requirements.

The CNN processes each 18 channel image through three convolutional layers (with 32, 64, and 64 filters, respectively), each followed by ReLU activation and max-pooling. The output is flattened and passed through a dense layer with 128 neurons, generating a 128 dimensional embedding vector that captures the most relevant spatial patterns from the imagery.

To incorporate environmental context, each embedding vector is concatenated with a set of engineered features derived from meteorological time series. These features consist of weekly summaries of temperature, humidity, wind speed, solar radiation and precipitation, computed for both the week immediately preceding the biological sampling and the week before that. By aligning the temporal references of the satellite and weather data, the model forms a consistent multimodal feature set.

The resulting fused representation comprising both spatial embeddings and temporal descriptors, is used as input to a predictive model. Three alternatives are evaluated: Random Forest, XGBoost and a transformer model. This hybrid design enables the model to exploit the complementary nature of spatial and temporal signals, improving its capability to detect complex patterns and enhancing the accuracy of pest forecasting, particularly during outbreak peaks.

3.3 Training of the Proposed Model

Each plot is treated independently, training a dedicated model per location using only its own data from 2017 to 2020. A specific CNN is trained per plot to extract spatial features from its fused satellite images. Once trained, this CNN generates a 128 dimensional embedding vector for each weekly image, which is then concatenated with the corresponding meteorological time series data. The resulting multimodal feature set is used to train a plot, specific predictive model, either a Random Forest, XGBoost or a transformer model. This strategy allows each model to focus on the unique environmental and biological dynamics of its respective plot, reducing the influence of interplot variability and improving local forecasting accuracy.

3.4 Machine Learning Algorithms

The multimodal hybrid algorithm is composed by a CNN-based embedding method and a machine learning algorithm. Both classic machine learning paradigms and transformer paradigms are used to evaluate the hybrid approach. Specifically, two tree-based ensemble approaches such as Random Forest and

XGBoost are chosen. Additionally, a transformer is also used to observe whether its performance varies compared to the classic machine learning approaches when its input data includes features extracted from images. Lag-Llama [12] is a foundation model designed for univariate probabilistic time series forecasting. It is based on a decoder-only Transformer architecture and leverages lagged values as covariates. The model is pretrained in a self-supervised manner on a large and diverse corpus of time series data from multiple domains, enabling strong generalization capabilities in zero-shot and few-shot scenarios. Lag-Llama tokenizes input sequences using fixed lag indices along with temporal features (e.g., hour-of-day, day-of-week), allowing the model to be frequency-agnostic and adaptable to unseen sampling rates. At inference time, it autoregressively outputs a probability distribution over future values using a parametric distribution head such as a Student's t-distribution thus capturing predictive uncertainty.

Random Forest is an ensemble of decision trees trained using bagging, where each tree is built from a random bootstrap sample and a subset of features. This approach increases robustness and reduces variance, producing stable predictions by averaging the outputs of multiple trees.

XGBoost is a gradient boosting method that builds trees sequentially, where each tree focuses on correcting the residuals of the previous ones. It incorporates regularization and shrinkage mechanisms to improve generalization and prevent overfitting, making it effective for complex regression tasks.

These models are evaluated to determine the most effective strategy for forecasting pest outbreaks based on fused multimodal features.

4 Experimentation and Results

This section presents the experimental results obtained when predicting the test set. Section 4.1 displays the configuration of the different algorithms used. Section 4.2 reports the results obtained by the multimodal hybrid methodology using different machine learning algorithms. Section 4.3 presents the results obtained by machine learning algorithms. Finally, Sect. 4.4 discusses the results obtained.

4.1 Experimental Settings

In this section, the values of the parameters that have been used for both the CNN and for all the machine learning algorithms tested in the proposed multimodal hybrid model are reported.

- CNN: The first convolutional layer applies 32 filters of size 3×3 while the second and third convolutional layers utilize 64 filters of size 3×3 each, and 2×2 max pooling operation to reduce spatial dimensions. The last dense layer has 128 neurons. The model is compiled using the Adam optimizer with a learning rate of 0.001. The Mean Squared Error (MSE) is used as the loss function. To prevent overfitting and improve generalization, the early stopping technique is used to monitor the validation loss. Training stops if no significant improvement defined by a threshold of 10^{-5} is observed for 15 consecutive epochs. Furthermore, the best recorded weights are restored, ensuring that the final model retains the optimal validation performance. The model is trained for a maximum of 100 epochs with a batch size of 32.

- Lag-Llama: The estimator, whose main function is to encapsulate all the aspects necessary to train and generate predictions, is initialized from a pretrained checkpoint and its configuration (including parameters such as input size, number of layers, embedding per head, and number of attention heads) is extracted directly from the checkpoint. The pretrained model is huggingface [9]. This strategy is in line with the approach detailed in the Lag-Llama [12], where pretraining on diverse time series data enables strong zero-shot and few-shot generalization. The model forecasts one week ahead using a context length of two weeks. Each model trained for 50 epochs. Recognizing that the optimal learning rate may vary depending on the data set, the experiments perform a grid search over multiple values (0.01, 0.05, 0.001, 0.005, 0.0001, 0.0005), said values being those reported by the authors in [12]. For each plot, the best learning rate is selected based on the lowest Mean Absolute Error (MAE) computed on the validation forecasts. During prediction, the model generates forecasts using 20 parallel samples, which facilitates robust estimation of the predictive distribution.
- Random Forest: 100 trees are considered in the ensemble and each tree within the ensemble is built without depth restrictions and is fitted to a randomly resampled dataset with replacement. The division of nodes is carried out until pure partitions or the minimum required samples are reached and at each split, all available features are considered to select the best partition, maximizing the model's predictive capacity. Additionally, the MSE criterion is used to minimize variance at each node.
- XGboost: 100 trees and a fixed seed of 1 to ensure result reproducibility are used. The learning rate has been set to 0.3, a value that balances convergence speed and generalization capacity. The maximum tree depth has been fixed at 6, as greater depths increase model complexity and may lead to overfitting. To prevent overfitting and enhance generalization, each tree has been trained using all available instances in each iteration. Similarly, all features have been used in each tree, avoiding restrictions in attribute selection during training. No penalties have been imposed on tree expansion, allowing the model to grow without additional constraints. Tree growth has also been regulated by establishing a minimum requirement on the sum of instance weights at each leaf node, preventing excessively specific partitions that could compromise generalization. Additionally, L2 regularization has been applied without extra constraints, ensuring a balanced penalization of coefficients. The algorithm has been configured to minimize the MSE.

4.2 Multimodal Hybrid Approach Results

In this section the results when predicting the number of flies caught in traps for each plot during the years of the test set from 2021 to 2023 are depicted, using the MAE as an evaluation metric.

Table 1. MAEs obtained for each plot when using Lag-Llama, Random Forest and XGBoost in the multimodal hybrid algorithm.

Plots	CNN&Lag-Llama	CNN&RF	CNN&XGBoost
Plot 1	**0.8104**	0.8923	0.9533
Plot 2	**1.3258**	1.6208	1.7236
Plot 3	**1.3770**	2.8583	2.8804
Plot 4	**1.1779**	2.4071	3.0670
Average	**1.1727**	1.9446	2.1560

We firstly conduct a comparative analysis of the results when use the multimodal hybrid algorithm with Lag-Llama, Random Forest and XGBoost.

Table 1 presents a comparison of the MAE values obtained using the hybrid multimodal methodology with the Lag-Llama, Random Forest, and XGBoost algorithms. This evaluation uses the fused dataset, which includes the image features extracted by the CNN along with time series containing weekly statistical and biological data. The MAE values represent the absolute difference between the actual and predicted values across the entire dataset, thus indicating the prediction error of fallen flies in traps produced by the different hybrid architectures. It can be observed that using Lag-Llama within the hybrid multimodal methodology yields better results compared to using Random Forest or XGBoost, both when applied individually to each plot and when generalized across all four plots. Moreover, Lag-Llama exhibits a very short execution time, as it is a Transformer-based model that leverages a pre-trained architecture.

4.3 Comparison with Benchmark Models

In this section, the best multimodal hybrid model, CNN&Lag-Llama, is compared to various benchmark models, in particular, the machine learning algorithms that have been used in the hybrid method have been selected as benchmark models to evaluate the relevance of data fusion from image-based features and meteorological time series and the predictive capacity of both images and meteorological data when used separately, using the MAE as an evaluation metric.

This means comparing the results obtained by the CNN when is applied to predict using only images, and the Random Forest, XGBoost and Lag-Llama model using only meteorological data, that is, using the same dataset that the hybrid method but without extracted features. In the case of the CNN to obtain predictions, the same CNN architecture was used, except for reducing the number of neurons in the flatten and the last dense layers from 128 to 64 and a final output layer is added with only one neuron, that represents the prediction generated by the model.

Table 2. MAEs obtained by the best multimodal hybrid model and benchmark models using only images or only meteorological data.

Plots	CNN&Lag-Llama	CNN	RF	XGBoost	Lag-Llama
Plot 1	0.8104	1.0173	**0.7656**	0.9410	0.8104
Plot 2	1.3258	1.7418	1.5553	1.5375	**1.3123**
Plot 3	1.3770	**1.1175**	1.4995	2.2572	1.8780
Plot 4	1.1779	**0.9948**	3.8427	2.9751	1.1244
Average	**1.1727**	1.2178	1.9157	1.9277	1.2812

The results are presented in Table 2, which reports the MAEs for the predictions generated by the CNN when using only images for training, and by Random Forest, XGBoost, and Lag-Llama when using meteorological data for training. As in the comparison presented in the previous section, the MAE values indicate the number of fallen flies in traps that were incorrectly predicted by the different algorithms. It can be observed that CNN&Lag-Llama outperforms all the methods that are used for comparative purposes. Although the CNN achieved competitive results in terms of MAE, it lacks consistency, as it produces the best results for some plots but, conversely, the worst for others. When comparing the evaluation metric obtained for Random Forest, XGBoost and Lag-Llama for each of the plots with the metrics reported for CNN&Lag-Llama and CNN, it can be concluded that the exclusive use of meteorological data leads to a decrease in predictive performance and that using only the images results in lower errors than using only the meteorological data. This confirms not only that the images provide additional valuable information beyond the meteorological data but also highlights the importance of integrating the image features with the meteorological data to improve the predictive capabilities of the model.

4.4 Discussion of Results

The experimental results show the effectiveness of the proposed multimodal hybrid methodology, which integrates CNN with machine learning algorithms for olive fruit fly prediction. The incorporation of spatial features extracted from Sentinel-2 satellite images significantly enhances the predictive accuracy when fused with meteorological data.

Comparative analyses confirm that the CNN&Lag-Llama hybrid model consistently achieves more accurate predictions compared to standalone machine learning models. While CNN alone provides useful spatial representations, their direct predictions exhibit high variance and instability. However, machine learning models relying solely on meteorological data do not capture the spatial dependencies present in satellite imagery. The proposed multimodal hybrid approach effectively combines these strengths, mitigating individual model weaknesses.

Furthermore, the experiments reveal that Lag-Llama outperforms Random Forest and XGBoost when used as the model in the hybrid pipeline.

Overall, the results validate the potential of multimodal data fusion for agricultural pest forecasting. The integration of CNN-based spatial feature extraction with structured numerical data from weather stations enhances predictive capabilities, providing a robust framework for proactive pest management. Despite these promising results, some limitations remain. The model's performance could be influenced by seasonal variations and data availability constraints, particularly in periods with missing satellite observations. Furthermore, while the proposed methodology effectively predicts pest outbreaks one week in advance, longer-term forecasting remains an open challenge.

5 Conclusions and Future Works

This work has presented a multimodal hybrid methodology that combines satellite imagery with meteorological data to improve the accuracy of the prediction of olive fruit fly infestations. The developed multimodal hybrid deep learning algorithm leverages a CNN for spatial feature extraction from fused Sentinel-2 images and integrates these features with time series data using advanced machine learning models. Experimental results have demonstrated that the hybrid approach, especially when employed by Lag-Llama, consistently outperforms standalone methods based solely on imagery or meteorological data, confirming the benefits of multimodal data fusion.

Despite the promising performance, several limitations merit further research. Seasonal variations and data availability, particularly during periods with reduced satellite observations, can impact model robustness. In future work, we plan to extend the forecasting horizon beyond one week and investigate the integration of additional data sources such as soil moisture indices and in situ pest monitoring to enrich the feature space. Furthermore, exploring alternative deep learning architectures and model interpretability techniques (e.g. SHAP analysis) could provide deeper insights into the predictive mechanisms, facilitating decision support in pest management. These enhancements aim to broaden the scope of the application and improve the generalizability of the proposed approach in various agricultural scenarios.

Acknowledgments. The authors would like to thank the Spanish Ministry of Science and Innovation for the support within the projects PID2020-117954RB-C21, TED2021-131311B-C22 and PID2023-146037OB-C22.

References

1. Allu, A.R., Mesapam, S.: Impact of remote sensing data fusion on agriculture applications: a review. Eur. J. Agron. **164**, 127478 (2025)
2. Alzubaidi, L., et al.: Review of deep learning: concepts, CNN architectures, challenges, applications, future directions. J. Big Data **8**(1), 1–74 (2021). https://doi.org/10.1186/s40537-021-00444-8
3. Barrile, V., Simonetti, S., Citroni, R., Fotia, A., Bilotta, G.: Experimenting agriculture 4.0 with sensors: a data fusion approach between remote sensing, UAVS and self-driving tractors. Sensors, 22(20):7910, 2022
4. Bayoudh, K.: A survey of multimodal hybrid deep learning for computer vision: architectures, applications, trends, and challenges. Inf. Fusion **105**, 102217 (2024)
5. Bhatt, D., et al.: CNN variants for computer vision: history, architecture, application, challenges and future scope. Electron. **10**(20), 2470 (2021)
6. Chacón-Maldonado, A., Melgar-García, L., Asencio-Cortés, G., Troncoso, A.: A novel method based on hybrid deep learning with explainability for olive fruit pest forecasting. Neural Computing and Applications, pp. 1–20, 2024
7. El Sakka, M., Ivanovici, M., Chaari, L., Mothe, J.: A review of CNN applications in smart agriculture using multimodal data. Sensors **25**(2), 472 (2025)
8. Fang, M., et al.: Pest-conformer: a hybrid CNN-transformer architecture for large-scale multi-class crop pest recognition. Expert Syst. Appl. **255**, 124833 (2024)
9. Jiang, W., et al.: An empirical study of pre-trained model reuse in the hugging face deep learning model registry. In: 2023 IEEE/ACM 45th International Conference on Software Engineering (ICSE), pp. 2463–2475. IEEE, 2023
10. Mehrish, A., Majumder, N., Bharadwaj, R., Mihalcea, R., Poria, S.: A review of deep learning techniques for speech processing. Inf. Fusion **99**, 101869 (2023)
11. Mira, J.L., Barba, J., Romero, F.P., Escolar, M.S., Caba, J., López, J. C.: Benchmarking of computer vision methods for energy-efficient high-accuracy olive fly detection on edge devices. Multimedia Tools and Applications, pp. 1–25, 2024
12. Rasul, K., et al.: Lag-llama: towards foundation models for probabilistic time series forecasting, 2024
13. Regional government of Andalucía (Spain). Phytosanitary Information and Alert Network (RAIF) 2020. https://www.juntadeandalucia.es/agriculturapescaydesarrollorural/raif
14. Rodríguez-Díaz, F., Chacón-Maldonado, A., Troncoso-García, A., Asencio-Cortés, G.: Explainable olive grove and grapevine pest forecasting through machine learning-based classification and regression. Results Eng. **24**, 103058 (2024)
15. V. S. Sardar, K. Yindumathi, S. S. Chaudhari, and P. Ghosh. Convolution neural network-based agriculture drought prediction using satellite images. In: IEEE Mysore Sub Section International Conference (MysuruCon), pp. 601–607, 2021
16. Sarkar, C., Gupta, D., Gupta, U., Hazarika, B.B.: Leaf disease detection using machine learning and deep learning: Review and challenges. Appl. Soft Comput. **145**, 110534 (2023)
17. Yadav, S., Tewari, A.S.: CONF-RCNN: a conformer and faster region-based convolutional neural network model for multi-label classification of tomato leaves disease in real field environment. J. Plant Dis. Prot. **132**(2), 61 (2025)

Infrared Driver Monitoring Systems – A Review, New Opportunities and Trends

Bogusław Cyganek(✉) and Mateusz Knapik

AGH University of Krakow, Al. Mickiewicza 30, 30-059 Kraków, Poland
cyganek@agh.edu.pl

Abstract. There has been a long history of research into the creation of effective driver surveillance systems to improve safety in moving vehicles. This problem is very important and requires the use of interdisciplinary scientific methods, including those from fields such as AI, but also electronics, psychology, and medicine. In this paper, we present an overview of current opportunities and new trends in driver monitoring systems operating in infrared light. Our second contribution is a system to analyze the driver condition while maintaining privacy of data.

Keywords: Driver monitoring systems · ADAS · thermovision

1 Introduction

In this article we focus on the use of thermal imaging in active driver fatigue monitoring systems. These are based on infrared (IR) cameras that are able to transform infrared thermal radiation, naturally generated from the surface temperature of ambient objects, into digital images. Compared to visible spectrum sensors, IR imaging has many advantages, the most important of which include the ability to operate in virtually any lighting conditions, i.e. day or night, as well as in difficult conditions in the vehicle cabin, such as sun glare etc. without the need to use an external source of radiation.

However, thermal imaging has its limitations and challenges. First, the resulting images have relatively low contrast. Second, thermal cameras often require calibration. Finally, there is a lack of well-tagged recordings of driver behavior under various driving conditions and fatigue, whereas effective training of modern deep learning classifiers requires large repositories of labeled data.

In this article, we address these and many other topics related to driver surveillance methods using thermal imaging. We present an overview of important works in this field, as well as the results of our research in this area. Also, in this paper we provide almost fifty references to important articles in this area.

2 Advanced Driver Assistance Systems Operating in IR

Night vision ADAS, based on Long-Wave Infrared (LWIR) image processing for automotive applications, have been developed by many automotive and cooperating companies. Veoneer is one of the companies working in this area, delivering automotive grade electronics [44]. Their out-cabin mounted thermovision systems focus on detection of pedestrians and animals, which are difficult to spot in night time conditions. On the other hand, BMW developed their own systems called Night Vision 1 and 2 [6]. These are equipped with the passive thermal cameras whose images are shown to the drivers in varying brightness depending on the temperature of objects. Another leading car manufacturer Mercedes-Benz in 2005 developed the Night View Assist system, which was mounted in the S-Class, and the contemporary Night View Assist Plus, which is debuting on the E-Class [5].

3 Object Detection in Infrared Spectrum

Thermal imaging operates by passively detecting infrared radiation emitted by objects as a function of their temperature [47]. Consequently, the resulting images exhibit texture, edge, and gradient characteristics that differ substantially from those of conventional RGB imagery. As a result, standard image processing techniques frequently are inappropriate.

3.1 Image Preprocessing

Due to these constraints, techniques of signal conditioning are often employed to mitigate the high intrinsic noise characteristic of thermal sensors.

Marzec et al. in [39] proposed a technique to eliminate the impact of background and interference caused by hair and hairline in face localization and facial landmarks detection task.

Similarly, Strąkowska et al. [42] employed a dynamic thresholding approach based on the average intensity of the thermal image to reduce the dependence on precise camera calibration. Knapik and Cyganek, in their paper [27], also utilized morphological filtering on thermal images to address the issue of outlier values in image intensity. This preprocessing step led to a reduction in the number of false positives generated by the algorithm responsible for identifying candidate regions of interest for eye corner detection [30]. In a subsequent publication [28], the authors introduced the novel concept of Virtual High Dynamic Range (VHDR) to enhance the clarity and contrast of thermal images. In contrast, Ye et al. [48] proposed a lightweight low-light visible spectrum image enhancement network specifically designed for automotive applications. The architecture combines the capabilities of the Swin Vision Transformer with a U-Net convolutional network, resulting in substantial improvements in environmental perception tasks under low-light conditions.

3.2 Feature-Based Object Detection Methods

In their earlier work, Marzec et al. [38] applied a combination of thresholding and the active contour method to localize human faces in thermal images. Similarly,

Cheong et al. [9] proposed a technique based on projecting a binarized image to determine the height and width of the head region for face localization.

Many studies have suggested the use of the standard Viola-Jones face detection algorithm [8,32], which has proven highly successful in images in the visible spectrum. Another classical computer vision algorithm applied to face detection in thermal images is the Histogram of Oriented Gradients (HOG). Originally proposed by Dalal and Triggs in [15], HOG has been effectively adapted for thermal imaging by several researchers [31,32,36]. The method's ability to capture edge and gradient structures has made it particularly suitable for overcoming the low-texture challenges of thermal images. Lin et al. in [35] discuss thermal face recognition under different conditions, such as normal, with added noise, wearing glasses, face mask, etc.

3.3 Deep Learning-Based Object Detection Methods

The thermal imaging pedestrian detection algorithm, based on attention guidance and a local cross-level network, was proposed by Yu et al. [49]. Gender detection based on thermal images of human faces is dealt with in the work by Jalil & Reda [25]. For this purpose, two different thermal image datasets were prepared, which were then used for training of a few variants of the ResNet CNN. Knapik et al. [31] proposed a custom face and facial landmark detection architecture based on YOLOv8, specifically adapted to address the unique challenges of thermal imaging and to support real-time inference on embedded hardware. The authors incorporated Convolutional Block Attention Modules (CBAMs) and a Bi-directional Feature Pyramid Network (BiFPN) to improve feature extraction from the low-resolution and low-contrast thermal images.

3.4 Datasets with Thermal Images for Driver Monitoring

Having a large enough and labeled dataset is crucial, especially when using deep learning methods. It is no different when analyzing various features that we use to infer the condition of drivers. In this regard, a fully annotated thermal infrared dataset for face recognition under various environmental conditions and distances was proposed by Ashrafi et al. [4]. Named Charlotte-ThermalFace, this dataset contains over 10000 of annotated infrared thermal images in different thermal conditions, several distances from the camera, as well as varying head positions.

Kopaczka et al. created a dataset of thermal faces with full annotations [32]. Another datasets SF-TL54 and TFW with annotated thermal faces in the wild conditions are available thanks to Kuzdeuov et al. [33,34]. Knapik & Cyganek created a dataset with thermal images for yawn detection [27]. Another annotated thermal dataset is also proposed in consecutive work by Knapik et al. [31].

4 Extracting Behavioral Signals

A very important area is the analysis of the psychophysical state of a human based on the analysis of thermal imaging signals. It turns out that signals of this type not only enable operation without an external source of lighting, but also enable detection of features invisible to standard RGB imaging.

4.1 Physiological Thermal Signals

Goulart et al. discuss methods of motion analysis in children through facial emissivity of infrared thermal imaging [22]. They show that physiological signals acquired in the far infrared spectrum can be used as objective markers to identify emotions. They propose an experimental setup to analyze 5 emotions: disgust, fear, happiness, sadness, and surprise, from facial thermal images of children aged 7–11 years. Their results indicate that emissivity variations constitute an efficient marker for analyzing emotions in facial thermal images. In this vein, Cruz-Albarran et al. analyze the detection of human emotions based on a smart thermal system of thermographic images [11]. They present a non-invasive method to obtain biomedical thermal imaging for the diagnosis of emotions. Recently Nowakowski & Kaczmarek discuss application of AI methods in IR thermal imaging and sensing for medical applications [40]. Especially useful is the presentation of the underlying theory of IR thermography in view of novel AI methods in medical diagnosis and treatment.

4.2 Respiratory Rate Monitoring

A survey on affective state recognition based on thermography is presented by Qudah et al. [3]. They show that thermovision allows for the non-invasive detection of psychphysiological signals, such as pulse rate and respiration rate. They also discuss the stages of thermal-based human affective state recognition.

In their 2017 study, Cho et al. [10] proposed DeepBreath, a deep learning-based model designed to automatically recognize an individual's psychological stress level from breathing patterns. Also Kopaczka et al. [32] proposed a system for respiratory rate monitoring and emotion classification, even under conditions of unconstrained and varying head poses. Novel face frontalization technique based on the application of piecewise affine transformations allows regions of interest (ROIs) to remain fixed in position within the frontalized view.

4.3 Eye and Eyelid Movement Monitoring

Monitoring eye and eyelid movements is an important metric for assessing cognitive state, fatigue, and attention levels, yet remains particularly challenging in thermal imaging. In this respect, Cyganek & Gruszczyński propsed a template based metod for eye detection, followed by a tensor based classifier [13].

In [39], Marzec et al. introduced a fast and efficient algorithm for eye localization in thermal images. The algorithm comprises two primary stages. The first stage involves finding hottest points on the image that describe potential eye regions within the image. In the second stage, a neural network-based decision module classifies these candidate regions to accurately identify eye locations.

Strąkowska and Strąkowski in [42] proposed a system for the automatic detection and tracking of eye corners in thermal images. The detection process begins by identifying local maxima within the image to establish candidate regions of interest (ROIs). Forczmański and Smoliński in [20] introduced novel eye state classification in thermal images. In the initial step, the eyes are localized, and regions of interest (ROIs) are extracted from the thermal image. Subsequently, a Gabor filtering-based approach is applied to classify the state of the eyes. Experimental evaluations conducted on video sequences demonstrated highly promising results. Knapik and Cyganek [28] proposed an alternative approach to eye detection in thermal images. Their method combines sparse image representation with a bag-of-visual-words framework and clustering techniques to achieve final object detection.

4.4 Gaze Tracking and Pose Estimation

Accurate estimation of head pose enhances the reliability of driver monitoring systems by providing insights into gaze direction and potential distraction levels.

Wang et al. [45] proposed a system for gaze tracking using thermal images. The method exploits the surface temperature difference between the eye cornea and the limbus to track corneal movements. Guo et al. propose a benchmark for identity-preserved human posture detection in infrared thermal images [23]. It consists of a large collection of data images, called the IPHPDT dataset, as well as a set of trained classifiers from the YOLO family of detectors. Head pose estimation, a critical signal to assess driver attention, has also been incorporated into numerous proposed systems. Knapik et al. [31] estimated head pose in 3D space by utilizing extracted facial keypoints. Similarly, Kopaczka et al. [32] employed an Active Appearance Model to fit 68-point facial landmarks within detected face regions of interest (ROIs), which were subsequently used to calculate head pose for further analysis.

4.5 Yawning Detection

In 2019, Knapik and Cyganek proposed a system for assessing driver fatigue levels by integrating yawning detection with thermal imaging [27]. The approach used yawning frequency as a key behavioral indicator of drowsiness. Yawning events were identified using an innovative thermal voxel counting model, which detects sudden thermal variations associated with the yawning reflex. The effectiveness of the method was validated using a custom annotated thermal image database specifically developed for the study.

Forczmański and Smoliński presented a multimodal system for driver physical state estimation based on thermal imaging in 2020 [21]. The system employs Haar-like features in conjunction with the Viola-Jones detector for initial face detection. Subsequently, regions corresponding to the mouth and eyes are extracted and Gabor filtering is applied to enable the detection of eyelid closure, blinking, and yawning events. Kajiwara presents a method for driver-condition detection using a thermal imaging camera and neural networks [26].

4.6 Additional Behavioral Indicators

Kamath et al. propose a robust emotion recognition systems, called TERNet, that relies on thermal images classified by a number of deep convolutional neural networks [41]. They report a top accuracy of 96.2% in recognition of thermal face expressions using VGG16 with custom layer, trained on face data from the TUFTS face database. Using phones while driving can also be very distracting and dangerous in effect. In this context, Wang et al. propose a method for fast detection of driver distraction caused by the use of a handheld phone [46].

5 Inference of Driver Alertness and Attentiveness

Based on information about multi-modal features, the next step is to infer the driver's fatigue state. Here, we describe multi-modal signal fusion modules and methods for their analysis.

5.1 Signal Fusion and Decision-Making Models

For the decision on the driver's state, Knapik and Cyganek in [31] proposed a state machine, designed to combine multiple signals, such as head pose, head movement events, and yawning frequency using predefined weights to trigger alerts when specific thresholds are exceeded. The role of thermal imaging in designing ADAS, developed under the European project Heliaus, is discussed in the paper by Farooq et al. [18]. They present the object detection and classification framework based on thermalvision with 7 main object classes in the task of scene understanding for ADAS. In their next paper [17] the authors analyze the usefulness of uncooled thermal infra-red (IR) sensors in designing thermal perception systems for in-cabin and out-cabin vehicular applications and as an alternative to visible spectrum sensors. In the subsequent article [19], the authors describe the structure and effects of the Heliaus project. Its goal was the development of in-cabin applications, as well as to prototype new intelligent thermal systems that enable the monitoring of driver activities by determining their soft biometrics, monitoring vital signs, and detecting drowsiness. Their main achievements in the area of thermal monitoring in cars are the GENNet gender classification network GENNet [16], which specific features can also be used in driver monitoring, as well as the NEXT2U module for driver stress and drowsiness detection [7]. Recently Hao et al. propose a lightweight and explainable model for the recognition of driver abnormal behavior [24]. They optimized the standard YOLOv8 detector to operate well in vehicular systems with relatively limited computational resources.

5.2 Large Language Models Approach for Behavioral Inference

Incorporating LLMs into the decision-making pipeline represents a significant step toward creating more intuitive and intelligent driver monitoring systems capable of contextual understanding. Knapik and Cyganek in [31] proposed the use of large language models (LLMs) to develop fusion modules to synthesize detection events into a coherent assessment of driver state. This approach enables the system to generate responses to queries that extend beyond its explicit training data, providing enhanced flexibility and adaptability. Experimental evaluations demonstrated the system's high accuracy in detecting and responding to indicators of driver fatigue and distraction. Tami et al. [1] proposed the use of multimodal LLMs for the detection of general safety-critical traffic events. The authors developed a framework that integrates textual, visual, and auditory modalities to enhance the detection and interpretation of such events.

6 Data Privacy Protection

Despite the rapid development of object detection algorithms, data protection remains an under-researched and under-prioritized topic in the field. Many research studies and commercial applications focus primarily on improving detection accuracy, robustness to various conditions, and computational efficiency, often neglecting the ethical and legal implications of disclosing personal data.

However, today, more than ever, there is a need for solutions that take data protection into account. The growing number of surveillance systems, intelligent vehicles, wearable devices, and public monitoring tools pose a serious risk of unauthorized data collection, identity recognition, and misuse of sensitive biometric information [12].

Techniques known as perceptual encryption (PE) [2], aims to balance privacy protection with the utility of data for training and inference tasks. The central concept involves encrypting images in such a way that their content remains unintelligible and unrecognizable to human observers, while still retaining sufficient structural information to allow machine learning models to detect and recognize patterns within them. One of the first learnable image encryption (LE) methods was proposed by Tanaka [43]. The technique divides the image into blocks, applies intensity inversion to randomly selected pixels, and performs random pixel shuffling. Madono et al. [37] extended Tanaka's original concept by introducing additional block shuffling and a learnable shuffling adaptation network (AdaptNet), further enhancing the system's privacy-preserving capabilities.

Knapik and Cyganek [29] introduced a fully operational general purpose object detector based on the YOLO architecture, capable of operating in encoded image space for privacy protection, with a primary focus on person detection in unconfined environments. The proposed hierarchical patch-based scrambling method was specifically designed to address the challenges of object detection under encryption. To further strengthen privacy, an additional layer combining an Exclusive-OR (XOR) operation with a Negative-Positive Transform (NPT) was implemented. This enhancement provides an adjustable balance between detection accuracy and privacy protection - see Sect. 7.

7 Experiments

This work introduces an integrated system that combines two independently validated solutions: a learnable perceptual encryption-based object detector and a thermal-spectrum fatigue detection framework. By uniting these technologies, the proposed system provides reliable real-time driver monitoring in challenging vehicle conditions while ensuring strict adherence to data privacy principles. To ensure privacy, visual encryption is applied immediately after image acquisition. This eliminates the risk of exposing unprocessed visual content and adheres to privacy-by-design principles.

Based on the hierarchical scrambling method from [29], the thermal image is divided into patches and blocks. Block positions within patches are permuted using key K_1, pixel positions within blocks using K_2, and selected pixel values are bitwise-negated using K_3 (Negative-Positive transform). Keys K_2 and K_3 may be optionally unique for each block to enlarge the key space. This results in a perceptually encrypted image for secure processing.

The face and landmark detector is built on the improved YOLOv8 face architecture [31], adapted to the ScrambledYOLO framework [29].

The complete architecture of the integrated system is shown in Fig. 1.

The hierarchical adaptation network increases both trainable parameters and computational cost per forward pass. However, the overhead is small: 2,656 (+0.3%) additional parameters with shared keys and 38,656 (+5%) with unique keys (4×4 block size). This adds only 0.16 GFLOPs (5% over baseline), allowing real-time performance even on devices like the NVIDIA Jetson Nano.

To validate the feasibility of our approach, we selected the SF-TL54 [34] data set, featuring detailed annotations of 54 facial landmarks, including the eyes, nose, mouth, and facial outline. For realistic deployment scenario, a 4×4 pixel block scrambling scheme was applied. This method provides a reasonable balance between sufficient anonymization and processing efficiency for inherently low resolution thermal images.

The baseline models evaluated are based on the architectures from [31]. After 300 epochs of pretraining, all models were fine-tuned for 120 epochs. For privacy-preserving variants, only the adaptation network and the first two YOLO backend layers were unfrozen, while the rest remained frozen. In contrast, all layers were unfrozen during fine-tuning of the baseline models.

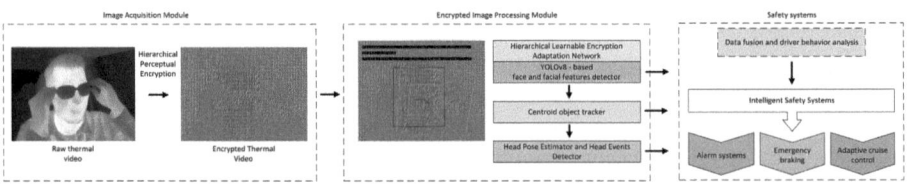

Fig. 1. Proposed privacy-preserving ADAS system overview

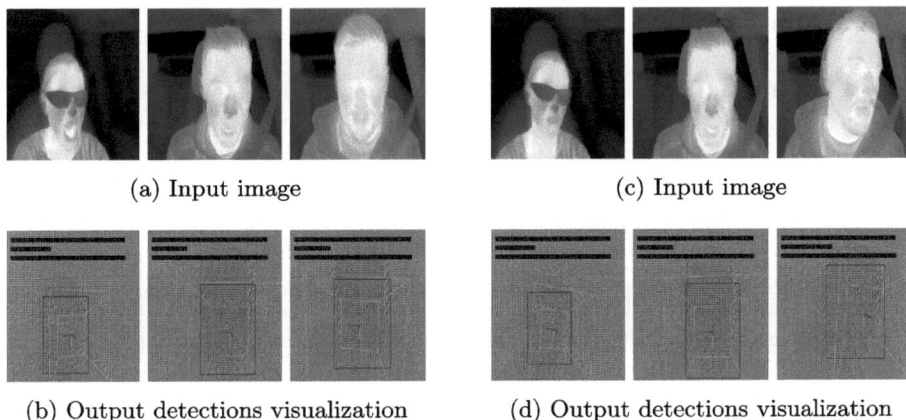

(a) Input image (c) Input image

(b) Output detections visualization (d) Output detections visualization

Fig. 2. Sample visualization of presented system

The results show that encrypted image input introduces additional complexity to the already challenging task of thermal image detection. All models incorporating privacy-preserving modifications experience some degradation in detection performance, particularly under stricter metrics such as pose mAP@0.5-0.95%. Models with attention modules are especially affected, likely due to overfitting to the original feature distributions. These attention blocks are not adequately adapted to the altered input, leading to suboptimal feature selection. The observed degradation may also be due to our training strategy, where most of the model weights remain frozen during adaptation. This suggests that fine-tuning a larger portion of the network or introducing data augmentations tailored to scrambled inputs could help mitigate the performance drop. This limitation warrants further investigation in future work. The comprehensive performance metrics are listed in Table 1. The visualizations of the samples can be seen in Fig. 2. In addition, qualitative examples can be seen in the additional video material available on YouTube [14].

Table 1. Comparison of baseline and privacy-preserving face and facial feature detectors on the SF-TL54 dataset. "Unique Keys" indicates the number of distinct K_2 and K_3 keys used per patch.

Model family	Backbone	Block Size	Unique Codes	Box mAP@0.5-0.95 (%)	Diff from baseline	Pose mAP@0.5 (%)	Diff from baseline	Pose mAP@0.5-0.95 (%)	Diff from baseline
Improved YOLOv8-face-tiny (baseline)	ShuffleNet v2 + CBAM + BiFPN	-	-	0.937	-	0.995	-	0.480	-
YOLOv8-face-tiny (baseline)	ShuffleNet v2	-	-	0.940	-	0.993	-	0.447	-
Improved YOLOv8-face-tiny (hierarchically scrambled image)	AdaptNet + ShuffleNet v2 + CBAM + BiFPN	4 × 4 px	1	0.908	-2.9 pp	0.979	-1.6 pp	0.421	-5.9 pp
		4 × 4 px	16	0.913	-2.4 pp	0.945	-5.0 pp	0.370	-11.0 pp
YOLOv8-face-tiny (hierarchically scrambled image)	AdaptNet + ShuffleNet v2	4 × 4 px	1	0.937	-0.3 pp	0.975	-1.8 pp	0.389	-5.8 pp
		4 × 4 px	16	0.924	-1.6 pp	0.966	-2.7 pp	0.372	-7.5 pp

8 Conclusions

The main contributions of this article are as follows: (i) A focused survey of current research directions and emerging technologies relevant to driver monitoring systems using infrared imaging. This overview helps position our contribution within the broader trends of driver monitoring systems and infrared analytics; (ii) An integrated system that combines privacy-preserving object detection with a robust thermal-based driver fatigue monitoring framework.

- **Results analysis** – By applying learnable perceptual encryption immediately after image acquisition, the system ensures end-to-end protection of sensitive visual data. Experimental evaluations demonstrate that the proposed pipeline maintains competent privacy-protection level, high detection performance and reasonable processing requirements, confirming its suitability for real-world, privacy-critical scenarios such as in-vehicle monitoring.
- **Future Work** – Looking ahead, we identify several emerging trends that are set to influence this domain. Polarimetric thermal imaging offers the potential to increase the extraction of more detailed information from thermal scenes. Furthermore, as demonstrated in our earlier work, the integration of LLMs into perception and reasoning pipelines opens new possibilities for adaptive, interpretable, and context-aware decision-making in ADAS.

Despite these advances, the availability of high-quality data sets for thermal vision remains a limiting factor. Promising research directions include the use of transfer learning from large-scale RGB datasets, the generation of realistic synthetic thermal data, and the use of teacher-student frameworks.

Acknowledgments. Research under project no. 10741, supported by program "Excellence initiative - research university" for the AGH University of Krakow.

References

1. Abu Tami, M., Ashqar, H.I., Elhenawy, M., Glaser, S., Rakotonirainy, A.: Using multimodal large language models (mllms) for automated detection of traffic safety-critical events. Vehicles **6**(3), 1571–1590 (2024)
2. Ahmad, I., Choi, W., Shin, S.: Comprehensive analysis of compressible perceptual encryption methods—compression and encryption perspectives. Sensors **23**(8) (2023)
3. Alqudah, M.: Affective state recognition using thermal-based imaging: a survey. Comput. Syst. Sci. Eng. **37**, 47–62 (2021)
4. Ashrafi, R., Azarbayjani, M., Tabkhi, H.: Charlotte-thermalface: a fully annotated thermal infrared face dataset with various environmental conditions and distances. Infrared Phys. Technol. **124**, 104209 (2022)
5. Autoexpress: Night vision - mercedes (2022). https://www.autoexpress.co.uk/car-reviews/39300/night-vision-mercedes
6. BMW: Night vision (2022). https://faq.bmw.co.uk/s/article/what-is-night-vision

7. Cardone, D., et al.: Driver stress state evaluation by means of thermal imaging: a supervised machine learning approach based on ecg signal. App. Sci. **10**(16) (2020)
8. Chakraborty, M., et al.: High precision automated face localization in thermal images: oral cancer dataset as test case. In: Medical Imaging 2017: Image Processing, vol. 10133, p. 1013326. Int. Society for Optics and Photonics, SPIE (2017)
9. Cheong, Y.K., Yap, V.V., Nisar, H.: A novel face detection algorithm using thermal imaging. In: 2014 IEEE Symposium on Computer Applications and Industrial Electronics (ISCAIE), pp. 208–213 (2014)
10. Cho, Y., Bianchi-Berthouze, N., Julier, S.J.: Deepbreath: deep learning of breathing patterns for automatic stress recognition using low-cost thermal imaging in unconstrained settings. In: 2017 Seventh International Conference on Affective Computing and Intelligent Interaction (ACII), p. 456–463. IEEE (2017)
11. Cruz-Albarran, I.A., Benitez-Rangel, J., Osornio-Rios, R., Morales-Hernández, L.: Human emotions detection based on a smart-thermal system of thermographic images. Infrared Phys. Technol. **81** (2017)
12. Cyganek, B.: An analysis of the road signs classification based on the higher-order singular value decomposition of the deformable pattern tensors. In: Blanc-Talon, J., Bone, D., Philips, W., Popescu, D., Scheunders, P. (eds.) ACIVS 2010. LNCS, vol. 6475, pp. 191–202. Springer, Heidelberg (2010). https://doi.org/10.1007/978-3-642-17691-3_18
13. Cyganek, B., Gruszczyński, S.: Hybrid computer vision system for drivers' eye recognition and fatigue monitoring. Neurocomputing **126**, 78–94 (2014)
14. Cyganek, B., Knapik, M.: Privacy-preserving adas system - demo videos (2025). https://www.youtube.com/playlist?list=PLlATNsaPJqAWNMP1d1l9GTygsr3dtlHJZ
15. Dalal, N., Triggs, B.: Histograms of oriented gradients for human detection. In: 2005 IEEE CVPR'05, vol. 1, pp. 886–893 (2005)
16. Farooq, M., Javidnia, H., Corcoran, P.: Performance estimation of the state-of-the-art convolution neural networks for thermal images-based gender classification system. J. Electron. Imaging **29** (2020)
17. Farooq, M., Shariff, W., O'Callaghan, D., Merla, A., Corcoran, P.: On the role of thermal imaging in automotive applications: a critical review. IEEE Access (2023)
18. Farooq, M.A., Corcoran, P., Rotariu, C., Shariff, W.: Object detection in thermal spectrum for advanced driver-assistance systems (adas). IEEE Access **9** (2021)
19. Farooq, M.A., Shariff, W., Corcoran, P.: Evaluation of thermal imaging on embedded gpu platforms for application in vehicular assistance systems. IEEE Trans. Intell. Veh. **8**(2), 1130–1144 (2023)
20. Forczmański, P., Smoliński, A.: Eyes state detection in thermal imaging. In: Choraś, M., Choraś, R.S. (eds.) IP&C 2019. AISC, vol. 1062, pp. 22–29. Springer, Cham (2020). https://doi.org/10.1007/978-3-030-31254-1_4
21. Forczmański, P., Smolinski, A.: Supporting driver physical state estimation by means of thermal image processing, pp. 149–163 (2021)
22. Goulart, C., Valadão, C., Rodriguez, D., Caldeira, E., Bastos, T.: Emotion analysis in children through facial emissivity of infrared thermal. PLOS ONE **14** (2019)
23. Guo, Y., Chen, Y., Deng, J., Li, S., Zhou, H.: Identity-preserved human posture detection in infrared thermal images: a benchmark. Sensors **23**(1) (2023)
24. Hao, J., Sun, X., Liu, X., Hua, D., Hu, J.: A lightweight and explainable model for driver abnormal behavior recognition. Eng. Appl. Artif. Intell. **139**(PA) (2025)
25. Jalil, A.J., Reda, N.M.: Infrared thermal image gender classifier based on the deep resnet model. Adv. Hum.-Comput. Interact. **2022**(1), 3852054 (2022)

26. Kajiwara, S.: Driver-condition detection using a thermal imaging camera and neural networks. Int. J. Autom. Technol. **22**, 1505–1515 (2021)
27. Knapik, M., Cyganek, B.: Driver's fatigue recognition based on yawn detection in thermal images. Neurocomputing **338**(C), 274–292 (2019)
28. Knapik, M., Cyganek, B.: Fast eyes detection in thermal images. Multimedia Tools Appl. **80**(3), 3601–3621 (2021)
29. Knapik, M., Cyganek, B.: Privacy-preserving people detection in the wild. Pattern Anal. Appl. **28**(2), 1–21 (2025)
30. Knapik, M., Cyganek, B.: Comparison of sparse image descriptors for eyes detection in thermal images. In: 14th International Joint Conference on Computer Vision, Imaging and Computer Graphics Theory and Applications (VISIGRAPP 2019) , vol. 5: VISAPP, pp. 638–644. INSTICC, SciTePress (2019)
31. Knapik, M., Cyganek, B., Balon, T.: Multimodal driver condition monitoring system operating in the far-infrared spectrum. Electronics **13**(17) (2024)
32. Kopaczka, M., et al.: A fully annotated thermal face database and its application for thermal facial expression recognition. In: 2018 IEEE International on Instrumentation and Measurement Technology Conference (I2MTC), pp. 1–6 (2018)
33. Kuzdeuov, A., Aubakirova, D., Koishigarina, D., Varol, H.A.: TFW: annotated thermal faces in the wild dataset. IEEE Trans. Inf. Forensics Secur. **17**, 2084–2094 (2022)
34. Kuzdeuov, A., Koishigarina, D., Aubakirova, D., Abushakimova, S., Varol, H.A.: Sf-tl54: a thermal facial landmark dataset with visual pairs. In: 2022 IEEE/SICE International Symposium on System Integration (SII), pp. 748–753 (2022)
35. Lin, S., Chen, L., Chen, W.S.: Thermal face recognition under different conditions. BMC Bioinf. **22** (2021)
36. Ma, C., Trung, N.T., Uchiyama, H., Nagahara, H., Shimada, A., Taniguchi, R.I.: Adapting local features for face detection in thermal image. Sensors **17**(12) (2017)
37. Madono, K., Tanaka, M., Onishi, M., Ogawa, T.: Block-wise scrambled image recognition using adaptation network (2020)
38. Marzec, M., Koprowski, R.: Wróbel: detection of selected face areas on thermograms with elimination of typical problems. J. Med. Inf. Technol. **16**, 151–159 (2010)
39. Marzec, M.E.A.: Automatic method for detection of characteristic areas in thermal face images. Multimedia Tools Appl. **74**(12), 4351–4368 (2015)
40. Nowakowski, A.Z., Kaczmarek, M.: Artificial intelligence in IR thermal imaging and sensing for medical applications. Sensors **25**(3) (2025)
41. Shreyas, K., et al.: TERNet: a deep learning approach for thermal face emotion recognition. In: Mobile Multimedia/Image Processing, Security, and Applications 2019, vol. 10993. International Society for Optics and Photonics, SPIE (2019)
42. Strąkowska, M., Strąkowski, R.: Automatic eye corners detection and tracking algorithm in sequence of thermal medical images. Meas. Autom. Monit. **61** (2015)
43. Tanaka, M.: Learnable image encryption (2018). https://arxiv.org/abs/1804.00490
44. Veoneer (2022). https://www.veoneer.com
45. Wang, Q., Boccanfuso, L., Li, B., Ahn, A.Y.J.: Thermographic eye tracking. In: 9th Biennial ACM Symposium on Eye Tracking Research & Applications, pp. 307–310 (2016)
46. Wang, R., Huang, L., Wang, C.: Fast detection of handheld phone-distracted driving by sensing the driver's hand-grip. IEEE Trans. Veh. Technol. **73**(8), 11136–11149 (2024)
47. Wikipedia: Thermography (2024). https://en.wikipedia.org/wiki/Thermography

48. Ye, L., Wang, D., Yang, D., Ma, Z., Zhang, Q.: Velie: a vehicle-based efficient low-light image enhancement method for intelligent vehicles. Sensors **24**(4) (2024)
49. Yu, L., Wang, Y., Sun, X., Han, S.: Thermal imaging pedestrian detection algorithm based on attention guidance and local cross-level network. J. Electr. Imaging **30**(5) (2021)

Ambient Intelligence Integration in Vocational Education: Evaluating Smart Learning Environments for Digital Skills Development

Ana Costa and Dalila Durães(✉)

ALGORITMI Centre/LASI, University of Minho, Braga, Portugal
pg53062@alunos.uminho.pt, dad@di.uminho.pt

Abstract. The rapid advancement of Artificial Intelligence (AI) and Internet of Things (IoT) technologies demands a fundamental transformation in vocational education curricula to prepare students for the evolving digital economy. This paper presents the evaluation of the AIM4VET project, an Erasmus+ funded initiative that integrates ambient intelligence and IoT technologies into Vocational Education and Training (VET) programs across Portugal, Spain, and Slovenia. The study focuses on the implementation and assessment of twelve modular teaching units centered around smart home energy management systems, utilizing Arduino-Raspberry Pi architectures and KNIME analytics platform. Employing project-based learning methodologies, the curriculum addresses critical competencies in sensor integration, data processing, machine learning, and ambient intelligence applications. Results from 14 VET students demonstrate significant improvements in technical understanding, with post-assessment scores showing mastery across all evaluation criteria. Student feedback revealed high satisfaction levels with instructional clarity, while teacher assessments confirmed strong performance in autonomy, creativity, and collaborative problem-solving. The majority of students rated module difficulty as appropriate, indicating well-calibrated instructional design. The findings validate the effectiveness of integrating ambient intelligence environments in VET curricula, demonstrating enhanced student engagement, practical skill development, and preparation for Industry 5.0 contexts. This research contributes to the growing body of knowledge on technology-enhanced vocational education and provides a scalable framework for implementing AI and IoT literacy across European VET systems.

Keywords: Ambient Intelligent · Digital Skills · Vocational Education · Internet of Things · Smart Learning Environments · Project-Based Learning

1 Introduction

The digital transformation of modern economies has fundamentally altered the skills landscape, with Artificial Intelligence (AI), Internet of Things (IoT), and ambient intelligence technologies becoming central to industrial processes, service delivery, and everyday life [7,18]. This technological revolution has created unprecedented demand for workers equipped with advanced digital competencies, capable of designing, implementing, and managing intelligent systems across diverse sectors including manufacturing, healthcare, transportation, and smart cities [12,19]. However, a significant gap persists between the rapid pace of technological advancement and the preparedness of educational systems to deliver relevant, future-oriented curricula [11,24].

Vocational Education and Training (VET) systems face particular challenges in addressing this skills mismatch. Unlike traditional academic pathways, VET programs are designed to provide direct entry into the labor market, making their alignment with industry needs critical for economic competitiveness and social mobility [1,20]. Yet many European VET institutions continue to operate with curricula that predate the digital revolution, lacking the depth and specialization required to prepare learners for emerging technological domains such as Industry 5.0, smart environments, and autonomous systems [5,8]. The transition towards human-centric, sustainable, and resilient industrial systems, as envisioned by Industry 5.0 frameworks, demands a complete redefinition of VET curricula [1,4]. Current approaches frequently focus on theoretical knowledge transfer rather than hands-on, experiential learning that characterizes effective vocational education. While projects such as AI4VET and SmartVET have explored digital technology integration in vocational programs [2,15], few have explicitly focused on embedding AI and ambient intelligence within comprehensive teaching frameworks targeted at the VET level.

1.1 Main Contribution

The AIM4VET (Artificial Intelligence Learning Modules to Adapt VET to the Digital Transformation of the Labour Market) project addresses the challenges posed by digital transformation by integrating formal, structured AI education into pre-university VET systems. Funded by the Erasmus+ programme, the project developed innovative teaching modules in three core areas of artificial intelligence: Robotics, developed by Spain; Computer Vision, developed by Slovenia; and Ambient Intelligence and the Internet of Things (IoT), developed by Portugal. These modules were piloted in VET institutions across Portugal, Spain, and Slovenia, involving interdisciplinary teams from academia and secondary education. This paper presents the evaluation results of the Portuguese module, focusing on its impact on learners in terms of usability, engagement, satisfaction, and perceived knowledge acquisition. Furthermore, the study explores the pedagogical implications of using ambient intelligence as a foundation for responsive, learner-centered education, and discusses future opportunities for scaling and integrating these approaches into broader European VET policies and practices. More specifically, this paper presents the development of a smart home system focused on energy management and optimization, based on data collected from the implemented sensors.

The remainder of this paper is structured as follows. Section 2 presents a review of the most relevant related work, highlighting the current state of the art and existing research gaps. Section 3 present the AIM4VET Framewotk, and Sect. 4 describes the methodology adopted, including the design, tools, and data sources used in this study. Section 5 outlines the results obtained through the proposed approach, followed by a detailed discussion and analysis. Finally, Sect. 6 concludes the paper by summarizing the main findings and proposing directions for future research.

2 Related Work

2.1 AI and Digital Literacy in Education

The integration of AI in education has gained increasing attention in recent years, with researchers and policymakers emphasizing the necessity of equipping learners with foundational AI literacy [12,18]. AI literacy extends beyond technical know-how, encompassing ethical reasoning, problem-solving, and the ability to critically interpret AI-driven systems [17]. Initiatives such as AI4K12 in the United States and Elements of AI in Europe represent early efforts to promote public understanding of AI through structured curricula [23].

Despite these advancements, the incorporation of AI in school curricula remains limited, particularly in pre-university and vocational education contexts. A recent UNESCO report indicates that AI education is often fragmented, unstandardized, and lacking in pedagogical coherence across countries [24]. The need for comprehensive, context-sensitive approaches to AI teaching is therefore pressing, especially in systems where students are prepared for immediate entry into the labor market.

2.2 Smart Environments and IoT in Learning Contexts

Smart environments, defined as digitally enhanced physical spaces embedded with sensors, actuators, and communication technologies, have shown great potential in educational settings. When combined with AI, these environments enable adaptive learning experiences, personalized feedback, and real-time monitoring of learner behavior and engagement [6,9].

Research in ambient intelligence has demonstrated its capacity to support inclusive, learner-centered pedagogy, especially through context-aware systems that adjust to learners' needs in real-time [21]. The use of IoT devices in vocational contexts allows for simulation of real-world industrial systems, thereby enhancing practical training and bridging the gap between school and workplace environments [14].

Several pilot projects have successfully implemented IoT-based learning environments in technical education, revealing improved learner motivation and retention of knowledge [13,16]. However, their scalability and integration into formal curricula remain limited, often due to infrastructure constraints and the lack of teacher training.

2.3 Vocational Education and Training for the Digital Economy

VET is uniquely positioned to respond to the challenges posed by digital transformation, especially in sectors such as advanced manufacturing, robotics, and smart logistics [5]. Yet many VET programs across Europe are still grounded in traditional frameworks that do not reflect the evolving needs of Industry 5.0, a vision that emphasizes human-centric, sustainable, and resilient industrial systems [1].

Recent research advocates for a redefinition of VET curricula, integrating digital competence frameworks like DigCompEdu and AI-specific learning outcomes [4,10]. Moreover, the European Skills Agenda and Digital Education Action Plan both highlight the role of VET in ensuring that future workers are prepared for technological innovation through applied, hands-on learning [8].

Projects such as AI4VET [2] and SmartVET [15] have explored the incorporation of digital technologies into vocational programs, yet few have explicitly focused on embedding AI and ambient intelligence within teaching units targeted at the VET level. The AIM4VET project fills this gap by offering a modular, cross-disciplinary curriculum that leverages smart environments for pedagogical innovation. On the Portuguese context, the curriculum comprises twelve teaching modules, each with a duration ranging from 10 to 15 h. These modules were designed following active learning methodologies, especially project-based learning (PBL), which encourages learners to apply concepts through real-world problem-solving scenarios (Thomas, 2000; Bell, 2010). Each module introduces a technical concept in alignment with a "Required Knowledge" segment, ensuring that students build on a solid foundation of prerequisite understanding. This pedagogical structure supports differentiated learning and scaffolds progression across increasingly complex topics.

The twelve modules include: (1) Sensors, (2) Actuators, (3) Data Visualization, (4) AI Computing, (5) IoT, (6) Intelligent Interface, (7) Machine Learning: Pre-processing, (8) Machine Learning: Supervised Learning, (9) Machine Learning: Unsupervised Learning, (10) Ambient Intelligence(AmI): Domotics, (11) AmI: Smart House, and (12) AmI Personalization. For this application, these modules converge in the simulation and partial implementation of a smart home system. Students design and manage a prototype energy-efficient intelligent house that responds dynamically to environmental data and user interaction, exemplifying the real-world application of AI and IoT in smart environments.

3 AIM4VET Framework

The AIM4VET project is a transnational initiative launched in January 2023 and it addresses the growing need to prepare vocational education students for the digital transformation of the labor market, particularly in emerging technological domains. While these technologies are increasingly shaping economic and industrial systems, their integration into formal pre-university curricula—especially in VET, remains limited and inconsistent across Europe [8,24].

AIM4VET responds to this educational gap by offering a structured and modular curriculum that fosters AI literacy, computational thinking, and system integration skills among VET students. The project is coordinated by the University of A Coruña (Spain) in collaboration with the University of Minho (Portugal) and the University of Ljubljana (Slovenia). Each university works closely with a local VET school: CIFP Rodolfo Ucha Piñeiro (Spain), Escola Secundária de Caldas das Taipas (Portugal), and Šolski center Velenje (Slovenia). This tri-national structure promotes a diverse, cross-cultural exchange of pedagogical practices and technological implementation models.

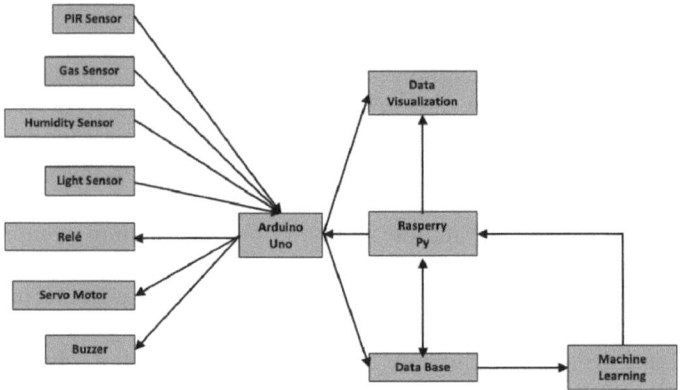

Fig. 1. Smart Home Framework.

The framework represents a smart home system centered around an Arduino Uno, represented on Fig. 1, which serves as the primary controller for various sensors and actuators. The Arduino is connected to multiple input devices, including a PIR sensor (motion detection), gas sensor, humidity sensor, and light sensor, as well as output devices such as a relay, servo motor, and buzzer. By the API of AdafruitIO, the Arduino send feed for data visualization. Using the API Firebase is possible to store the data. The Arduino communicates with a Raspberry Pi, which acts as a gateway for data processing visualization and analysis. The Raspberry Pi is responsible for data visualization and managing a database that stores sensor readings and system states. This database is further connected to a machine learning module, enabling intelligent analysis and decision-making based on historical and real-time data. This layered framework allows for real-time monitoring, automated control, and adaptive behavior, making it suitable for energy management and smart home applications.

On the software side, the project utilizes KNIME, an open-source data analytics platform that allows students to explore machine learning techniques through visual workflows. KNIME supports both supervised and unsupervised learning, including tasks such as data pre-processing, classification, clustering, and model evaluation. Its drag-and-drop interface makes it particularly suitable for VET students who may not yet be proficient in programming [3]. Additionally, data visualization tools and simple IoT dashboards were used to support the interpretation of sensor outputs and AI predictions, enhancing students' capacity to analyze and optimize the behavior of their smart home prototypes.

4 Implementation and Methodology

As presented on Fig. 2 the Curriculum Development was structured to include practical, hands-on activities following the principles of project-based learning (PBL). This methodology was chosen to foster student engagement, problem-solving, and collaboration—skills that are essential in technologically mediated work environments [22]. This module was organized around real-world challenges and included three key components: (1) a "Required Knowledge" section that presents prerequisite concepts; (2) a sequence of scaffolded learning activities; and (3) a final integrative task. The thematic progression of the modules mirrors the layered framework of a smart home system.

The Technological Implementation was centered on a simulated smart home environment with real hardware and software components. The framework was designed to provide an authentic context for learning and facilitate the practical integration of the previous modules. This technological ecosystem allowed students to experience a complete pipeline: from data acquisition and control (Arduino), to processing and visualization (Raspberry Pi), to intelligent analysis and decision-making (KNIME).

Fig. 2. Methodology Diagram.

The Pilot Implementation phase involved the partner VET institutions. Teachers were trained in advance to ensure fidelity of implementation and to support student learning with appropriate scaffolding. On the pilot classroom sessions teachers participated in periodic feedback sessions and implementation workshops to report challenges and suggest adjustments.

The Evaluation Strategy focused on three main dimensions: engagement, difficulty, and perceived learning outcomes. Data were collected using a combination of quantitative and qualitative instruments: (1) standardized questionnaires were administered at the end of each activity to measure student perceptions of content clarity and difficulty; (2) engagement metrics were inferred from teachers which analyse project completion rates, and classroom observations; and (3) knowledge assessments were used before and after the modules to determine learning gains, particularly in technical areas such as sensor integration, data interpretation, and AI principles.

5 Results and Discussion

As describe on previous section, the evaluation phase of this project was structured from different perspectives. These instruments were designed to assess learners' perceptions regarding several critical dimensions, including content clarity, perceived difficulty, engagement with the activity, and confidence in applying the concepts learned.

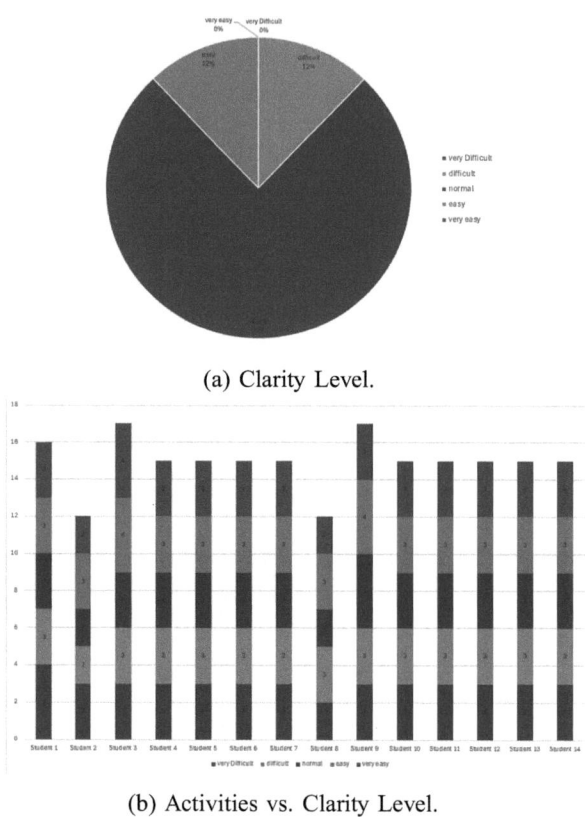

(a) Clarity Level.

(b) Activities vs. Clarity Level.

Fig. 3. Activity results. (Color figure online)

As we can observe on Fig. 3a each student's responses were recorded using a five-point scale, where 1 indicated "very difficult," 2 "difficult," 3 "normal," 4 "easy," and 5 "very easy." The data were then compiled to construct a profile of perceived difficulty across the student cohort.

The analysis revealed that the majority of responses clustered around the midpoint, with most students rating the activities as having a "normal" level of difficulty. This suggests that the instructional design and content delivery were appropriately calibrated to the students' skill level. Only 12% of students rated the activities as either "difficult" or "easy," indicating that while a small subset found the material either challenging or particularly straightforward, the overall perception was one of balanced and accessible complexity. These findings highlight the effectiveness of the module in maintaining instructional clarity while introducing technically demanding concepts.

Figure 3b illustrates students' perceptions of activity difficulty across all activities, using the same five-point Likert scale: 1 = very difficult, 2 = difficult, 3 = normal, 4 = easy, and 5 = very easy. Each bar represents an individual student's cumulative responses to the various module activities.

The distribution indicates a strong central tendency around the midpoint of the scale, with the majority of responses categorized as "normal" (level 3), represented by the green segment in each bar. This outcome reflects a well-balanced level of cognitive demand, suggesting that the activities were generally well-aligned with student capabilities and background knowledge.

Additionally, a consistent presence of "easy" (level 4, light blue) and "very easy" (level 5, purple) responses can be observed, particularly among Students 3, 9, and 10, indicating that for a subset of learners, some modules were perceived as straightforward or accessible. Conversely, a smaller portion of the responses falls into the "difficult" (level 2, orange) and "very difficult" (level 1, dark blue) categories, appearing with relative consistency across students. These ratings suggest that while the content was mostly clear, a minority of learners encountered challenges with specific tasks or concepts—particularly in technical modules such as data pre-processing or supervised learning.

Notably, no student rated all modules as exclusively difficult or very difficult, indicating that the instructional scaffolding and use of "Required Knowledge" segments successfully mitigated potential barriers to understanding. The overall pattern demonstrates that the activities were perceived as appropriately challenging without being inaccessible, thereby validating the instructional design in terms of clarity and gradual complexity.

Beyond self-reported perception data, the activities also employed teacher-assessed engagement metrics to provide a more holistic view of student participation and performance. These qualitative evaluations, drawn from Activity 1 to Activity 5, focused on observable behaviors and task outcomes across several criteria: autonomy, time management, solution design, creativity, debugging, programming, and teamwork. Each dimension was scored on a 0–5 scale, with descriptors corresponding to developmental levels: Not yet competent (0), Partially competent (2), Competent (4), and Expert (5).

The majority of students demonstrated a strong level of independence, with 8 out of 14 students achieving the highest score (5) in "Adequate selection of information before asking for help." This indicates that learners generally made active efforts to seek information and solve problems independently—an essential skill in AI and technical domains. A small number of students (e.g., Students 2 and 8) scored lower, suggesting some reliance on instructor guidance, which may be typical at this stage of skill development.

In the category of "Time Management", 6 students achieved expert-level performance (score of 5), while others ranged from 2 to 4. These results align with teacher observations indicating that most students completed their tasks within the allocated time, though a few struggled to maintain pace. These differences highlight the need for differentiated pacing or support mechanisms in future iterations.

In "Design and Construction of the Solution" and "Creativity", 6 students again received top scores (5), evidencing originality and initiative in the conception of their smart environment prototypes. The remaining students showed competent to developing performance (scores between 2 and 4), suggesting a generally high level of creative thinking, though some ideas could benefit from further elaboration or technical refinement.

The "Testing and Debugging" criterion reflected a strong distribution of capability. Approximately 50% of the students were able to efficiently identify and correct coding errors, a critical competency when integrating real-time sensor data and automation protocols. This is especially notable given the technical complexity of the Arduino-Raspberry Pi layered system.

Regarding "Programming", a majority of students produced clean, readable, and functional code. Six students were rated at the expert level, while others maintained solid competence. Similarly, in the "Teamwork" category, all students received mid to high scores, reflecting active collaboration, negotiation, and respectful peer interaction. This result reinforces the effectiveness of collaborative PBL strategies implemented in the activities.

Taken together, the teacher-reported engagement data offer a strong endorsement of the methodology. Most students not only completed their projects but did so with initiative, collaboration, and growing technical competence. The blend of structured scaffolding and hands-on exploration clearly supported student autonomy and peer-driven learning, which are critical for preparing VET learners for complex, intelligent systems design.

Based on the Fig. 4 titled "Positive Results by Question" summarizes the performance outcomes of 14 students across five assessment items, using binary indicators where 1 denotes a correct or satisfactory response and 0 denotes an incorrect or incomplete response. The analysis reveals a substantial improvement in student knowledge following the intervention. Most students achieved full marks (1) across all five items in the post-assessment phase, suggesting a robust comprehension of the concepts introduced during the modules. Specifically, Students 1, 3, 4, 5, 6, and 9 through 13 consistently demonstrated mastery across all evaluation points. These results indicate high retention and understanding of technical content such as configuring sensors, analyzing data flows, and applying logic to AI-controlled decision-making. A few students (e.g., Students 2, 7, 8, and 14) showed partial performance, with some items marked as 0. This suggests the presence of individual learning variability or potential difficulties with specific subtopics. Notably, Students 2 and 7 scored zero except on activity 2, potentially reflecting either a lack of prior knowledge, gaps in engagement, or barriers to comprehension during module delivery. These anomalies highlight the

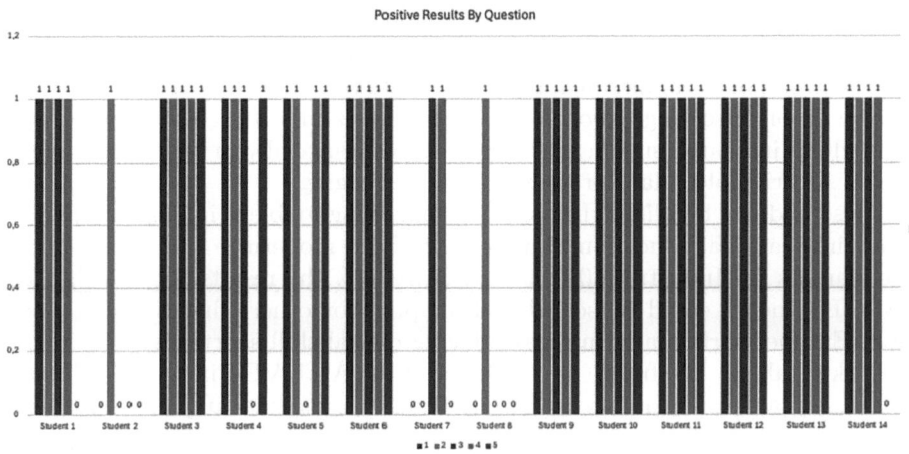

Fig. 4. Outcomes Students Results.

importance of personalized support mechanisms and formative feedback loops throughout the instructional cycle.

Furthermore, the post-assessment data validate the alignment between instructional goals and learning outcomes. The ability of the majority of students to correctly answer post-module questions reflects the clarity, relevance, and applicability of the learning activities. These findings reinforce the importance of pre- and post-assessment cycles in VET settings, not only to evaluate learning but also to inform future curriculum refinement and individual learning support.

6 Conclusions and Future Work

This project represents a significant step forward in addressing the skills gap in Artificial Intelligence (AI), the Internet of Things (IoT), and Ambient Intelligence (AmI) within the VET sector. Through the design and implementation of twelve structured, project-based modules, AIM4VET has demonstrated the pedagogical feasibility and technical effectiveness of integrating intelligent technologies into pre-university VET curricula.

The modular curriculum enabled students to engage with real-world applications in a smart home energy management system, facilitating hands-on learning across all levels of complexity—from sensor integration and control using Arduino and Raspberry Pi, to machine learning workflows implemented in KNIME. The pedagogical model adopted—centered on active learning and scaffolded knowledge—proved effective in ensuring high levels of engagement, understanding, and learner autonomy.

The multi-dimensional evaluation strategy employed in the project confirmed the impact of this approach. Questionnaire-based feedback revealed that students generally found the modules clear and well-calibrated in terms of difficulty. Teacher-based assessments further validated student engagement, evidencing strong performance in autonomy, collaboration, technical execution, and creative problem-solving. Knowledge assessments administered before and after the modules indicated significant learning gains, especially in technical domains such as AI principles, data processing, and debugging.

These findings highlight the value of embedding ambient intelligent environments in vocational education as a means to both modernize curricula and prepare learners for Industry 5.0 contexts. Moreover, the results suggest that the AIM4VET model could be scaled and adapted for other educational contexts across Europe, particularly in regions facing digital skill shortages.

Looking ahead, the future development of the AIM4VET initiative will focus on four key areas: scalability and replication, longitudinal impact assessment, integration of emerging technologies, and cross-cultural pedagogical research. To ensure broader impact, the curriculum will be adapted for deployment across a wider range of VET institutions, supported by customized guidelines and teacher training resources tailored to diverse educational contexts. In terms of impact assessment, future research will evaluate the long-term effects of the modules on students' career readiness, post-secondary education choices, and their transition into technologically advanced workplaces. Additionally, the curriculum will evolve to incorporate emerging technologies such as Generative AI, edge computing, and cybersecurity, ensuring alignment with the latest developments in digital transformation. Finally, as AIM4VET expands across Europe, further investigation will explore how cultural and institutional differences influence the implementation and effectiveness of intelligent learning environments in VET systems.

Acknowledgements. This work has been supported by Erasmus+ Programme of the European Union - Artificial Intelligence learning modules to adapt VET to labour market needs (AI4VET), AIM@VET - 2022-1ES01-KA220-VET-000089813.

References

1. Aeneas, E.I.T.D.F.: Industry 5.0: Towards a sustainable, human-centric and resilient european industry (2021). https://aeneas-office.org/2022/01/04/industry-5-0-towards-a-sustainable-human-centric-and-resilient-european-industry/
2. Barbas, M.P., Vieira, A.T., Branco, P.D.: Predict: jobs of the future with ai 4 vet inclusion. In: EDULEARN23 Proceedings, pp. 128–133. IATED (2023)
3. Berthold, M.R., et al.: Knime-the konstanz information miner: version 2.0 and beyond. ACM SIGKDD Explorat. Newsl. **11**(1), 26–31 (2009)
4. Cabero-Almenara, J., Gutiérrez-Castillo, J.J., Barroso-Osuna, J., Rodríguez-Palacios, A.: Digital teaching competence according to the digcompedu framework: comparative study in different Latin American universities. J. New Approaches Educ. Res. **12**(2), 276–291 (2023)
5. Cedefop: Empowering adults through upskilling and reskilling pathways, luxembourg: Publications office of the european union (2020). https://www.cedefop.europa.eu/en/publications/3081

6. Chang, M., Li, Y.: Smart Learning Environments. Springer, Heidelberg (2015)
7. Commission, E.: Artificial intelligence for Europe, com(2018) 237 final (2018). https://eur-lex.europa.eu
8. Commission, E.: Digital education action plan (2021–2027): Resetting education and training for the digital age, com(2020) 624 final (2020). https://education.ec.europa.eu/focus-topics/digital-education/action-plan
9. Dey, A.K.: Understanding and using context. Pers. Ubiq. Comput. **5**, 4–7 (2001)
10. Ghomi, M., Redecker, C.: Digital competence of educators (digcompedu): development and evaluation of a self-assessment instrument for teachers' digital competence. In: CSEDU (1). pp. 541–548 (2019)
11. Holmes, W.: Artificial intelligence in education: promises and implications for teaching and learning. Center for Curriculum Redesign (2019)
12. Holmes, W., Bidarra, J., Køhler Simonsen, H.: Artificial intelligence in higher education: a roadmap and future perspectives. Smart Learn. (2021)
13. Kassab, M., DeFranco, J., Laplante, P.: A systematic literature review on internet of things in education: benefits and challenges. J. Comput. Assist. Learn. **36**(2), 115–127 (2020)
14. Kim, P.W.: Ambient intelligence in a smart classroom for assessing students' engagement levels. J. Ambient. Intell. Humaniz. Comput. **10**(10), 3847–3852 (2019)
15. Koenraad, T., Whyte, S., Schmid, E.C.: itilt and smartvet: 2 eu projects to promote effective interactive whiteboard use in language and vocational education. Research-publishing. net (2013)
16. Ling, L., Yelland, N., Hatzigianni, M., Dickson-Deane, C.: The use of internet of things devices in early childhood education: a systematic review. Educ. Inf. Technol. **27**(5), 6333–6352 (2022)
17. Long, D., Magerko, B.: What is AI literacy? Competencies and design considerations. In: Proceedings of the 2020 CHI Conference on Human Factors in Computing Systems, pp. 1–16 (2020)
18. Luckin, R., Holmes, W.: Intelligence unleashed: an argument for ai in education (2016)
19. OECD: Preparing vocational education and training for the future of work: Ensuring vet is resilient to future labour market changes (2021). https://www.oecd.org/en/topics/vocational-education-and-training-vet.html
20. Pfeiffer, S.: Effects of industry 4.0 on vocational education and training. Institute of Technology Assessment, Vienna (2015)
21. Santos, O.C., Uria-Rivas, R., Rodriguez-Sanchez, M.C., Boticario, J.G.: An open sensing and acting platform for context-aware affective support in ambient intelligent educational settings. IEEE Sens. J. **16**(10), 3865–3874 (2016)
22. Thomas, J.W.: A review of research on project-based learning (2000)
23. Touretzky, D.: The ai4k12 initiative: developing national guidelines for teaching ai in k-12. GlobalSWEdu2020_Touretzky. pdf (2019)
24. UNESCO: Artificial intelligence and education: Guidance for policy-makers (2021). https://education.ec.europa.eu/focus-topics/digital-education/action-plan

Zero-Shot and Few-Shot Learning with Vision-Language Models for Post-disaster Structural Damage Assessment

Oriol Chacón-Albero[1](✉), Jaume Jordán[1], Vicent Botti[1,2], and Vicente Julian[1,2]

[1] Valencian Research Institute for Artificial Intelligence (VRAIN), Universitat Politècnica de València (UPV), Camí de Vera s/n, 46022 València, Spain
{odchaalb,vjulian}@upv.es, {jjordan,vbotti}@dsic.upv.es
[2] Valencian Graduate School and Research Network of Artificial Intelligence (VALGRAI), Universitat Politècnica de València (UPV), Camí de Vera s/n, 46022 València, Spain

Abstract. Structural damage assessment after natural disasters is a critical yet challenging task due to limited labeled data and the emergence of new damage patterns. In this work, we explore the use of vision-language models (VLMs) for post-disaster structural classification using the PeerHub ImageNet dataset. We evaluate several VLMs, including CLIP, OpenCLIP, SigLIP, and EvaCLIP, in a zero-shot setting across multiple structural tasks. Additionally, we investigate few-shot adaptation using Tip-Adapter and a simple prototype-based approach. Our results show that VLMs offer strong baseline performance, with few-shot methods improving reliability in low-data scenarios. To our knowledge, this is the first comprehensive study of VLMs for post-disaster structural assessment.

Keywords: Vision-Language models · Few-shot Learning · Post-disaster Assessment · Structural Health Monitoring

1 Introduction

Structural damage assessment following natural disasters is a critical task that directly impacts safety decisions, resource allocation, and recovery planning operations. The rapid and accurate evaluation of buildings and infrastructure in disaster-affected areas can mean the difference between life-threatening occupancy of compromised structures and efficient, targeted rehabilitation efforts.

As climate change continues to increase both the frequency and severity of extreme weather events worldwide [5], the need for efficient damage assessment methodologies has become increasingly urgent. Earthquakes, hurricanes, floods, and wildfires each present unique structural challenges, requiring assessment methods that can be quickly deployed and adapted to various damage patterns. Traditional inspection methods, relying heavily on manual expert evaluation, often struggle to scale in post-disaster scenarios where thousands of structures may require immediate assessment across affected regions with limited accessibility and resources. These challenges have motivated the use of Computer Vision (CV) systems to support and, eventually, automate structural health assessments [4].

Computer Vision techniques are becoming increasingly prevalent in structural health monitoring (SHM), enabling automated detection of surface defects (e.g., cracks, spalling, corrosion) and monitoring of global behaviors like displacement measurement or load estimation. These methods offer key advantages over traditional approaches, including non-contact sensing, low cost, and ease of deployment, particularly in hard-to-access areas [2]. However, the majority of proposed CV-SHM systems rely heavily on supervised learning, requiring large, task-specific labeled datasets. This dependence on domain-specific annotations limits their scalability, especially in dynamic post-disaster contexts where new damage types may appear, and labeled data is scarce or unavailable.

Focusing on post-disaster scenarios, computer vision plays a key role in assessing damage to buildings and infrastructure. A significant body of research leverages aerial and remote sensing imagery to map large-scale affected zones, compare pre and post-disaster scenes to quantify structural damage, and integrate geospatial data into 3D models for structural analysis [1]. Satellite and Unmanned Aerial Vehicle (UAV), equipped with technologies such as optical cameras, LiDAR, and Synthetic Aperture Radar, offer broad coverage and rapid situational awareness, making them ideal for identifying affected zones and guiding emergency response. Notably, datasets like FloodNet [8] have enabled research into flood scene understanding from high-resolution aerial imagery.

Complementing these methods, ground-level imagery provides critical close-up views of damage, capturing fine-grained features often invisible from above. The PeerHub ImageNet dataset [4] has emerged as the most widely used benchmark in this domain, offering thousands of images of earthquake damage, annotated for different classification tasks such as material type or damage severity.

Despite the utility and extensive work on datasets like PeerHub for earthquake-related damage classification, comparable datasets are scarce or nonexistent for other types of disasters, particularly for ground-level images capturing structural damage from floods, hurricanes, or wildfires. Each disaster scenario introduces distinct patterns of damage that are influenced by local construction practices and materials. As a result, existing models often fail to generalize across events without significant task-specific retraining. Building new datasets is time-consuming and expensive, as it requires rapid field deployment and domain-expert annotation, an especially difficult challenge in time-critical situations. Limitations such as the reliance on supervised learning, class imbalance, and the emergence of novel damage categories highlight the need for innovative solutions capable of operating under data-scarce and evolving conditions.

The recent development of Vision-language models (VLMs), such as CLIP [7], offers a promising alternative to traditional supervised approaches by leveraging large-scale pretraining on image-text pairs from the web. These models can associate visual features with natural language descriptions, enabling them to perform classification tasks without task-specific retraining. Their ability to operate in zero-shot or few-shot settings makes them particularly suited for disaster response scenarios. Moreover, VLMs support flexible integration of domain knowledge through prompt engineering, allowing experts to define custom labels and visual categories using natural language, opening new possibilities for rapid and scalable damage assessment across diverse disaster types.

A recent study [12] explored the use of CLIP for zero-shot and few-shot classification of common building defects, such as cracks, mildew, and peeling. Their work showed that prompts based on technical definitions significantly outperformed generic descriptions and even rivaled supervised baselines in certain tasks. While their results highlight the potential of VLMs in construction settings, the focus was limited to general defects in residential contexts and did not address the complex nature of post-disaster damage assessment. Moreover, despite their strong performance on some general tasks, VLMs still struggle with highly specialized domain-specific downstream tasks, especially those underrepresented in their pretraining data [3,7]. This limitation is particularly relevant in disaster scenarios.

In this work, we offer a novel exploration of VLMs for post-disaster structural damage assessment. Using the PeerHub-ImageNet dataset [4], we benchmark multiple VLMs (CLIP, SigLIP, EvaCLIP) across different classification tasks, including material type, structural component, and damage state. We systematically evaluate performance in zero-shot and few-shot settings, while varying the number of support images. In addition, we explore Tip-Adapter [14], a few-shot lightweight adaptation method, to better align the model with domain-specific tasks. All experiments are framed to simulate realistic post-disaster deployment, where only a small set of labeled examples may be available. Due to the constraints of existing datasets, our study focuses on earthquake damage classification as a proxy, evaluating selected classification tasks within the dataset.

The remainder of this paper is organized as follows. Section 2 introduces the VLMs used in our study and describes the experimental setup, including dataset details, prompt design, and evaluation protocol. Section 3 presents the results across zero-shot, few-shot, and adapter-based experiments. Finally, Sect. 4 discusses key trends and limitations, and outlines directions for future research.

2 Methodology

This section details the dataset, models, and experiments used to assess vision-language models for structural damage classification under limited supervision.

2.1 Dataset

We conduct our experiments using the PeerHub ImageNet dataset [4], an open-source benchmark for post-earthquake structural damage assessment. The dataset contains 36413 ground-level photographs of buildings affected by earthquakes, annotated with multiple classification labels relevant to structural evaluation.

The PeerHub dataset follows the φ-Net framework, which organizes recognition tasks into a hierarchical structure reflecting levels of scene understanding. Images are categorized into three scene levels—pixel, object, and structural—based on their scale and framing (e.g., close-ups of material loss vs. full-building shots). Corresponding classification tasks are assigned depending on the image level. For instance, spalling conditions are typically assessed at the pixel level, while component type and collapse mode are associated with the object or structural levels. These classification tasks are organized as nodes in a hierarchical decision tree, where each node represents a recognition task contributing to the overall structural characterization. Images are annotated with multiple attributes, making this a multi-task classification problem. This structured approach enables more context-aware and scalable damage assessment.

From the eight available tasks, we selected four representative classification problems (corresponding to Tasks 2, 3, 4, and 6 in the original taxonomy) that span different levels of the hierarchy and varying degrees of complexity relevant to emergency response scenarios. Table 1 summarizes these tasks and their corresponding dataset statistics. These selected tasks provide a comprehensive evaluation of VLM capabilities across both binary classification and multi-class problems, while covering different aspects of structural assessment. Note that the selected tasks are defined over distinct subsets of the full dataset, and some images may appear in more than one task.

Table 1. Selected PeerHub classification tasks with class distribution

Task	Class Distribution (%)	Total Images
Damage State	Damaged (53%), Unharmed (47%)	13,271
Spalling Condition	Spalling (37.7%), Non-spalling (62.3%)	7,735
Material Type	Steel (21.7%), Other (78.3%)	9,291
Component Type	Beam (10.7%), Column (34.2%), Wall (47.5%), Other (7.6%)	5,334

To evaluate few-shot capabilities, we employed a non-standard data split that more closely resembles real-world scenarios where labeled examples are scarce. For each classification task, we performed stratified sampling to maintain class distributions across splits, allocating 10% of the data for validation, 10% for training, and the remaining 80% for testing. From the training set, we randomly sampled small subsets to simulate few-shot learning conditions. This approach differs from typical machine learning evaluations, where most data is used for training; instead, our methodology prioritizes a comprehensive evaluation set while restricting the model's access to labeled examples. The validation set was used exclusively for hyperparameter tuning in the Tip-Adapter experiments.

2.2 Vision-Language Foundation Models

Despite the success of traditional models like Convolutional Neural Networks (CNNs) and Vision Transformers (ViTs), they often require large labeled datasets and retraining for even minor task changes, such as adding a new class. These models also tend to overfit domain-specific patterns and can struggle with distribution shifts. Vision-language models (VLMs) aim to address these challenges by enabling zero-shot and few-shot learning, allowing models to generalize to new tasks with minimal labeled data.

One of the most prominent VLMs is **CLIP** [7], introduced by OpenAI. CLIP is trained on a large collection of image-text pairs using a contrastive objective that aligns visual and textual representations in a shared embedding space. It consists of two encoders, one for images and one for text, which allow it to perform tasks like image classification or retrieval based on natural language prompts, without task-specific fine-tuning.

CLIP has shown strong zero-shot performance across a wide range of benchmarks and exhibits robustness to domain shifts. However, its generalization is constrained by its pretraining data, and performance often degrades on specialized tasks outside its training distribution [3]. To mitigate this, various strategies have been proposed, including prompt engineering [15], few-shot adaptation techniques [14], and lightweight fine-tuning methods [11].

Several recent models have extended or improved upon the CLIP architecture. **OpenCLIP** [6] is a community-driven implementation of CLIP that allows pretraining with a wider range of datasets (e.g., LAION-5B [9]), backbones (including ConvNeXt, ViT-G, and EfficientNet), and computational resources, enabling experimentation with more scalable and open alternatives to OpenAI's proprietary CLIP model. **SigLIP** (Sigmoid Loss for Language-Image Pretraining) differs fundamentally in its training objective: instead of CLIP's softmax-based contrastive loss, SigLIP uses a sigmoid loss that treats each image-text pair independently [13]. This change eliminates the need for negative sampling and leads to better performance in multi-label classification and long-tailed data, which are relevant challenges in structural damage datasets. **EvaCLIP** integrates the Eva visual backbone, a transformer architecture optimized for high-performance image understanding, with contrastive language-image pretraining. It retains the CLIP-style dual-encoder setup but benefits from more expressive visual representations, improved text alignment, and greater training efficiency through architectural and optimization enhancements [10]. EvaCLIP models are trained on massive image-text corpora (e.g., DataComp-1B), targeting better transfer to downstream tasks. These three models were selected to explore how differences in architecture, training objectives, and pretraining scale affect performance in low-data, domain-specific structural damage classification tasks.

2.3 Experimental Design

We designed three experiments to evaluate vision-language models under different supervision scenarios: zero-shot, few-shot classification, and few-shot adaptation using Tip-Adapter.

Zero-Shot Classification. In this setting, models classify input images without access to any labeled training data. We encoded category prompts such as *"a photo of a damaged structure"* or *"this is a photo of a column"*, based on default formats recommended by the model developers, and matched each image to the most similar class representation using cosine similarity in the shared embedding space. We compared several vision-language models (CLIP, OpenCLIP, SigLIP, and EvaCLIP), but report results only for the best-performing variant from each family: CLIP, OpenCLIP with LAION-G, SigLIP-400M, and EvaCLIP-8B.

Few-Shot Classification. To study the evolution of model performance as a function of the number of labeled examples, we conducted evaluations with 1, 2, 4, 8, 16, and 32 support images per class. Although the 32-shot falls outside the typical few-shot regime, it was included to observe performance saturation. For each class, we encoded support images and different textual definitions, including short labels and domain-specific descriptions (e.g., *"a photo of a beam: a horizontal or sloping structure used to transfer the load to structures below"*) as suggested in prior work [12]. All image and text embeddings for each class were averaged (mean pooling) to construct a class prototype. Classification was performed by computing cosine similarity between each test image and all class prototypes. Support samples were randomly drawn from the training set, and each experiment was repeated 30 times to account for sampling variability. Reported results include the mean and standard deviation across runs.

Few-Shot Adaptation with Tip-Adapter. We also evaluated the performance of Tip-Adapter [14], a lightweight adaptation method for CLIP. This method builds a cache model from support set embeddings and learns a small adapter on top of CLIP to better align predictions with downstream labels. We used the enhanced version that tunes hyperparameters on the validation set and report final performance on the test set. Based on our prior results, we fixed the number of support examples to 16 per class for this experiment.

3 Results

In this section, we present the results of the previously described zero-shot and few-shot experiments, organized by classification task.

3.1 Damage State Classification

In vision-based structural health monitoring, the binary classification of damage state is one of the most critical indicators. The definition is straightforward: any observable damage pattern on the structural surface is labeled as damaged, whereas images showing no visible signs of damage are labeled as unharmed. This task captures a fundamental distinction in post-disaster evaluation, often serving as a first step for triage-level structural assessment [4].

Table 2. Zero-shot performance of selected VLMs on Damage State classification.

Model	Accuracy	F1 Score	Precision	Recall
SigLIP-400M	**0.841**	**0.841**	**0.841**	**0.842**
CLIP	0.726	0.725	0.725	0.726
OpenCLIP (LAION-G)	0.699	0.699	0.709	0.705
EvaCLIP-8B	0.688	0.651	0.759	0.670

As shown in Table 2, the best zero-shot performance on this task was achieved by SigLIP-400M. Figure 1 shows the accuracy of few-shot experiments as a function of the number of samples, as well as the Tip-adapted baseline accuracy with 16 shots. Few-shot models show a consistent performance increase with more examples, especially between 1 and 8 shots, after which the gains become marginal. In the this setting, OpenCLIP (LAION-G) achieves the highest accuracy across shot counts. Tip-Adapter improves CLIP's accuracy from 72.6% to 76.2%. Overall, this task shows strong results, with both zero-shot and few-shot methods providing reliable performance. However, in this specific task zero-shot SigLIP-400M slightly outperforms all few-shot settings.

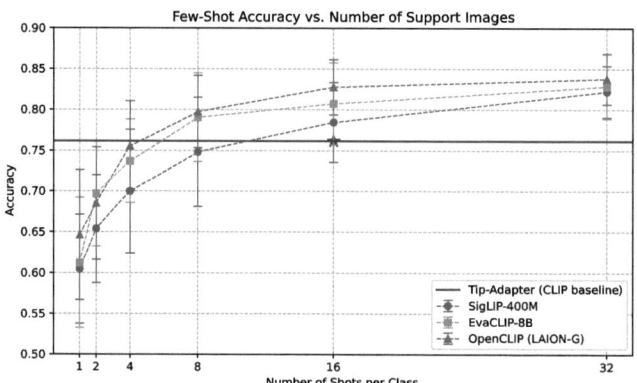

Fig. 1. Few-shot test acc. across different numbers of support images for the binary classification of damage state. Results averaged over 30 trials per configuration. TIP-Adapter result is plotted as a horizontal line (16-shot fixed baseline).

3.2 Spalling Condition Classification

Spalling refers to the loss of cover of a component's surface, due to flakes of material that break off, commonly observed in concrete or masonry elements. It can compromise structural integrity by reducing cross-sectional area and accelerating corrosion of embedded steel. This task is formulated as a binary classification problem, distinguishing between spalling and non-spalling conditions.

Table 3. Zero-shot performance on Spalling Condition classification

Model	Accuracy	F1 Score	Precision	Recall
SigLIP-400M	**0.663**	**0.652**	0.651	**0.661**
OpenCLIP (LAION-G)	0.597	0.597	0.647	0.644
EvaCLIP-8B	0.576	0.573	**0.663**	0.642
CLIP	0.590	0.511	0.528	0.521

As shown in Table 3, zero-shot performance on spalling condition classification proved more challenging than damage state classification, with baseline models achieving lower accuracy scores. This difficulty likely stems from the inherent challenge of defining negative classes (i.e., "structures without spalling") in natural language prompts, which requires models to recognize the absence rather than the presence of specific features. Furthermore, "Spalling" is a very specific, technical term that may not be well-represented in the web-scale training data of these models, unlike the more general concept of "damage". The best zero-shot result was also obtained by SigLIP-400M with 66.3% accuracy.

As illustrated in Fig. 2, few-shot learning patterns varied notably across models. LAION-G showed substantial performance improvements with increasing shot counts. In contrast, other models exhibited limited gains from few-shot learning, suggesting that spalling condition recognition may require more sophisticated adaptation strategies. The most significant improvement came from Tip-Adapter applied to CLIP, which enhanced performance from the baseline to 74.6% accuracy. Overall, this task highlights the variability in VLM performance across different structural damage types, with adaptation methods proving essential for achieving reliable classification of fine-grained damage conditions.

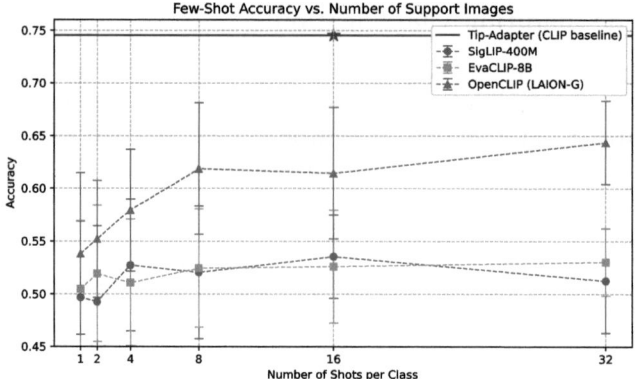

Fig. 2. Few-shot test acc. across different numbers of support images for the binary classification of spalling condition. Results averaged over 30 trials per conf. TIP-Adapter result is plotted as a horizontal line (16-shot fixed baseline).

3.3 Material Type Classification

Material identification is crucial for structural assessment, as different materials exhibit distinct mechanical properties and failure modes. While structural components are often covered by non-structural elements like plaster, exposed steel members can be identified through their characteristic shape and surface texture. This task was simplified to a binary classification problem in the original dataset, distinguishing between steel and other materials. To avoid the negative class definition challenges observed in the previous task, the "other" category was explicitly defined as "masonry, wood, or concrete structures".

Table 4. Zero-shot performance of selected VLMs on Material Type classification.

Model	Accuracy	F1 Score	Precision	Recall
SigLIP-400M	**0.950**	**0.931**	**0.928**	0.933
OpenCLIP (LAION-G)	0.936	0.913	0.904	0.923
EvaCLIP-8B	0.933	0.911	0.892	**0.937**
CLIP	0.703	0.681	0.704	0.786

As shown in Table 4, material type classification achieved excellent zero-shot performance, with most models exceeding 90% accuracy. This strong baseline performance is likely attributable to the prevalence of material concepts like "steel" and "concrete" in the web-scale training data of VLMs, making these terms well-represented in their learned visual-semantic associations. SigLIP-400M achieved the best zero-shot result with 95% accuracy. As illustrated in Fig. 3, few-shot learning provided modest but consistent improvements across models, with Tip-Adapter enhancing CLIP's performance from 70.3% to 93.8% accuracy. The highest overall performance was achieved by EvaCLIP-8B with 16 shots, reaching 97.7% accuracy. Few-shot performance gains were most pronounced between 1 and 4 shots, with diminishing returns beyond this point, suggesting that the strong zero-shot foundation required minimal additional supervision for near-optimal performance.

3.4 Component Type Classification

Identifying structural component types is essential for comprehensive damage assessment, as different elements (beams, columns..) serve distinct structural functions and exhibit different failure modes. This task represents the only multiclass problem in our study, distinguishing between four categories: beam, column, wall, and other components. The "other" category originally encompassed diverse elements, including joints, staircases, and non-structural components like windows or doors. Given the heterogeneous nature of this category and the challenges it poses for VLMs, we experimented with different prompt formulations. Our final approach defined the "other" class as "secondary structural elements".

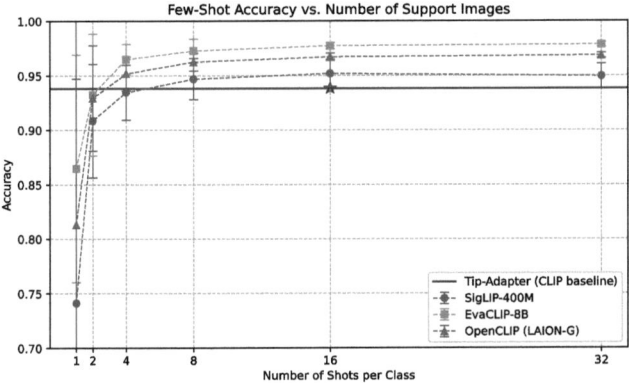

Fig. 3. Few-shot test acc. across different numbers of support images for the binary classification of material type. Results averaged over 30 trials per configuration. TIP-Adapter result is plotted as a horizontal line (16-shot fixed baseline).

Table 5. Zero-shot performance on Component Type classification

Model	Accuracy	F1 Score	Precision	Recall
SigLIP-400M	**0.490**	0.269	0.303	0.297
EvaCLIP-8B	0.489	**0.313**	**0.328**	**0.333**
OpenCLIP (LAION-G)	0.441	0.281	0.289	0.302
CLIP	0.407	0.287	0.311	0.303

As shown in Table 5, component type classification proved to be the most challenging task, with the best zero-shot performance reaching only 49% accuracy. This significant performance drop compared to binary classification tasks highlights the increased complexity of multi-class problems. The low F1-scores across all models (0.269-0.313) indicate challenges in achieving balanced classification performance across the four component categories, likely due to class imbalance and the heterogeneous nature of the "other" category. As illustrated in Fig. 4, few-shot learning showed modest improvements with increasing shot counts, but none of the few-shot prototype based approaches surpassed the best zero-shot baseline performance. However, the most significant improvement came from 16-shots Tip-Adapter applied to CLIP, which enhanced accuracy from 40.7% to 66.9%, representing a substantial 26.2% gain.

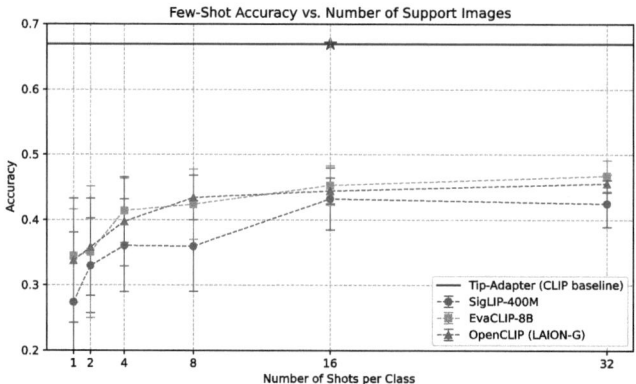

Fig. 4. Few-shot test acc. across different numbers of support images for the multiclass classification of component type. Results averaged over 30 trials per conf. TIP-Adapter result is plotted as a horizontal line (16-shot fixed baseline).

4 Conclusions

Our evaluation of vision-language models on structural damage classification demonstrates their significant potential for post-disaster assessment scenarios.

The strong zero-shot performance of SigLIP-400M across all tasks (reaching 95% accuracy on material classification) suggests VLMs can effectively support rapid damage assessment with minimal training data. However, performance varied substantially across tasks: while binary damage state classification achieved 84.1% zero-shot accuracy, multiclass component identification struggled at just 49.0%, revealing limitations in fine-grained recognition. The significant performance gap between different tasks further highlights how ambiguous ("other") or negative class definitions ("non-spalling") conflict with VLM reasoning patterns.

Few-shot adaptation delivered consistent but diminishing returns beyond 8-16 examples, with Tip-Adapter significantly boosting CLIP's accuracy across tasks. The high variance across trials, which decreased with the number of samples, underscores the critical importance of representative examples. Surprisingly, SigLIP's few-shot performance lagged behind its zero-shot capabilities, potentially due to token constraints limiting rich prompt engineering.

One limitation of our setup is that the TIP-Adapter experiments use a small labeled validation set (10% of data) for model selection, whereas prototype-based few-shot baselines are restricted to smaller support subsets. While both remain within a limited supervision setting, this difference may influence relative performance and should be considered in future benchmarking.

Our findings suggest key research directions, including: developing optimized adaptation techniques for high-performing zero-shot models like SigLIP; creating VLM-aligned benchmarks that address problematic class definitions; automating prompt engineering to dynamically optimize textual representations for specific models and tasks; and exploring hybrid approaches for complex multiclass recognition. Our work establishes VLMs as promising tools for disaster response, but underscores the need for domain-specific solutions before deployment in emerging scenarios like flood damage assessment. In particular, future work will explore adaptation to other disaster types, such as flood-related damage, where visual features and available data may differ significantly from earthquake scenarios.

Acknowledgments. This work is partially supported by grant PID2021-123673 funded by MCIN/AEI/10.13039/501100011033 and by "ERDF A way of making Europe", project TED2021-131295B-C32 from the State Research Agency, and DIGITAL2022 CLOUDAI02/S8760000 from the European Commission.

References

1. Al Shafian, S., Hu, D.: Integrating machine learning and remote sensing in disaster management: a decadal review of post-disaster building damage assessment. Buildings **14**, 2344 (2024)
2. Dong, C.Z., Catbas, F.N.: A review of computer vision based structural health monitoring at local and global levels. Struct. Health Monit. **20**, 692–743 (2021)
3. Fang, A., et al.: Data determines distributional robustness in contrastive language image pre-training (CLIP). In: International Conference on Machine Learning, pp. 6216–6234 (2022)

4. Gao, Y., Mosalam, K.: PEER Hub ImageNet: a large-scale multi-attribute benchmark data set of structural images. J. Struct. Eng. **146**, 04020198 (2020)
5. Glasser, R.: The climate change imperative to transform disaster risk management. Int. J. Disaster Risk Sci. **11**, 152–154 (2020)
6. Ilharco, G., et al.: Openclip (2021). https://doi.org/10.5281/zenodo.5143773
7. Radford, A., et al.: Learning transferable visual models from natural language supervision. In: ICML, pp. 8748–8763 (2021)
8. Rahnemoonfar, M., Chowdhury, T., Sarkar, A., Varshney, D., Yari, M., Murphy, R.R.: Floodnet: a high resolution aerial imagery dataset for post flood scene understanding. IEEE Access **9**, 89644–89654 (2021)
9. Schuhmann, C., et al.: LAION-5b: an open large-scale dataset for training next generation image-text models. In: 36th NeurIPS Conference, pp. 25278–25294 (2022)
10. Sun, Q., Fang, Y., Wu, L., Wang, X., Cao, Y.: EVA-CLIP: improved training techniques for CLIP at scale (2023). https://doi.org/10.48550/arXiv.2303.15389
11. Wortsman, M., et al.: Robust fine-tuning of zero-shot models. In: 2022 IEEE/CVF Conference on Computer Vision and Pattern Recognition (CVPR), pp. 7949–7961 (2022)
12. Yong, G., Jeon, K., Gil, D., Lee, G.: Prompt engineering for zero-shot and few-shot defect detection and classification using a visual-language pretrained model. Comput.-Aided Civil Infrastruct. Eng. **38**, 1536–1554 (2022)
13. Zhai, X., Mustafa, B., Kolesnikov, A., Beyer, L.: Sigmoid loss for language image pre-training. In: 2023 IEEE/CVF International Conference on Computer Vision, pp. 11941–11952 (2023)
14. Zhang, R., et al.: Tip-adapter: training-free adaption of clip for few-shot classification. In: European Conference on Computer Vision, pp. 493–510 (2022)
15. Zhou, K., Yang, J., Loy, C.C., Liu, Z.: Learning to prompt for vision-language models. Int. J. Comput. Vision **130**, 2337–2348 (2022)

Biomedical Applications

Analyzing the Impact of Data Augmentation on Tumor Detection and Classification in Mammograms

Mădălina Dicu[1(✉)], Enol García González[2], Camelia Chira[1], and José R. Villar[2]

[1] Faculty of Mathematics and Computer Science, Babeș-Bolyai University, Str. Mihail Kogălniceanu nr. 1, 400084 Cluj-Napoca, Romania
{madalina.dicu,camelia.chira}@ubbcluj.ro
[2] Department of Computer Science, University of Oviedo, C. Jesús Arias de Velasco, s/n, 33005 Oviedo, Spain
{garciaenol,villarjose}@uniovi.es

Abstract. Breast cancer remains one of the leading causes of mortality among women worldwide, making early detection crucial for improving survival rates. Deep learning-based approaches have shown remarkable potential in automating tumor detection from mammographic images; however, their effectiveness largely depends on the choice of data augmentation strategies and model architecture. In this study, we systematically investigate the impact of six data augmentation techniques and four object detection models on the task of breast tumor detection, using the publicly available DDSM dataset. Each model was trained on pre-processed mammographic images, with individual augmentation techniques applied separately to assess their isolated effects. The augmentations analyzed include Contrast Limited Adaptive Histogram Equalization, random rotation, random translation, horizontal flipping, Contrast Limited Adaptive Histogram Equalization combined with rotation, and Gaussian noise addition. Experimental results demonstrate that Faster Region-based Convolutional Neural Network consistently outperforms the YOLO variants, achieving the best detection result of 91.35% accuracy when combined with cache optimization. Additionally, we found that Contrast Limited Adaptive Histogram Equalization-based contrast enhancement significantly improves detection performance, whereas geometric transformations such as random rotation and horizontal flipping tend to degrade model accuracy.

Keywords: Breast cancer detection · Deep learning · Object detection · Faster R-CNN · YOLO

1 Introduction

Breast cancer continues to be one of the most widespread and deadly diseases affecting women worldwide, with millions of new cases diagnosed each year and a significant mortality rate [13]. Although advances in detection methods and treatments have improved survival rates in many regions, access to early diagnosis remains uneven, especially in areas with limited medical resources. Early detection of breast cancer is crucial for increasing the chances of effective treatment, highlighting the need for accurate and accessible diagnostic solutions.

In recent years, computer vision technologies, particularly convolutional neural networks, have become increasingly important in analyzing mammographic images, helping radiologists improve diagnostic accuracy and reduce interpretation time [12]. However, the performance of these models is influenced by several factors, such as the quality of input data, preprocessing techniques, data augmentation strategies, and the chosen network architecture.

In this study, we investigate how the choice of data augmentation techniques and neural network architecture affects performance in breast tumor detection. Using the publicly available Digital Database for Screening Mammography (DDSM) [6], we trained and evaluated four modern object detection models: Faster R-CNN [16], YOLOv8 [7], YOLOv9 [20], and YOLOv11 [8]. The study involved applying six different augmentation techniques individually to assess the impact of each method on detection accuracy and model robustness.

We address the following two research questions:

- **RQ1:** How do different object detection models (Faster R-CNN, YOLOv8, YOLOv9, YOLOv11) perform in breast tumor detection?
- **RQ2:** Which data augmentation techniques have a positive impact on detection accuracy?

The main contributions of this work are as follows: we conduct a systematic evaluation of the impact of six data augmentation techniques on the performance of object detection models applied to mammographic images; we compare four modern detection architectures, covering both one-stage and two-stage paradigms; and finally, we identify the optimal combinations of augmentation strategies and network architectures to improve breast tumor detection.

The structure of the paper is organized as follows: Sect. 2 reviews relevant literature, Sect. 3 describes the experimental methodology and dataset, Sect. 4 presents the experimental results, while Sect. 5 discusses and interprets the findings. Finally, Sect. 6 concludes the study and outlines directions for future work.

2 Related Work

Several studies have highlighted the importance of applying realistic augmentations to enhance model robustness. Oza et al. [14] emphasized that methods such as CLAHE, moderate rotations, and translations are effective in introducing natural variability without altering essential anatomical structures. Similarly, Prinzi et al. [15] demonstrated that the integration of augmentation techniques within a YOLO-based framework can improve the detection of complex formations, such as asymmetries and distortions.

Other directions have explored broader approaches. Alhsnony and Sellami [2] showed that combining augmentation with training on multiple datasets contributes to building more general and precise models. Furthermore, Alawee et al. [1] proposed GAN-based augmentation techniques to generate synthetic images, suggesting that enhancing data quality can have a positive impact on diagnostic performance.

Regarding model architectures, recent works have confirmed that contrast-based augmentations, such as CLAHE, are particularly valuable for detecting subtle structures, as illustrated by Shia and Ku [17] in their YOLOv8-based study on microcalcification detection. In contrast, more aggressive transformations like wide-angle rotations or horizontal flipping have been associated with performance degradation, particularly in breast mass detection tasks [3,11], indicating that perturbing the natural anatomical orientation can negatively affect model recognition capabilities.

Thus, existing literature supports the idea that selecting appropriate augmentation strategies is critical for the success of automatic tumor detection models in mammographic imaging. Moreover, a clear need emerges for a systematic investigation into the impact of different augmentation techniques on the performance of modern detection networks within the specific context of breast tumor analysis.

3 Methodology

This section details the dataset preparation, augmentation strategies, model selection, and experimental design carried out in this study. Our primary objective was to investigate the impact of various data augmentation techniques on the tumor detection performance of object detection models. We begin by outlining the dataset characteristics and the preprocessing methods used to standardize input images, and subsequently discuss the augmentation techniques employed to increase data variability. Finally, we introduce the selected deep learning models and outline the training and evaluation procedures used in our experiments.

3.1 Dataset and Image Preprocessing

In this study, we used the public *Digital Database for Screening Mammography (DDSM)* [6], which provides a large collection of mammograms from multiple medical centers. The dataset includes approximately 700 cases without tumors, 900 with benign tumors, and 900 with malignant tumors.

To minimize variability introduced by different scanning devices and resolutions, we selected only MLO (Mediolateral Oblique) views that were digitized using *HOWTEK* scanners at a standardized resolution of *43.5 microns*. Furthermore, we retained only images that contained benign or malignant tumors, ensuring consistent acquisition characteristics and focusing the study exclusively on tumor detection.

After applying these selection criteria, the final dataset consisted of *964* images, including *547* benign and *419* malignant cases. The dataset was divided into three subsets: 80% for training (772 images), 10% for validation (96 images), and 10% for testing (96 images).

We observed that many mammograms contained unwanted elements such as identification labels and scanning artifacts, which could interfere with the learning process of detection models. To address this, we applied a preprocessing pipeline designed to enhance tumor visibility and remove irrelevant components.

We adopted basic morphological operations—erosion and dilation [19]— following the recommendations of Omer et al. [10]. This approach was selected based on findings from a previous comparative study [5], where multiple preprocessing strategies, including morphological operations and the GrowCut algorithm [4], were evaluated. This preprocessing technique removes all image elements resulting from the scanner such as background labels and borders.

This preprocessing method was chosen for its simplicity, efficiency, and proven ability to improve model performance, especially in two-stage detectors [5].

Examples illustrating this process are shown in Fig. 1. Figure 1a presents the raw mammogram, where artifacts and labels are visible. Figure 1b shows the annotated tumor regions, and Fig. 1c displays the mammogram after preprocessing, with only the breast tissue retained.

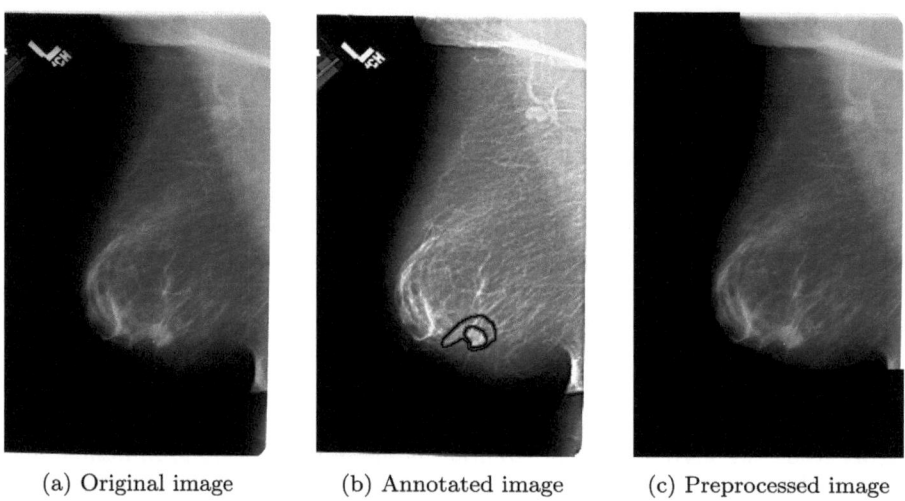

(a) Original image   (b) Annotated image   (c) Preprocessed image

Fig. 1. Example images from the DDSM dataset (Case ID: A_1171): (a) original raw image, (b) annotated tumor regions, and (c) image after morphological preprocessing.

3.2 Data Augmentation

After completing the preprocessing stage, which focused on isolating the breast tissue and removing artifacts, we further expanded the dataset through a series of data augmentation techniques. Because medical imaging datasets are often limited in size, applying augmentation was essential to help the models generalize better to unseen data, following best practices outlined in the literature [18].

The goal of these augmentations was to introduce natural and realistic variations while preserving the anatomical integrity of the tumor regions. By simulating different visual conditions, we aimed to expose the models to a broader range of tumor appearances, ultimately improving their robustness across different scanning environments.

The augmentation techniques applied in this study are summarized below:

- **Contrast Limited Adaptive Histogram Equalization (CLAHE)**: This technique enhances local contrast by dividing the image into 8×8 pixel tiles and applying histogram equalization with a clip limit of 2.0. This setting helps to reveal fine details without introducing excessive noise.
- **Random Rotation**: The images were rotated randomly by an angle between $-45°$ and $+45°$ to introduce geometric variability, while maintaining clinically plausible orientations.
- **CLAHE + Rotation**: In this case, CLAHE was first applied to enhance contrast, followed by a random rotation. This combination introduces variations in both image contrast and orientation.
- **Horizontal Flip**: Images were mirrored along the vertical axis (O_Y) to simulate natural left-right variations in breast positioning during mammography.
- **Random Translation**: Images were shifted horizontally and vertically by up to $\pm 10\%$ of their dimensions, introducing variability in tumor positioning within the field of view.
- **Gaussian Noise**: Random noise with a standard deviation of $\sigma = 0.05$ was added to the normalized pixel values, simulating noise that could arise from different scanning conditions.

Examples of each augmentation technique are illustrated in Fig. 2. These augmented images reflect the types of variations introduced during training, helping the models to become more resilient to visual changes while preserving the critical anatomical features needed for accurate tumor detection.

3.3 Deep Learning Models

For this study, we selected four object detection models that represent the two main paradigms in the field: two-stage and one-stage detectors. Our objective was to compare classical models, known for their high accuracy but slower processing, with more recent models designed for speed and real-time applications.

Faster Region-based Convolutional Neural Network (Faster R-CNN), introduced by Ren et al. [16], is a two-stage detector that combines a Region Proposal Network (RPN) with a Convolutional Neural Network (CNN)-based classifier. The RPN first generates candidate object regions, which are then classified and refined in a second stage. Due to its design, Faster R-CNN provides strong performance, particularly in detecting small objects, making it a

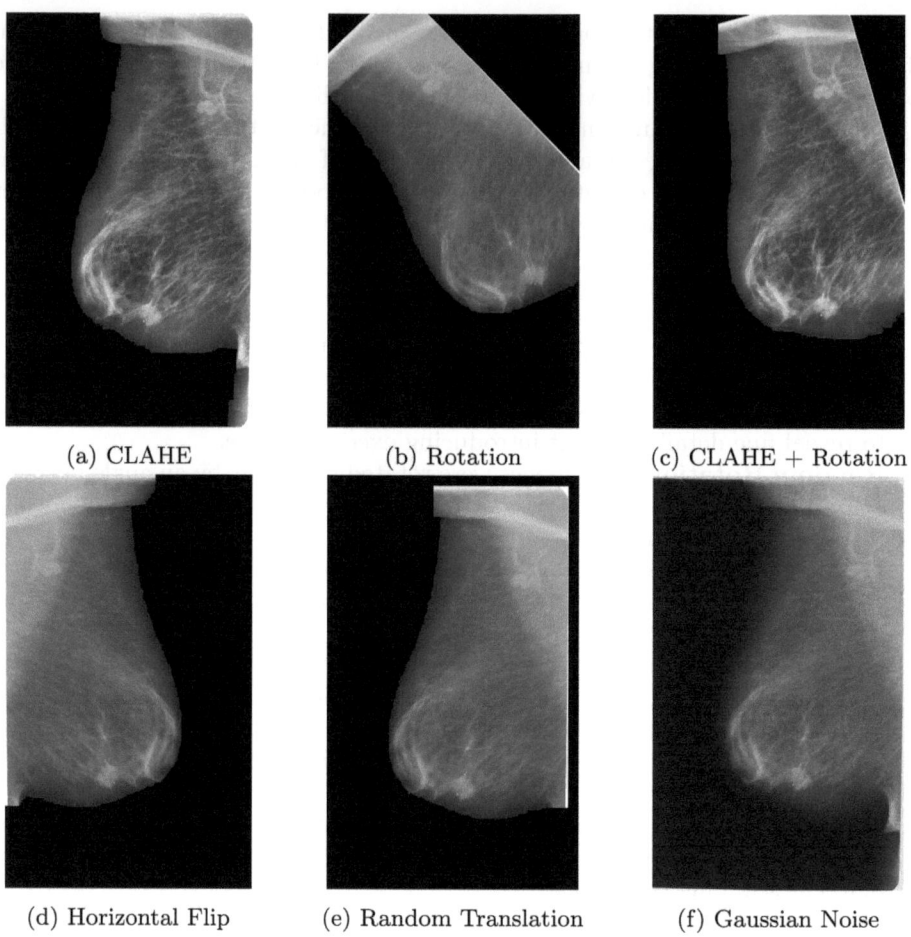

Fig. 2. Examples of augmented images using the techniques applied in this study (Case ID: A_1171).

good fit for precision-critical tasks such as medical imaging. However, this model typically requires more computational resources and has longer inference times compared to one-stage alternatives.

You Only Look Once (YOLO) is a family of one-stage detection models that predict bounding boxes and class labels in a single forward pass through the network [7]. This design makes YOLO models fast and efficient, which is particularly valuable for real-time applications. In this work, we used three recent YOLO versions: YOLOv8 [7], YOLOv9 [20], and YOLOv11 [8].

YOLOv8 introduced a new anchor-free architecture and a decoupled detection head, aiming to improve both speed and accuracy. **YOLOv9** built on this by incorporating transformer-based components and enhanced attention mechanisms, which help the model handle more complex and diverse datasets [20].

YOLOv11, the most recent version at the time of this study, further refines feature extraction and computational efficiency, achieving promising results across a wide range of object detection tasks.

We selected these models to represent different trade-offs between accuracy and computational efficiency. Faster R-CNN is well-known for its precision in detecting small or low-contrast objects, while the YOLO family offers much faster inference speeds. Including YOLOv8, YOLOv9, and YOLOv11 allowed us to explore how recent architectural improvements influence model performance, particularly in response to various data augmentation strategies.

3.4 Proposed Approach

To systematically assess the impact of each augmentation technique on model performance, we designed a series of independent experiments. In each experiment, the original training and validation sets were expanded by adding augmented versions of each image, generated using a single augmentation technique. The test set remained unchanged across all experiments to ensure a fair and consistent evaluation framework.

This experimental design allowed us to isolate the effect of each augmentation method, providing a clearer understanding of how individual transformations influence detection accuracy and model robustness. The overall structure of the datasets used in the experiments is summarized in Table 1.

Table 1. Structure of the datasets used in the experiments.

Dataset	Training	Validation	Testing
Original	772 images	96 images	96 images
Original + Augmentation	1544 images	192 images	96 images

In total, seven experimental configurations were defined. Each configuration corresponded either to the original dataset or to a combination of the original dataset with one specific augmentation technique. These configurations are listed in Table 2.

3.5 Experimental Setup and Evaluation Metrics

Based on the materials and methodologies described in the previous sections, the experimental work conducted in this study involved training four object detection models—YOLOv8, YOLOv9, YOLOv11, and Faster R-CNN—using both the original dataset and the six augmented versions created with different data augmentation techniques. In total, 28 models were trained to perform tumor detection and classification into benign and malignant categories.

Table 2. List of performed augmentation experiments.

Experiment	Applied Augmentation Technique
Exp_0	Original dataset without any augmentation
Exp_1	Original dataset + CLAHE
Exp_2	Original dataset + Random rotation between $-45°$ and $+45°$
Exp_3	Original dataset + CLAHE followed by random rotation
Exp_4	Original dataset + Horizontal flip
Exp_5	Original dataset + Random translation up to $\pm 10\%$
Exp_6	Original dataset + Addition of Gaussian noise

The hyperparameters for each model family were selected through a preliminary tuning process aimed at identifying configurations that offered the best trade-off between accuracy and convergence stability. The process to establish the value of the parameters consisted of running small training sessions of 5 epochs with each configuration and comparing the results obtained to analyze the trend towards the best parameters. Table 3 summarizes the main training parameters used during the experiments.

Table 3. Hyperparameters used for model training during experimentation.

Parameter	YOLO models	Faster R-CNN
Optimizer	AdamW (momentum: 0.9)	SGD (momentum: 0.9)
Learning Rate	1.667×10^{-3}	2.5×10^{-4}
Batch Size	16	128

Following the training phase, all models were evaluated on the same unaltered test set to ensure a consistent and fair comparison across all experimental configurations.

For model evaluation, we used the mean Average Precision (mAP) metric, calculated at two different Intersection over Union (IoU) thresholds: AP50 (at 50% IoU) and AP75 (at 75% IoU), following the evaluation protocol defined by the COCO dataset [9].

4 Results

This section presents the detection performance achieved by the YOLOv8, YOLOv9, YOLOv11, and Faster R-CNN models in the task of breast tumor detection, using preprocessed images and various data augmentation strategies. The complete performance results across all model and augmentation combinations are summarized in Table 4.

Table 4. Detection performance (%) of YOLOv8, YOLOv9, YOLOv11, and Faster R-CNN models trained on the original and augmented datasets. Results are reported as mean Average Precision at IoU thresholds of 0.5 (AP50) and 0.75 (AP75). The best result is highlighted in bold.

Dataset	YOLOv8		YOLOv9		YOLOv11		Faster R-CNN	
	AP50	AP75	AP50	AP75	AP50	AP75	AP50	AP75
Original	18.70	9.63	14.70	5.69	12.40	6.01	77.90	33.00
CLAHE	20.30	9.10	15.82	6.44	16.80	7.84	**91.35**	8.50
Rotation	3.50	1.16	2.46	0.83	1.44	0.72	33.20	14.40
CLAHE + Rotation	5.47	1.83	1.74	0.47	1.84	0.97	12.40	6.20
Horizontal Flip	1.99	0.62	1.05	0.49	2.56	0.60	12.10	9.90
Translation	1.43	0.46	1.39	0.70	1.11	0.39	42.70	12.40
Gaussian Noise	9.09	4.44	6.23	2.84	11.59	3.61	32.40	13.50

Without any augmentation, Faster R-CNN consistently outperformed the three YOLO variants at both AP50 and AP75 thresholds. This result highlights the robustness of two-stage architectures when detecting small and low-contrast objects, as is often the case in medical imaging. In contrast, the YOLO models obtained significantly lower scores, indicating challenges in generalizing from the original dataset without additional variability introduced through augmentation.

Applying CLAHE-based augmentation led to performance improvements across all models, with Faster R-CNN achieving the highest gains (Table 4, row *CLAHE*). This finding suggests that enhancing local contrast is particularly beneficial for detecting subtle structures in mammographic images.

By comparison, augmentations involving random rotation—either alone or combined with CLAHE—had a strong negative impact on performance. Following these transformations, AP50 scores dropped sharply, approaching minimal values, which indicates that altering the anatomical orientation of the breast significantly disrupts detection capabilities (see Table 4, rows *Rotation* and *CLAHE + Rotation*).

Similarly, applying horizontal flipping resulted in a notable decline in performance, particularly for Faster R-CNN, suggesting that models rely heavily on anatomical cues associated with natural breast orientation. Random translation had a more moderate impact: while performance degradation was less severe compared to rotations, YOLO models appeared more sensitive to tumor position changes within the image field.

Adding Gaussian noise produced relatively limited effects. Faster R-CNN remained notably more resilient than the YOLO variants, likely due to its two-stage design, which helps filter out minor perturbations in the input.

5 Discussion

Among all models, Faster R-CNN demonstrated the most consistent performance across different augmentations, especially when using contrast-enhanced images. Among the YOLO versions, YOLOv8 showed slightly better resilience under moderate perturbations, although the differences between YOLOv8, YOLOv9, and YOLOv11 remained small, with no major improvements in tumor detection across versions.

In analyzing the YOLO variants, it is notable that the detection performance decreases from YOLOv8 to YOLOv11 despite architectural improvements. This is mainly due to YOLOv11's use of lightweight Transformer blocks and anchor-free detection, which favor global context understanding over local feature precision. While beneficial for large-scale object detection, these changes reduce the model's sensitivity to small, low-contrast tumors typical in mammograms, leading to lower accuracy in specialized medical imaging tasks.

Overall, the results suggest that careful augmentations such as CLAHE can enhance model performance in tumor detection tasks, while aggressive geometric transformations (such as rotation or flipping) tend to confuse the models and degrade accuracy. Model selection also remains critical: Faster R-CNN proved to be the most robust option when faced with variations introduced during training.

The analysis of the obtained results provides clear answers to the two research questions formulated in this study.

In relation to **RQ1**, the comparison across all experimental scenarios highlights the superior performance of the Faster R-CNN architecture. Its two-stage design, which combines region proposal generation with refined classification, offers a distinct advantage for detecting breast tumors—especially given their small size and low contrast. While the YOLO models (YOLOv8, YOLOv9, and YOLOv11) are fast and computationally efficient, they showed greater sensitivity to perturbations in the data. In particular, their performance dropped significantly when augmentations introduced transformations that compromised clinical realism.

Regarding **RQ2**, the impact of data augmentation techniques on model accuracy varied considerably. Applying CLAHE was the only strategy that consistently improved performance, by enhancing local contrast without altering the overall structure of the images. In contrast, geometric transformations such as random rotation, horizontal flipping, and translation had a negative effect on model accuracy. These operations introduced anatomical variations that are unlikely to occur in real mammographic images, disrupting the models' ability to correctly recognize lesions. Adding Gaussian noise produced only a moderate impact on performance, with Faster R-CNN once again demonstrating better resilience compared to the YOLO variants—likely due to its region proposal and refinement mechanisms.

Overall, these findings emphasize that the effectiveness of augmentation strategies critically depends on preserving the clinical realism of the images. Models also need to be robust enough to handle minor variations without compromising their understanding of anatomical structures. Poorly chosen augmentations can significantly degrade performance, whereas careful preprocessing combined with appropriate model selection proves essential for successful tumor detection in medical imaging tasks.

6 Conclusions and Future Work

This study analyzed the impact of data augmentation techniques and network architecture selection on performance in breast tumor detection. The conducted experiments demonstrated that models based on the Faster R-CNN architecture achieved superior results compared to those from the YOLO family, exhibiting greater robustness to data variability and improved capability in detecting tumors, particularly small or low-contrast lesions. Regarding augmentation strategies, the application of the CLAHE technique led to significant performance improvements by enhancing the models' ability to detect subtle structures. In contrast, geometric augmentations such as random rotation and horizontal flipping negatively affected the results, highlighting the importance of preserving the clinical realism of images during the training process.

As a future work based on the analysis carried out in this work, we propose developing a new and improved data augmentation technique. In the data augmentation techniques evaluated in this work, basic mechanisms well known in the literature have been used to work with all types of vision problems. These methods are very generic and make slight variations in the generated images. The method to be worked on for future work will consist of developing an algorithm to create tumor images artificially. These images must be realistic and share characteristics with real cases to increase the dataset by masquerading as new cases.

Acknowledgements. This research has been funded by the Spanish Research Agency –grant PID2023-146257OB-I00–. Also, by Principado de Asturias, grant IDE/2024/000734, and by the Council of Gijón through the University Institute of Industrial Technology of Asturias grants SV-25-GIJÓN-1-23. This research was supported by the project "Romanian Hub for Artificial Intelligence - HRIA", Smart Growth, Digitization and Financial Instruments Program, 2021-2027, MySMIS no. 334906.

References

1. Alawee, W.H., Al-Haddad, L.A., Basem, A., Al-Haddad, A.A.: A data augmentation approach to enhance breast cancer detection using generative adversarial and artificial neural networks. Open Eng. **14**(1), 20240052 (2024)
2. Alhsnony, F.H., Sellami, L.: Enhancing breast cancer detection through advanced deep learning: an application of yolov8x on mammographic images. In: 2024 IEEE 7th International Conference on Advanced Technologies, Signal and Image Processing (ATSIP), vol. 1, pp. 128–133. IEEE (2024)
3. Famouri, S., Morra, L., Mangia, L., Lamberti, F.: Breast mass detection with faster R-CNN: on the feasibility of learning from noisy annotations. IEEE Access **9**, 66163–66175 (2021)

4. Ghosh, P., Antani, S.K., Long, L.R., Thoma, G.R.: Unsupervised grow-cut: cellular automata-based medical image segmentation. In: 2011 IEEE First International Conference on Healthcare Informatics, Imaging and Systems Biology, pp. 40–47 (2011). https://doi.org/10.1109/HISB.2011.44
5. González, E.G., Dicu, M., Villar, J.R., Chira, C.: Analyzing the impact of image preprocessing on tumor detection and classification in mammograms. In: Proceedings of the 2nd Olympiad in Engineering Science (OES 2025) (2025). https://indico.uis.no/event/50/papers/1265/files/252-conf_enolGarcia_OES2025.pdf
6. Heath, M., Bowyer, K., Kopans, D., Moore, R., Kegelmeyer, W.P.: The digital database for screening mammography. In: Yaffe, M.J. (ed.) Proceedings of the Fifth International Workshop on Digital Mammography, pp. 212–218. Medical Physics Publishing (2001)
7. Jocher, G., Chaurasia, A., Qiu, J.: YOLO by Ultralytics (2023). https://github.com/ultralytics/ultralytics. Accessed 20 Apr 2025
8. Jocher, G., Qiu, J.: Ultralytics yolo11 (2024). https://github.com/ultralytics/ultralytics. Accessed 20 Apr 2025
9. Lin, T.-Y., et al.: Microsoft COCO: common objects in context. In: Fleet, D., Pajdla, T., Schiele, B., Tuytelaars, T. (eds.) ECCV 2014. LNCS, vol. 8693, pp. 740–755. Springer, Cham (2014). https://doi.org/10.1007/978-3-319-10602-1_48
10. M. Omer, A., Elfadil, M.: Preprocessing of digital mammogram image based on Otsu's threshold. Am. Sci. Res. J. Eng. Technol. Sci. **37**(1), 220–229 (2017). https://asrjetsjournal.org/index.php/American_Scientific_Journal/article/view/3476
11. Moiz, A., et al.: Breast masses detection using yolov8. Int. J. Innov. Sci. Technol. **6**, 198–206 (2024)
12. Nasser, M., Yusof, U.K.: Deep learning based methods for breast cancer diagnosis: a systematic review and future direction. Diagnostics **13**(1), 161 (2023)
13. World Health Organization: Breast cancer factsheet (2024). https://www.who.int/news-room/fact-sheets/detail/breast-cancer
14. Oza, P., Sharma, P., Patel, S., Adedoyin, F., Bruno, A.: Image augmentation techniques for mammogram analysis. J. Imaging **8**(5), 141 (2022)
15. Prinzi, F., Insalaco, M., Orlando, A., Gaglio, S., Vitabile, S.: A yolo-based model for breast cancer detection in mammograms. Cogn. Comput. **16**(1), 107–120 (2024)
16. Ren, S., He, K., Girshick, R., Sun, J.: Faster R-CNN: towards real-time object detection with region proposal networks. In: Advances in Neural Information Processing Systems, vol. 28 (2015)
17. Shia, W.C., Ku, T.H.: Enhancing microcalcification detection in mammography with yolo-v8 performance and clinical implications. Diagnostics **14**(24), 2875 (2024)
18. Shorten, C., Khoshgoftaar, T.M.: A survey on image data augmentation for deep learning. J. Big Data **6**(1), 1–48 (2019)
19. Soille, P., et al.: Morphological Image Analysis: Principles and Applications, vol. 2. Springer (1999)
20. Wang, C.Y., Yeh, I.H., Liao, H.Y.M.: Yolov9: learning what you want to learn using programmable gradient information. arXiv preprint arXiv:2402.13616 (2024)

An Enhanced Hybrid Machine Learning Model for Plant Disease Detection and Classification

Mara Măcelaru[iD], Petrică C. Pop[✉][iD], Rareş Chiuzbăian, and Norbert Kovacs

Department of Mathematics and Computer Science, Technical University of Cluj-Napoca, North University Center of Baia Mare, 430122 Baia Mare, Romania
{mara.hajdu,petrica.pop}@mi.utcluj.ro

Abstract. Timely and precise detection of plant diseases plays a crucial role in ensuring good agricultural productivity and food security. Conventional methods of disease detection frequently depend on manual inspection, which may be time-consuming and susceptible to errors. In our paper, we develop an enhanced hybrid machine learning (ML) based model that combines Bayesian Convolutional Neural Networks (B-CNNs) for feature extraction with Gaussian Naïve Bayes (GNB) classification for final decision-making. In addition, we performed various data augmentation methods to strengthen the diversity of the training data and to improve its generalization. Our proposed hybrid ML-based model was trained and validated on the PlantVillage dataset. The performance metrics obtained were impressive, proving that it is highly competitive against existing state-of-the-art solution approaches and demonstrating the high potential of our hybrid ML-based model for real-world applications in smart agriculture.

Keywords: Plant disease detection and classification · Machine learning · Hybrid machine learning

1 Introduction

Maintaining crop yield and quality largely depends on the accurate and timely identification of plant diseases. According to the Food and Agriculture Organization (FAO) of the United Nations, around 40% of the annual crop yield is lost due to pests and pathogens that play an important role in the case of plant disease. Nowadays, plant pathologists mainly rely on optical observations to detect plant diseases. The multitude of plant diseases, influenced by various factors like plant species, environmental variables, and agricultural methods, represents a challenge even for experienced pathologists to diagnose these conditions extensively. To tackle these problems, in recent years, researchers have successfully used machine learning (ML) and deep learning (DL) methods for the detection and classification of plant diseases, achieving significant results.

In the last years, ML and DL models have been widely applied in agriculture to detect and classify plant diseases with high accuracy. These models analyze plant images to detect diseases in the early stages. Recently, several ML and DL techniques have been proposed to detect and classify plant diseases. In this section, we present some of the most important and relevant papers that used ML and DL for plant disease identification and classification.

Ramesh et al. [10] employed Random Forest (RF) for plant disease detection, differentiating between healthy and diseased leaves using datasets they created. Meshram et al. [8] presented a comprehensive survey of the applications of ML algorithms in the agricultural domain. They classified agricultural activities into three main categories: pre-harvesting, harvesting, and post-harvesting, and for each category the authors presented the existing ML approaches. Neelakantan [9] examined the performance of different ML algorithms: RF, SVM, Decision Tree (DT), KNN, and Naive Bayes (NB) on a tomato dataset, resulting in the fact that RF was the best algorithm achieving 89% accuracy. Recently, [7] evaluated, analyzed and tested five ML algorithms: KNN, Random Forest, Iterative Dichotomizer 3, Adaptive Boosting and Logistic Regression for plant disease identification, using a large data set containing 74798 images mainly from the PlantVillage dataset. Their results indicate that the traditional ML algorithms: KNN and RF performed well, achieving an accuracy of 92% across the entire data set and 97% on the Tomato dataset, respectively.

Abd Algani et al. [1] developed a novel DL model that combines ant colony optimization with the CNN to identify and appreciate the disease of the plant leaf. Their reported results indicate that their proposed model achieves only a 0.01% increase in accuracy compared to the regular CNN models. Ali et al. [3] proposed an ensemble of various deep learning architectures: DenseNet201, EfficientNetB0, InceptionResNetV2 and EfficientNetB3, to enhance the classification accuracy of plant leaf diseases. They introduced an innovative image-processing technique designed to enhance the efficiency of DL models. Their ensemble model developed achieved an accuracy of 99.89% on the PlantVillage dataset. Too et al. [12] compared the fine-tuning of VGG16, Inception-V4, and ResNet for plant disease classification, demonstrating that DenseNet achieved a maximum accuracy of 99.75%. Kaur and Bensal [6] evaluated different DL models, like DenseNet169, Xception, InceptionV3, MobileNetV2, and ResNet50V2 for plant disease identification and classification. Alqahtani [4] developed DL framework, called RefineDet, that uses ResNet-50 as the base network of the RefineDet approach to extract a representative set of sample keypoints. Recently, Aboelenin et al. [2] introduced a hybrid CNN and Vision Transformer (ViT) model that combines local and global feature extraction for superior classification. For a recent survey on ML or/and DL approaches for the detection and classification of plant disease, we refer to Sajitha et al. [11].

We developed an enhanced hybrid ML-based model with the objective of addressing the problem of detection and classification of plant diseases. Our key contributions, related to the existing state-of-the-art, are summarized as follows.

1. From the perspective of algorithm design, we developed a novel solution approach for efficient plant disease detection and classification. Our hybrid ML-based model combines Bayesian Convolutional Neural Networks (B-CNNs) for feature extraction with Gaussian Naïve Bayes (GNB) that ensures robust probabilistic classification for final decision-making. In addition, we performed various data augmentation methods to strengthen the diversity of the training data and to improve its generalization.
2. From the perspective of empirical evaluation, we performed extensive experiments on one of the most used datasets, namely PlantVillage dataset. Our results were analyzed, interpreted and evaluated against existing state-of-the-art approaches from the literature.

The rest of our paper has the following structure: Sect. 2 presents our proposed methodology that contains the architecture developed and the description of the used Bayesian CNNs (B-CNNs) and Gaussian Naïve Bayes (GNB) classifier. Section 3 contains the description of the used dataset, while in Sect. 4 we detail the dataset preprocessing step and the used augmentation methods. In Sect. 5, we present the results achieved and compare them with existing state-of-the-art results. Finally, in Sect. 6, we present the conclusions of our study and some future research directions.

2 Proposed Methodology

The evolution in the field of artificial intelligence, particularly in ML and DL, has led to significant improvements in the automatic detection of plant diseases. The use of these technologies helps us detect diseases with high accuracy, which will help farmers make faster and more efficient decisions regarding their crops.

Classic ML models, such as the Gaussian Naive Bayes (GNB) classifier, are based on probabilistic calculations, assuming that each feature of an image does not depend on the others. Although this model is fast and efficient, we will not obtain good results in cases where we have complex images, where the features are interconnected.

Similarly, CNNs, used in DL, provide very good results in image analysis because they can identify complex details and patterns. However, a main disadvantage of these models is that they cannot predict how certain their predictions are, which is a very important aspect when it comes to diagnosing plant diseases, where variations in the data can affect the results. To solve this issue, Bayesian CNNs use advanced statistical methods to also calculate the level of uncertainty of the predictions, using techniques such as Monte Carlo Dropout, etc.

In our paper, we designed a hybrid ML-based model, called B-CNNs-GNB, which combines the advantages of both technologies. Bayesian CNN helps to extract complex features from images and calculates how certain the predictions are, while Gaussian Naive Bayes makes the final decisions based on probabilities. The combination of the two methods offers a very good balance of accuracy and computational efficiency and may be used efficiently for plant disease detection.

A typical Bayesian CNN model has several layers, each of which has a specific role: the input layer receives the image, the convolutional layers analyze the details, the pooling layers reduce the data size, and the fully connected layers complete the classification. Using model tuning mechanisms, such as batch normalization and dropout, the model will become more stable and accurate.

We implemented a Bayesian CNN model with five convolutional layers. Our model architecture also includes a maximum pooling layer, batch normalization layers, and a Gaussian classifier that is used to estimate class probabilities. The dataset used to train and evaluate our hybrid ML-based model is the PlantVillage dataset, one of the most widely used and known datasets for plant disease classification.

In Fig. 1, we present the proposed plant disease detection flow, which follows a structured approach to classify diseased plant leaves using a Bayesian CNN and a Gaussian Naive Bayes classifier. The flow consists of five primary phases: the first phase is the data acquisition and preprocessing, the next one is the feature extraction with Bayesian CNN, the next phase involves estimation and probabilistic classification using Naive Bayes, and the final phase is disease prediction.

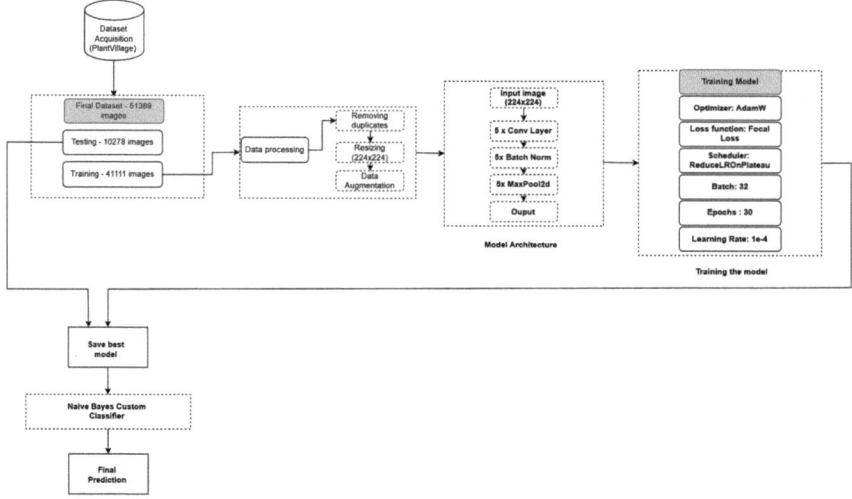

Fig. 1. The diagram flow of our developed hybrid ML-based model.

The input images used belong to the PlantVillage dataset, which contains 51389 images, of which 80% were used for training (41111 images) and the remaining 20% were used for testing (10278 images). The preprocessing phase deals with the removal of duplicates, image resizing (224×224 pixels), and data augmentation.

Through these phases, input images are standardized, and feature representation is improved. The preprocessed images are then sent to a Bayesian

CNN that uses five convolutional layers, five batch normalization layers, and five max-pooling layers, followed by fully connected layers. The Bayesian approach introduces stochastic regularization by applying Monte Carlo dropout during inference, allowing multiple forward passes per image, resulting in a collection of predictions, providing a measure of predictive uncertainty rather than a single deterministic output. By executing multiple stochastic forward passes, the Bayesian CNN generates a distribution of predictions for each input. The mean prediction is computed by aggregating these results, and the variance quantifies the uncertainty of the model.

This probabilistic inference ensures robust decision-making, particularly in ambiguous cases where multiple disease symptoms overlap. The final feature representations from the Bayesian CNN serve as input to a GNB classifier, which models the feature distributions for each disease class as independent Gaussian distributions. The likelihood function is computed per feature using the class-specific Gaussian parameters, and then the Bayes' theorem is applied to compute the posterior probability for each class. The arg max decision rule selects the disease class with the highest posterior probability.

The class of disease with the maximum posterior probability is selected as the final prediction. To optimize the training phase, the model is trained using the AdamW optimizer, Focal Loss function, and a ReduceLROnPlateau scheduler. The ReduceLROnPlateau scheduler is applied during the training phase to dynamically adjust the learning rate based on the validation loss. If the validation loss does not improve for a set number of epochs, the scheduler reduces the learning rate, allowing the optimizer to refine weight updates with finer adjustments. This approach helps prevent oscillations, avoids premature convergence, and ensures a better generalization to unseen data. The training is carried out with a learning rate of 1e-4, a batch size of 32, and 30 epochs. The best-performing model is saved and deployed for real-world inference, using its learned feature representations for accurate plant disease classification.

2.1 Model Arhitecture

A **convolutional layer** is the main component of CNNs that applies filters to an input image to extract important characteristics such as edges, textures, and patterns. Each filter overlays the image, making a **convolution operation** defined as:

$$y(i,j) = \sum_m \sum_n x(i-m, j-n) w(m,n) \tag{1}$$

where $x(i,j)$ represents the input feature map, $w(m,n)$ represents the convolutional filter (kernel) and $y(i,j)$ represents the output feature map.

These layers were improved by **five batch normalization layers** to increase stability and convergence during the training phase.

Batch normalization (BN) normalizes activations in a neural network using:

$$\hat{x} = \frac{x - \mu}{\sigma}, \quad y = \gamma \hat{x} + \beta \tag{2}$$

where μ and σ are the mean and standard deviation of the mini-batch, γ and β are learnable parameters that scale and shift the normalized output. The model retained a **single max-pooling layer** and a **dropout rate of 50%** to prevent overfitting.

Max-pooling is a down-sampling technique that reduces spatial dimensions while preserving important features:

$$y(i,j) = \max_{m,n} x(i+m, j+n) \tag{3}$$

Dropout randomly drops neurons during training with probability p:

$$y = \begin{cases} \frac{x}{1-p}, & \text{with probability } (1-p) \\ 0, & \text{with probability } p \end{cases} \tag{4}$$

Our model also included **two fully connected layers**, and the final predictions were calculated as the average of the results from **N stochastic forward passes**.

Fully connected layers compute a weighted sum of inputs:

$$y = Wx + b \tag{5}$$

where W represents the weight matrix, x the input vector, and b the bias term.

In Bayesian CNNs, multiple stochastic forward passes through the network allow uncertainty estimation. Predictions are obtained as follows:

$$\hat{y} = \frac{1}{N} \sum_{i=1}^{N} f(x, \theta_i) \tag{6}$$

where $f(x, \theta_i)$ is the output of the model with different stochastic weights θ_i due to dropout.

An important adjustment of our model is the use of a **Gaussian classifier**. A **Gaussian classifier** assumes that the characteristics follow a normal distribution:

$$P(x|C_k) = \frac{1}{\sqrt{2\pi\sigma_k^2}} e^{-\frac{(x-\mu_k)^2}{2\sigma_k^2}} \tag{7}$$

where μ_k and σ_k^2 are the mean and variance of class C_k, $P(x|C_k)$ is the likelihood of x given class C_k.

The posterior probability is calculated using the Bayes theorem:

$$P(C_k|x) = \frac{P(x|C_k)P(C_k)}{P(x)} \tag{8}$$

where $P(C_k)$ represents the prior probability of class C_k, $P(x)$ represents the marginal probability of the data.

Rectified Adam (Radam) is an adaptive optimizer that stabilizes training, mainly in the early stages, using a rectified variance term:

$$m_t = \beta_1 m_{t-1} + (1 - \beta_1) g_t \tag{9}$$

$$v_t = \beta_2 v_{t-1} + (1 - \beta_2) g_t^2 \tag{10}$$

$$\theta_t = \theta_{t-1} - \eta \frac{m_t}{\sqrt{\hat{v}_t} + \epsilon} \tag{11}$$

where m_t and v_t are estimates of the first and second moment, β_1, β_2 are momentum coefficients, and η is the learning rate.

3 Dataset Description

The dataset used in this article is PlantVillage dataset, which is one of the most used dataset for plant disease classification. The dataset has 51389 images that combine healthy and unhealthy plant leaves with several diseases. This dataset contains high-resolution images from different plant species and disease types and is one of the most detailed datasets used in agricultural deep learning applications. The dataset is organized in such a way as to facilitate the training and evaluation of machine learning models for automatic plant disease detection, making it an essential resource for precision agriculture and crop monitoring systems.

The PlantVillage dataset serves as a base for advancing ML and DL applications in agriculture, providing a diverse, well-labeled, and scalable dataset that helps with real-time disease detection and early intervention strategies.

4 Dataset Preprocessing and Augmentation Techniques

The **Data augmentation** process involves multiple techniques to improve the diversity of the training data and improve generalization. These transformations enhance dataset diversity by modifying images in ways to improve model generalization and robustness.

In Fig. 2, we illustrate the sequence of data augmentation transformations applied to plant images during the training phase to enhance dataset diversity and improve model generalization.

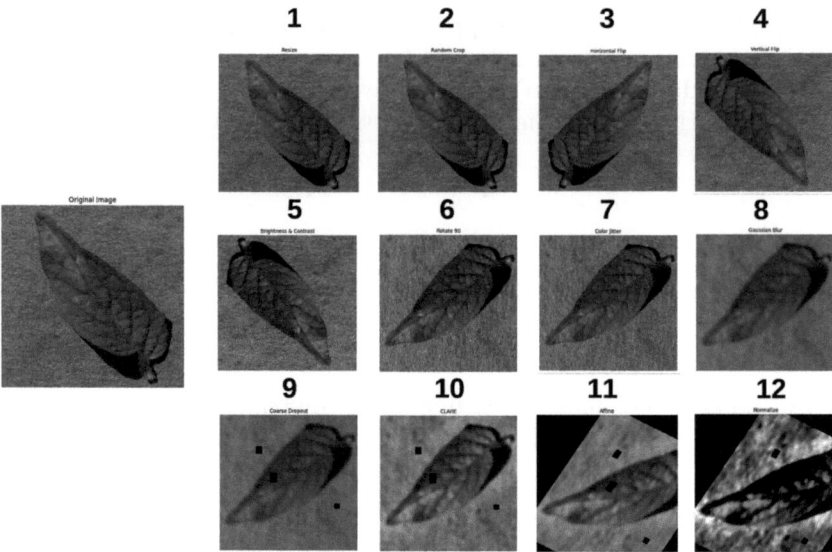

Fig. 2. Data Augmentation Techniques Applied to Plant Images.

The performed operations are:

1. **Resizing.** Resize the image to a fixed **224 × 224 pixels** size, so that all images have the same size
2. **Random Cropping.** Obtains a **random 224 × 224 crop** from the image, to make sure that the model learns important features from different sections.
3. **Horizontal Flip.** Flips the image **horizontally** with a probability of **100%** (p=1.0), which is very useful for symmetry-based data augmentation.
4. **Vertical Flip.** Flips the image **vertically** with a probability of **100%**, further increasing variability.
5. **Random Brightness and Contrast Adjustment.** Modifies **brightness and contrast** by ±20%, so that the model learns to recognize patterns even under **several lighting conditions**.
6. **Random Rotation by 90 Degrees.** Rotates the image by 90° at a probability of **100%**, which is very useful for datasets where orientation is not fixed.
7. **Color Jitter.** Introduces variations in **brightness, contrast, saturation, and hue**, to make the model robust to **color variations** in real-world images.
8. **Gaussian Blur.** Applies a **Gaussian blur** with a kernel size randomly chosen between **3 and 7**, so that the model learns to manage **blurred images**.
9. **Coarse Dropout.** Randomly removes **rectangular regions** from the image (similar to **Cutout**), making the model to learn features **without relying on specific areas**.

10. **Contrast Limited Adaptive Histogram Equalization (CLAHE).** Improves **local contrast** in small grid regions (**8 × 8 tiles**) to enhance feature detection in **low-contrast images**.
11. **Affine Transformations.** Applies **scaling (zooming)**, **translation (shifting)**, **rotation** ($-45°$ to $45°$), and **shear distortions** ($-10°$ to $10°$) to add variations in image **perspective**.
12. **Normalization.** Standardizes pixel values using the **mean and standard deviation** of the **ImageNet dataset**, so that the model receives **normalized inputs** to improve convergence during training.

These augmentations improve model generalization and prevent overfitting, ultimately leading to improved performance when used on real-world plant disease detection.

5 Results and Performance Evaluation

Several comparative experiments were conducted to assess the efficiency of our proposed hybrid ML-based model for plant disease detection and classification on PlantVillage dataset. The results obtained are presented and analyzed in this section. In our computational experiments 80% of the dataset was allocated for training purposes, with the remaining 20% allocated for testing to evaluate the performance of the proposed hybrid ML model.

Our application was developed and tested on an ASUS TUF F15 FX506HE laptop, running Ubuntu 24.04.2 LTS. The system has an 11th generation Intel Core i5-11400H processor, with a maximum frequency of 4.50 GHz, along with 15.35 GB of available RAM. For graphics processing, the system uses an NVIDIA GeForce RTX 3050 Ti Mobile video card (discrete), along with an integrated Intel UHD Graphics unit.

In our paper, we measure the performance of the developed hybrid ML-based model using accuracy, precision, recall, and F1-score.

In Table 1, we displayed the results obtained by our developed hybrid ML model for plant disease identification and classification on the PlantVillage dataset consisting of 51389 images divided into 38 classes.

Analyzing the values obtained by our hybrid ML-based model, we can see that we have a very good classification performance, obtaining an average precision of 99.83%, a recall of 99.85%, an F-1 score of 99.84%, and an accuracy of 99.85%. These values show an almost perfect classification for all disease categories.

In conclusion, the results obtained by testing our hybrid ML-based model show that the DL approach combined with probabilistic classification increases classification efficiency and reduces uncertainty. The model's ability to extract disease-specific features through deep convolution layers, together with the probabilistic decision of the Naive Bayes classifier, greatly helps to increase robustness. Its near-perfect performance gives us confidence that there is a high potential for its use in the real world, especially in precision agriculture, where fast and accurate identification of plant diseases is essential for crop protection.

Table 1. The Performance Metrics obtained by our enhanced hybrid ML model for all 38 classes of the plants from PlantVillage

Class	Precision	Recall	F1-Score	Accuracy
Apple_scab	99.52	99.68	99.6	99.68
Apple_Black_rot	99.84	100	99.92	100
Apple_Cedar_apple_rust	100	100	100	100
Apple_Healthy	99.82	99.82	99.82	99.82
Background_without_leaves	99.91	100	99.96	100
Blueberry_Healthy	99.93	99.93	99.93	99.93
Cherry_Powdery_mildew	100	100	100	100
Cherry_Healthy	100	100	100	100
Grape_Black_rot	100	99.66	99.83	99.66
Grape_Esca_(Black_Measles)	99.71	99.86	99.78	99.86
Grape_Leaf_blight_(Isariopsis_Leaf_Spot)	99.91	100	99.95	100
Grape_Healthy	100	100	100	100
Orange_Haunglongbing_(Citrus_greening)	100	100	100	100
Peach_Bacterial_spot	99.96	99.96	99.96	99.96
Peach_Healthy	100	100	100	100
Pepper_bell_Bacterial_spot	100	99.9	99.95	99.9
Pepper_bell_Healthy	99.93	99.86	99.9	99.86
Potato_Early_blight	100	99.9	99.95	99.9
Potato_Late_blight	99.8	99.6	99.7	99.6
Potato_Healthy	99.35	100	99.67	100
Raspberry_Healthy	99.73	99.73	99.73	99.73
Soybean_Healthy	99.9	99.88	99.89	99.88
Squash_Powdery_mildew	99.89	100	99.95	100
Strawberry_Leaf_scorch	100	100	100	100
Strawberry_Healthy	100	99.78	99.89	99.78
Tomato_Bacterial_spot	99.86	99.81	99.84	99.81
Tomato_Early_blight	99.2	99	99.1	99
Tomato_Late_blight	99.6	99.6	99.6	99.6
Tomato_Leaf_Mold	100	99.79	99.89	99.79
Tomato_Septoria_leaf_spot	99.89	99.89	99.89	99.89
Tomato_Two-spotted_spider_mite	99.88	99.46	99.67	99.46
Tomato_Target_Spot	98.94	99.64	99.29	99.64
Tomato_Yellow_Leaf_Curl_Virus	99.94	99.98	99.96	99.98
Tomato_Mosaic_virus	99.73	100	99.87	100
Tomato_Healthy	99.87	99.94	99.91	99.94
Mean	99.83	99.85	99.84	99.85

We assess the efficiency of our developed hybrid ML-based model by comparing it against state-of-the-art algorithms on the PlantVillage dataset. We used the accuracy as the primary evaluation metric. The comparison of the results is presented in Table 2.

Table 2. Comparison between our proposed hybrid ML-based model and state-of-the-art models from literature

Reference	Proposed model	Accuracy	Our accuracy
Aboelenin et al. [2]	Hybrid model	99.24%	**99.85%**
Kaur and Bansal [6]	ResNet50V2	99.42%	**99.85%**
Alqahtani [4]	DL-PlantRefineDet	**99.94%**	99.85%
Too et al. [12]	DenseNET121	**99.98%**	99.85%

Analyzing the values displayed in Table 2, we may notice that the results obtained by our developed hybrid ML-based model confirm the high competitiveness of our innovative solution approach, compared to the current state-of-the-art methods for plant disease detection and classification.

The accuracy of our hybrid model is 99.85%, a competitive result compared to existing models. Although the value obtained by our model is slightly lower than DenseNet121 (99.98%) and DL-PlantRefineDet (99.94%), our model outperforms other hybrid and CNN-based approaches, such as the hybrid model of Aboelenin et al. (99.24%) and ResNet50V2 (99.42%). Although DenseNet121 has a higher reported accuracy of 99.98%, the difference with our model is only 0.13%, which may not be statistically significant in practical applications. The small difference in accuracy between the models suggests that we can work on further improvements, to improve the accuracy but also to test on more existing datasets.

6 Conclusion

In our paper, we develop an enhanced hybrid ML-based model that combines Bayesian Convolutional Neural Networks (B-CNNs) for feature extraction with Gaussian Naïve Bayes (GNB) classification for final decision-making. The integration of Bayesian inference enhances the robustness of the hybrid model, allowing predictive uncertainty estimation and ensuring more reliable classifications in real-world agricultural applications.

The results obtained indicate high values of precision, recall and F1-score in all disease classes, with an overall accuracy of 99.85%. The minimal error rates and consistent accuracy trends highlight the reliability of this approach in detecting plant diseases, achieving a near-perfect classification. However, the hybrid model exhibits minimal errors in classifying certain diseases, whose images show visual similarities with other disease categories.

In the future, we plan to improve the model's accuracy by creating extended datasets based on real-world scenarios, to increase reliability and performance in diverse conditions, and by testing the model on other existing datasets.

Acknowledgments. This work was supported by the project "Collaborative Framework for Smart Agriculture" – COSA that received funding from Romania's National Recovery and Resilience Plan PNRR-III-C9-2022-I8, under grant agreement 760070 and the project "New Tool Based on Intelligent Algorithms and Machine Learning for Detecting Plant Diseases from Images", funded through the National Research Grant Competition – GNaC ARUT 2023.

References

1. Abd Algani, Y.M., Caro, O.J.M., Bravo, L.M.R., Kaur, C., Al Ansari, M.S., Bala, B.K.: Leaf disease identification and classification using optimized deep learning. Measur. Sensors **25**, 100643 (2023)
2. Aboelenin, S., Elbasheer, F.A., Eltoukhy, M.M., El-Hady, W.M., Hosny, K.M.: A hybrid framework for plant leaf disease detection and classification using convolutional neural networks and vision transformer. Complex Intell. Syst. **11**, 142 (2025)
3. Ali, A.H., Youssef, A., Abdelal, M., Raja, M.A.: An ensemble of deep learning architectures for accurate plant disease classification. Eco. Inform. **81**, 102618 (2024)
4. Alqahtani, Y., Nawaz, M., Nazir, T., Javed, A., Jeribi, F., Tahir, A.: An improved deep learning approach for localization and recognition of plant leaf diseases. Expert Syst. Appl. **230**, 120717 (2023)
5. Hughes, D.P., Salathé, M.: An open access repository of images on plant health to enable the development of mobile disease diagnostics. arXiv preprint arXiv:1511.08060 (2015)
6. Kaur, K., Bansal, K.: Enhancing plant disease detection using advanced deep learning models. Indian J. Sci. Technol. **17**, 1755–1766 (2024)
7. Macelaru, M., Pop, P.C., Barata, J.: A comparative study of machine learning models for plant disease identification. In: Quintián, H., et al. (eds.) SOCO 2024. Lecture Notes in Networks and Systems, vol. 889, pp. 107–116 (2025)
8. Meshram, V., Patil, K., Meshram, V., Hanchate, D., Ramkteke, S.: Machine learning in agriculture domain: a state-of-art survey. Artif. Intell. Life Sci. **1**, 100010 (2021)
9. Neelakantan, P.: Analyzing the best machine learning algorithm for plant disease classification. Mater. Today Proc. **80**(3), 3668–3671 (2023)
10. Ramesh, S., Hebbar, R., Niveditha, M., Pooja, R., Shashank, N., Vinod, P.V.: Plant disease detection using machine learning. In: Proceedings of 2018 International Conference on Design Innovations for 3Cs Compute Communicate Control (ICDI3C), pp. 41–45. IEEE (2018)
11. Sajitha, P., Andrushia, A.D., Anand, N., Naser, M.Z.: A review on machine learning and deep learning image-based plant disease classification for industrial farming systems. J. Ind. Inf. Integr. **38**, 100572 (2024)
12. Too, E.C., Yujian, L., Njuki, S., Yingchun, L.: A comparative study of fine-tuning deep learning models for plant disease identification. Comput. Electron. Agric. **161**, 272–279 (2019)

Interpretable ML for Stress Detection from Vital Signs Using SHAP

Samson Mihirette[1](✉), Enrique Antonio De la Cal Martin[1], and Qing Tan[2]

[1] University of Oviedo, Oviedo, Spain
uo298476@uniovi.es
[2] Athabasca University, Athabasca, Canada

Abstract. Stress is a major health concern, contributing to cardiovascular and mental health issues, as well as reduced productivity. Wearable technologies enable continuous monitoring of vital signs—such as heart rate (HR), respiratory rate (RR), and heart rate variability (HRV)—supporting real-time stress detection. Although machine learning (ML) methods have shown strong predictive capabilities, interpretability remains essential for clinical and personal health use.

This study integrates SHapley Additive exPlanations (SHAP) with an XGBoost classifier to enhance transparency in stress prediction from physiological signals. Using data from three wearable datasets, SHAP identified HR, RR intervals, and HRV metrics—particularly the LF/HF ratio—as key predictors. The method also revealed the impact of temporal and individual differences on predictions.

These findings highlight the potential of SHAP to deliver both accurate and interpretable stress monitoring, advancing trustworthy AI integration in wearable health systems.

Keywords: SHAP · Stress prediction · Vital signs · Machine learning

1 Introduction

Stress is a significant public health issue, contributing to cardiovascular disease, mental health disorders, and decreased workplace productivity. Traditional assessment methods, such as self-reports and laboratory-based tests, often lack real-time insight and are vulnerable to subjective bias. With the advancement of wearable technologies, it is now possible to continuously monitor physiological signals like heart rate (HR), respiratory rate (RR), and heart rate variability (HRV), offering new opportunities for real-time stress detection outside controlled environments [3,5,18].

Machine learning (ML) models have shown strong potential in detecting stress by uncovering complex, nonlinear patterns within physiological data. However, many high-performing models operate as "black boxes," providing limited transparency into how predictions are made. In clinical and health-related applications, this lack of interpretability presents a major barrier to adoption. We integrate SHAP, a model-agnostic explanation method, to provide both global and local interpretability—enhancing model transparency and user trust. By attributing each feature's contribution to a prediction, SHAP facilitates both global understanding across a dataset and local explanations for individual instances. Integrating SHAP with a strong predictive model like XGBoost can achieve a balance between performance and interpretability, supporting more transparent and clinically useful stress monitoring systems.

Our objectives in this study are fourfold. First, we develop an XGBoost-based machine learning model trained on HR, RR, and both time- and frequency-domain HRV features to detect stress from wearable data. Second, we apply SHAP to interpret the model's global feature importance and individual-level predictions. Third, we examine whether the physiological patterns highlighted by SHAP align with established knowledge of stress responses, such as autonomic nervous system activity. Lastly, we assess whether SHAP explanations promote model trustworthiness and transparency without compromising predictive performance.

By focusing on both accuracy and explainability, this work aims to contribute to the development of trustworthy, wearable-based stress detection systems that can support clinical decision-making and personalized health management.

2 Related Works

2.1 Machine Learning in Stress Prediction

Machine learning (ML) techniques have become increasingly popular in stress prediction due to their ability to uncover complex, nonlinear relationships in physiological data that traditional statistical models often miss. In particular, features derived from heart rate variability (HRV) and respiratory patterns have shown strong potential for detecting stress under both controlled and real-world conditions.

Previous studies have used a variety of classification algorithms such as support vector machines (SVMs), random forests, and neural networks, yielding promising results. However, these models often act as "black boxes," making it challenging to interpret the reasoning behind individual predictions. This lack of interpretability poses a significant barrier to their adoption in clinical and health-monitoring applications. [7]. In this study, we do not introduce a novel machine learning algorithm. Instead, we train a widely used, high-performing algorithm—XGBoost—on physiological features extracted from wearable data. The core contribution lies in enhancing the interpretability of this model using SHAP. SHAP is not used to train or modify the architecture of the XGBoost model itself; rather, it is applied post hoc to explain the model's output, revealing the contribution of each physiological feature to both individual and global predictions. This dual-layered approach allows us to retain the predictive strength of XGBoost while making its decision-making process transparent and clinically interpretable [16,17,19].

2.2 Feature Importance and Explainability in ML

Interpretability is critical for the adoption of machine learning models in health-related applications, where clinical decision-making demands transparency and accountability. While many explainable AI (XAI) techniques have been developed to make models more understandable, they vary significantly in terms of scope, granularity, and reliability. This section provides a comparative overview of commonly used interpretability methods, highlighting why SHAP was selected for this study.

- XGBoost Feature Importance: Built-in importance scores such as gain, cover, or frequency offer a fast way to rank features globally. However, they lack local interpretability (i.e., explaining individual predictions), are sensitive to multicollinearity, and provide no indication of the direction of a feature's effect on the outcome [4].
- Partial Dependence Plots (PDPs) and Individual Conditional Expectation (ICE): These tools visualize the marginal effect of a feature on the prediction by averaging or isolating its impact. While intuitive, PDPs assume feature independence and may obscure heterogeneity in individual responses. ICE improves on this by showing instance-level variation but becomes hard to interpret with high-dimensional data [6].
- LIME (Local Interpretable Model-Agnostic Explanations): LIME approximates a black-box model locally using a simple interpretable model (e.g., linear regression). It provides fast, instance-level explanations but can yield inconsistent results depending on perturbation sampling and is sensitive to data locality and feature correlations [15].
- Skater: Skater is a Python library that wraps various interpretability tools, including feature importance, PDPs, and surrogate models. However, it acts more as a wrapper than a stand-alone technique, and its interpretability still depends on the underlying model-agnostic methods it employs.
item SHAP (SHapley Additive exPlanations): SHAP provides both global and local explanations by assigning each feature a "Shapley value," reflecting its contribution to a prediction. Unlike other methods, SHAP is grounded in cooperative game theory, ensuring consistency and local accuracy. When used with tree-based models (like XGBoost), SHAP's TreeExplainer variant computes exact values efficiently, even for large datasets. Crucially, SHAP accounts for feature interactions and is robust to correlated features—making it well suited for interpreting physiological data, where such dependencies are common [11,13,14].

SHAP values are derived from Shapley values in cooperative game theory. For a model f, input instance x, and feature set N, the SHAP value ϕ_i for feature i is computed as [11]:

$$\phi_i(f, x) = \sum_{S \subseteq N \setminus \{i\}} \frac{|S|! \cdot (|N| - |S| - 1)!}{|N|!} \left[f_{S \cup \{i\}}(x_{S \cup \{i\}}) - f_S(x_S) \right] \quad (1)$$

where:

- S is a subset of all features excluding i,
- $f_S(x_S)$ is the expected model output when only the features in subset S are known (others are marginalized),
- $|N|$ is the total number of features,
- The weighting term $\frac{|S|! \cdot (|N|-|S|-1)!}{|N|!}$ ensures fair distribution based on permutations.

For example, suppose we have a model f trained to predict stress using three features: HR, MEAN_RR, and LF/HF. To compute the contribution of HR for a specific instance x, we consider all subsets $S \subseteq N \setminus \{HR\}$ (i.e., $\{MEAN\_RR\}, \{LF/HF\}$). For each subset S, we compare the expected prediction $f_{S \cup \{HR\}}(x_{S \cup \{HR\}})$ against $f_S(x_S)$. These differences, weighted by the appropriate permutation factor, yield the SHAP value ϕ_{HR}, representing the marginal impact of HR on the model's output.

2.3 SHAP in Healthcare AI

SHAP has been increasingly applied in healthcare AI, including studies on cardiovascular risk prediction, ICU mortality, and stress detection from wearable devices. Its ability to reveal physiologically meaningful feature interactions has made it a valuable tool in health monitoring applications. In stress-related research, SHAP has helped validate that features like HR, RR, and HRV metrics meaningfully contribute to stress classification [14]. Moreover, the growing demand for explainable AI (XAI) is being driven by regulatory frameworks such as the EU AI Act and FDA guidelines for clinical AI systems [1]. Transparent models, like those augmented with SHAP, are more likely to gain acceptance in clinical and consumer health applications, where interpretability is essential for accountability, safety, and ethical deployment.

3 Materials and Methods

This section outlines the experimental design and analytical procedures used to develop an interpretable ML model for stress detection. We adopted a structured pipeline that integrates multiple publicly available and custom physiological datasets, rigorous preprocessing techniques, a tree-based classification algorithm (XGBoost), and SHAP-based interpretability. The methodology is designed to ensure both robustness of predictions and transparency of model outputs, aligning with the needs of clinical and consumer-grade health applications.

3.1 Dataset Description

This study utilizes two publicly available stress datasets: WESAD, SWELL, and our own dataset: Genius–Stress_Harshini. These datasets were selected for their rich collection of physiological signals recorded during various stress-inducing tasks, making them ideal for cross-dataset evaluation of model generalizability and feature importance:

- WESAD (Wearable Stress and Affect Detection Dataset): Contains multimodal physiological and motion data from 15 participants exposed to baseline, stress, and amusement conditions. Relevant features extracted include HR, RR, and HRV metrics derived from chest-worn devices [2].
- SWELL: Includes data from office workers under three working conditions: normal, time pressure, and interruption. Signals such as ECG and respiration were collected from which HR and HRV parameters were derived [10].
- Genius–Stress: A custom dataset focused on stress among students while driving a medical automobile, recording physiological metrics such as HR and RR during exams and high-pressure tasks.

Across datasets, the primary features used for model training include:

- Vital signs: HR, RR.
- Time-domain HRV features: Mean RR interval, median RR, RMSSD, SDNN.
- Frequency-domain HRV features: LF power, HF power, LF/HF ratio.
- Temporal features: Time index to capture circadian or task-based stress variation.

3.2 Data Preprocessing

To ensure consistency across datasets, a unified preprocessing pipeline was implemented:

- Signal Processing: Raw ECG and respiratory signals were filtered using a band-pass filter (0.5–40 Hz) to remove noise. RR intervals were extracted using peak detection algorithms and used to compute HRV features.
- Handling Missing Data: Missing values due to sensor dropout or motion artifacts were imputed using forward-fill for short gaps (less than 5 s) and removed for longer gaps.
- Label Harmonization: Stress labels were aligned across datasets using experimental condition annotations. For binary classification, data were labelled as "stress" vs. "non-stress".
- Feature Extraction Windowing: A sliding window of 60 s with 50% overlap was applied to extract stable statistical features while preserving temporal dynamics.
- Class Imbalance Handling: To address imbalanced class distributions, SMOTE (Synthetic Minority Oversampling Technique) was applied during training.

3.3 Model Selection

We selected XGBoost as the primary classification model for stress prediction due to its robustness, efficiency, and proven success with structured, tabular data. XGBoost is an ensemble learning method based on gradient-boosted decision trees, offering several advantages: it handles missing values internally, scales well with large datasets, supports parallel processing for faster computation, and is less prone to overfitting due to regularization techniques. These characteristics make it particularly well-suited for physiological data collected from wearable sensors, which often include non-linear patterns, noise, and missing segments. Furthermore, its tree-based structure allows for seamless integration with SHAP for model interpretability, enabling transparent and trustworthy analysis critical for healthcare applications.

XGBoost was selected due to its exceptional predictive capabilities in stress detection tasks. Its gradient boosting framework effectively captures complex, non-linear relationships among physiological features such as HR, RR, and HRV. This aligns with findings from related studies where XGBoost outperformed other machine learning models in classifying stress states using wearable sensor data [12].

- Hyperparameter Optimization: Grid search with 5-fold cross-validation was used to tune parameters including max depth, learning rate, and number of estimators.
- Evaluation Metrics: Model performance was assessed using accuracy, precision, recall, F1-score, and AUC-ROC. Cross-validation was performed both within each dataset and across datasets (leave-one-dataset-out) to test generalizability.

3.4 SHAP Explanation Framework

To interpret the trained XGBoost models, we employed SHAP using the TreeExplainer algorithm.

- Global Interpretability: SHAP summary plots were generated to identify the most influential features across the entire dataset. These plots help visualize how individual feature values (e.g., high HR or low MEAN_RR) contribute to predictions.
- Local Interpretability: SHAP force plots were used to examine individual predictions, allowing for the inspection of personalized stress explanations, essential for user-specific feedback in wearable health systems.

This methodology enables a transparent and reproducible analysis pipeline that combines performance-focused modelling with interpretable AI, setting the stage for trust-based deployment in real-world health monitoring applications.

4 Results and Discussions

This section presents the outcomes of the SHAP-based interpretability analysis and discusses their physiological and clinical implications. By combining results and discussion, we provide an integrated view of the model's predictive behavior, the relevance of key features, and potential real-world applications.

4.1 SHAP Feature Importance Results

The SHAP analysis revealed a clear hierarchy of physiological feature importance in stress prediction. Heart rate (HR) emerged as the most influential predictor, consistently contributing to stress classification across all datasets. In addition to HR, several heart rate variability (HRV) metrics demonstrated significant influence, particularly low-frequency (LF) power, the mean RR interval, and the LF/HF ratio.

As shown in Fig. 1, features derived from both the time domain (e.g., MEAN RR, MEDIAN RR) and frequency domain (e.g., LF power, LF/HF ratio) contributed meaningfully to stress detection. This finding underscores the physiological basis for combining multiple domains of HRV analysis when developing wearable-based stress monitoring systems.

Temporal features, although not explicitly modeled as sequential inputs, also showed relevance, suggesting that future models could benefit from incorporating time-aware or recurrent architectures.

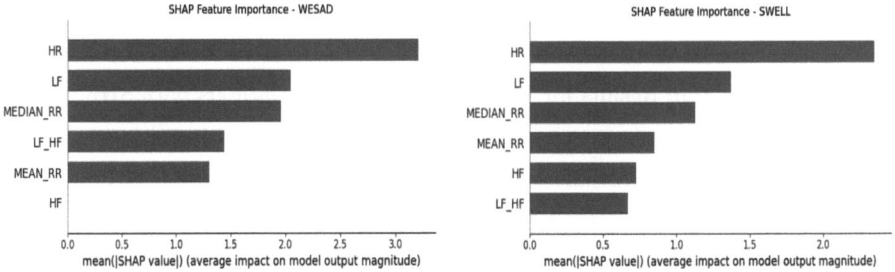

Fig. 1. Global SHAP feature importance plot ranking physiological features by their average contribution to stress prediction across the dataset. The top contributors are heart rate (HR) and HRV metrics such as LF, MEAN_RR, and LF/HF ratio.

4.2 Physiological Interpretation of Key Features

The physiological relevance of the top-ranked features aligns with established stress response mechanisms. Elevated HR is a hallmark of increased sympathetic nervous system activity, typically observed during acute stress. Similarly, a decrease in MEAN RR and MEDIAN RR intervals reflects faster heart rates and reduced parasympathetic tone under stress conditions.

The LF/HF ratio, which captures the balance between sympathetic and parasympathetic influences, varied depending on individual responses. In some participants, a heightened LF/HF ratio corresponded with stress, while in others, shifts were less pronounced. This variability suggests the need for personalized baseline measurements in future wearable stress models to capture individual differences in autonomic regulation.

The ability of SHAP to uncover these physiologically grounded patterns demonstrates its value not just in model interpretability but also in reinforcing biological validity.

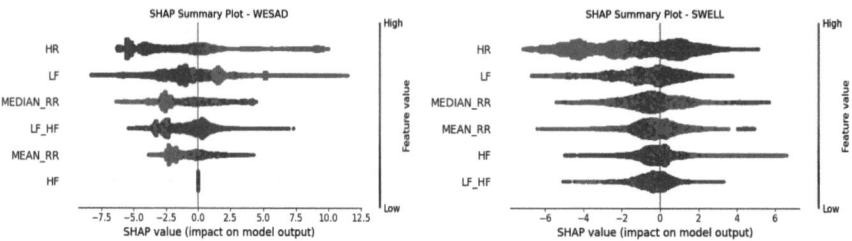

Fig. 2. SHAP summary plot showing the impact of feature values on model predictions. Red dots represent high feature values, and blue dots represent low values. HR, MEAN_RR, and LF/HF ratio show directional influence consistent with known physiological stress responses. (Color figure online)

Table 1. Classification Results for WESAD and SWELL Datasets with SHAP Explanation

Dataset	Class	Precision	Recall	F1-Score	Support	Accuracy	AUC Score	SHAP Used
WESAD	0	0.97	0.97	0.97	64712	0.97	0.9998	Yes
	1	0.99	0.98	0.99	13616			
SWELL	0	0.99	0.97	0.99	28678	0.99	0.9995	Yes
	1	0.99	0.98	0.98	8178			

4.3 SHAP vs. Traditional Feature Importance

Compared to traditional XGBoost feature importance measures, such as gain-based rankings, SHAP provided more detailed and clinically meaningful insights. While gain-based methods quantify how often and how significantly a feature contributes to tree splits, they fail to indicate the direction of influence or explain individual predictions.

In contrast, SHAP assigned each feature a contribution value for every prediction, revealing whether a higher or lower value of a feature increased the likelihood of stress classification. This level of detail is essential for health monitoring applications where users and clinicians require transparent explanations of AI-driven decisions.

Table 2 summarizes the key differences between SHAP and traditional feature importance methods, highlighting the advantages of SHAP in healthcare-oriented machine learning models.

Table 2. Comparison of Feature Importance Methods in Stress Prediction Models

Criteria	SHAP (SHapley Additive Explanations)	Gain-Based Feature Importance (XGBoost)
Interpretability	High: Provides both global and local (per-instance) interpretability	Low: Only provides global importance
Theoretical Foundation	Based on cooperative game theory (Shapley values)	Based on how much each feature improves model splits
Direction of Influence	Shows whether a feature increases or decreases the prediction	Only shows importance, not direction
Handles Feature Interactions	Accounts for interactions between features	Assumes independence between features
Instance-Level Explanation	Explains predictions for individual samples	Not available
Robustness to Feature Correlation	More robust due to conditional expectations	Can overestimate importance of correlated features
Visualizations	SHAP summary plots, force plots, dependence plots	Bar charts only
Computation Time	Higher (especially on large datasets)	Lower (faster to compute)
Use in Regulatory/Clinical Settings	Suitable for transparent, explainable AI required in healthcare	Limited transparency; not recommended alone for clinical use
Applicability Across Models	Model-agnostic (works with tree, linear, DL, etc.)	Model-specific (e.g., XGBoost, LightGBM)

4.4 Limitations and Future Directions

While promising, this study has several limitations. The datasets used were relatively small and may not fully capture the diversity of stress responses across broader populations. Experimental conditions and self-reported stress labels may not reflect the complexity of real-world stressors.

Additionally, SHAP computation adds processing overhead, which may limit real-time deployment on low-power wearable devices. Future research should explore optimization techniques for lightweight SHAP approximation and investigate sequential modeling approaches that account for temporal dynamics in physiological signals.

Expanding datasets to include more diverse demographics and incorporating contextual information, such as physical activity or environmental factors, could further improve model generalizability and ecological validity.

This study reinforces the value of using wearable-derived physiological signals for real-time stress detection. The SHAP analysis revealed that HR and HRV features—particularly LF, MEAN_RR, and LF/HF ratio—are the most influential predictors of stress. These results are consistent with established physiological research linking stress to autonomic nervous system activity, validating the use of these signals in stress monitoring systems. Importantly, SHAP enabled not only the identification of the most impactful features but also insight into how and why these features influence model predictions. This level of interpretability is crucial for the development of trustworthy AI systems in health applications, particularly in consumer wearables and clinical monitoring tools where users may require transparency in predictions [9]. SHAP's ability to provide both global insights and individual-level explanations positions it as a valuable framework for enhancing the interpretability of real-time AI in wearable health platforms.

While subject ID was not directly included in the current model, the results suggest substantial variability in physiological stress responses across individuals [8]. The SHAP summary plot indicates a spread of feature contributions, hinting at personalized physiological profiles. Incorporating subject-specific factors—such as baseline HRV, age, fitness level, or context of stressors—could improve the sensitivity and specificity of predictions. Future work should explore personalized modelling approaches that adapt thresholds and feature importance per user, enhancin.

One of the ongoing debates in machine learning is the trade-off between interpretability and performance. However, this study demonstrates that high interpretability can coexist with strong model performance. The XGBoost classifier achieved a nearly perfect AUC of 0.9998, while still allowing for detailed SHAP-based interpretability. That said, the use of SHAP introduces some computational overhead, which may limit its feasibility in ultra-low-power or real-time edge computing environments unless appropriately optimized.

5 Conclusion and Future Work

This study demonstrated the effectiveness of using interpretable ML models for stress prediction based on wearable-derived physiological signals. By training an XGBoost classifier on features including HR, RR, and various HRV metrics, we achieved exceptionally high predictive performance (AUC: 0.9998). To address the critical need for transparency in health-related AI systems, we employed SHAP to interpret model decisions. SHAP revealed that HR, LF power, MEAN_RR, and LF/HF ratio were the most influential features in stress classification. These findings align with well-established physiological responses to stress and support the reliability of SHAP as an explanation framework in this context. Furthermore, the visualization of temporal heart rate trends illustrated distinct HR dynamics under stress and non-stress conditions, highlighting the potential for time-aware modelling in future wearable stress detection systems. Building on these findings, several areas for future research are identified:

- Dataset Expansion and Diversity: Incorporating larger and more diverse datasets—across demographics, environments, and wearable devices—will improve model generalizability and robustness.

- Context-Aware Features: Including external contexts such as physical activity, environmental factors, and self-reported emotions could enhance the ecological validity of predictions.
- Real-Time Deployment: Further work is needed to optimize SHAP or similar interpretability tools for real-time, on-device inference in wearable platforms, ensuring both speed and transparency.

Overall, this work illustrates the promise of combining interpretable machine learning with physiological sensing for trustworthy, personalized health monitoring and lays the groundwork for the future development of clinically relevant wearable stress analytics.

Acknowledgments. This research was supported by the "Genius Case I" project funded by Antolin Company (Ref. FUO-23-145), the Spanish Centre for the Development of Technology and Innovation (CDTI) under the 'Missions Science and Innovation 2021' call (Ref. MIG-20211008 – INMERBOT consortium); the Spanish Ministry of Economic Affairs and Industry (Ref. MCINN-24-PID2023-146257OB-I00); the Foundation for the Promotion of Applied Scientific Research and Technology in Asturias (FICYT) under the GRUPIN program (Ref. SEK-25-GRU-GIC-24-055).

References

1. Eur-lex - 52021pc0206 - en - eur-lex. https://eur-lex.europa.eu/legal-content/EN/TXT/?uri=celex:52021PC0206. Accessed 12 Apr 2025
2. WESAD (Wearable Stress and Affect Detection) - UCI Machine Learning Repository. https://archive.ics.uci.edu/dataset/465/wesad+wearable+stress+and+affect+detection
3. Castaldo, R., Melillo, P., Bracale, U., Caserta, M., Triassi, M., Pecchia, L.: Acute mental stress assessment via short term HRV analysis in healthy adults: a systematic review with meta-analysis. Biomed. Signal Process. Control **18**, 370–377 (2015). https://doi.org/10.1016/J.BSPC.2015.02.012
4. Chen, T., Guestrin, C.: XGBoost: a scalable tree boosting system. In: Proceedings of the ACM SIGKDD International Conference on Knowledge Discovery and Data Mining, 13–17 August 2016, pp. 785–794 (2016). https://doi.org/10.1145/2939672.2939785/SUPPL_FILE/KDD2016_CHEN_BOOSTING_SYSTEM_01-ACM.MP4. https://dl-acm-org.uniovi.idm.oclc.org/doi/10.1145/2939672.2939785
5. Gjoreski, M., Gjoreski, H., Luštrek, M., Gams, M.: Continuous stress detection using a wrist device - in laboratory and real life. In: UbiComp 2016 Adjunct - Proceedings of the 2016 ACM International Joint Conference on Pervasive and Ubiquitous Computing, pp. 1185–1193 (2016). https://doi.org/10.1145/2968219.2968306. https://dl-acm-org.uniovi.idm.oclc.org/doi/10.1145/2968219.2968306
6. Goldstein, A., Kapelner, A., Bleich, J., Pitkin, E.: Peeking inside the black box: visualizing statistical learning with plots of individual conditional expectation. J. Comput. Graph. Stat. **24**(1), 44–65 (2015). https://doi.org/10.1080/10618600.2014.907095. https://www.tandfonline.com/doi/abs/10.1080/10618600.2014.907095

7. Harms, M.B.: Stress and exploitative decision-making. J. Neurosci. **37**(42), 10035 (2017). https://doi.org/10.1523/JNEUROSCI.2169-17.2017. https://pmc.ncbi.nlm.nih.gov/articles/PMC5647765/
8. Healey, J.A., Picard, R.W.: Detecting stress during real-world driving tasks using physiological sensors. IEEE Trans. Intell. Transp. Syst. **6**(2), 156–166 (2005). https://doi.org/10.1109/TITS.2005.848368
9. Kim, H.G., Cheon, E.J., Bai, D.S., Lee, Y.H., Koo, B.H.: Stress and heart rate variability: a meta-analysis and review of the literature. Psychiatry Investig. **15**(3), 235 (2018). https://doi.org/10.30773/PI.2017.08.17. https://pmc.ncbi.nlm.nih.gov/articles/PMC5900369/
10. Koldijk, S., Sappelli, M., Verberne, S., Neerincx, M.A., Kraaij, W.: The swell knowledge work dataset for stress and user modeling research. In: ICMI 2014 - Proceedings of the 2014 International Conference on Multimodal Interaction, pp. 291–298 (2014). https://doi.org/10.1145/2663204.2663257/SUPPL_FILE/ICMI2189-FILE3.MP4. https://dl-acm-org.uniovi.idm.oclc.org/doi/10.1145/2663204.2663257
11. Lundberg, S.M., et al.: From local explanations to global understanding with explainable AI for trees. Nat. Mach. Intell. **2**(1), 56–67 (2020). https://doi.org/10.1038/s42256-019-0138-9. https://www.nature.com/articles/s42256-019-0138-9
12. Mihirette, S., De La Cal, E.A., Tan, Q., Sedano, J.: Cross-contextual stress prediction: simple methodology for comparing features and sample domain adaptation techniques in vital sign analysis. Appl. Intell. **55**, 420 (2025). https://doi.org/10.1007/s10489-025-06277-9
13. Molnar, C.: Interpretable machine learning (2025). https://christophm.github.io/interpretable-ml-book/. Accessed 22 Mar 2025
14. Rajkomar, A., Dean, J., Kohane, I.: Machine learning in medicine. New Engl. J. Med. **380**(14), 1347–1358 (2019). https://doi.org/10.1056/NEJMRA1814259. https://pubmed.ncbi.nlm.nih.gov/30943338/
15. Ribeiro, M.T., Singh, S., Guestrin, C.: "Why should i trust you?" Explaining the predictions of any classifier. In: Proceedings of the ACM SIGKDD International Conference on Knowledge Discovery and Data Mining, 13–17 August 2016, pp. 1135–1144 (2016). https://doi.org/10.1145/2939672.2939778/SUPPL_FILE/KDD2016_RIBEIRO_ANY_CLASSIFIER_01-ACM.MP4. https://dl-acm-org.uniovi.idm.oclc.org/doi/10.1145/2939672.2939778
16. Samek, W., Wiegand, T., Müller, K.R.: Explainable artificial intelligence: understanding, visualizing and interpreting deep learning models. arXiv preprint (2017). https://arxiv.org/abs/1708.08296v1
17. Schmidt, P., Reiss, A., Duerichen, R., Van Laerhoven, K.: Introducing WeSAD, a multimodal dataset for wearable stress and affect detection. In: ICMI 2018 - Proceedings of the 2018 International Conference on Multimodal Interaction, pp. 400–408 (2018). https://doi.org/10.1145/3242969.3242985. https://dl-acm-org.uniovi.idm.oclc.org/doi/10.1145/3242969.3242985
18. Schneiderman, N., Ironson, G., Siegel, S.D.: Stress and health: psychological, behavioral, and biological determinants. Ann. Rev. Clin. Psychol. **1**, 607 (2005). https://doi.org/10.1146/ANNUREV.CLINPSY.1.102803.144141. https://pmc.ncbi.nlm.nih.gov/articles/PMC2568977/
19. Tonekaboni, S., Joshi, S., McCradden, M.D., Goldenberg, A.: What clinicians want: contextualizing explainable machine learning for clinical end use. Proc. Mach. Learn. Res. **106**, 359–380 (2019). https://arxiv.org/abs/1905.05134v2

Learning from Normal Brain Activity for Automatic Detection of Photoparoxysmal Responses as Electroencephalogram Anomalies

Fernando Moncada Martins[1,3](✉), Víctor M. González[2,3],
José R. Villar[1,3], María Antonia Gutiérrez[4], Pablo Calvo Calleja[4],
Sara Urdiales Sánchez[4], Ricardo Díaz Pérez[4], and Alinne Dalla-Porta Acosta[4]

[1] Computer Science Department, University of Oviedo, Gijón, Spain
{moncadafernando,villarjose}@uniovi.es
[2] Electrical Engineering Department, University of Oviedo, Gijón, Spain
vmsuarez@uniovi.es
[3] Biomedical Engineering Center, University of Oviedo, Gijón, Spain
[4] Neurophysiology Service, Cabueñes University Hospital, Gijón, Spain
pablo.calvo@sespa.es

Abstract. Photosensitivity is a neurological condition in which the brain produces epileptiform reactions to visual stimuli known as Photoparoxysmal Responses (PPR). These events are typically diagnosed through Intermittent Photic Stimulation (IPS) while monitoring brain signals with electroencephalography (EEG). Manual analysis of PPR is time-consuming and subjective, which motivates the development of automated detection methods. In this work, we propose an unsupervised anomaly detection (AD) approach using a Variational Autoencoder (VAE) trained exclusively on normal EEG segments from non-photosensitive patients. The model is evaluated on EEG recordings from photosensitive patients to identify PPR activity as deviations from normal patterns. In previous research, this VAE model outperformed other unsupervised AD models in the literature for this task; however, it generated a large number of False Positives that were later confirmed as EEG anomalies that were not labelled. This research represents the first step in an EEG anomaly detection and multi-classification framework, aiming not only to detect PPR but to automatically label all Positive instances as the different types of anomalous EEG patterns in future work. Results reveal that the model performed well, reaching 83% Accuracy, Sensitivity and Specificity, despite producing numerous False Positives as expected due to the lack of labels. This research is carried out with real EEG recordings gathered at Cabueñes University Hospital, Spain.

This research has been funded by the Spanish Research Agency –grant PID2023-146257OB-I00–. Also, by Principado de Asturias, grant IDE/2024/000734, and by the Council of Gijón through the University Institute of Industrial Technology of Asturias grants SV-23-GIJON-1-09, SV-23-GIJÓN-1-17, and SV-24-GIJÓN-1-05.

© The Author(s), under exclusive license to Springer Nature Switzerland AG 2026
E. Corchado et al. (Eds.): HAIS 2025, LNAI 16202, pp. 115–126, 2026.
https://doi.org/10.1007/978-3-032-08465-1_10

Keywords: EEG · Electroencephalogram · PPR · Photoparoxysmal Response · Anomaly Detection · Photosensitivity · Epilepsy

1 Introduction

Photosensitivity is a neurological condition in which the brain produces epileptic discharges as a reaction to specific visual stimuli, such as flashing lights or rapidly changing visual patterns. In worst cases, these abnormal responses can trigger epileptic seizures, resulting in photosensitive epilepsy. According to [2], approximately 30% of epileptic patients are photosensitive, and around 6% of the general population also suffers from this condition, as reported by [20]. Currently, the internationally standardized clinical protocol for diagnosing photosensitivity is called Intermittent Photic Stimulation (IPS) [19], which consists of exposing patients to flashing white light at fixated frequencies in the range 1 Hz–50 Hz while recording the patient's brain activity with Electroencephalography (EEG) to visualize how the brain reacts to these flashes. A patient is diagnosed with photosensitivity if the stimulation session triggered epileptic responses. The stimulation is first performed by increasing the frequencies from 1 Hz until an epileptic reaction is produced; then, the frequencies are decreased from 50 Hz until another abnormal response is generated. These reactions must be triggered without inducing full seizures, which requires careful monitoring and control by trained clinical staff to stop the procedure if necessary.

These responses are known as Photoparoxysmal Responses (PPR). In [21], PPR discharges were categorized into four types, ranging from Type-1 to Type-4, as shown in Fig. 1: the higher the Type, the increased the severity and the likelihood of a seizure occurrence. However, real-world PPR often exhibit a mixture of these types, and EEG morphology can vary significantly across patients and even across sessions for the same individual. Factors such as treatment, sleep quality, and time of day can all influence this variability [1]. Consequently, identifying and labelling PPR requires manual inspection by clinical neurophysiologists, making the diagnostic process labour-intensive and complex.

Moreover, despite its clinical utility, the IPS procedure has several limitations [2]. It demands significant human oversight to monitor for PPR activity. Given the low prevalence of photosensitivity in the general population [20] and the need to interrupt stimulation once any paroxysmal activity is detected, the quantity of recorded PPR data is inherently limited. This results in a highly imbalanced dataset, which poses a challenge for developing and training Machine Learning and Deep Learning models. To address this issue, an alternative approach is to frame PPR detection as an Anomaly Detection (AD) problem, treating PPR discharges as brief bursts of irregular brain activity occurring amongst normal EEG patterns.

The present study proposes the use of a Variational Autoencoder (VAE) following an AD approach. The model is first trained only with normal and healthy brain activity segments extracted from EEG recordings from non-photosensitive patients. Since the photosensitivity condition has a very low prevalence among

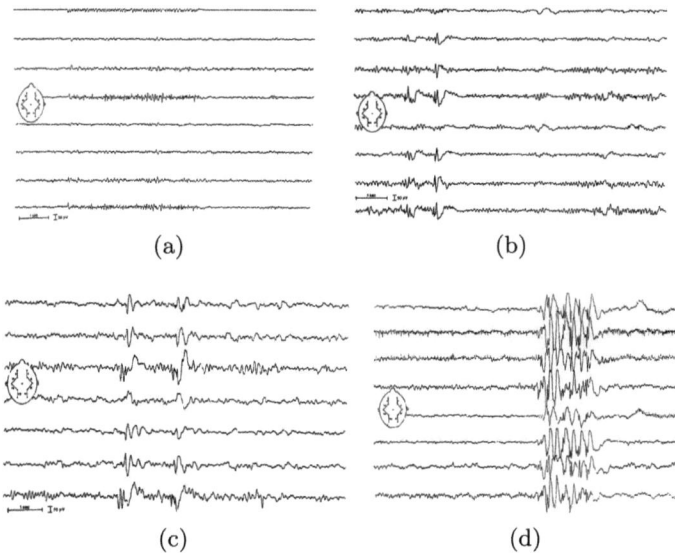

Fig. 1. PPR types: **a)** Type-1, **b)** Type-2, **c)** Type-3, and **d)** Type-4. Each type presents more intensity in terms of both amplitude and spread, as they become more accentuated and start appearing in more channels.

the population, it is easier to gather real EEG recordings from other patients who were submitted to the IPS procedure but did not show PPR activity. The objective is to evaluate whether the current approach effectively marks the EEG recordings for photosensitive patients by labelling anomalies –PPR events among them–. However, due to the current lack of labels for anomalous activity in photosensitive recordings, this first step into that approach will focus on the PPR detection task.

The structure of this study is as follows: the next section provides a brief overview of the state-of-art and related work in AD techniques for clinical applications in epilepsy and photosensitivity; Sect. 3 describes the VAE architecture for time-series analysis following for AD; Sect. 4 details the dataset created for this project and describes the experimental setup used throughout the study; Sect. 5 presents the results along with a comprehensive discussion; and finally, Sect. 6 summarizes the key findings and suggests directions for future work.

2 Related Work

Accurately identifying anomalies is essential in clinical diagnosis, where deviated samples are detected by comparison with healthy and normal values. For this reason, AD models have gained prominence in recent years. For instance, Generative Adversarial Networks (GAN) have been used to reconstruct intermediate brain MRI slices to highlight abnormalities at various stages [3], while autoencoders have been applied to detect subtle irregularities in chest X-rays and lymph metastasis images [15]. In time-series EEG analysis for seizure detection in epileptic patients, Recurrent Neural Network models show promise in identifying temporal anomalies [11], and unsupervised GAN and semi-supervised VAE have been with behind-the-ear EEG recordings [13,14]. Simple ML approaches also continue to be explored in this domain [5].

To date, limited work has investigated PPR analysis specifically for diagnosing photosensitivity beyond our previous studies. On the one hand, [4] proposed a prediction method based on spectral analysis using Fourier Transforms of EEG segments immediately before the onset of PPR during the IPS procedure. On the other hand, [16] investigated high-frequency brain oscillations of brain reactions when applying a light stimulation protocol different from the clinical IPS protocol. Our previous research has focused on automatically detecting PPR discharges during IPS sessions, exploring basic ML techniques [6], or mitigating class imbalance through Data Augmentation [9] or Transfer Learning for a more complex Inception-based model [10].

This study is a continuation of our most recent work: we conducted a comparative study of various unsupervised ML and DL algorithms configured as AD models for PPR detection [7] that showed that a VAE model incorporating Recurrent layers [14] significantly outperformed other state-of-the-art techniques, and later confirmed that diverse EEG anomalies were often unintentionally detected despite not being considered during training, thus increasing the rate of False Positives and affecting detection performance [8]. In both studies, the VAE model was trained with both normal and abnormal EEG instances labelled as non-PPR data to perform a PPR detection. Despite that, EEG anomalies were still being detected and categorized as PPR. In this study, the VAE model learns from normal brain activity by removing all EEG anomalies from the training set to perform only a PPR detection –a high number of False Positives produced by EEG anomalies is expected–. In the following steps, a multilabel classification or multiclassification will be applied over all detected anomalies to distinguish between all possible abnormalities present in EEG recordings.

3 Variational Autoencoder for Time-Series Anomaly Detection

The approach proposed in this study is built upon the method designed in [14], which presents a semi-supervised AD model based on a VAE for epileptic seizures. A VAE architecture consists of two core components: an encoder and a decoder. The former processes an input instance X_i to reduce it into a latent space z represented by a pair of mean μ_i and standard deviation σ_i vectors. The latter samples a value from the generated latent space and attempts to reconstruct the original instance $\widehat{X_i}$. During training, the model must be optimized to minimize the reconstruction error between the original instance X_i and its reconstruction $\widehat{X_i}$.

Anomalies are identified based on their deviation from normal patterns. Therefore, for AD tasks, the model is trained exclusively with normal instances. As a result, the latent space z created by the encoder is composed solely by normal representations, and the decoder learns to accurately reconstruct only normal patterns. When a new instance is presented to the model, anomalies can be detected either by using the reconstruction loss –where a high loss suggests that the input deviates significantly from the normal latent space– or the distance between the new latent representation and the rest of the normal latent space –the greater the distance, the less similarity between the data and the more likelihood of being an anomaly instance–.

Moreover, two additional structures are integrated into the model to enhance performance: on the one hand, a Recurrent-based layer using GRU cells is added as the first layer of both the encoder and the decoder to capture the temporal dependencies of the consecutive instances [17]; on the other hand, k normalizing flow layers are stacked after the encoder to apply transforms such as contractions or expansions to the latent space, enriching and increasing the flexibility of the latent distribution [12].

4 Materials and Methods

This section describes the dataset used in this research in Sect. 4.1, and the experimentation design in Sect. 4.2. The experiments were implemented in Python.

4.1 Dataset Description

Cabueñes University Hospital collected two datasets for this research: the first one, referred as *PhotData*, contains EEG recordings from 9 photosensitive patients who exhibited PPR discharges during the IPS session; the second one, named *HealthyData*, includes EEG signals from 5 non-photosensitive patients who showed no PPR activity during stimulation. Each EEG session recorded brain activity continuously for 1 to 2.5 h (with the exception of two sessions lasting approximately 30 min), with the IPS session occupying only the final 5 min in each case. All were recorded using the clinical equipment, a Natus Nicolet EEG cap ©, employing 19 electrodes placed according to the International 10–20 System [18] as illustrated in Fig. 2. The clinical neurophysiologists visually examined the EEG recordings using the System 98 Viewer ©clinical software to find and annotate the onsets and offsets of any PPR discharge in *PhotData* –for a total of 22 discharges of durations from 0.8 s to 3.4 s–, and every EEG anomaly in *HealthyData*, including artifacts from electrode, muscular and ocular sources as well as random epileptiform spikes that are distinct from visually triggered PPR. Note that EEG anomalies present in *PhotData* have not been annotated yet and are currently a work in progress.

PhotData was recorded at a sampling rate of 256 Hz, while 128 Hz were used for *HealthyData*. To address this difference, cubic spline interpolation is applied in *HealthyData* to increase the number of samples per second from 128 up to

256, aligning it with *PhotData*. Following the original design outlined in [14], two cross-head channels are constructed employing the four channels most relevant to PPR analysis, as determined by clinical expertise: F3–F4 and O1–O2, as illustrated in Fig. 2. After preprocessing the signals with a 6th order Butterworth band-pass filter (0.5–120 Hz) and a 50 Hz Notch filter to remove power line interference, a sliding window technique with 1-second window length and 90% overlap is applied to segment all EEG recordings. Each resulting instance is then manually labelled based on the marks provided by the clinical specialists, resulting in two binary classification schemes: "PPR" vs. "non-PPR" for *PhotData* and "anomaly" vs. "normal" for *HealthyData*. Positive labels are assigned to those EEG windows that contain abnormal activity from 50% to 100% of their length. The class distribution for each dataset is summarized as follows:

- *PhotData*
  - Number of non-PPR windows: 539,886 (**99.94%**)
  - Number of PPR windows: 314 (**0.06%**)
- *HealthyData*
  - Number of normal windows: 261,635 (**90.00%**)
  - Number of anomalous windows: 29,086 (**10.00%**)

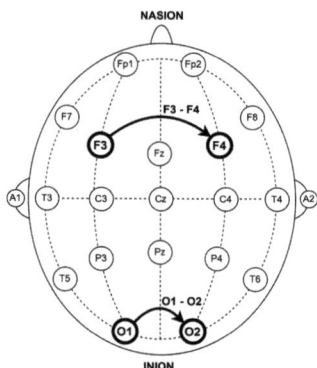

Fig. 2. Placement of the 19 electrodes used for EEG recording following the 10–20 international standardized system, as well as the construction of the two cross-head channels F3-F4 and O1-O2. The Nasion is located at the centre of the frontonasal area; the Inion is located at the centre of the back of the neck.

4.2 Experimentation Design

The experimentation workflow designed for this research is shown in Fig. 3. For each EEG window, Short-Time Fourier Transform is applied to each cross-head channel to obtain the frequency bands corresponding to key brain rhythms: *Delta*

(0.5–4 Hz), *Theta* (4–8 Hz), *Alpha* (8–16 Hz), *Beta* (16–40 Hz), *Gamma* (40–80 Hz), and *High-Gamma* (80–120 Hz), as proposed by [14]. Then, the band power ratio for each frequency band is computed, yielding 12 spectral features per window. All values are standardized (mean = 0, standard deviation = 1) individually for each channel.

For the AD task, the VAE model is trained exclusively on normal EEG windows. Since *HealthyData* contains instances from non-photosensitive patients labelled as "normal" or "anomaly", only the "normal" windows from all patients are used for the training process, ensuring that the model learns to accurately identify and reconstruct normal instances. Then, the model is evaluated for each patient from *PhotData*. However, the anomalies to detect are limited to PPR events because EEG anomalies have not been fully annotated. As demonstrated in previous research [8], a high rate of False Positive instances is expected, corresponding to the unlabelled EEG anomalies. Moreover, a calibration step was used to adapt the VAE model to the particular brain activity patterns of each patient in those prior studies, but the absence of anomaly marks *PhotData* makes it impossible to remove EEG anomalies and perform the tuning with only normal data. Nevertheless, this limitation allows us to analyze the impact and necessity of the calibration step. The VAE architecture used in this research is illustrated in Fig. 4. The model was trained for 20 epochs using a batch size of 256 instances. The initial learning rate was 0.001 and was updated to 90% of its value every 5 epochs.

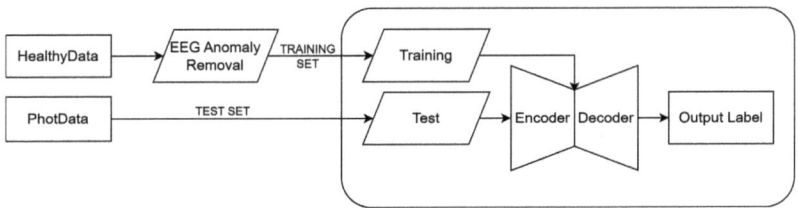

Fig. 3. Experimentation workflow: the VAE model was trained using normal EEG instances from *HealthyData* and then evaluated with each photosensitive patient from *PhotData*.

5 Results and Discussion

The evaluation metrics used to assess the PPR detection performance of the VAE model are Accuracy (*Acc*), Sensitivity (*Sens*), and Specificity (*Spec*). Table 1 shows the results obtained by the model for each photosensitive patient.

Overall, the model performed well, achieving values of around 83% in most cases. The large number of "non-PPR" instances in *PhotData* makes the Spec metric particularly robust against misclassification, while also heavily influencing Acc. The values of these two metrics indicate a notable rate of False Positives,

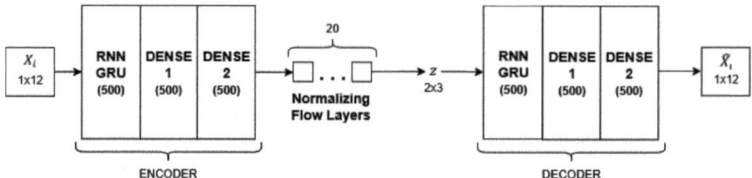

Fig. 4. VAE architecture for time-series AD task. The first layer of the encoder and the decoder is a GRU-based Recurrent layer to consider the temporal dependencies from 100 consecutive instances.

Table 1. PPR detection results obtained in photosensitive patients by the VAE model after learn normal brain activity exclusively from non-photosensitive patients. Includes the mean (Mn), median (Mnd) and standard deviation (StD) of each metric.

P_i	Acc	Sens	Spec
P_1	0.9723	0.6868	0.9767
P_2	0.8909	0.8389	0.8912
P_3	0.8352	0.7754	0.8367
P_4	0.9438	0.6563	0.9487
P_5	0.9624	0.8006	0.9837
P_6	0.2026	1.0000	0.1975
P_7	0.9708	0.9492	0.9813
P_8	0.7346	0.9499	0.7296
P_9	0.9412	0.8210	0.9429
Mn	0.8282	0.8309	0.8320
Mdn	0.9412	0.8210	0.9429
StD	0.2332	0.1116	0.2378

which was expected due to the yet unlabeled EEG anomalies present in *Phot-Data*. In terms of Sens, it is important to highlight that False Negatives do not represent PPR discharges that have not been properly detected, but EEG windows that contain some degree of PPR presence within. The misclassified instances usually correspond to border instances where PPR activity doesn't occupy the full window. Given the scarce amount of PPR-labelled instances in the dataset, Sens is far more sensitive to variations in detection. Despite not identifying all PPR instances, the model successfully detected all PPR discharges across all patients.

Figure 5 compares the current results in PPR detection performance with those obtained in previous research, where the VAE model was not trained on general "non-PPR" data from photosensitive patients (including unlabeled EEG anomalies) and a calibration step was added to fine-tune the model for each patient. In contrast, the present study is based on training the model exclusively on normal data from non-photosensitive patients, after excluding all "EEG anomaly" windows, making the calibration impossible because of the lack of anomaly labels in *PhotData*. As can be seen, Sens values and the robustness improve with calibration, proving the importance of patient-specific tuning for better learning of individual brain patterns. Furthermore, in both studies, the model exhibited abnormal behaviour for photosensitive patient number 6 (P_6): in the current experiment, it struggled to distinguish between normal and PPR activity, while in the previous study it achieved only 50% Sens. This consistent difficulty is likely due to the markedly different brain patters produced by this patient compared to the others, further emphasizing the value of the calibration process, as illustrated in Fig. 6.

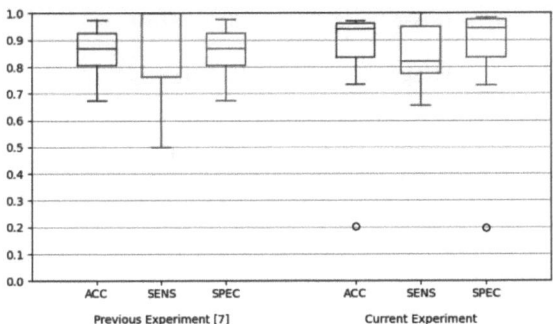

Fig. 5. Comparison of performance results between the VAE model when trained on normal data from non-photosensitive patients without a calibration step (current research), and when trained with other photosensitive patients with a calibration step (previous research [7]).

6 Conclusions and Future Work

This study proposes the use of a VAE model –originally designed by [17] and later applied by [14] as an AD procedure for epileptic seizures– for identifying PPR discharges in EEG time-series. Two datasets were collected: *PhotData*, comprising EEG recordings from photosensitive patients that exhibited PPR activity during the diagnostic procedure, and *HealthyData*, which contains recordings from non-photosensitive patients and the marks of all EEG anomalies that occurred during the recording session.

To perform the AD task, the VAE model is trained exclusively on normal EEG windows from *HealthyData* and then evaluated on each patient in *PhotData*. A calibration step to tune the model for each target patient is not possible due to the impossibility of removing the anomalous instances, as in training. All previous research was focused on training and evaluating AI model for automatic PPR detection with patients from the same domain, i.e., photosensitive or, in their absence, epileptic patients. Yet this study proposes to use healthy patients,

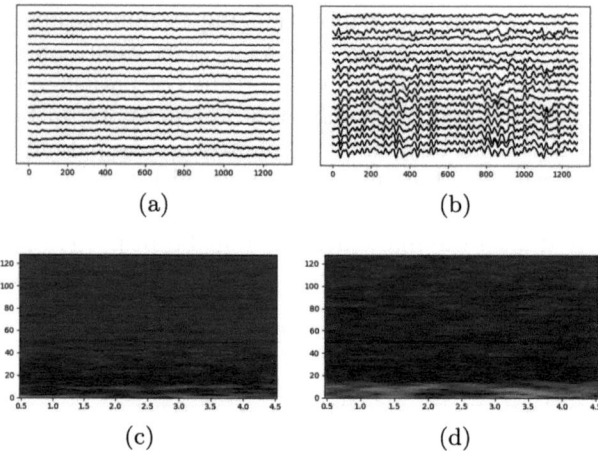

Fig. 6. Comparison of EEG segments between patient P_6 and another photosensitive patient (P_4). The upper row shows a 5-second length normal brain activity EEG segment from **a)** P_4 and **b)** P_6. The lower row includes the corresponding spectrograms, being **c)** from P_4 and **d)** from P_6.

who are larger in number and availability, to train a model to be used on ill patients. The results indicate that the model effectively detects PPR instances despite the lack of patient-specific calibration, which has been shown to improve performance.

Furthermore, computational efficiency and scalability are critical in clinical applications such as the automatic detection of epileptiform events in EEG recordings. EEG data are usually high-dimensional in a continuous recording, so detection algorithms require minimal latency to support immediate clinical decision-making. The system must also adapt to patient-specific variability and integration with hospital monitoring systems.

For this purpose, future work should prioritize the exhaustive annotation of EEG anomalies in *PhotData*, mirroring the methodology used in *HealthyData* The clinical team is currently working on this task to greatly improve the available dataset. In the meantime, a promising alternative is to automatically detect and remove anomalies during training. Multiclass classifiers could be integrated into the latent space of the VAE, detecting and classifying anomalous latent vectors of new training instances and excluding them from the training process, not only allowing for a patient-specific calibration, but also distinguishing multiple EEG abnormalities at once, including pathological activity, whether all annotations are available for manual instance labelling or not. Lightweight models also require attention due to their real-time capabilities.

Author contributions. Fernando Moncada Martins, Víctor M. González, and José R. Villar designed the methodology and experiments and executed all technical and computer work. They all wrote the paper.

Clinical specialists Antonia Gutiérrez, Pablo Calvo, Sara Urdiales, Ricardo Díaz, and Alinne Dalla-Porta Acosta collected the data at the Cabueñes University Hospital's Neurophysiology Service, recorded and anonymised the data, and also studied the VAE results and interpreted them.

Ethical Approval. The study was carried out according to the Declaration of Helsinki and approved by the Ethics Committee of the University Hospital of Burgos (Protocol Code CEIm2467, 23 February 2021).

Informed consent was obtained from all subjects involved in the study. Written informed consent was obtained from the patients to publish this paper.

References

1. Dong, H., et al.: Mixed neural network approach for temporal sleep stage classification. IEEE Trans. Neural Syst. Rehabil. Eng. **26**(2), 324–333 (2018). https://doi.org/10.1109/TNSRE.2017.2733220
2. Fisher, R.S., et al.: Visually sensitive seizures: an updated review by the epilepsy foundation. Epilepsia (2022). https://doi.org/10.1111/epi.17175
3. Han, C., et al.: Madgan: unsupervised medical anomaly detection GAN using multiple adjacent brain MRI slice reconstruction. BMC Bioinform. **22** (2021). https://doi.org/10.1186/s12859-020-03936-1
4. Kalitzin, S., et al.: Enhancement of phase clustering in the EEG/MEG gamma frequency band anticipates transitions to paroxysmal epileptiform activity in epileptic patients with know visual sensitivity. IEEE Trans. Bio-Med. Eng. **49**, 1279–86 (2002). https://doi.org/10.1109/TBME.2002.804593
5. Karpov, O.E., et al.: Evaluation of unsupervised anomaly detection techniques in labelling epileptic seizures on human EEG. Appl. Sci. **13**(9) (2023). https://doi.org/10.3390/app13095655. https://www.mdpi.com/2076-3417/13/9/5655
6. Moncada, F., et al.: Virtual reality and machine learning in the automatic photoparoxysmal response detection. Neural Comput. Appl. (2022). https://doi.org/10.1007/s00521-022-06940-z
7. Moncada, F., et al.: Anomaly detection comparison for photo-paroxysmal response detection. Logic J. IGPL (2024)
8. Moncada, F., et al.: Evaluation of an AI-EEG based photo-paroxysmal response solution on healthy subjects: when false positive really matters. In: 2nd Olympiad in Engineering Science (OES 2025) (2025)
9. Moncada Martins, F., et al.: Sensors **23**(4) (2023). https://doi.org/10.3390/s23042312. https://www.mdpi.com/1424-8220/23/4/2312
10. Moncada Martins, F., et al.: Inception networks, data augmentation and transfer learning in EEG-based photosensitivity diagnosis. Mach. Learn. Sci. Technol. **6**(1), 015034 (2025). https://doi.org/10.1088/2632-2153/adb008
11. Pilcevic, D., et al.: Performance evaluation of metaheuristics-tuned recurrent neural networks for electroencephalography anomaly detection. Front. Physiol. **14** (2023). https://doi.org/10.3389/fphys.2023.1267011
12. Rezende, D., Mohamed, S.: Variational inference with normalizing flows. In: Bach, F., Blei, D. (eds.) Proceedings of the 32nd International Conference on Machine Learning. Proceedings of Machine Learning Research, Lille, France, vol. 37, pp. 1530–1538. PMLR (2015). https://proceedings.mlr.press/v37/rezende15.html

13. You, S., et al.: Unsupervised automatic seizure detection for focal-onset seizures recorded with behind-the-ear EEG using an anomaly-detecting generative adversarial network. Comput. Methods Programs Biomed. (2020). https://doi.org/10.1016/j.cmpb.2020.105472
14. You, S., et al.: Semi-supervised automatic seizure detection using personalized anomaly detecting variational autoencoder with behind-the-ear EEG. Comput. Methods Programs Biomed. (2022). https://doi.org/10.1016/j.cmpb.2021.106542
15. Shvetsova, N., et al.: Anomaly detection in medical imaging with deep perceptual autoencoders. IEEE Access **9**, 118571–118583 (2021). https://doi.org/10.1109/ACCESS.2021.3107163
16. Strigaro, G., et al.: Flash-evoked high-frequency EEG oscillations in photosensitive epilepsies. Epilepsy Res. **172**, 106597 (2021). https://doi.org/10.1016/j.eplepsyres.2021.106597. https://linkinghub.elsevier.com/retrieve/pii/S0920121121000504
17. Su, Y., et al.: Robust anomaly detection for multivariate time series through stochastic recurrent neural network. In: Proceedings of the 25th ACM SIGKDD International Conference on Knowledge Discovery & Data Mining, KDD 2019, pp. 2828–2837. Association for Computing Machinery, New York (2019). https://doi.org/10.1145/3292500.3330672
18. International Federation of Clinical Neurophysiology: Report of the committee on methods of clinical examination in electroencephalography. Electroencephalography and Clinical Neurophysiology **10**(2) (1958). https://doi.org/10.1016/0013-4694(58)90053-1
19. Trenité, D.G.N., et al.: Photic stimulation: standardization of screening methods. Epilepsia **40**(9) (1999). https://doi.org/10.1111/j.1528-1157.1999.tb00911.x
20. Trenité, D.K.N.: Photosensitivity in epilepsy. electrophisiological and clinical correlates. Acta Neurologica Scandinavica **125**(Suppl.), 3–149 (1989)
21. Waltz, S., et al.: The different patterns of the photoparoxysmal response - a genetic study. Electroencephalogr. Clin. Neurophysiol. **83**(2) (1992). https://doi.org/10.1016/0013-4694(92)90027-F

Subsymbolic and Symbolic Pipeline for an Explainable EEG Authentication System

Marcos Rodriguez-Vega[✉] and Pino Caballero-Gil

Department of Computer Engineering and Systems, University of La Laguna, Tenerife, Spain
mrodrive@ull.edu.es

Abstract. Biometric systems based on electroencephalography (EEG) are increasingly used for user authentication due to the uniqueness and difficulty in replicating brain signals. However, current systems, particularly those relying on subsymbolic one-class neural networks, face challenges in explainability and robustness against noisy or synthetic inputs. In this work, we introduce a hybrid subsymbolic and symbolic pipeline for an explainable EEG authentication system. The system first applies a symbolic coherence-checking module to evaluate signal quality, using neurophysiological criteria such as interchannel consistency and temporal stability. Inputs failing this stage, often corresponding to noisy or improperly measured signals, are immediately rejected. High-coherence signals are then processed in parallel by two components: a one-class neural network trained on legitimate user data, and a symbolic module based on Inductive Logic Programming (ILP). The symbolic module derives and applies logic rules grounded in EEG feature distributions of the honest user, offering transparent justifications for acceptance or rejection decisions. In cases of disagreement between modules, the system combines their outputs through a weighted decision strategy. This approach enhances security against adversarial input and resilience to noisy measurements, and is enriched by symbolic logs for explainability, which promotes interpretability, defining a way for trustworthy EEG-based authentication in practical deployments.

Keywords: EEG Biometrics · Symbolic Reasoning · Explainable AI

1 Introduction

Authentication systems are the foundation of modern digital security, ensuring that only authorized users gain access to sensitive resources [6,12]. While traditional methods based on passwords or tokens are vulnerable to theft and impersonation, biometric approaches offer a promising alternative that relies on intrinsic physiological or behavioral traits [2]. Among them, electroencephalography (EEG) has emerged as a compelling biometric modality [15,17] due to its uniqueness, nonvolitional nature, and difficulty of externally replicating brain signals [13].

Despite this potential, EEG-based authentication systems face important challenges [9]. In particular, many recent proposals rely on subsymbolic machine learning models, such as one-class neural networks, which, although effective, often act as black boxes and lack transparency [7]. This makes it difficult to interpret or audit their decisions, especially in safety-critical or privacy-sensitive applications.

This work proposes a hybrid approach that combines subsymbolic models with symbolic reasoning to improve explainability and robustness. By integrating interpretable logic-based modules alongside neural components, this system provides both high authentication performance and human-readable justifications. This is especially valuable for detecting invalid or adversarial inputs and for facilitating system audits and forensic analysis. Through the case of EEG-based authentication, this system demonstrates how hybrid pipelines can contribute to trustworthy biometric security systems that are not only accurate, but also transparent and auditable.

To realize this, this work designs a multi-stage pipeline that includes a symbolic filtering module for detecting low-quality EEG inputs based on neurophysiological criteria, producing detailed logs of signal anomalies. Then, this work explores several neural architectures, such as CNNs, MLPs, and LSTMs, to construct subsymbolic one-class models capable of learning the distribution of the legitimate user's EEG signals. In parallel, a symbolic predictor is implemented based on rule-driven comparisons to the user's characteristic feature distributions, offering inherently interpretable decisions. Finally, the predictions from both components are combined into a single decision strategy that balances performance and explainability, enabling informed acceptance or rejection of each authentication attempt.

2 Background and Related Works

EEG-based biometrics leverage the uniqueness and complexity of brain signals to authenticate individuals [9]. Compared to traditional biometrics such as fingerprints or facial recognition, EEG offers advantages in terms of resistance to forgery, especially since brain activity is inherently not externally observable and influenced by internal cognitive states [13]. However, the design of reliable EEG authentication systems presents multiple challenges, including inter-session variability, noise sensitivity, and the need for real-time performance. To address these, various studies have explored both handcrafted features and deep learning models [14]. While the latter can achieve high accuracy, they often lack interpretability, which is critical in contexts requiring auditability and trust.

Electroencephalography (EEG) is a non-invasive technique that captures the brain's electrical activity through sensors placed on the scalp. From a mathematical perspective, an EEG signal can be described as a multichannel time series $x(t) = [x_1(t), x_2(t), \ldots, x_C(t)]$, where $x_c(t)$ denotes the signal measured at channel c at time t, and C is the total number of channels. These signals encode subtle fluctuations in neural activity and are typically sampled at high temporal resolution, allowing for the analysis of rhythmic patterns across various frequency bands. This temporal richness makes EEG a compelling candidate for biometric authentication, this requires robust and interpretable processing pipelines to account for its variability and complexity.

One fundamental step in EEG processing pipelines is feature extraction [5,16], which transforms raw signals into informative representations for classification. This system extracts both temporal and spectral features, including a frequency-weighted power (FWP) descriptor that captures the spectral energy distribution across standard EEG bands [11]. Formally, given an EEG epoch $x_c(t)$ for each channel c, the relative power in each band b is denoted $\text{relpow}_{c,b}$ and used to compute the global FWP vector:

$$\mathbf{fwp}(E) = \sum_{b \in \mathcal{B}} w_b \cdot \text{relpow}_b(E),$$

where $\mathcal{B}$ represents the set of canonical EEG bands (e.g., delta, theta, alpha, beta, gamma), and w_b are predefined weights reflecting the physiological relevance of each band. This FWP representation is central to several symbolic rules used later in the system. Other works have employed related frequency features, but typically lack symbolic interpretability or rule-based reasoning. By integrating these features into both symbolic and neural decision modules, this system aligns with recent efforts in explainable EEG biometrics [3] [8], while offering a more auditable and structured approach.

In contrast to neural models, symbolic systems refer to approaches that operate using explicit, human-interpretable rules, often encoded through logic-based formalisms such as first-order logic, decision trees, or rule sets. These systems are typically grounded in domain knowledge and enable transparent reasoning about the conditions under which a particular decision is made. While symbolic AI has been successfully applied in fields such as expert systems, legal reasoning, and diagnostics, it remains rarely adopted in biometric authentication, where data-driven methods dominate. This is primarily due to the complexity and variability of biometric signals, which are often assumed to be better captured by flexible statistical or neural models. Nonetheless, symbolic reasoning offers valuable advantages in terms of explainability and auditability, key properties for trustworthy AI in security critical domains [10]. This work aims to bridge this gap by introducing symbolic modules that operate alongside neural components, providing rule-based justifications for authentication decisions.

3 Authentication System Architecture

The architecture of the proposed hybrid EEG-based authentication system is illustrated in Fig. 1. The process begins with the acquisition of EEG data from a user trying to authenticate. Each signal segment is first passed through a symbolic signal validation module, which applies rule-based checks to detect common artifacts and measurement anomalies. These rules, grounded some in neurophysiological principles (e.g., amplitude thresholds, interchannel coherence, or flat-line detection), ensure that only signals of sufficient quality proceed further. Invalid segments are immediately rejected and recorded by the system's logging mechanism, which maintains symbolic explanations of rejections for future auditability.

If the signal is asserted as valid, it is passed simultaneously to two parallel decision branches. The first is a subsymbolic decision module, implemented as a one-class neural network trained exclusively on the genuine user's data. This model outputs a confidence score in the range $[0, 1]$, computed via a sigmoid activation function, representing the estimated similarity between the input signal and the distribution of legitimate user patterns. In parallel, a symbolic decision module evaluates the input against a set of personalized logic rules, derived from the user's own EEG feature distributions (e.g., spectral profiles, global field power, Hjorth parameters). This symbolic path adds interpretability to the system by generating logical justifications for each prediction.

Both modules send their outputs, the subsymbolic score and the symbolic decision, to a final integration step, where a weighted fusion strategy produces the system's final authentication decision $\hat{y}$. Importantly, all symbolic modules contribute to a unified log system, enabling the generation of transparent, human-readable explanations for both rejections and acceptances decision. This pipeline is designed not only for accurate authentication, but also for resilience against adversarial inputs and full auditability.

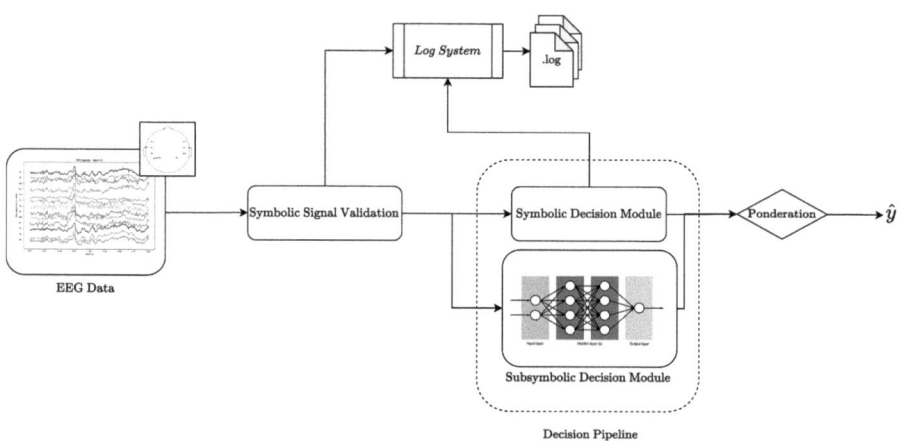

Fig. 1. Overall architecture of the proposed EEG authentication system

4 Initial Signal Validation

Before making any authentication decision, the system performs an initial symbolic validation as seen in Sect. 3 to assess the quality of each EEG epoch.

This stage is critical to ensure that only physiologically plausible and properly acquired signals are considered, thereby protecting the decision modules from spurious or adversarial inputs. The filtering mechanism relies on a set of logic-based rules, each designed to detect specific types of common artifacts or measurement issues. These rules are listed in Table 1 and formally defined through the symbolic predicate `valid_epoch`. The first condition, **Amplitude threshold**, checks whether any channel in the input epoch exceeds a predefined maximum absolute amplitude θ_{amp}. Excessive amplitudes often indicate artifacts caused by eye blinks, muscle activity, or faulty electrodes. If such a peak is detected, the signal is discarded. The second condition, **Variance threshold**, examines the variability within each channel. If the variance of any channel exceeds θ_{var}, the epoch is rejected. High variance may reflect sudden, erratic fluctuations inconsistent with typical neural activity. The third rule, **Flat-line detection**, identifies channels that remain almost constant during the epoch. Specifically, if the difference between the maximum and minimum values of a channel falls below ϵ_{flat}, the channel is considered flat, which is usually caused by disconnected or non-functional electrodes. Such epochs are deemed invalid. Lastly, the **Inter-channel coherence** rule evaluates the degree of correlation between pairs of channels. If the minimum pairwise correlation across all channel combinations falls below θ_{coh}, the epoch is assumed to lack sufficient spatial consistency and is discarded. This coherence check helps detect improperly placed electrodes or corrupted spatial patterns.

These four conditions are logically combined in the following symbolic rule:

$$\begin{aligned}
\texttt{valid\_epoch}(E) \Leftarrow &\ \neg\,\texttt{amp\_exceed}(E, \theta_{\text{amp}}), \\
& \neg\,\texttt{var\_exceed}(E, \theta_{\text{var}}), \\
& \neg\,\texttt{flatline}(E, \epsilon_{\text{flat}}), \\
& \neg\,\texttt{low\_coherence}(E, \theta_{\text{coh}}).
\end{aligned}$$

That is, an epoch E is considered valid only if none of the rejection conditions are triggered. For example, the predicate `amp_exceed` is defined as:

$$\texttt{amp\_exceed}(E, \theta) \Leftarrow \max_{c,t}|x_c(t)| > \theta.$$

All rejections at this stage are recorded in symbolic logs, which include the violated condition and the specific metric that caused the failure. This logging facilitates interpretability and makes the system auditable, allowing practitioners to trace back decisions to clearly defined physiological rules. The formal definitions of these rules are described in Table 1.

5 Decision Pipeline: Symbolic and Neural Models

Once an EEG epoch passes the initial quality validation, it is forwarded to the decision pipeline as seen in Sect. 3, which combines symbolic and subsymbolic models to determine whether the signal corresponds to the legitimate user. This stage is divided into two parallel modules: a symbolic decision module and a

Table 1. Symbolic initial filtering rules for artifact rejection (θ = threshold).

Rule	Condition	Description
Amplitude threshold	$\max_{c,t} |x_c(t)| > \theta_{\text{amp}}$	Reject if any channel's peak amplitude exceeds θ_{amp}
Variance threshold	$\text{Var}(x_c) > \theta_{\text{var}}$	Reject if any channel's variance exceeds θ_{var}
Flat-line detection	$\exists c : \max_t x_c(t) - \min_t x_c(t) < \epsilon_{\text{flat}}$	Reject if any channel is nearly constant (flat)
Inter-channel coherence	$\min_{i \neq j} \text{Corr}(x_i, x_j) < \theta_{\text{coh}}$	Reject if the lowest pairwise correlation is below θ_{coh}

subsymbolic neural module. Each produces an independent prediction, and their outputs are later combined through a weighting mechanism to produce the final authentication decision.

Symbolic Decision Module. This module relies on a set of explainable logic rules grounded in feature statistics derived from the training data of the legitimate user. As shown in Table 2, these rules compare the input epoch's features to the expected distribution of features for the genuine user. If any rule is violated, the symbolic module rejects the epoch and logs the corresponding reasoning trace. The symbolic rules include a set of threshold-based comparisons between the features of the input epoch and the expected distributions derived from the legitimate user's data. First, the frequency-weighted power (FWP) vector of the input is compared to the user's mean FWP μ_{fwp}, requiring that their Euclidean distance remains below a threshold θ_{fwp}. Second, the relative power across frequency bands and channels must not deviate from the user's average values by more than a specified tolerance θ_{rel}. Additionally, the global field power (GFP) of the epoch must remain close to the user's typical GFP, bounded by θ_{gfp}, while Hjorth activity metrics, which characterize the signal's spatial complexity, must also fall within a user-specific range defined by θ_{hj}. Finally, the complete feature vector of the epoch is required to maintain a minimum correlation θ_{corr} with the prototype representation of the user. All threshold values (θ_{fwp}, θ_{rel}, θ_{gfp}, θ_{hj}, and θ_{corr}) were computed solely from the statistics of the legitimate user's training data. Specifically, each threshold was set based on the user's mean feature values, following a one-class validation approach that does not rely on impostor examples. This strategy is consistent with the overall one-class setting of the system. These conditions together define whether the symbolic module accepts an input as a valid instance of the target user's EEG pattern.

Formally, an input epoch E is accepted by the symbolic module if all the following hold:

```
valid_user_epoch(E) ⇐ fwp_ok(E),
                      relpow_ok(E),
                      gfp_ok(E),
                      hj_ok(E),
                      corr_ok(E).
```

These symbolic rules that are used in this module were automatically generated using an Inductive Logic Programming (ILP) approach. Specifically, descriptive EEG features (e.g., frequency-weighted power, relative band power, GFP, Hjorth activity) were computed for each training epoch and converted into Prolog-compatible facts. Positive examples corresponded to epochs from the legitimate user, and negative examples were drawn from other users. The resulting ILP training files consist of mode declarations and example facts defining the honest/1 predicate in terms of low-level numerical features. Although the final system applies manually defined threshold-based rules for efficiency and transparency, their structure and feature selection were informed by this ILP-derived representation.

Table 2. Generic symbolic rules for identifying a legitimate user based on feature statistics (μ = mean).

Rule	Generic Condition	Description
Deviation of weighted power	$\|\mathbf{fwp}(E) - \mu_{\text{fwp}}\|_2 < \theta_{\text{fwp}}$	Reject if the Euclidean θ_{fwp}. distance between the frequency-weighted power of E and the user's mean exceeds
Range of relative power	$\max_{c,b}\|\text{relpow}_{c,b}(E) - \mu_{\text{relpow},b}\| < \theta_{\text{rel}}$	Reject if any channel $\mu_{\text{relpow},b} \pm \theta_{\text{rel}}$. band relative power deviates outside
GFP consistency	$\|\text{gfp}(E) - \mu_{\text{gfp}}\| < \theta_{\text{gfp}}$	Reject if the global field potential of E deviates by more than θ_{gfp} from the user's mean
Hjorth activity	$\|\text{hj}(E) - \mu_{\text{hj}}\| < \theta_{\text{hj}}$	Reject if the Hjorth activity of E (per channel) deviates by more than θ_{hj} from the user's mean
Correlation with prototype	$\text{Corr}(\mathbf{f}(E), \mu_f) > \theta_{\text{corr}}$	Accept only if the correlation θ_{corr}. between the full feature vector of E and the user's prototype exceeds

Subsymbolic Decision Module. In parallel, the input is evaluated by a one-class neural network trained to recognize the legitimate user. These models are optimized to output a high confidence score when the input resembles the training data of the user and a low score otherwise. Three neural architectures were explored: a Multi-Layer Perceptron (MLP), a Convolutional Neural Network (CNN), and a Long Short-Term Memory (LSTM) network.

Each model receives a preprocessed feature vector and is trained exclusively on data from the target user, following a one-class classification approach. The models were optimized with constraints that enforce perfect recall (i.e., no false rejections of genuine user inputs) while minimizing false acceptances.

The symbolic and subsymbolic outputs are finally fused using a weighted strategy. If both agree, their shared decision is adopted. In cases of disagreement, the system favors the symbolic module when confidence in the subsymbolic prediction is low, or vice versa. This integration allows for robust and explainable predictions, while maintaining the flexibility and accuracy of neural networks.

Fusion Strategy. To combine the outputs of the symbolic and subsymbolic modules, the system employs a weighted decision mechanism. Let $s_{\text{sym}} \in \{0,1\}$ denote the binary decision of the symbolic module, and $s_{\text{sub}} \in [0,1]$ the confidence score output by the neural model. The final authentication decision $\hat{y}$ is computed as:

$$\hat{y} = \begin{cases} 1, & \text{if } \alpha \cdot s_{\text{sym}} + \beta \cdot s_{\text{sub}} \geq \tau, \\ 0, & \text{otherwise}, \end{cases}$$

where α and β are fusion weights satisfying $\alpha + \beta = 1$, and $\tau \in [0,1]$ is a decision threshold. In this work, we set $\alpha = 0.5$ and $\beta = 0.5$ to give equal importance to both modules. Future extensions may explore adaptive or learned fusion weights based on confidence calibration or user-specific behavior.

6 Experimental Setup

All experiments were conducted on a workstation equipped with an Intel Core i7-11700KF processor running at 3.60 GHz, a NVIDIA RTX 4070 GPU, 32 GB of RAM, and Ubuntu 24.04 as the operating system. The dataset used in this work was the publicly available PhysioNet EEG corpus, which includes multi-channel EEG recordings across different subjects. To evaluate the effectiveness of one-class models for user authentication, each model was trained to recognize a single legitimate user while treating all other inputs as unknown or adversarial.

The dataset was split into two disjoint partitions: 80% of the data was reserved for training and validation (trainval), and the remaining 20% was held out for final testing. Stratification was applied to preserve the class balance between genuine and impostor epochs. During hyperparameter tuning, a 5-fold cross-validation was performed over the trainval partition to robustly estimate model performance. This design ensures that the final evaluation on the test set reflects generalization to unseen data.

Hyperparameter optimization was carried out using the Optuna framework [1], which efficiently explores high-dimensional parameter spaces through Bayesian optimization. Each model architecture (CNN, MLP, and LSTM) was tuned independently over 20 trials. The search space included model-specific architectural choices, such as the number of convolutional filters for CNNs or hidden units for LSTMs, as well as global parameters like dropout rate and learning rate.

The present approach prioritizes minimizing the False Acceptance Rate (FAR) as the primary optimization objective. This reflects a more security-oriented perspective, in which the system is designed to minimize the risk of granting access to unauthorized users, even at the cost of occasionally rejecting legitimate ones.

7 Results and Discussion

To evaluate authentication performance in a domain-appropriate way, we adopted standard biometric evaluation metrics: False Acceptance Rate (FAR), False Rejection Rate (FRR), and Equal Error Rate (EER). These metrics quantify the system's ability to discriminate between legitimate and illegitimate users and are defined as follows:

The False Acceptance Rate is defined as

$$\text{FAR} = \frac{\text{FP}}{\text{FP} + \text{TN}},$$

and measures the proportion of impostor attempts (false positives) that were incorrectly accepted by the system. Conversely, the False Rejection Rate is given by

$$\text{FRR} = \frac{\text{FN}}{\text{FN} + \text{TP}},$$

capturing the proportion of legitimate attempts (true positives) that were wrongly rejected. Finally, the Equal Error Rate (EER) corresponds to the operating point at which FAR and FRR become equal:

$$\text{EER} = \text{FAR} = \text{FRR}.$$

This point is identified by sweeping the decision threshold and finding the value where both error rates intersect. A lower EER reflects a better overall trade-off between security (minimizing FAR) and usability (minimizing FRR), and is widely used as a global summary of system performance.

Figure 2 shows the comparative performance of the CNN, MLP, and LSTM models, where each bar corresponds to a biometric metric sorted in ascending order per model. This visualization highlights that the CNN achieves the lowest overall error rates, with a particularly favorable EER of 2.07%, and minimal FRR. The MLP shows slightly higher error rates across the board, while the LSTM presents the highest FAR among all models, indicating a greater tendency to incorrectly accept illegitimate users.

Table 3 summarizes the mean biometric scores obtained during cross-validation, along with the best hyperparameter configuration selected by Optuna for each architecture. Notably, while the LSTM achieves the lowest FRR (0.53%), it does so at the cost of a significantly higher FAR (11.4%), which undermines security by allowing more unauthorized users. In contrast, the CNN balances a low FAR (9.1%) and FRR (0.8%), resulting in the lowest EER overall, making it the most reliable option in terms of both security and usability.

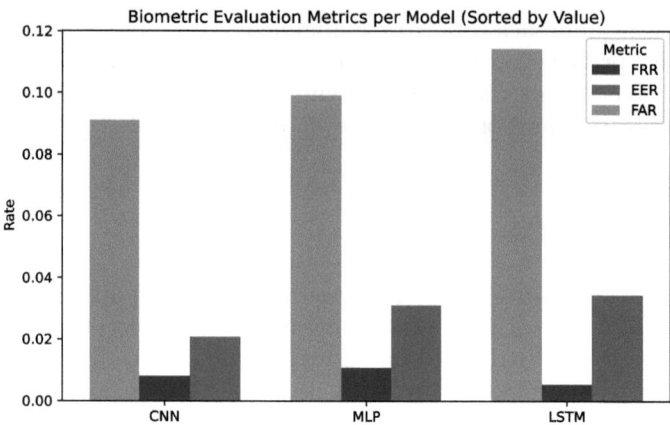

Fig. 2. Biometric evaluation metrics for CNN, MLP, and LSTM models (FAR, FRR, EER), sorted in ascending order for each model.

Table 3. Biometric performance and best hyperparameters for each model (5-fold cross-validation).

Model	FAR	FRR	EER	Best hyperparameters
CNN	0.0911	0.0081	0.0208	Convolution filters: 48, kernel size: 5, pooling fraction: 0.573, learning rate: 0.0094
MLP	0.0992	0.0107	0.0311	Hidden layers: [114, 75], dropout: 0.034, learning rate: 0.0007
LSTM	0.1144	0.0054	0.0343	Hidden size: 64, LSTM layers: 2, learning rate: 0.0005

These results illustrate a critical trade-off: while minimizing false rejections (FRR) ensures usability, excessively high false acceptance rates (FAR) can compromise security. The CNN achieves a strong balance, outperforming other models in EER while maintaining a low FAR and very low FRR. This suggests that, under a one-class setup, CNNs are particularly well-suited for learning distinctive EEG patterns of a legitimate user without overfitting.

Compared to recent EEG-based authentication systems, our approach offers a competitive trade-off between usability and security. For instance, Bidgoly et al. propose a deep learning-based system using only three EEG channels (Oz, T7, Cz), achieving 98.04% accuracy with an Equal Error Rate (EER) of 1.96%, even for users not seen during training—highlighting their model's universality and privacy-preserving design via EEG fingerprinting hashes [4]. Similarly, Zeynali and Seyedarabi explored single-channel systems using optimized electrode placement and neural networks, obtaining up to 98.3% accuracy depending on the mental task [18]. While our best model (CNN) achieves an EER of 2.08% using a conventional training setup and cross-validation, it does so under a one-class constraint and without exploiting privileged task-based information or multi-day/session matching, demonstrating robustness with minimal overfitting and good generalization. Moreover, unlike [18], our evaluation incorporates standard biometric metrics (FAR, FRR, EER) and separates training from validation using independent folds, aligning more closely with deployment-ready authentication scenarios.

Future work will explore integrating session-aware data, performing statistical significance tests across folds, and extending to more complex architectures such as transformer-based encoders to enhance generalization under realistic and adversarial settings.

8 Conclusion

This work presents a hybrid EEG-based authentication system that integrates symbolic and subsymbolic reasoning to improve explainability, robustness, and trustworthiness. By combining interpretable logic rules with powerful one-class neural models, the system enables both accurate classification and transparent justifications for acceptance or rejection decisions. Such explainable mechanisms are essential for real-world deployments where accountability and auditability are critical, particularly in security-sensitive contexts.

The proposed architecture illustrates the potential of hybrid AI systems in bridging the gap between performance and interpretability. However, further research is required to enhance scalability and robustness, especially when facing more heterogeneous datasets or adversarial attempts to impersonate legitimate users. Moreover, as EEG data is highly personal and privacy-sensitive, future directions must also address secure processing frameworks such as homomorphic encryption or federated learning to ensure compliance with ethical and legal standards. Ultimately, this line of work contributes toward building biometric authentication systems that are not only effective but also reliable, interpretable, and privacy-preserving.

Acknowledgements. This research has been possible thanks to the research projects PID2022-138933OB-I00 ATQUE and 2023DIG28 IACTA, and the Cybersecurity Chair C065/23 ULL-INCIBE, funded by MCIN/ EI/10.13039/501100011033, Cajacanarias la Caixa Fundations, and the European Union NextGenerationEU/PRTR, respectively.

Code and Data Availability. The code used in our experiments is available at our GitHub repository. The EEG dataset employed can be accessed from PhysioNet (EEG Motor Movement/Imagery Dataset).

References

1. Akiba, T., Sano, S., Yanase, T., Ohta, T., Koyama, M.: Optuna: a next-generation hyperparameter optimization framework. In: Proceedings of the 25th ACM SIGKDD International Conference on Knowledge Discovery & Data Mining, KDD 2019, pp. 2623–2631. Association for Computing Machinery, New York (2019). https://doi.org/10.1145/3292500.3330701

2. Alrawili, R., AlQahtani, A.A.S., Khan, M.K.: Comprehensive survey: biometric user authentication application, evaluation, and discussion. Comput. Electr. Eng. **119**, 109485 (2024). https://doi.org/10.1016/j.compeleceng.2024.109485. https://www.sciencedirect.com/science/article/pii/S0045790624004129
3. Apicella, A., Isgrò, F., Pollastro, A., Prevete, R.: Toward the application of XAI methods in EEG-based systems (2024). https://arxiv.org/abs/2210.06554
4. Bidgoly, A.J., Bidgoly, H.J., Arezoumand, Z.: Towards a universal and privacy preserving EEG-based authentication system. Sci. Rep. **12**(1), 2531 (2022). https://doi.org/10.1038/s41598-022-06527-7
5. Boonyakitanont, P., Lek-uthai, A., Chomtho, K., Songsiri, J.: A review of feature extraction and performance evaluation in epileptic seizure detection using EEG. Biomed. Signal Process. Control **57**, 101702 (2020). https://doi.org/10.1016/j.bspc.2019.101702. https://www.sciencedirect.com/science/article/pii/S1746809419302836
6. Chenchev, I., Aleksieva-Petrova, A., Petrov, M.: Authentication mechanisms and classification: a literature survey. In: Arai, K. (ed.) Intelligent Computing, pp. 1051–1070. Springer, Cham (2021)
7. Dobson, J.E.: On reading and interpreting black box deep neural networks. Int. J. Digit. Humanit. **5**(2), 431–449 (2023). https://doi.org/10.1007/s42803-023-00075-w
8. Hussain, I., et al.: An explainable EEG-based human activity recognition model using machine-learning approach and lime. Sensors **23**(17) (2023). https://doi.org/10.3390/s23177452. https://www.mdpi.com/1424-8220/23/17/7452
9. Jalaly Bidgoly, A., Jalaly Bidgoly, H., Arezoumand, Z.: A survey on methods and challenges in EEG based authentication. Comput. Secur. **93**, 101788 (2020). https://doi.org/10.1016/j.cose.2020.101788. https://www.sciencedirect.com/science/article/pii/S0167404820300730
10. Kaur, D., Uslu, S., Rittichier, K.J., Durresi, A.: Trustworthy artificial intelligence: a review. ACM Comput. Surv. **55**(2) (2022). https://doi.org/10.1145/3491209
11. Monsy, J.C., Vinod, A.P.: EEG-based biometric identification using frequency-weighted power feature. IET Biometrics **9**, 251–258 (2020). https://doi.org/10.1049/iet-bmt.2019.0158. https://digital-library.theiet.org/doi/abs/10.1049/iet-bmt.2019.0158
12. Patel, S.S., Jaiswal, A., Arora, Y., Sharma, B.: Survey on graphical password authentication system. In: Jeena Jacob, I., Kolandapalayam Shanmugam, S., Piramuthu, S., Falkowski-Gilski, P. (eds.) Data Intelligence and Cognitive Informatics, pp. 699–708. Springer, Singapore (2021)
13. Pavlov, Y.G., et al.: #eegmanylabs: investigating the replicability of influential EEG experiments. Cortex **144**, 213–229 (2021). https://doi.org/10.1016/j.cortex.2021.03.013. https://www.sciencedirect.com/science/article/pii/S0010945221001106
14. Roy, Y., Banville, H., Albuquerque, I., Gramfort, A., Falk, T.H., Faubert, J.: Deep learning-based electroencephalography analysis: a systematic review. J. Neural Eng. **16**(5), 051001 (2019). https://doi.org/10.1088/1741-2552/ab260c
15. Vadher, H., et al.: EEG-based biometric authentication system using convolutional neural network for military applications. Secur. Privacy **7**(2), e345 (2024). https://doi.org/10.1002/spy2.345. https://onlinelibrary.wiley.com/doi/abs/10.1002/spy2.345
16. Azlan, W.A., Low, Y.F.: Feature extraction of electroencephalogram (EEG) signal - a review. In: 2014 IEEE Conference on Biomedical Engineering and Sciences (IECBES), pp. 801–806 (2014). https://doi.org/10.1109/IECBES.2014.7047620

17. Yassine, F.A., Abdelkader, G.: EEG-based biometric authentication using machine and deep learning approachs: a review. In: 2024 8th International Conference on Image and Signal Processing and their Applications (ISPA), pp. 1–8 (2024). https://doi.org/10.1109/ISPA59904.2024.10536762
18. Zeynali, M., Seyedarabi, H.: EEG-based single-channel authentication systems with optimum electrode placement for different mental activities. Biomed. J. **42**(4), 261–267 (2019). https://doi.org/10.1016/j.bj.2019.03.005

Cybersecurity and Network Protection

Analyzing DoS Attacks on CoAP Networks Using Low-Dimensional Latent Representations

Álvaro Michelena[1], Jose Aveleira-Mata[2(✉)],
Marta-María Álvarez-Crespo[1], Emilio Lima-Bullones[1],
Agustín García-Fischer[1], Carmen Benavides[2], and José Luis Calvo-Rolle[1]

[1] CTC, CITIC, Department of Industrial Engineering, University of A Coruña, Avda. 19 de febrero s/n, 15405 Ferrol, A Coruña, Spain
{alvaro.michelena,marta.maria.alvarez.crespo,emilio.limab,jlcalvo}@udc.es
[2] Department of Electric, Systems and Automatics Engineering, University of León, León, Spain
{jose.aveleira,carmen.benavides}@unileon.com

Abstract. Internet of Things systems are growing rapidly, offering services in diverse environments but also posing important security challenges. Among the most common threats are denial of service attacks, which compromise the availability of resource-constrained devices. One of the most widely used protocols in these settings is the Constrained Application Protocol, whose features can be exploited to amplify such attacks. In this work, we compare three unsupervised techniques for reducing dimensionality: Isometric Mapping, t-distributed stochastic neighbor embedding, and Uniform Manifold Approximation and Projection, for visual analysis, detection, and characterization of denial of service attacks on networks using that protocol. We use a real traffic dataset obtained in an experimental setup under denial of service attack conditions. The results show that t-distributed stochastic neighbor embedding and Uniform Manifold Approximation and Projection enable clear visual separation between legitimate and malicious traffic. These findings support the use of low-dimensional latent representations as an exploratory tool to detect anomalous behavior in Internet of Things networks.

Keywords: CoAP · Dimensionality Reduction Techniques · DoS attacks

1 Introduction

The rapid expansion of the Internet of Things (IoT) has led to an exponential increase in the number of connected devices, with 17.2 billion devices connected globally in 2025, representing an 11.7% increase compared to 2024 [18]. This proliferation spans critical sectors such as healthcare, agriculture, and industry, integrating devices that handle sensitive data and operate essential infrastructure.

However, this growth also increases the attack surface, exposing vulnerabilities in systems with limited security measures. The diversity of devices, platforms, and protocols in the IoT ecosystem complicates the implementation of unified security standards, making it difficult to ensure data confidentiality, integrity, and availability [16].

CoAP (Constrained Application Protocol) is one of the most widely used protocols in this context. It is designed to provide RESTful services over UDP, with low overhead and support for features such as Observe and resource discovery [17]. In addition to CoAP, IoT environments may use protocols like MQTT, AMQP, or DDS, which follow different communication models and address specific functional requirements [6]. Depending on the deployment constraints, IoT systems may also rely on non-IP-based communication technologies such as Zigbee or LoRa, Zigbee is a low-power, short-range mesh-networking standard built on IEEE 802.15.4, and is commonly deployed in home automation, building control, and industrial sensor networks. LoRa (Long Range) is a low-power wide-area network (LPWAN) technology, which are designed for low-power, short-range or long-range wireless communication in constrained environments [1].

Denial-of-Service (DoS) attacks target the availability of networked systems by sending large volumes of traffic or requests that consume processing, memory, or bandwidth resources. In UDP-based protocols, where there is no handshake or connection state, services may process incoming messages without verifying their legitimacy or source [14]. This increases exposure to DoS scenarios, especially in constrained IoT environments where endpoints operate with limited resources and cannot implement advanced mitigation mechanisms such as connection tracking or per-client rate limiting [11]. A specific type of DoS attack is amplification. In this case, the attacker sends a small request to a server that produces a significantly larger response, and redirects it to a victim by spoofing the source IP address. This allows a small amount of attacker-controlled traffic to generate a large volume of traffic toward the target. In IoT environments, amplification attacks can be particularly effective, as many devices support UDP-based discovery or management protocols with predictable responses [5]. A device with limited network or processing capacity may become unavailable after receiving a small number of amplified messages. While UDP enables lightweight and efficient communication, it also exposes protocols to specific attack vectors. CoAP is vulnerable to this type of attack due to its support for confirmable messages and block-wise transfers, which can generate large responses from small requests. The risk of amplification and the need to limit response sizes and validate endpoints is explicitly mentioned in the CoAP specification [17].

Mitigating amplification-based DoS attacks requires the ability to detect anomalous traffic patterns that deviate from normal protocol behavior [2]. A realistic test environment is used to evaluate amplification attacks against CoAP services. The resulting traffic is captured and labeled to distinguish between normal and attack scenarios. Using low-dimensional latent representations generated by an autoencoder, the model is trained to capture the typical structure of CoAP exchanges. The objective is to evaluate whether these representations can distinguish legitimate CoAP traffic from anomalies caused by amplification, enabling early detection of such attacks in constrained environments.

Denial of Service attacks that originate from multiple coordinated devices are called Distributed Denial of Service (DDoS) attacks, as they involve several sources targeting a single service.

This work focuses on amplification-based Denial of Service attacks, to which the Constrained Application Protocol (CoAP) is particularly vulnerable due to its request/response design and block-wise transfers. We explore the use of unsupervised dimensionality reduction techniques—Isomap, t-SNE, and UMAP—as tools to detect abnormal traffic behavior without prior labeling

Section 2: Case Study, we describe the experimental setup and dataset collection used to generate and capture Constrained Application Protocol traffic under DoS and DDoS conditions. Section 3: Applied Techniques introduces the three unsupervised dimensionality reduction methods—Isomap, t-distributed stochastic neighbor embedding, and Uniform Manifold Approximation and Projection—used for visual analysis. Section 4: Experimental Setup and Results Analysis presents the preprocessing steps, the configuration and execution of each technique, and discusses the results of detecting and characterizing Denial of Service and Distributed Denial of Service attacks on CoAP networks. Finally, Sect. 5: Conclusions and Future Research Lines concludes the paper and outlines directions for future work.

2 Case Study

CoAP (Constrained Application Protocol) is a lightweight application-layer protocol designed to enable RESTful communication between constrained devices over UDP [17]. It follows the client/server model and supports standard methods such as GET, POST, PUT, and DELETE. One of its key features is the "Observe" extension, which allows clients to subscribe to resources and receive notifications when those resources are updated [8]. These characteristics make CoAP suitable for IoT scenarios where bandwidth, memory, and energy are limited.

To analyze CoAP network traffic under amplification-based DoS conditions, a test environment was used with real traffic exchanges. The server, developed in Node.js using the "node-coap" library, provides RESTful endpoints and supports block-wise transfers. A NodeMCU board programmed with "ESP-CoAP" [15] periodically sends sensor data. A JavaScript client running on a Raspberry Pi 3 interacts with observable resources, and additional Copper4Cr clients [9] are used to send CoAP requests and observe responses through a graphical interface. This setup allows the generation and capture of real CoAP traffic in .pcap format for further analysis and labeling.

The amplification attack targets the client by exploiting CoAP's block-wise transfer mechanism. In this setup, the attacker runs a virtual machine with Linux and uses IP spoofing to impersonate the legitimate client. Requests are sent from the attacker to the CoAP server, which then replies to the actual client.

By negotiating small block sizes in the request, the server is forced to split the response into multiple packets, increasing the total traffic sent to the client.

To execute the attack, the attacker configures IP address spoofing using the iptables tool. The following command is used on the attacker's machine:

```
iptables -t nat -A POSTROUTING -p udp -o eth0 -j SNAT -to
CLIENT_IP:PORT
```

where CLIENT_IP and PORT match the CoAP client's address and port. Copper4Cr is then launched on the attacker's side, emulating the client's behavior and sending requests with a block size set to 16, the smallest available. Although the attacker does not receive the server's responses, the legitimate client is overwhelmed by a high number of CoAP response packets corresponding to a request it never initiated.

To execute the attack, a Node.js script was developed using the native-dns-packet library [19], which allows manual editing of DNS packet fields to align their structure with the format of CoAP messages.

The cross-protocol attack was executed while capturing all network traffic in a .pcap file. A custom dissection tool, developed in previous works [13], was used to process the capture and extract all relevant fields associated with the CoAP protocol. The tool outputs a structured .csv file where each frame is labeled with a "type" field indicating whether it corresponds to normal traffic or to traffic generated during the attack, based on its timestamp.

The resulting dataset, CoAP_DoS.csv, contains 30.319 records, each representing a captured CoAP frame. Each row includes 85 attributes, such as timing features (frame delta time, displayed delta time, epoch timestamp, and relative time), network-layer fields (IP source and destination addresses, TCP/UDP source and destination ports), Ethernet MAC addresses, packet metadata (capture length, coloring rule), and CoAP-specific fields (message type, version, token, token length, payload length and description, response time and response code). Of these records, 21.269 correspond to normal traffic and 9.050 to traffic generated during Denial of Service attack scenarios.

3 Applied Techniques

In this contribution, three dimensional reduction techniques are used to visualize and analyze the behavior of denial of service (DoS) attacks in data networks operating under the CoAP protocol. In this way, the projection to latent spaces allows to facilitate their interpretation, to identify possible clustering and to detect anomalous behavior. The selected techniques combine linear and nonlinear approaches to preserve different aspects of the original data structure. This section briefly describes each of them: Isomap, Uniform Manifold Approximation and Projection, and t-Distributed Stochastic Neighbor Embedding.

3.1 Isomap

Isomap is a nonlinear dimensionality reduction method designed to preserve the intrinsic geometry of data by maintaining geodesic distances between samples. Unlike linear techniques such as Principal Component Analysis (PCA), which emphasize variance preservation, Isomap focuses on capturing the manifold structure underlying high-dimensional data [4].

The core of the Isomap algorithm lies in estimating geodesic distances (approximations of true manifold distances) between all pairs of points. This is achieved by first constructing a neighborhood graph using the k-nearest neighbors of each sample. Then, Dijkstra's algorithm (or FloydâĂŞWarshall, depending on implementation) is applied to compute the shortest paths between all points in the graph, effectively yielding the geodesic distance matrix [3].

Once the geodesic distance matrix is obtained, classical Multidimensional Scaling (MDS) is employed to embed the data into a lower-dimensional space. MDS seeks a configuration of points in the target space that best preserves the pairwise geodesic distances, resulting in a low-dimensional representation that reflects the nonlinear structure of the original data manifold.

3.2 Uniform Manifold Approximation and Projection (UMAP)

UMAP is a powerful nonlinear dimensionality reduction technique grounded in principles of Riemannian geometry and algebraic topology [12]. It aims to preserve both local and global structures of high-dimensional data by constructing a topological representation of the data manifold.

UMAP begins by building a weighted graph in the original high-dimensional space, where edges reflect neighborhood relationships based on a chosen distance metric. This graph is then mapped onto a low-dimensional space through an optimization process that minimizes the divergence between fuzzy set representations of the original and projected graphs. The result is a latent representation where distances reflect the underlying data structure as faithfully as possible.

Two key hyperparameters guide UMAP's behavior: the number of neighbors, which determines the size of the local neighborhood used for manifold approximation, and the minimum distance, which controls how tightly points are packed in the lower-dimensional space. By adjusting these parameters, UMAP can be tuned to favor either local detail preservation or a more global view of the data distribution.

3.3 T-Distributed Stochastic Neighbor Embedding (t-SNE)

t-SNE is a nonlinear dimensionality reduction method developed by van der Maaten and Hinton in 2008, widely used for visualizing high-dimensional data [10]. It models pairwise similarities between data points using conditional probabilities and projects them into a lower-dimensional space by minimizing the Kullback-Leibler divergence between the original and projected distributions [7].

This technique effectively preserves local structures, making it particularly useful for revealing clusters. However, due to its non-convex cost function, results may vary between runs.

A key aspect of t-SNE's performance is its sensitivity to several hyperparameters, most notably the perplexity, which influences the number of effective nearest neighbors used when modeling similarities. Lower perplexity values emphasize local relationships, while higher values capture broader structure. Other important parameters include the learning rate and the number of iterations, which affect convergence and stability.

4 Experimental Setup and Results Analysis

This section describes the experimental framework used to evaluate the behavior of different applied dimensionality reduction techniques. It includes a description of the preprocessing steps, the configuration and execution of each technique, and a comparative analysis of the resulting visualizations.

4.1 Dataset Preprocessing and Experimental Configuration

This section describes the dataset preprocessing steps and the configuration used to apply and evaluate the dimensionality reduction techniques considered in this research work.

Before applying the dimensionality reduction methods, a thorough preprocessing pipeline was applied to ensure the quality and consistency of the data. The following steps were carried out:

- **Removal of constant features:** Variables with no variance across samples were discarded as they provide no discriminatory information.
- **Elimination of high-missing-rate features:** Features with more than 50% missing values were removed to avoid unreliable patterns.
- **Exclusion of potentially biased attributes:** Fields such as IP and MAC addresses or message content were discarded to prevent bias and ensure model generalization.
- **Encoding of categorical variables:** Categorical features were converted into numerical form using natural (ordinal) encoding.
- **Removal of incomplete records:** Any remaining samples with missing values were excluded from the dataset.
- **Z-score normalization:** All numerical features were standardized using z-score normalization to facilitate the application of dimensionality reduction techniques.

With the data properly preprocessed and normalized, the dimensionality reduction techniques described in the previous section were applied. In all cases, the projection was configured to reduce the data to two components, allowing for a simple and intuitive visualization of behavioral patterns associated with normal and DoS traffic.

Each technique was tested under different hyperparameter configurations to evaluate its ability to separate and characterize the traffic classes. Specifically:

- For Isomap, the effect of varying the number of nearest neighbors was analyzed. Values of 10, 25, 50, 75, 100, 200, and 500 were tested to explore the balance between local and global structure preservation.

- For t-SNE, different values of the perplexity parameter were explored: 5, 10, 15, 20, 25, 30, 40, 50, 75, 100, 200, and 400. These configurations were used to assess how neighborhood size affected the clustering and separation of normal and malicious traffic samples.
- For UMAP, experiments were conducted with varying values for the number of neighbors (10, 25, 50, 100) and the minimum distance parameter (0.0, 0.1, 0.25, 0.5).

Each technique and its corresponding configurations were analyzed independently to identify those settings that most clearly revealed differences between normal and attack traffic. The selection of optimal configurations was conducted by the visual separability of the two traffic types, aiming to improve the compactness of each group and to enhance the distinction between benign and malicious behavior patterns.

Figure 1 gives an overview of a flowchart with each of the stages carried out in this research work.

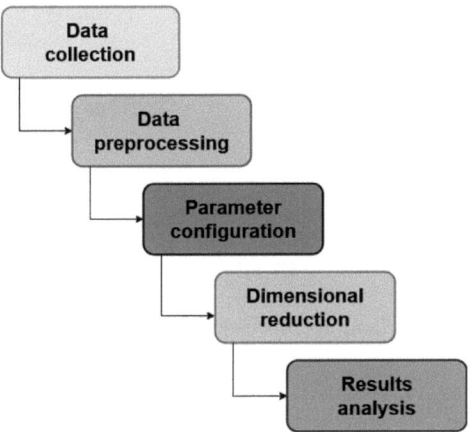

Fig. 1. Experimental steps.

4.2 Results Analysis and Discussion

In this section, the results obtained through the implementation of the selected dimensionality reduction techniques are presented, focusing on the configurations that yielded the best performance according to the previously established evaluation criteria. Figures 2, 4 and 3 display the outcomes corresponding to Isomap, t-SNE, and UMAP, respectively. In all the visualizations, scatter plots are shown where each point represents an individual network packet. Green points correspond to legitimate traffic packets, while red points indicate packets associated with DoS attack activity.

Figure 2 presents the best projection obtained with Isomap, considering a tuning parameter of 500 neighbors. In this visualization it can be seen how the samples corresponding to DoS attacks are concentrated in specific regions of the latent space. However, the separation of these samples with the data associated with normal traffic is neither complete nor clearly defined. There are significant overlaps between the two classes, which complicates direct visual identification of attack patterns. Although Isomap succeeds in capturing some global relationships in the dataset structure, its effectiveness as a visualization tool for distinguishing between normal traffic and DoS attacks in this scenario is limited.

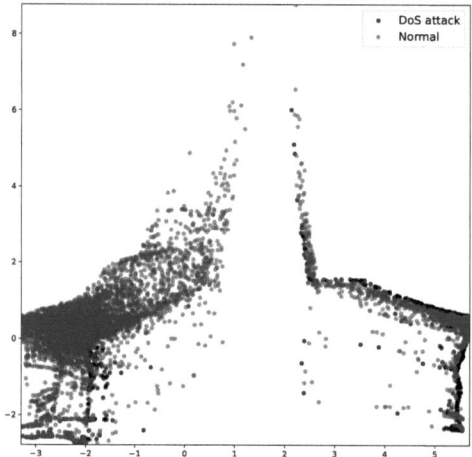

Fig. 2. Isomap representation in 2D space.

Figure 3 shows the 2D representation obtained using the UMAP technique, configured considering a minimum distance of 0.1 and 50 neighbors, which yielded the best results among the configurations tested. With these parameters, UMAP generates several compact groups. A main cluster concentrates most of the network traffic, predominantly consisting of normal packets, although some DoS packets are also present within it. Additionally, a set of smaller peripheral clusters is formed, which mostly contain either DoS packets or legitimate traffic, showing a partial but useful separation between classes.

This structure allows many packets from both classes to be clearly distinguishable. However, the presence of DoS and normal packets interspersed in some clusters suggests that under certain conditions, malicious traffic can emulate the behavior of legitimate packets. This overlap may hinder the effectiveness of detection systems and highlights the complexity of distinguishing DoS attacks based solely on traffic patterns.

Figure 4 shows the two-dimensional representation obtained using the t-SNE technique, configured with a perplexity value equal to 10. Similar to UMAP,

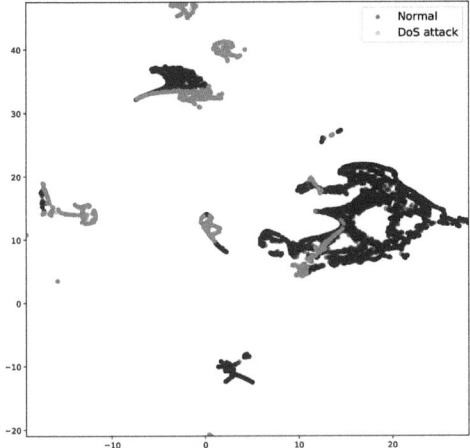

Fig. 3. UMAP representation in 2D space.

t-SNE allows observing a evident separation between both classes. DoS attacks tend to cluster in regions of latent space that are clearly defined and differentiated from normal traffic, making them easier to identify visually. This ability of t-SNE to effectively differentiate between the two classes provides an effective tool for exploratory analysis of this type of data.

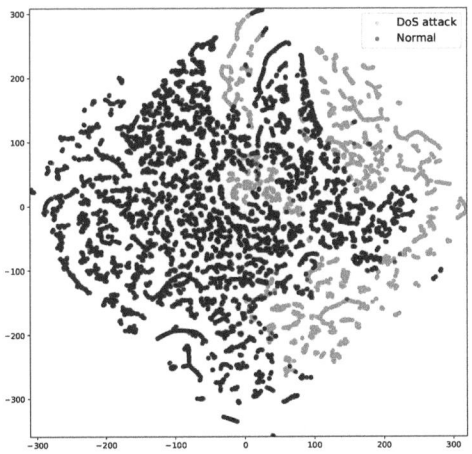

Fig. 4. t-SNE representation in 2D space.

5 Conclusions and Future Research Lines

In this paper several dimensionality reduction techniques were evaluated for the visual representation and analysis of traffic behavior patterns in networks using the CoAP protocol, with the objective of detecting denial of service (DoS) attacks. The results showed that t-SNE and UMAP effectively differentiate legitimate traffic from that associated with DoS attacks. In particular, UMAP stood out for its ability to generate compact and well-separated clusters, which produced a main cluster predominantly composed of normal traffic and several peripheral clusters that captured more specific patterns, often related to anomalous behavior. However, the presence of interspersed DoS and legitimate packets in some clusters that, under certain conditions, malicious traffic can mimic the behavior of normal packets, making detection based solely on visual or structural features more complex.

These results reinforce the value of visualization as a complementary tool for security analysis in CoAP-based IoT networks. As future work, we propose to use these latent representations as a preprocessing step in machine learning-based attack detection models, as well as to extend the study to other protocols, attack types and dimensionality reduction techniques.

Acknowledgments. This research is the result of the Strategic Project "Critical infrastructures cybersecure through intelligent modeling of attacks, vulnerabilities and increased security of their IoT devices for the water supply sector" (C061/23), as a result of the collaboration agreement signed between the National Institute of Cybersecurity (INCIBE) and the University of A Coruña. This initiative is carried out within the framework of the funds of the Recovery Plan, Transformation and Resilience Plan funds, financed by the European Union (Next Generation).

Álvaro Michelena's research was supported by the Spanish Ministry of Universities (https://www.universidades.gob.es/), under the "Formación de Profesorado Universitario" grant with reference FPU21/00932.

CITIC, as a center accredited for excellence within the Galician University System and a member of the CIGUS Network, receives subsidies from the Department of Education, Science, Universities, and Vocational Training of the Xunta de Galicia. Additionally, it is co-financed by the EU through the FEDER Galicia 2021-27 operational program (Ref. ED431G 2023/01)

Xunta de Galicia. Grants for the consolidation and structuring of competitive research units, GPC (ED431B 2023/49). This work has been funded by the Recovery, Transformation, and Resilience Plan, financed by the European Union (Next Generation) thanks to the "Internet of Things Security in Home and Business Environments in the Context of 5G-IoT Technology".

References

1. Abderrahmane, T., Nourredine, A., Mohammed, T.: Experimental analysis for comparison of wireless transmission technologies: Wi-Fi, Bluetooth, Zigbee and Lora for mobile multi-robot in hostile sites. Int. J. Electr. Comput. Eng. (IJECE) **14**(3), 2753–2761 (2024)

2. Almeghlef, S.M., Alghamdi, A., Ramzan, M.S., Ragab, M.: Application layer-based denial-of-service attacks detection against IoT-coap. Electronics **12**, 2563 (2023). https://doi.org/10.3390/electronics12122563. https://www.mdpi.com/2079-9292/12/12/2563
3. Geng, X., Zhan, D.C., Zhou, Z.H.: Supervised nonlinear dimensionality reduction for visualization and classification. IEEE Trans. Syst. Man Cybern. Part B (Cybern.) **35**(6), 1098–1107 (2005)
4. Ghojogh, B., Ghodsi, A., Karray, F., Crowley, M.: Multidimensional scaling, sammon mapping, and isomap: tutorial and survey. arXiv preprint arXiv:2009.08136 (2020)
5. Hassan, A., Nizam-Uddin, N., Quddus, A., Hassan, S.R., Rehman, A.U., Bharany, S.: Navigating IoT security: insights into architecture, key security features, attacks, current challenges and AI-driven solutions shaping the future of connectivity. Comput. Mater. Continua (Print) 1–10 (2024). https://doi.org/10.32604/cmc.2024.057877
6. Hosny, K.M., El-Hady, W.M., Samy, F.M.: Technologies, protocols, and applications of internet of things in greenhouse farming: a survey of recent advances. Inf. Process. Agric. (2024)
7. Ji, S., Zhang, Z., Ying, S., Wang, L., Zhao, X., Gao, Y.: Kullback-leibler divergence metric learning. IEEE Trans. Cybern. **52**(4), 2047–2058 (2020)
8. Khalil, K., Mohaidat, T., Darwich, M., Kumar, A., Bayoumi, M.: An efficient hardware design of coap protocol for the internet of things. In: 2024 IEEE 17th Dallas Circuits and Systems Conference (DCAS), pp. 1–5. IEEE (2024)
9. Kovatsch, M.: Github - mkovatsc/copper4cr: Copper (cu) coap user-agent for chrome (javascript implementation) (2022). https://github.com/mkovatsc/Copper4Cr
10. Van der Maaten, L., Hinton, G.: Visualizing data using t-SNE. J. Mach. Learn. Res. **9**(11) (2008)
11. Mahajan, R.A.: Enhancing MQTT security in the internet of things with an enhanced symmetric algorithm. Deleted J. **20**, 126–137 (2024). https://doi.org/10.52783/jes.758
12. McInnes, L., Healy, J., Melville, J.: Umap: uniform manifold approximation and projection for dimension reduction. arXiv preprint arXiv:1802.03426 (2018)
13. Narciandi-Rodríguez, D., Aveleira-Mata, J., Corcoba, A.M., Rubiños, M., Arcano-Bea, P., Alaiz-Moretón, H.: Herramienta de disección de tramas para protocolos iot. Jornadas de Automática (45) (2024)
14. Newman, S.: UDP flood DDoS attack (2024). https://www.corero.com/what-is-udp-flood-ddos-attack/
15. lovelesh patel: Commits · automote/esp-coap · github (2024). https://github.com/automote/ESP-CoAP/commits?author=lovelesh
16. Selvaraj, M., Uddin, G.: A large-scale study of IoT security weaknesses and vulnerabilities in the wild. ACM Trans. Softw. Eng. Methodol. **34**(2), 1–40 (2025)
17. Shelby, Z., Hartke, K., Bormann, C.: The constrained application protocol (coap) (2014). https://doi.org/10.17487/RFC7252. https://www.rfc-editor.org/info/rfc7252
18. Singhvi, H.: The internet of things in 2025: trends, business models, and future directions for a connected world. Int. J. Internet Things **3**(1), 17–24 (2025). https://doi.org/10.34218/IJIOT_03_01_003
19. Slepak, G.: Native-dns-packet (2014). https://github.com/netbeast/react-native-dns-packet. Accessed 26 Mar 2025

An Approach to Anomaly Detection with Dynamic Threshold Definition for Real-World Environments

Gabriel Souza Marques[1](✉), Maynara Souza[1], Flávio Arthur Oliveira Santos[1], Cleber Zanchettin[1], and Paulo Novais[2]

[1] Universidade Federal de Pernambuco (UFPE), Recife, PE, Brazil
{gsm3,mds3,faos,cz}@cin.ufpe.com
[2] University of Minho, Braga, Portugal
pjon@di.uminho.pt

Abstract. This paper introduces the Memory-based Streaming Classification for Anomaly Detection (MSCAD), which combines supervised memory updates with adaptive thresholding to enhance performance in streaming data environments. Evaluations were conducted on three publicly available datasets: KDD Cup 1999 (KDD99), NSL-KDD, and UNSW-NB15. MSCAD consistently outperforms the baseline MemStream model, especially in recall and F1-score. The proposed dynamic thresholding mechanism enhances adaptability to evolving data distributions, addressing limitations of fixed-threshold approaches. Results demonstrate MSCAD's robustness across datasets of varying complexity, establishing it as a reliable solution for real-world anomaly detection tasks.

Keywords: Anomaly Detection · Unsupervised Learning · Adaptive Threshold

1 Introduction

Anomaly detection plays a critical role in real-world applications such as cybersecurity [1,11], financial fraud prevention [10], and healthcare diagnostics [9]. In these domains, timely identification of atypical patterns is essential to mitigate risks, reduce economic loss, and enable early interventions.

Traditional machine learning approaches typically frame anomaly detection as either a supervised classification problem or an unsupervised modeling task. While supervised methods can be accurate in controlled environments, they depend on labeled data—which is often scarce, expensive, or unavailable in real-world scenarios [2]. Unsupervised methods are more suitable for discovering unknown or evolving threats, but they often suffer from overfitting or poor generalization in high-dimensional, multi-aspect data streams.

In streaming environments, these challenges are magnified due to the continuous arrival of data, latency constraints, and the presence of concept drift—non-stationary changes in data distributions [5,7]. This motivates the need for models that are both adaptive and capable of learning incrementally over time.

In this work, we propose MSCAD (MemStream Combined to Adaptive Network Anomaly Detection), a novel architecture that synthesizes supervised memory updates, dynamic thresholding, and adaptive pseudo-labeling strategies. MSCAD is designed to enhance robustness, interpretability, and real-time adaptability in non-stationary data streams, particularly for security-critical environments.

The key contributions of this work are:

1. An open-source[1] deep architecture for real-time anomaly detection with dynamic memory and adaptive pseudo-labeling, capable of handling concept drift through continuous memory updates.
2. The introduction of MSCAD, integrating supervised memory updates with dynamic thresholding to improve detection in streaming data.
3. Demonstration of significant performance improvements over the MemStream baseline across three benchmark datasets, with emphasis on recall and F1-score.
4. A detailed analysis of thresholding strategies, highlighting the benefits of adaptive methods over fixed thresholds, and validating MSCAD's robustness and practical applicability in diverse, imbalanced environments.

2 Related Work

Recent advances in deep learning have significantly influenced anomaly detection, especially in streaming scenarios. Architectures such as DeepLog [4] and Kitsune [8] utilize LSTMs and autoencoders to model temporal and distributed patterns in real time, even under resource constraints. While effective, these models generally depend on static representations and fixed thresholds, which limits their adaptability in evolving environments.

MemStream [2] addressed some of these limitations by incorporating an adaptive memory module and partial supervision. However, its reliance on fixed decision thresholds makes it vulnerable to performance degradation under concept drift [6,13].

To enhance flexibility, Adaptive NAD [12] proposed combining pseudo-labeling strategies with online learning. This hybrid approach significantly reduces false positives and improves model responsiveness to evolving threats. Despite its strengths, Adaptive NAD lacks an integrated memory mechanism, which can be beneficial in streaming anomaly detection tasks.

Our work builds upon these developments by combining the architectural advantages of MemStream with the learning flexibility of Adaptive NAD, introducing a unified framework that addresses dynamic memory management, adaptive thresholding, and online pseudo-labeling.

---

[1] https://github.com/gabrielsm0405/MemStream-AdaptiveNad.

3 Proposed Framework

Before introducing our proposed framework, it is essential to understand the individual characteristics and mechanisms of the two techniques that inspired it: MemStream and Adaptive NAD. Each of these methods addresses specific challenges in streaming anomaly detection. MemStream leverages memory-based representations to adaptively detect anomalies in evolving data streams, while Adaptive NAD introduces an online self-supervised learning strategy through pseudo-labeling to improve adaptability and reduce reliance on labeled data. By analyzing their core components, we lay the groundwork for understanding how their integration leads to a more robust and flexible solution.

3.1 Foundations: MemStream and Adaptive NAD

MemStream: Anomaly Detection with Adaptive Memory. MemStream is a framework designed for anomaly detection in continuous data streams, particularly in environments affected by concept drift. Its architecture consists of two main components: an autoencoder, responsible for extracting compact data representations, and an adaptive memory module, which stores representations associated with normal patterns for future comparisons [2].

After an initial training phase using a small set of normal data, MemStream processes each new instance in two steps. In the first step, it calculates the anomaly score by comparing the compressed representation of the instance with its K nearest neighbors stored in memory, using a weighted average of L1 distances—known as the discounted score. In the second step, the memory is updated: if the anomaly score is below a fixed threshold β, the instance is considered normal and its representation is added to memory, replacing the oldest entry based on a FIFO (First In, First Out) policy.

This approach proves effective in scenarios with gradual changes in the data. However, its reliance on a fixed threshold can hinder its adaptability in the presence of abrupt distribution shifts or more intense concept drift scenarios.

Adaptive NAD: Online Detection Framework with Dynamic Thresholding. Adaptive NAD was proposed as a general framework for online and unsupervised anomaly detection, with a focus on security applications. Its main distinction lies in two key strategies.

The first is the two-layer detection strategy, in which the first layer employs a deep unsupervised model—such as LSTM-VAE—to estimate the loss, while the second layer uses a supervised and interpretable model, such as a Random Forest [3], trained with dynamically generated pseudo-labels.

The second strategy involves online learning with adaptive thresholds, where two dynamic thresholds, T_1 and T_2, are periodically recalculated based on the distributions of loss values for normal and anomalous samples. This continuous update allows the model to adapt to new data patterns over time, effectively reducing both false positives and false negatives [12].

Algorithm 1: MSCAD

Input: Initial dataset X_0; data stream $x_t{}_{t=1}^{N}$; thresholding technique T
Output: Trained MS (unsupervised) and trained neural network M' (supervised)

1. Randomly initialize MS;
2. Randomly initialize M';
3. **TrainMSAutoencoder**(X_0);
4. **InitMSMemory**(X_0);
5. **foreach** $x_0^i \in X_0$ **do**
6. $Loss \leftarrow MS(x_0^i)$;
7. $LossDB_{normal} \leftarrow LossDB_{normal} \cup \{Loss\}$;
8. $T_1 \leftarrow AdaptiveThreshold(LossDB_{normal}, T)$;
9. $T_2 \leftarrow Null$;
10. **while** *inputting* x_t **do**
11. $Loss \leftarrow MS(x_t)$;
12. $BatchDB \leftarrow BatchDB \cup \{x_t, Loss\}$;
13.   **if** $T2 == Null$ **then**
14. $X \leftarrow X \cup \{x_t\}$;
15.   **if** $Loss < T_1$ **then**
16. $LossDB_{normal} \leftarrow LossDB_{normal} \cup \{Loss\}$;
17. $Y \leftarrow Y \cup \{normal\}$;
18. $X_{normal} \leftarrow X_{normal} \cup \{x_t\}$;
19.   **else**
20. $LossDB_{abnormal} \leftarrow LossDB_{abnormal} \cup \{Loss\}$;
21. $Y \leftarrow Y \cup \{abnormal\}$;
22.   **continue**
23.   **if** $Loss < T_1$ **then**
24. $LossDB_{normal} \leftarrow LossDB_{normal} \cup \{Loss\}$;
25. $X \leftarrow X \cup \{x_t\}$;
26. $Y \leftarrow Y \cup \{normal\}$;
27. $X_{normal} \leftarrow X_{normal} \cup \{x_t\}$;
28.   **else if** $Loss > T_2$ **then**
29. $LossDB_{abnormal} \leftarrow LossDB_{abnormal} \cup \{Loss\}$;
30. $X \leftarrow X \cup \{x_t\}$;
31. $Y \leftarrow Y \cup \{abnormal\}$;
32.   **else**
33. $y_t \leftarrow M'(x_t)$;
34.   **if** $y_t = normal$ **then**
35. $X_{normal} \leftarrow X_{normal} \cup \{x_t\}$;
36.   **if** $Size(BatchDB) == MSmemoryLength$ **then**
37. $T_1 \leftarrow AdaptiveThreshold(LossDB_{normal}, T)$;
38. $T_2 \leftarrow AdaptiveThreshold(LossDB_{abnormal}, T)$;
39.   **TrainMSAutoencoder**(X_{normal});
40.   **UpdateMSMemory**(X_{normal});
41.   **Train**(X, Y, M');
42.   **Empty**($X, Y, X_{normal}, BatchDB$);

Unlike MemStream, Adaptive NAD leverages dynamic thresholding and maintains a continuous pseudo-labeling mechanism to retrain its models, resulting in improved robustness when faced with concept drift or evolving definitions of normality.

3.2 MSCAD

This section introduces MSCAD, a hybrid anomaly detection technique that integrates the memory-based unsupervised detection capabilities of MemStream with the adaptive pseudo-supervised learning framework of Adaptive NAD. The primary motivation behind this integration is to leverage the strengths of both approaches: MemStream's ability to compute robust reconstruction losses in non-stationary environments, and Adaptive NAD's capacity to dynamically adjust decision thresholds and learn from data streams in an online fashion.

The experiments involving MSCAD were structured in three distinct phases. **In the first phase**, MemStream (MS) was executed in isolation using a fixed decision threshold, as outlined in its original formulation. **In the second phase**, MS was embedded into the Adaptive NAD framework, replacing its original unsupervised model with MS's autoencoder-based loss computation. **In third phase**, after, integration we adjust dynamically the threshold and improved adaptability to concept drift and evolving data patterns.

In the integrated setup, MS functions as the first layer, responsible for generating anomaly scores (i.e., reconstruction losses) from incoming samples. These scores are compared against adaptive thresholds to decide whether an instance is normal, anomalous, or ambiguous. For ambiguous cases, the second layer—a supervised model trained with pseudo-labeled data—is employed to make the final decision. In addition to the Random Forest model originally proposed in Adaptive NAD, we also experimented with replacing the supervised component with a neural network (MLPClassifier with hidden_layer_sizes = (100, 100)), aiming to capture more complex decision boundaries.

The complete procedure is formalized in Algorithm 1, which outlines how the two layers interact, how adaptive thresholds are recalculated, and how the model is continuously updated as new data points arrive.

4 Experiments and Results

To assess the effectiveness of the MSCAD framework, we conducted a series of experiments using the approaches described in Sect. 3.1.

Datasets. We evaluated our framework on three widely used cybersecurity anomaly detection datasets: KDD99, NSL-KDD, and UNSW-NB15. These benchmarks offer diversity in attack types, structure, and temporal behavior. KDD99 is a classic dataset known for its class imbalance; NSL-KDD improves upon it with better balance and generalization; and UNSW-NB15 provides modern, realistic network traffic and complex attack scenarios.

Table 1. Performances obtained for each dataset in MSCAD.

Dataset	Technique	Threshold	Precision	Recall	F1-Score	Accuracy	AUC
KDD99	MS	$\beta = 1$	0.90	0.50	0.45	0.80	0.96
	MSCAD	Default	0.90	0.91	0.91	0.94	0.98
	MSCAD	Percentile	**0.96**	**0.92**	**0.94**	**0.96**	**0.98**
NSL-KDD	MS	$\beta = 0.1$	0.73	0.50	0.32	0.47	0.98
	MSCAD	Default	0.94	0.93	0.93	0.93	0.98
	MSCAD	Mean	**0.97**	**0.97**	**0.97**	**0.97**	**0.98**
UNSW-NB15	MS	$\beta = 0.1$	0.56	0.50	0.11	0.13	0.98
	MSCAD	Default	0.94	0.98	0.96	0.98	0.98
	MSCAD	Percentile	**0.94**	**0.99**	**0.96**	**0.98**	**0.98**

"Default" refers to default Adaptive NAD setting.

All datasets were preprocessed according to the standardization and normalization protocols defined by the MemStream study [2], ensuring comparability across datasets and model configurations.

Evaluation Metrics. The performance of each method was assessed using the following metrics: Area Under the Receiver Operating Characteristic Curve (AUC-ROC), precision, recall, F1-score, accuracy, and confusion matrix. These metrics offer a comprehensive evaluation of both detection capability and classification quality, particularly in imbalanced or stream-based anomaly detection contexts. The threshold parameter, as introduced in Sect. 3.2, is a key tunable component of the anomaly scoring process. Table 1 reports results for both the default threshold and the best-performing adaptive threshold (mean- or percentile-based). Additional threshold analysis and ablation studies are presented in Sect. 5.

Results on Individual Datasets. On the *KDD99 dataset*, the baseline MemStream (MS) model achieved high precision (0.90) and AUC (0.96), but suffered from low recall (0.50) and a poor F1-score (0.45), indicating limited sensitivity to anomalies. In contrast, MSCAD significantly improved recall (0.91) and F1-score (0.91), while maintaining high precision (0.90) and increasing accuracy (0.94) and AUC (0.98). When applying a percentile-based threshold, MSCAD further improved precision to 0.96 and F1-score to 0.94, highlighting the benefit of adaptive thresholding.

MS performed poorly on *NSL-KDD*, with accuracy at 0.47 and a low F1-score of 0.32, despite an AUC of 0.98. These results suggest overfitting or poor generalization under stream conditions. MSCAD addressed this gap, achieving balanced and high metrics: precision (0.94), recall (0.93), F1-score (0.93), and accuracy (0.93). With a mean-based threshold, MSCAD achieved even higher scores (all metrics at 0.97), demonstrating the synergy between adaptive thresholding and memory supervision.

The *UNSW-NB15 dataset* proved the most challenging. MS showed severe degradation, with accuracy at 0.13, F1-score at 0.11, and recall at 0.50, despite a high AUC of 0.98. This reflects poor classification reliability under complex network behaviors. MSCAD, however, exhibited dramatic improvement: recall reached 0.98, precision 0.94, and F1-score 0.96. The use of a percentile-based threshold further increased recall to 0.99 and maintained an accuracy of 0.98, demonstrating the model's robustness even under more realistic and heterogeneous data conditions.

Table 2. Performances obtained changing the threshold.

Dataset	Threshold	Precision	Recall	F1-Score	Accuracy	AUC
KDD99	Default	0.90	0.91	0.91	0.94	0.98
	Percentile	**0.96**	**0.92**	**0.94**	**0.96**	**0.98**
	Mean	0.94	0.91	0.92	0.95	0.98
	Median	0.93	0.89	0.91	0.95	0.98
	Mode	0.93	0.88	0.91	0.94	0.98
	QR	0.94	0.90	0.92	0.95	0.98
	Std	**0.96**	**0.92**	**0.94**	**0.96**	**0.98**
NSL-KDD	Default	0.94	0.93	0.93	0.93	0.98
	Mean	**0.97**	**0.97**	**0.97**	**0.97**	**0.98**
	Percentile	0.93	0.91	0.92	0.92	0.98
	Median	0.93	0.94	0.93	0.93	0.98
	Mode	0.91	0.91	0.90	0.90	0.98
	IQR	0.91	0.91	0.90	0.90	0.98
	Std	0.91	0.90	0.90	0.90	0.98
UNSW-NB15	Default	0.94	0.98	0.96	0.98	0.98
	Percentile	**0.94**	**0.99**	**0.96**	**0.98**	**0.98**
	Mean	**0.94**	**0.99**	**0.96**	**0.98**	**0.98**
	Median	0.94	0.99	0.96	0.98	0.98
	Mode	0.88	0.97	0.92	0.96	0.98
	IQR	0.94	0.98	0.96	0.98	0.98
	Std	0.94	0.98	0.96	0.98	0.98

"Default" refers to default Adaptive NAD setting.

5 Ablation: Impact of the Threshold

A core component of MSCAD is its dynamic thresholding, converting continuous anomaly scores into binary decisions. We conducted an ablation study to evaluate various thresholding strategies based on MemStream's anomaly scores.

Besides the original Adaptive NAD method—which fits a distribution to scores and sets thresholds via percentiles—we tested simpler statistical alternatives: fixed percentiles, mean, median, mode, interquartile range (IQR) –or anomalous data, it is 0.5, and for normal data, it is 0.95– and standard deviation. Algorithm 2 formalizes this threshold computation, adjusting dynamically to normal or anomalous data. This analysis isolates the threshold's impact on MSCAD's performance and demonstrates the value of adaptive, distribution-aware methods for robust anomaly detection in streaming data.

Table 2 demonstrates that the choice of thresholding method substantially affects MSCAD's performance across datasets. Thresholds based on percentiles and standard deviation consistently yield superior precision and F1-scores on KDD99, indicating their effectiveness in managing class imbalance and score variability. For NSL-KDD, the mean-based threshold attains the best results, reflecting the dataset's improved balance and reduced redundancy. In the more complex UNSW-NB15 dataset, percentile and mean thresholds again provide the highest recall and F1-scores, while mode-based thresholds perform comparatively worse, likely due to multimodal score distributions.

These results underscore the necessity of adapting thresholding strategies to dataset characteristics. Methods incorporating distributional information generally enhance detection robustness, whereas simpler statistics may suffice for less complex data. Consequently, threshold selection is critical for optimizing anomaly detection in streaming environments.

6 Discussions

6.1 On the Dataset Impact

MSCAD consistently outperforms the baseline MemStream, particularly in recall and F1-score, due to its supervised memory updates and adaptive thresholding. The largest improvements occur on UNSW-NB15, a complex and imbalanced dataset where traditional memory-based methods fail to detect anomalies effectively.

KDD99, being simpler and more redundant with clearly separable anomalies, yields the highest scores for all models. NSL-KDD, which introduces greater balance and diversity compared to KDD99, presents a more realistic challenge, slightly reducing performance but better reflecting real-world conditions.

The dynamic thresholding strategies in MSCAD enhance adaptability to evolving data distributions, proving critical for sustained anomaly detection across varied dataset characteristics.

6.2 On Model Performance and Thresholding Limitations

Although the MemStream model achieved a high AUC-ROC of 0.98 on the UNSW-NB15 dataset, a more detailed analysis reveals its limited practical effectiveness. As shown in Fig. 1a, the model predominantly classified samples as anomalous, correctly identifying only 9 normal instances. This resulted in a low

Algorithm 2: Adaptive Threshold with Selectable Technique

Input: Loss database $LossDB$; T threshold technique
Output: Calculated threshold $\mathcal{T}$

1 **if** $Size(LossDB) > 0$ **then**
2   **if** $LossDB$ is *normal* **then**
3      $p \leftarrow 0.95$
4   **else**
5      $p \leftarrow 0.05$
6   **if** T is **adaptiveNad** **then**
7      $FitDist \leftarrow FitBestDistribution(LossDB)$;
8      $\mathcal{T} \leftarrow ComputePercentile(FitDist, p)$;
9   **else if** T is **percentile** **then**
10      $\mathcal{T} \leftarrow percentile(LossDB, p*100)$;
11   **else if** T is **mean** **then**
12      $\mathcal{T} \leftarrow mean(LossDB)$;
13   **else if** T is **median** **then**
14      $\mathcal{T} \leftarrow median(LossDB)$;
15   **else if** T is **mode** **then**
16      $\mathcal{T} \leftarrow mode(LossDB)$;
17   **else if** T is **iqr** **then**
18      $Q_1 \leftarrow 25^{\text{th}}$ percentile of $LossDB$;
19      $Q_3 \leftarrow 75^{\text{th}}$ percentile of $LossDB$;
20      $IQR \leftarrow Q_3 - Q_1$;
21      $\mathcal{T} \leftarrow Q_3 + 1.5 \cdot IQR$;
22   **else if** T is **stdDev** **then**
23      $\mu \leftarrow mean(LossDB)$;
24      $\sigma \leftarrow std(LossDB)$;
25      $\mathcal{T} \leftarrow \mu + k \cdot \sigma$;   // k is adjustable
26
27 **else**
28    $\mathcal{T} \leftarrow \emptyset$;

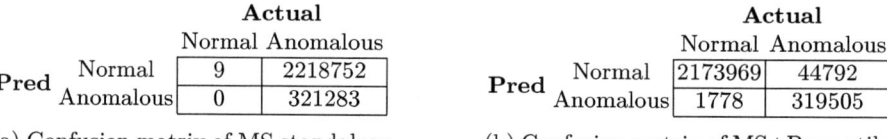

		Actual	
		Normal	Anomalous
Pred	Normal	9	2218752
	Anomalous	0	321283

(a) Confusion matrix of MS standalone

		Actual	
		Normal	Anomalous
Pred	Normal	2173969	44792
	Anomalous	1778	319505

(b) Confusion matrix of MS+Percentile

Fig. 1. Confusion matrix comparison between MS and MS+Percentile.

accuracy of 13%, highlighting that the high AUC value can be misleading. Specifically, AUC reflects the model's ability to rank samples by anomaly score but does not guarantee reliable binary classification in highly imbalanced datasets.

Conversely, incorporating MemStream within Adaptive NAD, which employs dynamic thresholding based on percentile adjustments, substantially improves detection quality. Figure 1b presents a more balanced confusion matrix with clearer separation between normal and anomalous classes. Additionally, Fig. 2 demonstrates the dynamic behavior of anomaly scores alongside adaptive thresholds enabling effective response to data stream variations. This qualitative comparison underscores the need for cautious interpretation of AUC metrics in anomaly detection, particularly under class imbalance. Complementary measures—such as accuracy, F1-score, confusion matrices, and visual inspection of score distributions—are crucial for a comprehensive assessment of model performance and real-world applicability.

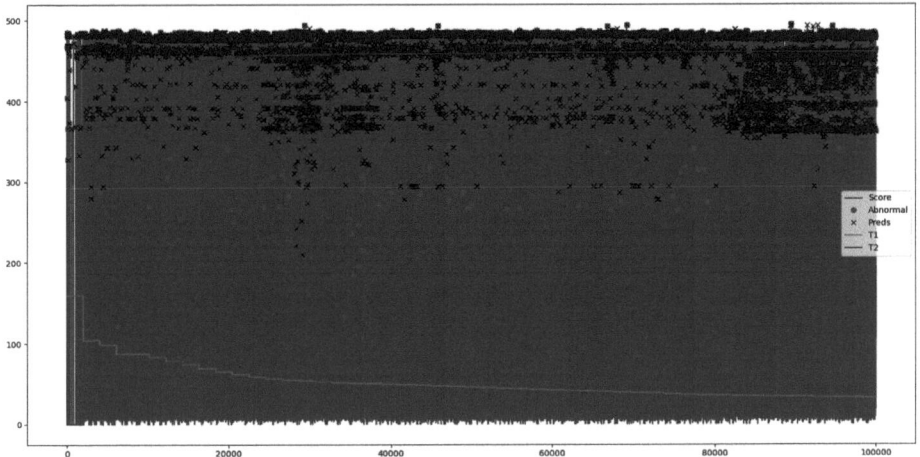

Fig. 2. Anomaly detection results using the MSCAD method. The blue area represents the anomaly scores assigned to each sample. Red dots indicate true abnormal events, while green crosses denote predicted anomalies. Thresholds T1 (orange) and T2 (dark green) are shown for reference. The x-axis corresponds to sample indices, and the y-axis shows score values. (Color figure online)

7 Conclusion

This work presented MSCAD, an anomaly detection framework that integrates supervised memory updates with adaptive thresholding to improve detection in streaming data scenarios. Our experiments on three benchmark datasets (KDD99, NSL-KDD, and UNSW-NB15) demonstrated MSCAD's superior performance compared to the baseline MemStream model, particularly in recall and F1-score —two critical metrics in anomaly detection, as anomalies typically represent rare events where identifying all positive cases (high recall) while minimizing false positives (reflected in F1-score) is essential.

The results highlight MSCAD's robustness and adaptability: it excels in complex, imbalanced environments such as UNSW-NB15, where traditional memory-based approaches struggle. Meanwhile, on simpler and more redundant datasets like KDD99, MSCAD maintains high accuracy, confirming its effectiveness across varying data complexities.

Dynamic thresholding proved essential, enabling the model to adjust decision boundaries in response to changing data distributions, thereby improving practical detection capabilities beyond static threshold methods.

Overall, MSCAD represents a significant advancement in memory-based anomaly detection, offering a flexible and reliable approach suitable for diverse and evolving network environments. While the current evaluation focused on comparison with MemStream as a relevant baseline, future work will extend this analysis to include other state-of-the-art methods to provide a more comprehensive benchmarking.

Although the approach showed significant improvements in experiments using public datasets, it has not yet been tested in real-world environments with dynamic and unpredictable traffic. This raises questions about the robustness of the method when facing concept drift and the noise typically found in real networks. Future works should focus on it.

Acknowledgments. The work of Paulo Novais has been supported by FCT – Fundação para a Ciência e Tecnologia within the R&D Units Project Scope of the Unit 00319.

References

1. Bhatia, S., Hooi, B., Yoon, M., Shin, K., Faloutsos, C.: Midas: microcluster-based detector of anomalies in edge streams (2020). https://arxiv.org/abs/1911.04464
2. Bhatia, S., Jain, A., Srivastava, S., Kawaguchi, K., Hooi, B.: Memstream: memory-based streaming anomaly detection (2022). https://arxiv.org/abs/2106.03837
3. Breiman, L.: Random forests. Mach. Learn. **45**(1), 5–32 (2001). https://doi.org/10.1023/A:1010933404324
4. Du, M., Li, F., Zheng, G., Srikumar, V.: Deeplog: anomaly detection and diagnosis from system logs through deep learning. In: Proceedings of the 2017 ACM SIGSAC Conference on Computer and Communications Security (CCS), pp. 1285–1298. ACM (2017). https://doi.org/10.1145/3133956.3134015
5. Guha, S., Mishra, N., Roy, G., Schrijvers, O.: Robust random cut forest based anomaly detection on streams. In: Proceedings of the 33rd International Conference on International Conference on Machine Learning, ICML 2016, vol. 48, pp. 2712–2721. JMLR.org (2016)
6. Han, D., et al.: Deepaid: interpreting and improving deep learning-based anomaly detection in security applications. In: Proceedings of the 2021 ACM SIGSAC Conference on Computer and Communications Security, CCS 2021, pp. 3197–3217. ACM (2021). https://doi.org/10.1145/3460120.3484589
7. Hariri, S., Kind, M.C., Brunner, R.J.: Extended isolation forest. IEEE Trans. Knowl. Data Eng. **33**(4), 1479–1489 (2021). https://doi.org/10.1109/TKDE.2019.2947676
8. Mirsky, Y., Doitshman, T., Elovici, Y., Shabtai, A.: Kitsune: an ensemble of autoencoders for online network intrusion detection (2018). https://arxiv.org/abs/1802.09089

9. Schlegl, T., Seeböck, P., Waldstein, S.M., Schmidt-Erfurth, U., Langs, G.: Unsupervised anomaly detection with generative adversarial networks to guide marker discovery (2017). https://arxiv.org/abs/1703.05921
10. Srivastava, A., Kundu, A., Sural, S., Majumdar, A.: Credit card fraud detection using hidden Markov model. IEEE Trans. Dependable Secure Comput. **5**(1), 37–48 (2008). https://doi.org/10.1109/TDSC.2007.70228
11. Tan, S.C., Ting, K.M., Liu, T.F.: Fast anomaly detection for streaming data. In: Proceedings of the Twenty-Second International Joint Conference on Artificial Intelligence, IJCAI 2011, vol. 2, pp. 1511–1516. AAAI Press (2011)
12. Yuan, Y., Huang, Y., Yuan, Y., Wang, J.: Adaptive nad: online and self-adaptive unsupervised network anomaly detector (2025). https://arxiv.org/abs/2410.22967
13. Zhang, P., et al.: Real-time malicious traffic detection with online isolation forest over SD-wan. IEEE Trans. Inf. Forensics Secur. **18**, 2076–2090 (2023). https://doi.org/10.1109/TIFS.2023.3262121

Loss Functions for Time Series Forecasting in Network Security Situation Awareness

Richard Staňa[⊙], Pavol Sokol[✉][⊙], and Jakub Nižník

Institute of Computer Science, Faculty of Science, Pavol Jozef Šafárik University
in Košice, Jesenná 5, 040 01 Košice, Slovakia
{richard.stana,pavol.sokol,jakub.niznik}@upjs.sk,
https://ics.science.upjs.sk/en/

Abstract. The choice of loss function is a critical factor in machine learning, particularly when training neural networks, as it directly influences model convergence, generalization, and forecasting performance. In this paper, we conduct a comprehensive comparison of 20 existing regression-based loss functions in the context of training Long Short-Term Memory (LSTM) neural networks for time series forecasting. In addition, this paper introduces a novel loss function, Angle Loss, designed in the context of Network Security Situational Awareness (NSSA) forecasting. The experimental evaluation is based on real-world time series data representing cybersecurity alerts collected by the Warden system. The performance of each loss function is assessed using standard forecasting accuracy metrics, including Mean Absolute Error (MAE*) and Mean Absolute Scaled Error (MASE*), and visualized through box plots to highlight robustness and variability. The results provide insights into the impact of loss function choice on predictive performance and inform future applications of neural networks in NSSA forecasting.

Keywords: Loss function · LSTM · Time series · NSSA · Cybersecurity

1 Introduction

Over the past several years, a clear trend has emerged, shifting from reactive incident response to proactive cybersecurity strategies. In this context, it is essential to consider an organization's Cyber Situational Awareness (CSA), which can be defined as the perception of elements in the cyber environment in time and space (perception level), the comprehension of their meaning (comprehension level), and the projection of their future status (projection level) [3].

A crucial aspect of the current perspective on cybersecurity is the projection of future states, which represents the third and highest level of CSA. Predictive analysis methods play a key role in anticipating specific security incidents, forecasting the next steps of attackers, or predicting the overall security situation of an organization. In this regard, three main approaches to predictive methods in cybersecurity are commonly recognized: attack projection, attack prediction, and security situation forecasting [7].

In this paper, we focus on forecasting one specific part of CSA—Network Security Situational Awareness (NSSA) forecasting [3]. Rather than targeting ongoing attacks or specific intrusion events, our goal is to assess the holistic state of an information system, network, or even the entire organization's security.

NSSA can be analyzed using time series analysis, which captures current attack volumes, event frequencies, or other relevant indicators. However, the complex and temporal nature of network traffic and security logs presents a significant challenge for accurate forecasting. To address this, we employ neural network - Long Short-Term Memory (LSTM). An essential component of these models is the loss function [6], which governs the learning process, guides optimization, and directly affects model convergence, generalization ability, and predictive performance.

The choice of an appropriate loss function is thus critical. The authors in [18] note that loss functions are often not studied as rigorously as other training parameters, resulting in inconsistencies in model performance evaluation. Given the noisy and imbalanced nature of NSSA-related data, selecting the proper loss function is even more crucial, as different functions may yield significantly different results in terms of accuracy and robustness. Since we use the MAE* and MASE* metrics for evaluating the results, which are also used as loss functions, we decided to highlight this difference by adding an asterisk to the metrics - MAE, MASE represent loss functions, and MAE*, MASE* represent metrics.

Most existing time series forecasting research relies on the Mean Squared Error (MSE), Mean Absolute Error (MAE), or Huber [11] as loss functions. This paper aims to explore alternative existing loss functions to identify the most appropriate ones for NSSA forecasting. To summarize the problems outlined above, we emphasize the following research questions:

1. To describe and analyze a new loss function (Angle Loss) in the context of NSSA forecasting,
2. To compare the performance of various loss functions in combination with LSTM neural networks in the context of NSSA forecasting.

To address these research questions, we focus on the role of loss functions in time series forecasting within the context of the NSSA. This work builds upon prior research on time series analysis [21], where NSSA forecasting was explored using neural networks and three different loss functions.

Recent advancements in machine learning have highlighted neural networks as promising tools for NSSA forecasting [7]. Among them, Long Short-Term Memory (LSTM) networks stand out due to their ability to capture long-term dependencies in sequential data. This makes them especially well-suited for modeling complex patterns typical in cybersecurity datasets, which often exhibit non-linear and temporally dependent behaviors. This study explicitly investigates the application of LSTM networks for NSSA forecasting.

Our primary contribution lies in the analysis of loss functions, a crucial component of LSTM neural networks. Unlike other research papers, this paper focuses on NSSA forecasting. Additionally, the paper proposes a new loss function with the potential to serve as a suitable complement to existing loss functions.

This paper is structured into six sections. Following the introduction, Sect. 2 provides an overview of existing research focused on loss functions for time series forecasting. Based on insights from related literature, Sect. 3 presents the proposed methodology, the dataset used, the compared loss functions, and the newly introduced Angle Loss function. Section 4 describes the experimental evaluation framework. The results, their interpretation, and implications are discussed in Sect. 5. Finally, Sect. 6 provides the conclusions and outlines potential directions for future research and improvements.

2 Related Works

Since the main objective of this paper is to compare various loss functions in the domain of NSSA forecasting, we identified several related studies [6,10,11,18,22,23] that focus on evaluating well-established loss functions used in time series forecasting. Research groups have investigated the mathematical foundations of loss functions, analyzed their performance across different datasets and application domains, and identified their strengths and weaknesses depending on the nature of the data and the model architecture.

The above-mentioned studies confirm that the choice of loss function is a critical aspect of many machine learning models, particularly in deep neural networks. However, there is no universal loss function that is suitable for all types of data or complex objectives, such as time-series forecasting. The appropriate selection of a loss function depends on multiple factors, including the presence of outliers, data skewness, and specific model and performance requirements. In our paper, we focus specifically on the area of NSSA forecasting.

The second group of research papers related to this work consists of studies focused on designing custom loss functions [11,14–17,24]. These functions can be developed to improve forecasting performance by reducing computational complexity and training time [11]. The authors of the mentioned papers introduce novel loss functions that explicitly incorporate terms for shape and temporal distortion [15], enable models to better capture the overall shape of time-series sequences [16], account for both distortions and temporal trends [17], reduce overfitting to outliers by leveraging the properties of the arctangent function [24], or enhance structural alignment by comparing time-series data at the patch level [14].

3 Methodology

3.1 Dataset

The dataset used in this research was created from data we used in our previous research [20,21]. Although it is an older dataset, it remains a suitable resource for research purposes in the field of NSSA, encompassing various aspects essential for forecasting in this area. As source data, we used the Warden system [13]. This system collects, stores, and shares detected cybersecurity events in networks. The sources of security events include intrusion detection systems (IDS), honeypots, and third-party sources, among others. Events are stored in IDEA format [12], which stores data in a JSON-like file with some mandatory keys (form, ID, detect time, category). The source data are the same as those in the previous research; however, we identified a minor error in the processing timestamps. We repaired it and created a 20-time series based on various criteria, selecting sensors from the Warden system. However, for this paper, we chose only one time series based on the criterion Port 445 (alerts related to services running on port 445/TCP). In the paper [20], we analyzed the suitability of the time series created from the Warden system for NSSA purposes. It turned out that there are three groups, with one group of time series being suitable for NSSA forecasting. The time series representing port 445 is representative of this group. This time series has a 30-minute period and contains data from 2017-12-13 at 00:00 to 2018-12-09 at 16:30 (17,362 values). The 30-minute period was chosen based on the analysis in [19]. Every value represents the number of cybersecurity events that occurred within a 30-minute period (for example, at 2018-12-09 15:30, the value is 12068, indicating that between 15:30:00 and 15:59:59, 12068 events occurred). There are missing (NaN) values between 2018-10-31 at 00:00 and 2018-10-31 at 23:30 (48 values). Additionally, after visual analysis of the dataset, we set values lower than 50 (the 25th percentile of the dataset is 3455.25) to NaN because they were close to zero (20 values).

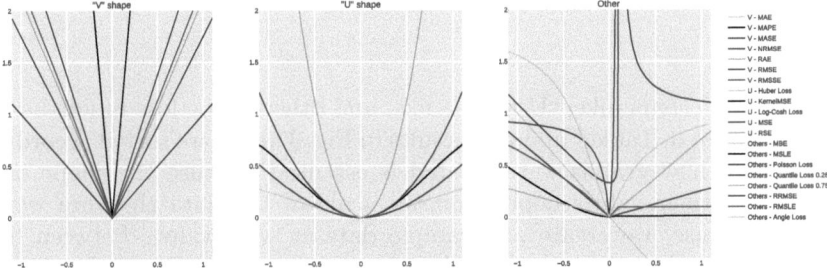

Fig. 1. Graphical comparison of loss functions. In this example, in the case of "V" shape, the MAE and RMSE have the same graph. (Color figure online)

3.2 Loss Functions

The primary purpose of this work is to validate the influence of different loss functions on neural network training. We use a combination of the LSTM network with different parameters (explained in Sect. 4) and 20 loss functions. The choice of loss functions was influenced by the survey [10]. They described 14 well-known regression loss functions and tested them on four datasets. We take these loss functions and also add other loss functions. All used loss functions with their sources are in Table 1.

Most of the described loss functions are not typically used as loss functions for forecasting tasks, but rather as metrics for comparing results. We provide a graph in Fig. 1 for a better picture of each loss function. For a better graphical comparison, we divided the used loss functions into three categories based on

Table 1. Loss functions used in this research.

Loss function	Shape	Definition	Source
Mean Absolute Error (MAE)	V	1	[10]
Mean Absolute Percentage Error (MAPE)	V	2	[10]
Mean Absolute Scaled Error (MASE)	V	3	[9]
Normalized Root Mean Squared Error (NRMSE)	V	4	[10]
Relative Absolute Error (RAE)	V	5	[10]
Root Mean Squared Error (RMSE)	V	6	[10]
Root Mean Squared Scaled Error (RMSSE)	V	18	[8]
Huber Loss	U	8	[10]
Kernel Mean Squared Error (KernelMSE) Loss	U	9	[5]
Log-Cosh Loss	U	10	[10]
Mean Squared Error (MSE)	U	11	[10]
Relative Squared Error (RSE)	U	12	[10]
Mean Bias Error (MBE)	Other	13	[10]
Mean Squared Logarithmic Error (MSLE)	Other	14	[10]
Poisson Loss	Other	15	[1]
Quantile Loss	Other	16	[10]
Relative Root Mean Squared Error (RRMSE)	Other	7	[10]
Root Mean Squared Logarithmic Error (RMSLE)	Other	17	[10]
Angle Loss	Other	19, 20, 21, 22	our work

their shape: "V" shape-like, "U" shape-like, and other shape loss functions. This division is shown in Table 1 and also results in Fig. 3 and 4 are sorted accordingly.

Explaining how graphs were created is essential because the shape of loss functions and their values depend on the scale of the data they are working with. In this case, we create an example dataset with values between 0 and 100 and take the last value (10) as the actual value. Then, we create an array containing all integer values between -100 and 120, which will serve as predicted values. The dataset and predicted values were normalized to the range of 0 to 1. This way, we plot the error between the predicted and actual values on the x-axis. On the y-axis, we plot the calculated loss value between the actual value and every predicted value from the created array.

We will mathematically define the loss functions as they were used in our research or as used in computing through batch processing. We will not go through the descriptions, pros, and cons of every loss function, as this information can be easily found in the provided literature. To save space, the equations are in two-column style, and we introduce recurring symbols in equations from 1 to 22: y is the real value, $\hat{y}$ is the predicted value, N is batch size.

"V" shape-like loss functions:

$$\text{MAE} = \frac{1}{N} \sum_{i=1}^{N} |y_i - \hat{y}_i| \qquad (1)$$

$$\text{MAPE} = \frac{1}{N} \sum_{i=1}^{N} \left| \frac{y_i - \hat{y}_i}{y_i} \right|, \qquad (2)$$

we do not use the percentage representation (multiplying by 100) because it is only multiplying by a constant.

$$\text{MASE} = \frac{\text{MAE}}{\bar{p}}, \quad (3)$$

where $\bar{p} = \frac{1}{n-1}\sum_{j=2}^{n}|y_j - y_{j-1}|$, where n is size of train part of the dataset.

$$\text{NRMSE} = \frac{\sqrt{\text{MSE}}}{\bar{o}}, \quad (4)$$

"U" shape like functions:

$$H = \frac{1}{N}\sum_{i=1}^{N}\begin{cases}\frac{1}{2}(y_i - \hat{y}_i)^2 \\ \text{if } |y_i - \hat{y}_i| < \delta, \\ \delta(|y_i - \hat{y}_i| - \frac{1}{2}\delta) \\ \text{if } otherwise\end{cases}, \quad (8)$$

where δ is a parameter that splits the function into linear and quadratic. In our experiments, we use half of the mean of the training part of the dataset as δ value.

$$\text{KernelMSE Loss} =$$
$$\sum_{i=1}^{N}\left(1 - \exp\left(-\frac{(y_i - \hat{y}_i)^2}{2\sigma^2}\right)\right), \quad (9)$$

Other loss functions:

$$\text{MBE} = \frac{1}{N}\sum_{i=1}^{N}(y_i - \hat{y}_i) \quad (13)$$

$$\text{MSLE} = \frac{1}{N}\sum_{i=1}^{N}(\log(1+y_i) - \quad (14)$$
$$\log(1+\hat{y}_i))^2$$

where $\bar{o}$ is the mean of the train part of the dataset.

$$\text{Poisson Loss} =$$
$$\frac{1}{N}\sum_{i=1}^{N}(\hat{y} - y + \log(\hat{y})) \quad (15)$$

$$\text{RAE} = \frac{\sum_{i=1}^{N}|y_i - \hat{y}_i|}{\sum_{i=1}^{N}|y_i - \bar{o}|}, \quad (5)$$

where $\bar{o}$ is the mean of the train part of the dataset.

$$\text{RMSE} = \sqrt{\text{MSE}} \quad (6)$$

$$\text{RRMSE} = \sqrt{\frac{\text{MSE}}{\frac{1}{N}\sum_{i=1}^{N}\hat{y}_i^2}} \quad (7)$$

where $\sigma = \frac{\sqrt{2}}{2}$.

$$\text{LogCosh Loss} =$$
$$\frac{1}{N}\sum_{i=1}^{N}(\log(\cosh(y_i - \hat{y}_i))) \quad (10)$$

$$\text{MSE} = \frac{1}{N}\sum_{i=1}^{N}(y_i - \hat{y}_i)^2 \quad (11)$$

$$\text{RSE} = \frac{\sum_{i=1}^{N}(y_i - \hat{y}_i)^2}{\sum_{i=1}^{N}(y_i - \bar{o})^2}, \quad (12)$$

where $\bar{o}$ is the mean of the train part of the dataset.

$$\text{Quantile Loss} = \sum_{i=1}^{N}\max(\quad (16)$$
$$(q-1)(y - \hat{y}), q(y - \hat{y})$$
$$),$$

where q is the required quantile.

$$\text{RMSLE} =$$
$$\sqrt{\frac{1}{N}\sum_{i=1}^{N}(\log(1+y_i) - \log(1+\hat{y}_i))^2} \quad (17)$$

$$\text{RMSSE} = \sqrt{\frac{\text{MSE}}{\bar{m}}}, \quad (18)$$

where $\bar{m}$ is $\frac{1}{n-1}\sum_{j=2}^{n}(y_j - y_{j-1})^2$, where n is size of train part of the dataset.

3.3 Angle Loss

Additionally, we have created a loss function named Angle loss. This loss function is inspired by the Cosine Similarity Loss, which is commonly used for comparing vectors where magnitude is unimportant. The idea is to measure the angle between the actual, previous, and predicted values. The Fig. 2, where angle α, shows explanations of angle loss function. The Angle Loss function is defined by Eqs. 19, 20, 21, and 22, where the symbols used are the same as in Fig. 2.

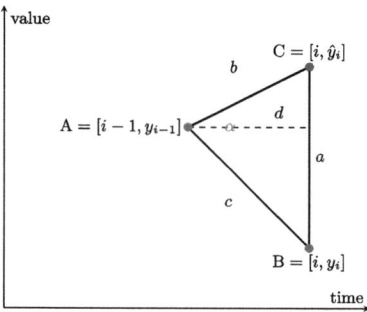

Fig. 2. Example plot for explaining Angle Loss. Blue points A and B are real values at time i and $i-1$, red point is the predicted value, d is the distance between time i and $i-1$, and α is the angle calculated in radians. (Color figure online)

$$a = |y_i - \hat{y}_i| \qquad (19)$$

$$b = \sqrt{d^2 + (\hat{y}_i - y_{i-1})^2} \qquad (20)$$

$$c = \sqrt{d^2 + (y_i - y_{i-1})^2} \qquad (21)$$

$$\text{Angle Loss} = \frac{1}{N} \sum_{i=1}^{N} (\arccos(\frac{b^2 + c^2 - a}{2bc})) \qquad (22)$$

We created this loss function with the idea of penalizing the neural network for making naive predictions (outputting the last value as a prediction), which is often observed in practice. As can be seen in Fig. 2, the angle α is big because the prediction point is close to the previous value. The angle size will be lower if the predicted value is closer to the real value. It will also be lower (in case described in Fig. 2) if the predicted value is greater by a than the real one.

This loss function depends significantly on the scale of the data, or more precisely, of the d parameter in Fig. 2 and the Eqs. 20 and 21. If we set this parameter to a high value, the angle will be low even if the absolute error is high, and vice versa. In our experiments, we set the value parameter d to the mean absolute error of naive prediction on the train part of the (scaled) dataset. So $d = \bar{p}$ where $\bar{p}$ is defined in MASE Loss in Eq. 3.

4 Experiment Evaluation

In this research, we focus solely on one-step-ahead forecasting. The dataset described in the previous section was stored in a Pandas Dataframe object. In this Dataframe, we add 384 columns with time lags ranging from 1 to 384. It means that we use the last eight days for forecasting one value 30 min into the future. The visual analysis reveals seasonal patterns in the dataset, but we did not account for them; instead, we allowed the neural network to discover and learn features independently. Point 2018-11-21 21:30 was chosen to create the train and test parts of the dataset. After removing rows that contain NaN values, we were left with 14,183 samples in the training set and 856 samples in the testing set. Before training, the dataset was normalized using a min-max scaler to normalize the values to a range of 0 to 1.

We chose an LSTM network for our experiments, and all network variants were trained using the Optuna framework [2]. The networks were trained in two stages. In the first stage, we choose 108 sets of parameters for training. Table 2 describes the chosen parameters in detail. These parameters were manually added to the Optuna study as enqueued trials and were set not to be pruned. In the second stage, we allowed the Optuna framework to choose parameters for 92 additional trials. The range of possible parameters for Optuna to choose is also described in Table 2. 4,000 LSTM networks were trained with different parameters, using 200 networks for each of 20 loss functions (Quantile Loss was used with parameter $q = 0.25$ and $q = 0.75$ in Eq. 16). Every network was trained for 200 epochs. During training, we employ techniques such as automatic pruning of non-promising trials using the Optuna framework, learning rate scheduling to reduce the learning rate, and early stopping of training if metrics do not improve over 30 consecutive epochs. The training process was documented using the Weights & Biases platform [4], making it easier to evaluate the results. Two commonly used metrics, MAE* and MASE*, were employed for evaluating forecast accuracy. LSTM networks were implemented in Python 3.11, using the PyTorch 2.6 library, and the Adam optimizer was chosen. We implemented 16 loss functions ourselves. The standard implementation from PyTorch was used for MAE, MSE, and Huber Loss.

5 Results and Discussion

We evaluated the results based on the best MAE* and MASE* metric values compared to naive forecasting, as well as the distribution of all MAE* metrics across all 200 training sessions for each loss function. The best results from every loss function compared to the naive forecast can be seen in Table 3. These values do not provide sufficient explanatory value because the values from 857.65 (1) to 888.38 (1.04) are not significantly different. Box plots of the results from every trained network provide a clearer view of the results and help categorize the loss function according to usability. Figure 3 shows box plots for every loss function. Each box plot was created from 200 MAE* values obtained by calculating MAE*

Table 2. Parameters used for training. In the first part, all possible combinations of the provided parameters were explored (108 combinations). In the second part, the Optuna framework chooses parameters from the provided integer ranges in the first three rows. In the case of shuffle batches (temporal continuity has been preserved), Optuna chose between True and False. In the last two lines, the chosen parameters were continuous values from the provided intervals.

Parameter	First part	Second part
Batch size	4, 16, 64	(4, 256)
Hidden size	128, 256	(4, 1024)
Stacked layers	1, 2, 4	(1, 8)
Shuffle batches	True	{True, False}
Dropout	0, 0.25	(0, 0.5)
Learning rate	5e−4, 1e−3, 5e−3	(1e−6, 1e−1)

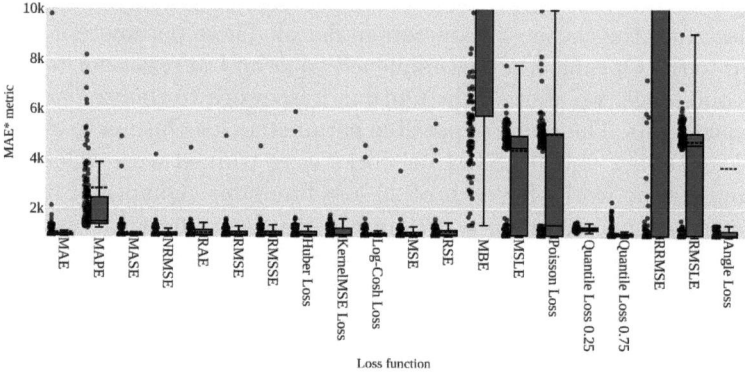

Fig. 3. Box plots MAE* values from predictions of every trained network. The actual distribution of loss values is shown on the left side of each box plot.

metrics for every trained LSTM network with its corresponding loss function. Due to some MAE* values from MBE Loss exceeding one million, for better clarity, we have cropped Fig. 3 to 10,000 on the y-axis. We divided loss functions into three categories: **unsuitable**, **suitable**, and **most suitable** for training an LSTM network for the forecasting task. According to Fig. 3, we will categorize the loss functions MAPE, MBE, MSLE, Poisson Loss, RRMSE, and RMSLE as **unsuitable**. Although these loss functions sometimes produce acceptable results, their performance is inconsistent and varies significantly across training runs. Consequently, their use is not recommended.

For a better view of other loss functions, we create Fig. 4. In this figure, we removed unsuitable loss functions from the previous paragraph and excluded MAE* metric values greater than 1600 from all remaining loss functions, assuming they are statistically insignificant outliers. This removed the following numbers of values for individual loss functions from Fig. 4 (values or their description

Table 3. Comparison of best results from each loss function and the naive forecast.

Loss function	MAE*	MASE*
MAE	857.65	1.00
RAE	859.16	1.00
RMSSE	862.84	1.01
MSE	865.76	1.01
KernelMSE Loss	865.85	1.01
RRMSE	867.98	1.01
MASE	868.14	1.01
RMSE	869.01	1.01
Angle Loss	869.36	1.01
Poisson Loss	872.36	1.02
RMSLE	873.97	1.02
Quantile Loss 0.75	876.00	1.02
NRMSE	880.71	1.03
Huber Loss	882.68	1.03
Log-Cosh Loss	885.20	1.03
MSLE	888.33	1.04
RSE	888.38	1.04
Quantile Loss 0.25	1052.03	1.23
MAPE	1219.19	1.42
MBE	1345.43	1.57
Naive forecasting	1647.66	1.92

are in the brackets): Huber Loss - 3 (1639.92, 5094.84, 5877.17), KernelMSE Loss - 13 (between 1652.78 and 479,686.1), Log-Cosh Loss - 3 (1603.8, 4072.96, 4544.69), MAE - 3 (1703.15, 2108.11, 9784.73), MASE - 2 (3670.24, 4874.77), MSE - 1 (3526.3), NRMSE - 1 (4166.36), Quantile Loss 0.25 - 0, Quantile Loss 0.75 - 14 (between 1617.53 and 2286.26), RSE - 3 (3959, 4375.12, 5421.43), RAE - 1 (4439.14), RMSE - 1 (4910.68), RMSSE - 1 (4507.31), and Angle Loss - 2 (178,337.88, 355,750.51).

In Fig. 4, we can see that both Quantile Losses will also be classified as **unsuitable**. Quantile Loss 0.25 due to poor MAE* metrics across all trained neural networks. In the case of a Quantile Loss of 0.75, only two trained neural networks achieved an MAE* metric value smaller than 900. Also, 14 values between 1617.53 and 2286.26 are not shown in Fig. 4 as described in the previous paragraph. Results from Quantile Losses are interesting because in review [10] Quantile Loss achieved very good results. This review described Quantile loss as a suitable choice when generating interval predictions rather than point estimates. However, in our case, we are focusing on point forecasting, and it appears that

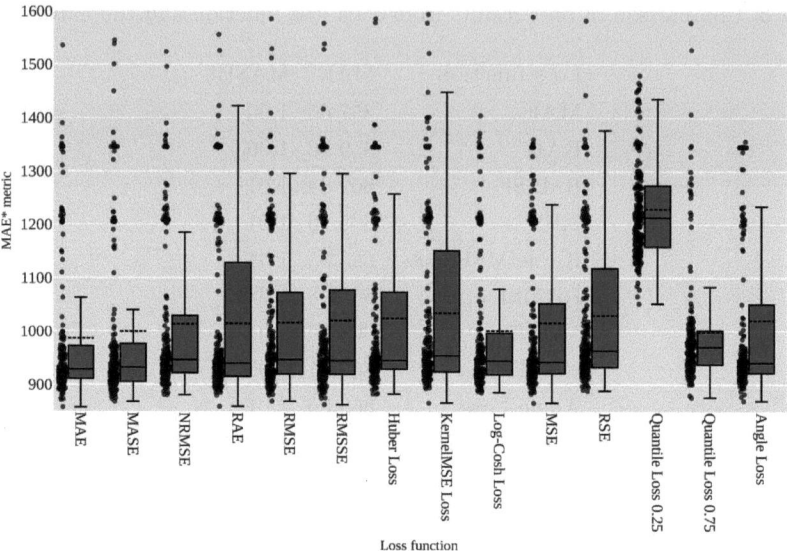

Fig. 4. Box plots MAE* values from predictions of trained networks. The actual distribution of loss values is shown on the left side of each box plot.

the parameter q from equations 16 may depend on the dataset or may be an interesting training parameter for future research.

The following loss functions fall into the category of **suitable**: Huber Loss, KernelMSE Loss, Log-Cosh Loss, MSE, NRMSE, RSE, RAE, RMSE, RMSSE, and Angle Loss. All these functions achieve similar results. From the box plots in Fig. 4, we can see that they have similar means (about 1018) and medians (about 943) for the MAE* metric. KernelMSE Loss and RSE Loss functions are at the upper fence of this category because their mean, median, and best results (except for one point at approximately 865 MAE* in KernelMSE Loss) are somewhat poorer than those of other loss functions in this category. The KernelMSE loss function even yields 11 results with MAE* exceeding 70,000.

The category **most suitable** contains MAE and MASE loss functions. These two were chosen based on the lowest statistical parameters (q1, q3, mean, and median) in Fig. 3, low best metric values (the lowest from all in the case of MAE Loss), and overall, the most stable results, as indicated by the distributions of results in Fig. 3. The resemblance of the results of the two loss functions lies in the similarity of their mathematical expressions. Both the MAE Eq. 1 and the MASE Eq. 3 are essentially the same. MASE can be interpreted as the MAE adjusted by a constant that depends on the training data.

In Fig. 3, we can find two interesting vertical lines. The first is around the MAE* metrics at approximately 1345, and the second is at about 1210. It appears that in training, neural networks tend to fall into local minima regardless of the loss function used.

For further analysis and tests, code examples and all results can be found on the GitHub repository: https://github.com/Kr1zA/loss_comparison.

6 Conclusion and Future Works

From a practical perspective, our experiments suggest that the MAE loss function remains a favorable choice for training LSTM networks in the task of NSSA forecasting. This is mainly due to its reliable performance, ease of implementation, and lower computational complexity compared to more complex metrics. The results suggest that the analyzed loss functions can be categorized into three groups, as described in Sect. 5. The results in the paper were analyzed on a single time series, the characteristics of which were suitable for NSSA forecasting [20]. The presented results provide a suitable basis for further analysis and research. To generalize the results, it would be appropriate to analyze loss functions from the perspective of other time series within NSSA forecasting as well.

Additionally, we proposed a novel loss function, Angle Loss. Our results demonstrate that Angle Loss achieves results comparable to established loss functions, highlighting its potential as an alternative approach in this area. However, the broader applicability of Angle Loss extends beyond the scope of our current experiments. Further research is necessary to analyze the strengths and limitations of Angle Loss. Specifically, future work should evaluate Angle Loss on datasets from various fields, investigate the characteristics of time series data, such as volatility, seasonality, and noise levels, that influence the effectiveness of Angle Loss, compare Angle Loss with other loss functions under different forecasting scenarios, including long-term forecasting, and multi-step forecasting, or even try combinations of loss functions with Angle Loss. It can also be helpful to provide an alternative perspective on forecast accuracy, for example, by utilizing statistical tests such as the Diebold-Mariano test or other relevant techniques.

Acknowledgements. This research was supported by the Slovak Recovery and Resilience Plan, funded by the European Union – NextGenerationEU, under the project "Competence Center for Cybersecurity at Pavol Jozef Šafárik University in Košice", project code: 17R05-04-V01-00007.

References

1. Tensorflow keras poisson loss. https://www.tensorflow.org/api_docs/python/tf/keras/losses/Poisson. Accessed 17 May 2025
2. Akiba, T., Sano, S., Yanase, T., Ohta, T., Koyama, M.: Optuna: a next-generation hyperparameter optimization framework. In: Proceedings of the 25th ACM SIGKDD International Conference on Knowledge Discovery and Data Mining (2019)
3. Bass, T.: Intrusion detection systems and multisensor data fusion. Commun. ACM **43**(4), 99–105 (2000)

4. Biewald, L.: Experiment tracking with weights and biases (2020). https://www.wandb.com/, software available from wandb.com
5. Bommidi, B.S., Teeparthi, K., Kosana, V.: Hybrid wind speed forecasting using iceemdan and transformer model with novel loss function. Energy **265**, 126383 (2023)
6. Elharrouss, O., et al.: Loss functions in deep learning: a comprehensive review. arXiv preprint arXiv:2504.04242 (2025)
7. Husák, M., Bartoš, V., Sokol, P., Gajdoš, A.: Predictive methods in cyber defense: current experience and research challenges. Futur. Gener. Comput. Syst. **115**, 517–530 (2021)
8. Hyndman, R.J., Athanasopoulos, G.: Forecasting: principles and practice. OTexts, Melbourne, Australia, 3rd edn. (2021). https://otexts.com/fpp3. Accessed 20 May 2025
9. Hyndman, R.J., Koehler, A.B.: Another look at measures of forecast accuracy. Int. J. Forecast. **22**(4), 679–688 (2006)
10. Jadon, A., Patil, A., Jadon, S.: A comprehensive survey of regression-based loss functions for time series forecasting. In: International Conference on Data Management, Analytics & Innovation, pp. 117–147. Springer, Cham (2024)
11. Jaiswal, R., Singh, B.: A comparative study of loss functions for deep neural networks in time series analysis. In: International Conference on Big Data, Machine Learning, and Applications, pp. 147–163. Springer, Singapore (2021)
12. Kácha, P.: Idea: security event taxonomy mapping. In: 18th International Conference on Circuits, Systems, Communications and Computers, pp. 17–21 (2014)
13. Kacha, P., Kostenec, M., Kropacova, A.: Warden 3: security event exchange redesign. In: 19th International Conference on Computers: Recent Advances in Computer Science (2015)
14. Kudrat, D., Xie, Z., Sun, Y., Jia, T., Hu, Q.: Patch-wise structural loss for time series forecasting. arXiv preprint arXiv:2503.00877 (2025)
15. Le Guen, V., Thome, N.: Shape and time distortion loss for training deep time series forecasting models. In: Advances in Neural Information Processing Systems, pp. 4189–4201 (2019)
16. Lee, H., Lee, C., Lim, H., Ko, S.: Tilde-q: a transformation invariant loss function for time-series forecasting. arXiv preprint arXiv:2210.15050 (2022)
17. Liao, H., Hu, Y., Yuan, L.: Time series forecasting with trend loss function (2024), available at SSRN 4960118
18. Malhathkar, S., Thenmozhi, S.: Deep learning for time series forecasting – with a focus on loss functions and error measures. In: 2022 IEEE World Conference on Applied Intelligence and Computing (AIC), pp. 646–651. IEEE (2022)
19. Pekarčík, P., Gajdoš, A., Sokol, P.: Forecasting security alerts based on time series. In: International Conference on Hybrid Artificial Intelligence Systems, pp. 546–557. Springer, Cham (2020)
20. Sokol, P., Staňa, R., Gajdoš, A., Pekarčík, P.: Network security situation awareness forecasting based on statistical approach and neural networks. Logic J. IGPL **31**(2), 352–374 (2023)
21. Staňa, R., Pekarčík, P., Gajdoš, A., Sokol, P.: Network security situation awareness forecasting based on neural networks. In: International Conference on Time Series and Forecasting, pp. 255–270. Springer, Cham (2021)
22. Terven, J., Cordova-Esparza, D.M., Romero-González, J.A., Ramírez-Pedraza, A., Chávez-Urbiola, E.A.: A comprehensive survey of loss functions and metrics in deep learning. Artif. Intell. Rev. **58**(7), 195 (2025)

23. Wang, Q., Ma, Y., Zhao, K., Tian, Y.: A comprehensive survey of loss functions in machine learning. Ann. Data Sci. **9**(2), 187–212 (2022)
24. Zhang, Y., Zhou, X., Zhang, Y., Li, S., Liu, S.: Improving time series forecasting in frequency domain using a multi resolution dual branch mixer with noise insensitive arctanloss. Sci. Rep. **15**(1), 12557 (2025)

A Hybrid Feature Selection Approach Using Filter-Wrapped Evaluation (FWE) for Attack Detection in SDN

Chin Jia Wen and Tan Saw Chin[✉]

Faculty of Computing and Informatics, Multimedia University, Cyberjaya, Malaysia
Sctan1@mmu.edu.my

Abstract. Software-Defined Networking (SDN), with its centralized control architecture, enhances network management flexibility but remains vulnerable to Distributed Denial of Service (DDoS) attacks, which can disrupt communication between the application and data planes. Effective attack detection is therefore essential. Feature Selection (FS) plays a vital role in improving intrusion detection systems by reducing computational overhead while maintaining high accuracy. This article proposes a hybrid FS method, Filter-Wrapped Evaluation (FWE), which combines Pearson Correlation and Recursive Feature Elimination (RFE) using XGBoost to improve DDoS detection in SDN environments. The proposed FWE method enhances detection performance by selecting the most relevant features and eliminating redundancy, thereby boosting accuracy and reducing processing time. Experimental evaluations on four benchmark datasets demonstrate that using the remaining features, FWE achieved 99.99% accuracy on CICIDS2017 and 100% accuracy on CICIoT2023 when paired with Decision Tree and Random Forest classifiers. When reduced to the top 10 selected features, FWE maintained high performance, achieving 99.99% accuracy on the APA-DDoS dataset with significantly lower execution time as low as 0.0871 s with Decision Tree. These results confirm FWE's effectiveness in balancing detection accuracy with real-time efficiency. Future work will focus on optimizing feature thresholds and evaluating performance with deep learning models.

Keywords: Software-defined Network (SDN) · Distributed Denial of Service (DDoS) · Feature Selection (FS) · Data diversity

1 Introduction

Software-Defined Networking (SDN) is one of the most significant network paradigms, offering a more flexible and efficient design compared to traditional networking [1]. SDN architecture is structured into three layers: the infrastructure layer, which contains physical switches; the application layer, which holds network applications and programs; and the control plane, which serves as a centralized layer to facilitate communication between the application and infrastructure layers [1]. This centralized control simplifies network administration and enhances performance in large-scale, high-speed computing systems. However, the decoupling of the control plane also introduces security vulnerabilities, particularly the risk of Distributed Denial of Service (DDoS) attacks. DDoS attacks pose a significant threat to SDN security, especially targeting the control plane, which is the core of the SDN network [2]. Attackers can exploit this vulnerability to hinder or take control of the entire network, leading to severe disruptions and financial losses. According to the Cloudflare Radar DDoS attack report in 2024 [3], the number of DDoS attacks has increased drastically, reaching 6.9 million requests per second (rps), which represent that 16% increase quarter-over-quarter and 83% year-over-year. This alarming rise highlights the necessity for advanced security mechanisms to mitigate such threats effectively.

One of the primary countermeasures against DDoS attacks in SDN is the use of Intrusion Detection Systems (IDS). IDS monitors network traffic to detect and prevent malicious activities. Many researchers have applied Feature Selection (FS) techniques to IDS to enhance detection accuracy and efficiency [4–6]. FS is a machine learning method that eliminates irrelevant or redundant features, reducing dataset dimensionality while preserving essential features for classification. However, traditional FS methods have certain limitations. Filter-based FS methods do not account for the correlation between features and classifiers, while wrapper-based FS methods iteratively evaluate feature subsets, potentially overlooking important features in the early stages [7, 8]. These limitations affect IDS performance in detecting DDoS attacks. To address these challenges, this research proposes a hybrid FS method called Filter-Wrapped Evaluation (FWE). This method leverages the efficiency of filter-based techniques and the classifier correlation consideration of wrapper-based approaches to enhance IDS performance. The proposed FWE method improves computational efficiency and optimize detection accuracy. Furthermore, data diversity plays a crucial role in machine learning model effectiveness. Studies have shown that model performance depends significantly on dataset diversity and size. Therefore, this research also investigates the impact of data diversity on IDS performance by evaluating different feature subsets across multiple datasets.

The contribution of this research are as follows:

1. Propose a Filter-Wrapped Evaluation (FWE) method for Feature Selection to enhance IDS performance by improving the detection speed and efficiency of DDoS attacks.
2. Investigate the impact of data diversity on IDS performance by evaluating how different feature subsets influence classification accuracy across multiple datasets. From the result, it is showing that FWE improves classification accuracy across datasets.
3. Results shows that FWE able to reduce the computational time compared with the results of remaining features and top 10 features while maintaining the accuracy and scalability among 4 datasets.

The remainder of this paper is organized as follows: Sect. 2 discusses related work on SDN attack detection and FS methods. Section 3 explains the proposed FWE feature selection scheme. Section 4 presents the experimental results and compares FWE with existing FS methods using performance metrics. Finally, Sect. 5 concludes the paper and discusses future research directions.

2 Related Works

In the current era of advanced networking, the detection of Distributed Denial of Service (DDoS) attacks in Software-Defined Networks (SDNs) presents a persistent challenge. SDNs, while enabling flexibility and centralized management, introduce vulnerabilities at the control plane—often exploited by attackers to disrupt communication between the data and application layers. As the scale and complexity of modern networks increase, conventional detection techniques struggle with real-time responsiveness, high false alarm rates, and scalability limitations, necessitating more efficient and accurate detection mechanisms. To address these challenges, various researchers have adopted machine learning (ML)-based intrusion detection systems (IDS) for DDoS attack detection. Dong et al. [9] proposed DDADA and DDAML—two detection algorithms built using improved KNN approaches. Their methods demonstrated enhanced detection rates; however, they lacked analysis regarding the computational cost and real-time feasibility in SDN environments. In a similar vein, Lei et al. [10] introduced TSMASAM, a hybrid ensemble model combining stacking and self-attention mechanisms, which significantly improved detection accuracy. Yet, the trade-off was increased detection time, making the solution less practical for low-latency networks. Tan et al. [11] addressed the need for timely detection through a DDoS trigger mechanism that dynamically reacts to abnormal flows in the network. While effective in reducing resource strain during attack detection, the model's performance decreased in large-scale traffic conditions, revealing its scalability limitations. Sangodoyin et al. [12] compared multiple classifiers—GNB, QDA, k-NN, and CART—and identified CART as the most effective for SDN-based flood attack detection. Nonetheless, the lack of hyperparameter optimization in the model design limited its full potential. Al-Dunainawi et al. [13] applied a 1D-Convolutional Neural Network (1D-CNN) to classify network traffic in SDNs and achieved superior results compared to traditional ML models like SVM and RF. However, their evaluation was conducted in simulated settings, which may not capture the complexities of real-world network environments.

In recent years, the integration of Feature Selection (FS) into ML-based IDS has been explored to improve classification performance while reducing computational overhead. Roopak et al. [14] applied a multi-objective optimization FS technique, which enhanced DDoS detection accuracy, yet the approach was tested on only one dataset, limiting its general application. Kim et al. [15] demonstrated that applying FS in multiclass ML classification in a 5G environment improved detection accuracy and reduced complexity, though their study's reliance on a single gNB setup compromised result generalization. Nadeem et al. [16] showed that Recursive Feature Elimination (RFE) using Random Forest enhanced performance, but the method consumed excessive resources and lost accuracy under high traffic loads. Other works have proposed diverse FS strategies. Alashhab et al. [17] introduced an ensemble-based classifier integrating SGD, EBM, and MLP for attack detection. Although performance gains were observed, the lack of computational time analysis left efficiency claims unsupported. Bouke et al. [18] enhanced the Gini index for FS within a decision-tree model, improving detection while reducing features, but similarly omitted processing time evaluations. Polat et al. [19] compared models trained on raw and FS-enhanced datasets, reporting accuracy improvements over 80% for FS models; however, only limited DDoS types were considered. Eldhai et al. [20]

used Boruta FS and stream classification for SDNs, improving performance but without handling class imbalance. Türkoğlu et al. [21] combined MRMR FS with Bayesian optimization for SD-VANETs but did not address runtime efficiency. Rahman et al. [22] evaluated ML algorithms like J48 and RF in small-server SDN setups, but their results may not translate to large-scale infrastructure due to hardware constraints.

In addition to traditional machine learning methods, deep learning (DL) models have been widely explored for DDoS detection in SDNs due to their ability to automatically extract hierarchical patterns from raw network data. Al-Dunainawi et al. [14] employed a 1D-Convolutional Neural Network (1D-CNN) and achieved superior accuracy compared4 to traditional ML models like SVM and RF. However, the model was only evaluated in a simulated SDN environment, raising concerns about generalizability to real-world traffic. Mehmood et al. [23] proposed an optimizer-equipped CNN-MLP architecture, which yielded 99.95% accuracy on CICDDoS2019 and InSDN datasets, demonstrating strong detection performance. Nonetheless, its heavy reliance on computational resources makes it unsuitable for real-time, low-latency SDN environments. Goud and Rao [24] introduced a CNN-GRU fusion model that enhanced the learning of both spatial and temporal features, but the added complexity increased computational overhead. Wang et al. [25] designed a hybrid DL model combining CNN, LSTM, and transformer components, which improved detection performance in realistic SDN scenarios, but again suffered from long training time and architectural complexity. Ataa et al. [26] also proposed a CNN-GRU-based architecture for real-time DDoS detection in SDNs, achieving high detection rates but with reduced scalability in resource-constrained systems.

In summary, while the literature presents numerous FS-based methods for improving SDN attack detection, key challenges remain. Many existing works do not justify FS hyperparameters such as correlation thresholds or number of selected features, nor do they conduct sensitivity analyses. Others neglect the computational cost or scalability across diverse datasets and ignore comparisons with modern baselines such as deep learning (DL) models. Furthermore, despite the known benefits of combining filter-based and wrapper-based FS methods, few studies implement such hybrids effectively. These limitations form the basis for our proposed approach, Filter-Wrapped Evaluation (FWE) which integrates Pearson Correlation and Recursive Feature Elimination using XGBoost. This hybrid strategy aims to strike a balance between computational efficiency and detection performance, selecting only the most relevant features while maintaining model generalizability across multiple benchmark datasets. Table 1 provided summary of DDoS detection methods in SDN while Table 2 provided summary of Feature Selection method in SDN. The comparison of deep learning models is presented in Table 3.

Table 1. Summary of DDoS Detection Methods in SDN

Reference	Method Proposed	Key Findings	Challenges
[9]	TSAMSAM (Ensemble Learning)	Captures correlation between features, improves integration effect	High time consumption
[10]	DDoS detection trigger mechanism	Effectively detects abnormal flows, saves SDN resources	Scalability issues under large-scale traffic
[11]	ML-based detection (GNB, QDA, k-NN, CART)	CART performed the best, all models showed good classification results	No application for hyperparameter tuning and optimization for CART and k-NN
[12]	FlowTrAPP (DDoS mitigation in data centers)	Outperformed OpenFlow-based QoS approach for DDoS mitigation	Effectiveness against other types of networks is undetermined
[13]	Optimized 1D-CNN	Outperformed ML models like Logistic Regression, RF, SVM, k-NN	Simulated environments may not capture real-world complexities such as diverse attack patterns, and dynamic network conditions

Table 2. Summary of Feature Selection Methods in SDN environments

References	FS Method	Classifier	Key Findings	Challenges
[14]	Multi-objective optimization-based FS	ELM classifier	Best feature selection performance for DDoS detection in IDS	Only evaluated on a single dataset
[15]	Feature selection applied in ML-based multiclass classification	DT, RF, k-NN	Improves detection performance and reduces time complexity	Only tested with only one gNB in 5G, which limits generalizability.

(*continued*)

Table 2. (*continued*)

References	FS Method	Classifier	Key Findings	Challenges
[16]	Filter method and Wrapper method Feature selection	SVM, k-NN, NB, RF, DT	RFE-based RF performs well in SDN for DDoS detection	Resource consumption increased and accuracy for large-scale traffic reduced
[17]	Enhanced Feature Selection method	SGD, EBM, MLP (Ensemble)	Improved model performance and computational efficiency	Computational time not addressed
[18]	Enhanced Gini index	Decision Tree (DT)	Outperforms baseline models in accuracy while reducing features	Did not address computational time
[19]	Specific feature extraction	SVM, k-NN, ANN, NB	FS improved model performance, which exceeded 80%	Only tested on ICMP, TCP, and UDP Flood, missing other DDoS attack types
[20]	Boruta Feature Selection	Voting and k-NN classifier	Improved classification accuracy and reduced complexity	Did not address imbalanced data streams
[21]	MRMR feature selection	k-NN, SVM, and DT	Demonstrates MRMR and Bayesian optimization effectiveness	Computational time not addressed
[22]	Address resolution protocol (ARP)	J48, SVM, k-NN, and Random Forest	J48 Performs best in SDN	Only tested on small server

3 Filter Wrapped Evaluation (FWE)

The section will be described the steps of the approach for detecting DDoS attacks in SDN with using the proposed Filter Wrapped Evaluation (FWE) feature selection in machine learning models as shown in Fig. 1. It consists of 3 parts: Data Collection, Cleaning and Preprocessing, FWE Feature Selection and Performance Metrics. The detail description of each part as below.

Table 3. Comparison of Deep Learning Models

Reference	Deep Learning Models	Key Findings	Challenges
[13]	Optimizer-equipped CNN-MLP	99.95% accuracy, effective feature learning	Requires GPU, high training time
[23]	1D-CNN	High accuracy over SVM/RF	Tested only in simulation
[24]	CNN-GRU Fusion	Captures spatial + temporal patterns	Computationally intensive
[25]	CNN-GRU Hybrid	Real-time capability, high accuracy	Limited scalability on low-resource systems
[26]	CNN + LSTM + Transformer	Improved generalization, high detection	Long training time, complex architecture

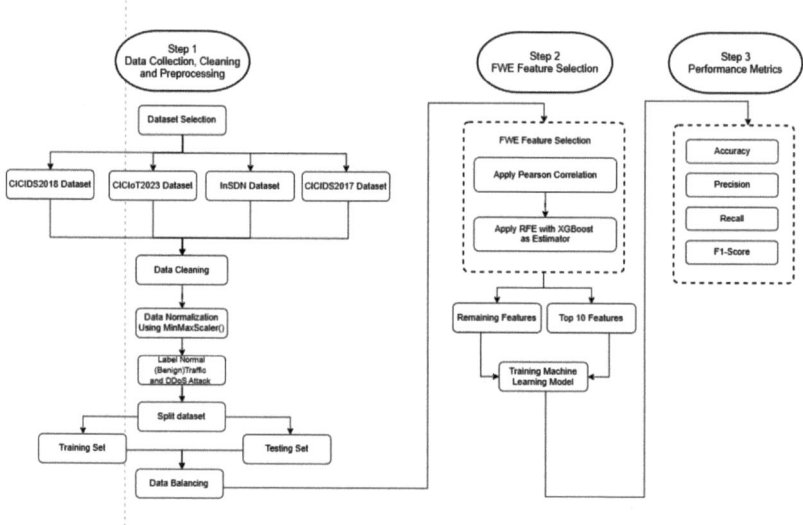

Fig. 1. Filter Wrapped Evaluation (FWE) Flow Diagram

3.1 Step 1 Data Collection, Cleaning and Preprocessing

The process will begin with data selection. These four datasets have been chosen as it contains DDoS attacks which are relevant for training and evaluating the IDS system in detecting DDoS attacks within SDN environment.

A. InSDN Dataset: InSDN dataset [27] was created by Elsayed, M. S. et al. [28] in 2020 to identify the attacks in SDN system. There are 3 csv files for the InSDN datasets with having total 343,889 data instances and 84 features per instance, which are normal_data.csv with having 68424 total number of instance records, OVS.csv with having 136743 total number of instance, and metasploitable-2.csv with having

138772 total number of instance. These datasets consist of many attacks' directories such as DoS, DDoS, Exploit, web attack, probe attack, and brute force. For the normal traffic, there are 68424 instances, while 275,465 instances belong to attack traffic, and there are 121,942 instances of DDoS attack traffic.

B. CICIDS2017: CICIDS2017 [29] was generated by Canadian Institute for Cybersecurity (CIC) in 2017 and details outlined by Sharafaldin, I. et al. [30] in 2018. It contains five days of network traffic starting from 9 a.m. Monday, July 3, 2017, and ended at 5 p.m. on Friday July 7, 2017. This dataset included the most common attacks such as Web based, Brute force, DoS, DDoS, Infiltration, Heart-bleed, Bot, and Scan. As the objective is to detect DDoS attacks, the only files which contain DDoS attacks which are on Friday, July 7, 2017. This dataset consists of 79 features per instance.

C. APA DDoS: The APA DDoS Dataset [31] comprises 151,201 entries and includes 23 features per record [32]. These features encompass various network traffic attributes such as source and destination IP addresses, TCP ports, protocol numbers, frame lengths, TCP flags (e.g., SYN, ACK, PSH), IP flags, TCP sequence and acknowledgment numbers, as well as aggregated metrics like packet and byte counts for each connection. Each record is labeled to indicate whether it represents benign traffic or a specific type of DDoS attack, including categories like DDoS-ACK and DDoS-PSH-ACK.

D. UNBCICIOT2023: The UNB-CIC IoT 2023 dataset [33] is developed by E. C. P. Neto et al. [34] and designed for intrusion detection in IoT networks. It includes a diverse set of attack scenarios targeting IoT devices, including DDoS, Botnet, and Infiltration attacks. This dataset provides up-to-date network traffic characteristics reflecting modern IoT security threats. Table 4 show for the characteristics of these 5 datasets.

Table 4. Summary of datasets

Dataset	Year	Total Instances	Features	Attack Types
InSDN	2020	343889	84	DoS, DDoS, Exploit, Web Attack, Probe Attack, Brute Force
CICIDS2017	2017	223082	78	Web-based, Brute Force, DoS, DDoS, Infiltration, Heartbleed, Bot, Scan
APA-DDoS	2020	151200	23	DDoS-PSH-ACK, DDOS-ACK
UNB-CIC-IoT2023	2023	238687	47	DDoS, Botnet, Infiltration

Firstly, data Cleaning will be applied to these datasets to ensure there are no missing values, duplicates value or infinite values which will affect the final results if the datasets did not clean. It followed by data normalization using min-max normalization technique, a method that scales the values of a feature to a range between 0 and 1. Normalize the data is important as it can ensures all the features are contributed equally in model's learning process. Then, each dataset will labelled Normal Traffic, which also called benign traffic as 0 and DDoS attack traffic will be labelled as 1. Subsequently, dataset splitting using train-test split procedure as it is used to estimate the performance of machine learning models with using training sets and predict on training sets. Finally, for each dataset, it will split into a 7:3 ratio, while 70% is used for training and the remaining 30% is used for model testing for prediction. For the datasets, it is required that data needs to be balanced. As data imbalance will lead to poor performance on the minority class which will affect the results 's accuracy. Therefore, Synthetic Minority Oversampling Technique (SMOTE) which is a statistical technique by increasing the number of minority classes in a balanced way as final step in the process.

3.2 Step 2 FWE Feature Selection

This paper presents a new FS method called FWE which is aimed at improving IDS detection effectiveness and saving computational time. For this FWE feature selection, it combines two feature selection methods, which is filter method with Pearson Correlation, and wrapper method with Recursive Feature Elimination (RFE) having XGBoost as estimator which can ensure the top 10 features are retained. These extracted features can improve model performance and help reduce the chances of overfitting. It will be useful working with datasets with having the number of features large or the complexity of the relationship between features and target variables. The first step in this FWE method is the application of Pearson Correlation to search for the relationship between each feature and the target variable. Pearson Correlation Coefficient, which usually denotes as r, is a measurement searching for the strength of the relationship between two variables. Pearson Correlation Coefficient will remove the features that are weakly correlated with the target. The following will show the steps for applying Pearson Correlation. Figure 2 shows for the first step which is apply Pearson Correlation.

Figure 2 showing the process of Correlation-Based Feature Selection with begins by combining the resampled training datasets, which includes the features, $X_{resampled}$ and the target variable $Y_{resampled}$ into a single dataset. The next steps is computing the correlation of each feature between the target variable to assess the strength of their relationship. Feature with a correlation magnitude exceeding with a predefined threshold ($t = 0.1$, chosen empirically) will be selected as relevant features. The dataset will be separated into two parts, which are $X_{selected}$, containing the chosen features, and $X_{remaining}$, containing less relevant features. The process ends with the extraction of selected features. The extracted features will be next applied to the Recursive Feature Elimination (RFE). RFE is being used as it needs to identify the most important features from the strongly correlated set and using XGBoost model as estimator. These are the steps for the extracted features applied to RFE as shown in Fig. 3.

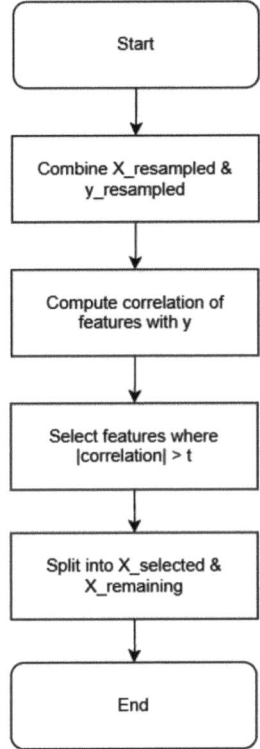

Fig. 2. Workflow for Correlation-Based Feature Filtering. This process begins by combining the resampled dataset (features and labels), computes the correlation of each feature with the target variable, selects features with correlation magnitude greater than a defined threshold ttt, and separates the selected from non-selected features.

Figure 3 showing another process of feature selection using Recursive Feature Elimination (RFE) with XGBoost as estimator. The process begins by initializing XGBoost classifier which serves as base model for evaluating feature importance. Next, RFE with XGboost will specify the desired number of features (num_features) to be selected. The RFE model is then fitted with selected feature set (X_selected) and the target variable, y iteratively removing the least important features until the optimal subset is obtained. Finally, the process extracts the final selected features, completed for the feature selection step.

3.3 Step 3 Performance Metrics

After using the training sets to train the model, the testing sets will be used to evaluate the performance of a classification model. In this paper, we will calculate the accuracy, precision, recall, f1-score [9].

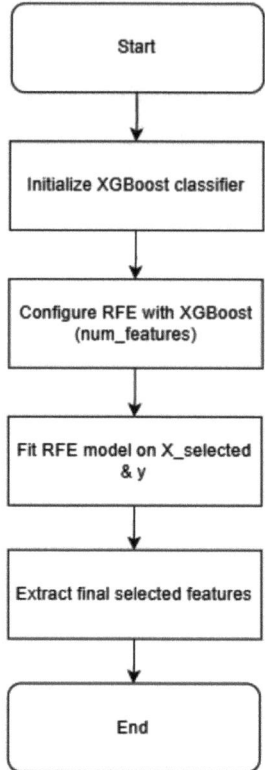

Fig. 3. Workflow for Recursive Feature Elimination (RFE) with XGBoost. This process initializes the XGBoost classifier, configures the RFE to retain a defined number of features, and iteratively removes the least important ones to extract the final feature subset.

4 Results and Discussion

The experimental setup and the environment play a crucial role in determining a reliable result. For this section, it will describe the details of the hardware, and the software used for this experiment. This article uses the Scikit-learn library which is included in the Python programming language to test the proposed FW method and evaluate the performance of the DDoS attack detection model. The hardware and software details will be shown in Table 5.

Table 5. Experimental Environment

Hardware and Software	Specification
Operating System	Windows 11 Version 23H2
Memory	24GB
CPU Processor	AMD Ryzen 7 6800H with Radeon Graphics 3.20 GHz
Ananconda Navigator	Version 2.6.3
Jupyter Lab	Version 4.2.5
Python	Version 3.12.7
Scikit Learn	Version 1.5.1

To comprehensively evaluate the performance of the proposed feature selection FWE, the experiment is tested under the following conditions:

1. Dataset Diversity & Model Generalization

    FWE is tested on four different datasets to analyze its effectiveness in handling diverse data distribution to ensure that the selected features are robust and contribute to better model generalization across various network traffic scenarios.

2. Feature Selection Conditions

    Two feature selection conditions are applied, which are top 10 features which being extracted from original features and remaining features which are not being selected. These conditions will help assess the trade-off between using a larger feature set versus a more compact, optimized subset for detection performance.

3. Detection Techniques

    After selecting the features, three machine learning models are used for attack detection, which are Random Forest (RF), Support Vector Machine (SVM) and Decision Tree (DT), these classifiers are chosen for their ability to effective handle high-dimensional data and the performance.

4. Feature Selection Comparison

    The results will be obtained from 3 machine learning models with using proposed Filter Wrapped Evaluation (FWE) method will also be compared with another 2 different feature selection methods, which are Random Forest and XGBoost. The comparison will provide insight into how different feature selection techniques will impact model accuracy, computational efficiency, and overall detection performance.

Table 6 shows the results of remaining features using proposed FWE compared to others FS approach under different detection approaches in various datasets.

For the InSDN dataset, Random Forest-DT and XGBoost-DT exhibit the best balance, achieving an accuracy of 99.9965% and 99.9947%, respectively, with near-perfect precision, recall, and F1-score. However, Random Forest-DT is the most efficient with an execution time of 0.7432 s, making it the optimal choice for speed and accuracy. For CICIDS2017, FWE-RF slightly outperforms other methods with an accuracy of 99.9982%, maintaining high precision, recall, and F1-score while being computationally efficient at 26.1575 s. However, if time is a concern, XGBoost-DT is a strong

Table 6. Results of remaining features using different FS methods on four datasets

FS Method	Model	InSDN					Features remaining
		Acc	Pre	Rec	F1	Time	
Random Forest	RF	99.9965	100.0000	99.9945	99.9973	6.8004	67
	SVM	99.9685	99.9564	99.9945	99.9755	1.2676	
	DT	99.9965	100.0000	99.9945	99.9973	0.7432	
XGBoost	RF	99.9965	100.0000	99.9945	99.9973	9.9684	67
	SVM	99.9650	99.9482	99.9973	99.9727	1.4658	
	DT	**99.9947**	**99.9973**	**99.9945**	**99.9959**	**1.6087**	
FWE	RF	99.9965	100.0000	99.9945	99.9973	13.2586	67
	SVM	99.5815	99.3581	99.9945	99.6753	1.1256	
	DT	99.9930	99.9945	99.9945	99.9945	1.1293	
FS Method	Model	CICIDS2017					Features remaining
		Acc	Pre	Rec	F1	Time	
Random Forest	RF	99.9925	100.0000	99.9870	99.9935	21.6681	68
	SVM	98.8928	98.1478	99.9584	99.0448	1.6349	
	DT	99.9806	99.9818	99.9844	99.9831	2.2572	
XGBoost	RF	99.9925	100.0000	99.9870	99.9935	31.3178	68
	SVM	98.9003	99.1530	99.9662	99.0513	1.7776	
	DT	99.9895	99.9922	99.9896	99.9909	1.4306	
FWE	**RF**	**99.9982**	**99.9922**	**99.9977**	**99.9844**	**26.1575**	68
	SVM	98.5103	97.5705	99.8933	98.7182	1.6373	
	DT	99.9806	99.9792	99.9870	99.9831	2.9814	
FS Method	Model	APA-DDoS					Features remaining
		Acc	Pre	Rec	F1	Time	
Random Forest	RF	85.9083	100.0000	71.8749	83.6363	2.5936	11
	SVM	68.4744	100.0000	37.0792	54.0990	0.2168	
	DT	85.9083	100.0000	71.8749	83.6363	0.1072	
XGBoost	RF	100.0000	100.0000	100.0000	100.0000	2.6503	11
	SVM	100.0000	100.0000	100.0000	100.0000	0.1779	
	DT	**100.0000**	**100.0000**	**100.0000**	**100.0000**	**0.1152**	
FWE	RF	85.9083	100.0000	71.8749	83.6363	3.0019	11
	SVM	68.4744	100.0000	37.0792	54.0990	0.0793	
	DT	85.9083	100.0000	71.8749	83.6363	0.0577	

(*continued*)

Table 6. (*continued*)

FS Method	Model	CICIoT2023					Features remaining
		Acc	Pre	Rec	F1	Time	
Random Forest	RF	100.0000	100.0000	100.0000	100.0000	16.4528	36
	SVM	98.7234	99.8778	98.8026	99.3373	1.5851	
	DT	99.9294	99.9789	99.9482	99.9635	2.1252	
XGBoost	RF	99.7789	99.9904	99.7813	99.8857	36.2901	36
	SVM	98.9408	99.8800	99.0252	99.4508	1.8272	
	DT	99.8030	99.9462	99.8503	99.8983	3.1380	
FWE	RF	100.0000	100.0000	100.0000	100.0000	24.0720	36
	SVM	98.8869	99.8548	98.9945	99.4228	6.4180	
	DT	**99.9182**	**99.9750**	**99.9405**	**99.9578**	**4.4496**	

alternative with 99.9895% accuracy and a faster execution time of 1.4306 s. In the APA-DDoS dataset, XGBoost-DT and XGBoost-RF perform exceptionally well, achieving 100% accuracy, precision, recall, and F1-score. Additionally, XGBoost-DT is the most efficient with an execution time of only 0.1152 s, making it the best choice for both effectiveness and speed. For CICIoT2023, Random Forest-RF and FWE-RF deliver 100% accuracy, precision, recall, and F1-score. However, Random Forest-RF is more efficient with an execution time of 16.4528 s, while FWE-RF takes 24.0720 s. If execution time is critical, XGBoost-DT offers a slightly lower accuracy of 99.8030% but with a more reasonable execution time of 3.1380 s. Regarding the consistency of the proposed FWE method across different classifiers, FWE performs competitively overall, especially when combined with Random Forest (FWE-RF) and Decision Tree (FWE-DT), where it consistently achieves high accuracy and detection metrics. However, its performance with SVM tends to be lower, particularly in complex datasets like APA-DDoS and CICIDS2017, where precision or recall can drop. Thus, while FWE is effective, it is most reliable when used with tree-based classifiers, and less consistent with margin-based classifiers like SVM. Overall, XGBoost-DT emerges as a consistently strong choice across datasets, balancing performance and efficiency, while FWE-RF and Random Forest-DT excel in specific scenarios where high accuracy or computational efficiency is prioritized. Table 7 shows the results of top 10 features using proposed FWE compared to others FS approach under different detection approaches in various datasets.

Across all datasets, XGBoost with Random Forest (RF) consistently delivers the best overall performance. In the InSDN dataset, it achieves 99.9982% accuracy, 100% precision, 99.9973% recall, and 99.9986% F1-score, making it the most reliable model for traffic classification. For CICIDS2017, FWE with Decision Tree (DT) attains an accuracy of 99.9851%, with precision, recall, and F1-score at 99.9870%, demonstrating its ability to balance detection performance effectively. In the APA-DDoS dataset, multiple models, including Random Forest (RF), XGBoost RF, and FWE RF, achieve 100% accuracy, precision, recall, and F1-score, indicating that APA-DDoS is well-separated and

Table 7. Results of top 10 Features using different FS methods on four datasets

FS Method	Model	InSDN				
		Acc	Pre	Rec	F1	Time
Random Forest	RF	99.9930	100.0000	99.9891	99.9945	4.4732
	SVM	98.4626	99.9275	97.6775	98.7897	0.2921
	DT	99.9912	100.0000	99.9864	99.9932	0.1781
XGBoost	RF	99.9982	100.0000	99.9973	99.9986	9.4148
	SVM	99.3766	99.9752	99.0541	99.5125	0.7267
	DT	**99.9982**	**100.0000**	**99.9973**	**99.9986**	**0.6822**
FWE	RF	99.9965	100.0000	99.9945	99.9973	4.4623
	SVM	99.0457	99.5465	99.9891	99.2626	0.3429
	DT	99.9965	100.0000	99.9945	99.9973	0.2301
FS Method	Model	CICIDS2017				
		Acc	Pre	Rec	F1	Time
Random Forest	RF	99.9952	96.9688	99.9532	99.9610	5.3448
	SVM	89.6048	84.7022	99.9506	91.6968	0.6504
	DT	99.9537	99.9662	99.9532	99.9597	0.2483
XGBoost	RF	99.9851	99.9870	99.9870	99.9870	12.3541
	SVM	92.0852	91.1507	95.4884	93.2691	0.8768
	DT	99.9597	99.9610	99.9688	99.964	0.5911
FWE	RF	99.9701	99.9896	99.9584	99.9740	6.5160
	SVM	97.5077	95.8795	99.9558	97.8752	1.5787
	DT	**99.9686**	**99.9870**	**99.9584**	**99.9727**	**0.2289**
FS Method	Model	APA-DDoS				
		Acc	Pre	Rec	F1	Time
Random Forest	RF	100.0000	100.0000	100.0000	100.0000	3.3081
	SVM	100.0000	100.0000	100.0000	100.0000	0.2480
	DT	100.0000	100.0000	100.0000	100.0000	0.1379
XGBoost	RF	100.0000	100.0000	100.0000	100.0000	2.9521
	SVM	100.0000	100.0000	100.0000	100.0000	0.2367
	DT	100.0000	100.0000	100.0000	100.0000	0.1915
FWE	RF	100.0000	100.0000	100.0000	100.0000	2.8166
	SVM	100.0000	100.0000	100.0000	100.0000	0.1369
	DT	**100.0000**	**100.0000**	**100.0000**	**100.0000**	**0.0871**
FS Method	Model	CICIoT2023				
		Acc	Pre	Rec	F1	Time
Random Forest	RF	99.8383	99.9827	99.8503	99.9165	33.7242
	SVM	99.5466	99.9461	99.5855	99.7655	0.3930
	DT	99.8551	99.9674	99.8830	99.9251	1.7767
XGBoost	RF	100.0000	100.0000	100.0000	100.0000	13.7542
	SVM	96.7536	99.9683	96.6785	98.2959	0.3784
	DT	99.9758	99.9923	99.9827	99.9875	0.8889
FWE	RF	99.8606	99.9942	99.8618	99.9280	17.5841

(*continued*)

Table 7. (*continued*)

FS Method	Model	CICIoT2023				
		Acc	Pre	Rec	F1	Time
	SVM	98.0526	99.9843	98.0044	98.9845	0.2749
	DT	**99.8755**	**99.9770**	**99.8945**	**99.9357**	**0.8479**

easily classifiable. However, for real-time attack detection, FWE with Decision Tree (DT) is the fastest model, requiring only 0.0871 s for classification. In CICIoT2023, XGBoost RF again achieves 100% across all metrics, proving to be the most effective model, though its computation time (13.75 s) is relatively high. If speed is a critical factor, FWE with Decision Tree (DT) offers a strong alternative with 99.8755% accuracy and a significantly lower processing time of 0.8479 s.

The FWE method shows strong and consistent performance, especially when used with tree-based classifiers such as DT and RF. It maintains high detection accuracy across datasets while remaining computationally efficient. To validate this consistency, statistical analyses were conducted using one-way ANOVA and Tukey HSD post-hoc testing on accuracy scores. Results show that there were no statistically significant differences between FWE, XGBoost, and Random Forest in CICIDS2017 with F = 0.2781 and p = 0.7665, CICIoT2023 with F = 0.3442 and p = 0.7219), and APA-DDoS, where all models achieved perfect classification performance, confirming that FWE performs competitively. Additionally, a sensitivity analysis was conducted by varying the Pearson correlation threshold (0.05, 0.1, 0.2) and the number of top features selected (5 and 10). The configuration of threshold = 0.1 and top-10 features resulted in the best performance, achieving 99.9982% accuracy on the InSDN dataset. This analysis supports the effectiveness of the original parameter choice in balancing performance and feature compactness. While FWE performs well with DT and RF, results with Support Vector Machine (SVM) are more variable, particularly in CICIDS2017 and CICIoT2023, where accuracy and precision are lower. This is likely due to the wrapper stage of FWE using a tree-based model (XGBoost) to guide feature elimination, producing a feature set optimized for tree-based classifiers. SVM, which relies on maximizing margins in transformed feature spaces, may not benefit as much from this selection. Even with Min-Max scaling applied, SVM's sensitivity to feature distribution and kernel compatibility may affect its performance.

5 Conclusion and Future Work

This study introduced a hybrid feature selection method, Filter-Wrapped Evaluation (FWE) that integrates Pearson Correlation and Recursive Feature Elimination (RFE) with XGBoost to enhance DDoS attack detection in Software-Defined Networks (SDN). FWE effectively reduces feature dimensionality while preserving relevant information, leading to improved detection accuracy and efficiency. Extensive evaluation on four benchmark datasets (InSDN, CICIDS2017, APA-DDoS, CICIoT2023) demonstrated that FWE, particularly when used with tree-based classifiers like Decision Tree (DT) and Random Forest (RF), achieved consistently high performance. Notably, FWE-DT attained execution times as low as 0.0871 s while maintaining 99.99% accuracy, indicating its suitability for real-time applications. However, this study does not include deep leaning-based baselines, which limits comparative comprehensiveness. Future works should be explore integrating deep learning models, evaluating real-time deployment feasibility, and benchmarking FWE on streaming data scenarios.

References

1. Wabi, A.A., Idris, I., Olaniyi, O.M., Ojeniyi, J.A.: DDOS attack detection in SDN: method of attacks, detection techniques, challenges and research gaps. Comput. Secur. **139**, 103652 (2024)
2. Xu, Y., Liu, Y.: DDoS attack detection under SDN context. In: IEEE INFOCOM 2016 – The 35th Annual IEEE International Conference on Computer Communications, pp. 1–9. IEEE (2016)
3. Yoachimik, O., Pacheco, J.: Record-breaking 5.6 Tbps DDoS attack and global DDoS trends for 2024 Q4. The Cloudflare Blog (2025). https://blog.cloudflare.com/ddos-threat-report-for-2024-q4/
4. El Sayed, M.S., Le-Khac, N.A., Azer, M.A., Jurcut, A.D.: A flow-based anomaly detection approach with feature selection method against DDoS attacks in SDNs. IEEE Trans. Cogn. Commun. Netw. **8**(4), 1862–1880 (2022)
5. Eliyan, L.F., Di Pietro, R.: DoS and DDoS attacks in Software Defined Networks: a survey of existing solutions and research challenges. Future Gener. Comput. Syst. **122**, 149–171 (2021)
6. Karan, B.V., Narayan, D.G., Hiremath, P.S.: Detection of DDoS attacks in software defined networks. In: 2018 3rd International Conference on Computational Systems and Information Technology for Sustainable Solutions (CSITSS), pp. 265–270. IEEE (2018)
7. Manso, P., Moura, J., Serrão, C.: SDN-based intrusion detection system for early detection and mitigation of DDoS attacks. Information **10**(3), 106 (2019)
8. Wang, B., Zheng, Y., Lou, W., Hou, Y.T.: DDoS attack protection in the era of cloud computing and software-defined networking. Comput. Netw. **81**, 308–319 (2015)
9. Dong, S., Sarem, M.: DDoS attack detection method based on improved KNN with the degree of DDoS attack in software-defined networks. IEEE Access **8**, 5039–5048 (2019)
10. Lei, L., Kou, L., Zhan, X., Zhang, J., Ren, Y.: An anomaly detection algorithm based on ensemble learning for 5G environment. Sensors **22**(19), 7436 (2022)
11. Tan, L., Pan, Y., Wu, J., Zhou, J., Jiang, H., Deng, Y.: A new framework for DDoS attack detection and defense in SDN environment. IEEE Access **8**, 161908–161919 (2020)
12. Sangodoyin, A.O., Akinsolu, M.O., Pillai, P., Grout, V.: Detection and classification of DDoS flooding attacks on software-defined networks: a case study for the application of machine learning. IEEE Access **9**, 122495–122508 (2021)
13. Al-Dunainawi, Y., Al-Kaseem, B.R., Al-Raweshidy, H.S.: Optimized artificial intelligence model for DDoS detection in SDN environment. IEEE Access (2023)
14. Roopak, M., Tian, G.Y., Chambers, J.: Multi-objective-based feature selection for DDoS attack detection in IoT networks. IET Netw. **9**(3), 120–127 (2020)
15. Kim, Y.E., Kim, Y.S., Kim, H.: Effective feature selection methods to detect IoT DDoS attack in 5G core network. Sensors **22**(10), 3819 (2022)
16. Nadeem, M.W., Goh, H.G., Ponnusamy, V., Aun, Y.: DDoS detection in SDN using machine learning techniques. Comput. Mater. Continua **71**(1) (2022)

17. Alashhab, A.A., Edrah, A., Zahid, M.S.M., Rahman, M.S.: Ensemble based detection model for DDoS attacks in SDNs using advanced feature selection. In: 2024 17th International Conference on Signal Processing and Communication System (ICSPCS), pp. 1–5. IEEE (2024)
18. Bouke, M.A., Abdullah, A., ALshatebi, S.H., Abdullah, M.T., El Atigh, H.: An intelligent DDoS attack detection tree-based model using Gini index feature selection method. Microprocess. Microsyst. **98**, 104823 (2023)
19. Polat, H., Polat, O., Cetin, A.: Detecting DDoS attacks in software-defined networks through feature selection methods and machine learning models. Sustainability **12**(3), 1035 (2020)
20. Eldhai, A.M., et al.: Improved feature selection and stream traffic classification based on machine learning in software-defined networks. IEEE Access (2024)
21. Türkoğlu, M., Polat, H., Koçak, C., Polat, O.: Recognition of DDoS attacks on SD-VANET based on combination of hyperparameter optimization and feature selection. Expert Syst. Appl. **203**, 117500 (2022)
22. Rahman, O., Quraishi, M.A.G., Lung, C.H.: DDoS attacks detection and mitigation in SDN using machine learning. In: 2019 IEEE World Congress on Services (SERVICES), vol. 2642, pp. 184–189. IEEE (2019)
23. Mehmood, S., Amin, R., Mustafa, J., Hussain, M., Alsubaei, F.S., Zakaria, M.D.: Distributed Denial of Services (DDoS) attack detection in SDN using Optimizer-equipped CNN-MLP. PLoS ONE **20**(1), e0312425 (2025)
24. Goud, K.S., Rao, G.S.: Towards an efficient DDoS attack detection in SDN: an approach with CNN-GRU fusion. In: 2024 Fourth International Conference on Advances in Electrical, Computing, Communication and Sustainable Technologies (ICAECT), pp. 1–10. IEEE (2024)
25. Wang, J., Wang, L., Wang, R.: A method of DDoS attack detection and mitigation for the comprehensive coordinated protection of SDN controllers. Entropy **25**(8), 1210 (2023)
26. Ataa, M.S., Sanad, E.E., El-Khoribi, R.A.: Intrusion detection in software defined network using deep learning approaches. Sci. Rep. **14**(1), 29159 (2024)
27. InSDN Dataset. https://www.kaggle.com/datasets/badcodebuilder/insdn-dataset/data. Accessed 09 Apr 2025
28. Elsayed, M.S., Le-Khac, N.A., Jurcut, A.D.: InSDN: a novel SDN intrusion dataset. IEEE Access **8**, 165263–165284 (2020)
29. IDS 2017 | Datasets | Research | Canadian Institute for Cybersecurity | UNB. https://www.unb.ca/cic/datasets/ids-2017.html. Accessed 09 Apr 2025
30. Sharafaldin, I., Lashkari, A.H., Ghorbani, A.A.: Toward generating a new intrusion detection dataset and intrusion traffic characterization. In: 4th International Conference on Information Systems Security and Privacy (ICISSP), Portugal (2018)
31. APA-DDoS Dataset (n.d.). www.kaggle.com. https://www.kaggle.com/datasets/yashwanthkumbam/apaddos-dataset
32. Kethineni, K., Pradeepini, G.: Intrusion detection in internet of things-based smart farming using hybrid deep learning framework. Clust. Comput. **27**(2), 1719–1732 (2024)
33. IoT Dataset 2023 | Datasets | Research | Canadian Institute for Cybersecurity | UNB. https://www.unb.ca/cic/datasets/iotdataset-2023.html. Accessed 09 Apr 2025
34. Neto, E.C.P., Dadkhah, S., Ferreira, R., Zohourian, A., Lu, R., Ghorbani, A.A.: CICIoT2023: a real-time dataset and benchmark for large-scale attacks in IoT environment. Sensors (2023, submitted)

RAG Embeddings Storage Optimization Through Quantization and Dimensionality Reduction

Naamán Huerga-Pérez, Rubén Álvarez, Álvaro Sánchez-Fernández, and Javier Díez-González[✉]

Department of Mechanical, Computer and Aerospace Engineering,
Universidad de León, 24071 León, Spain
`javier.diez@unileon.es`

Abstract. Retrieval-Augmented Generation is a powerful framework that enhances language models by retrieving relevant information from large external knowledge bases, relying heavily on high-dimensional vector embeddings. However, storing these embeddings at scale poses significant challenges due to their substantial memory requirements. To address this, we investigate two complementary strategies: quantization of embeddings using low-bit floating point formats, and dimensionality reduction via Principal Component Analysis (PCA). Our experiments, measuring performance using $nDCG@10$ (the standard MTEB Retrieval benchmark metric for ranking quality) relative to the *float32* baseline, show that low-bit formats like *float8* achieve 4x storage reduction with minimal (<0.3%) performance loss, significantly outperforming *int8* at the same compression level. Notably, combining *float8* with moderate PCA (e.g., retaining 50% dimensions) yields even better trade-offs, achieving 8x total compression with less performance degradation than *int8* alone (e.g., a 0.62% drop vs 1.53% for nomic-embed-text-v1.5) while requiring only half the storage space. These findings highlight the effectiveness of combining *float8* quantization and dimensionality reduction for efficient RAG embedding storage with minimal impact on retrieval quality.

Keywords: Artificial Intelligence · Machine Learning · Retrieval-Augmented Generation · Quantization · Dimensionality Reduction · Storage Optimization

1 Introduction

Natural Language Processing (NLP) is the field enabling computers to understand and process human language. It has become pivotal in modern artificial intelligence, driven significantly by the rise of Large Language Models (LLMs) [4,16].

LLMs exhibit remarkable capabilities in understanding context, generating coherent text, answering questions, and even performing complex reasoning tasks

[2]. However, LLMs suffer from inherent limitations that hinder their applicability in certain scenarios. Primarily, their knowledge is static, frozen at the time of their last training, making them unaware of events or information that emerged afterward. Furthermore, they typically lack access to private, domain-specific, or proprietary data sources, limiting their utility in enterprise settings. Finally, LLMs can sometimes generate plausible but incorrect or nonsensical information, a phenomenon often referred to as *hallucination* [12].

Retrieval-Augmented Generation (RAG) systems address these issues by retrieving relevant, up-to-date information from external knowledge sources before generation, grounding the output of the LLM in specific contexts [8]. The RAG process typically involves retrieving text snippets pertinent to the query of the user and providing them as additional context to the LLM alongside the original prompt.

Central to the functioning of RAG systems is the concept of embeddings and the use of specialized Vector Databases. Textual information from external sources is converted into dense numerical representations, known as embeddings, using dedicated embedding models [3,13]. These embeddings capture the semantic meaning of the text, such that similar concepts are represented by vectors that are close to each other in a high-dimensional space. Vector databases are optimized data stores designed to efficiently index, store, and query these high-dimensional embedding vectors based on similarity metrics (e.g., cosine similarity [8]). When a query is received, its embedding is computed, and the vector database rapidly retrieves the embeddings (and associated text) of the most semantically similar documents from the knowledge source.

However, a significant practical challenge arises from the high dimensionality of the embeddings generated by state-of-the-art models (often 1536 dimensions or more) [1]. Storing these vectors, typically using standard 32-bit floating-point precision, demands substantial memory resources, leading to high operational costs and hinders the deployment on resource-constrained devices [14]. While existing solutions like quantization to lower-precision formats (*float16*, *textitint8*) or even *binary* representations offer memory savings (2x, 4x, up to 32x respectively), they often involve trade-offs in retrieval performance and may not represent the optimal balance. [14].

While these existing quantization methods provide partial solutions, there is a need for a more systematic evaluation, particularly concerning specialized low-bits data formats and the combined effects of quantization and dimensionality reduction specifically for embedding vectors in RAG systems is still yet to be explored. In this paper, we address this gap by:

- Evaluating the impact of alternative, reduced-precision floating-point formats, such as *float8* variants, on the performance of embedding retrieval.
- Systematically investigating the effectiveness of applying dimensionality reduction techniques, specifically Principal Component Analysis (PCA) to embedding vectors, both independently and in combination with various quantization schemes, to further optimize storage.

2 Related Works

The challenge of efficiently storing and retrieving high-dimensional embedding vectors has spurred research into various compression techniques. Current approaches primarily fall into two categories: quantization, which reduces the number of bits stored for each vector component, and dimensionality reduction, which decreases the number of components per vector. Typically, these embeddings are represented and stored using standard 32-bit floating-point numbers [6], which serve as the baseline for how compression ratios and performance trade-offs are measured.

Quantization is the most common strategy, borrowing heavily from techniques used in deep learning model compression [17]. Standard reduced-precision formats like *float16* offer a 2x storage reduction compared to *float32*. Scalar quantization, typically converting *float32* to 8-bit integers (*int8*), achieves 4x compression and can leverage optimized CPU instructions (SIMD) for faster comparisons, though it often requires a calibration step and may incur some accuracy loss [14]. More aggressively, binary quantization reduces each component to a single bit (*0* or *1*) for 32x compression and extremely fast bitwise comparisons. However, as demonstrated by Shakir et al. (2024) [14], the significant precision loss from binary quantization usually necessitates a re-scoring step (re-ranking initial binary results using higher-precision vectors) to maintain acceptable accuracy, recovering performance from 92.5% to 96% in their experiments.

Dimensionality reduction offers an alternative approach. Techniques like PCA reduce the number of stored dimensions post-hoc. For instance, Wang (2019) [18] proposed using PCA not just for reduction, but as a method to efficiently select the optimal embedding dimension by training only once with a high dimension count and evaluating subsets of principal components. Other methods like Matryoshka Representation Learning (MRL), introduced by Kusupati et al. (2022) [7], allow selecting the embedding size post-training by optimizing nested lower-dimensional representations during the initial training phase. This differs from the purely post-hoc application of quantization or standard PCA investigated here. However, this technique requires specific modifications during the model's training phase, differing from the post-hoc application of quantization or standard PCA investigated here. Another common strategy involves simply training embedding models designed to output fewer dimensions inherently. However, as evaluated by Muennighoff et al. (2022) [5], this might trade off some representational capacity. While effective, reducing dimensions can risk discarding information crucial for fine-grained semantic distinctions.

While these techniques provide valuable tools, they are often studied in isolation. For instance, studies on quantization often focus on *int8* and *binary* formats [14], overlooking the potential of newer floating-point formats. Similarly, dimensionality reduction is either treated as a standalone post-hoc step [18] or integrated into the model's training phase [7], which limits its application to pre-existing models. Crucially, the synergistic effects of applying both quantization and dimensionality reduction post-hoc are not typically analyzed together.

Thus, our work extends these efforts by (1) evaluating low-precision floating-point formats, specifically *float8* variants, for embedding storage, balancing int8-level compression with float properties; (2) analyzing the effects of applying PCA for dimensionality reduction on retrieval performance; and (3) analyzing the *combined* effects of quantization and PCA-based dimensionality reduction to provide clear, data-driven insights into the performance trade-offs at various compression levels.

By exploring these novel formats and their interaction with dimensionality reduction, and by providing a structured selection methodology, this paper aims to offer more nuanced and effective strategies for optimizing embedding storage in RAG systems.

3 Problem Definition

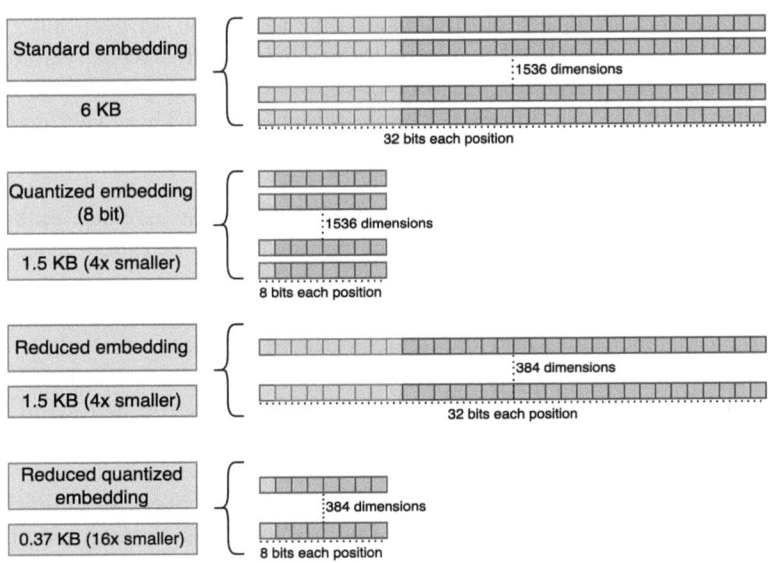

Fig. 1. Illustration of embedding storage optimization. Top: A standard high-dimensional embedding (e.g., 1536 dimensions in float32, 6 KB). Second: The same embedding after 8-bit quantization (1.5 KB, 4x smaller). Third: The embedding after dimensionality reduction (e.g., keeping 384 dimensions in float32, 1.5 KB, 4x smaller). Bottom: Combining dimensionality reduction and quantization (e.g., 384 dimensions in 8-bit, 0.37 KB, 16x smaller). The colors visually distinguish the components of the numerical formats: for float types, blue denotes the sign, green the exponent, and red the mantissa; for 8-bit integers, purple represents the value.

As introduced previously, RAG systems rely on high-dimensional vector embeddings to represent the semantic meaning of text. The core challenge this paper addresses, illustrated in Fig. 1, is the substantial storage cost associated with these vectors, particularly when operating at a large scale.

These embeddings are stored and indexed in specialized Vector Databases, optimized for efficient retrieval based on vector similarity. When a user poses a query, the RAG system first generates an embedding for the query text. It then performs a similarity search within the vector database to find the k document embeddings closest to the query embedding. Common similarity metrics include cosine similarity, calculated as $\frac{q \cdot v_i}{\|q\|\|v_i\|}$, where q is the query vector and v_i is a document vector. The text snippets corresponding to these top-k retrieved embeddings are then used to augment the original query.

Specifically, the retrieved text snippets are typically used to form an expanded prompt that provides the LLM with relevant context. This augmented prompt allows the LLM to generate a more informed, accurate, and grounded response by leveraging the provided external information.

However, the effectiveness of this approach introduces a significant scalability challenge: the storage of embedding vectors. State-of-the-art embedding models often generate vectors with high dimensionality (e.g. 1536, or even 3072 dimensions [5]) to capture nuanced semantic relationships effectively. While higher dimensionality often correlates with better representational quality and retrieval performance [5], it directly impacts storage requirements. These vectors are typically stored using standard 32-bit floating-point numbers (*float32*), where each dimension consumes 4 bytes [6].

Consequently, storing large collections of high-dimensional embeddings demands substantial memory for efficient retrieval. For instance, a knowledge base containing one million documents embedded into 1536-dimensional *float32* vectors would require approximately $1,000,000 \times 1536 \times 4$ bytes ≈ 6.1 GB of RAM, excluding metadata and indexing overhead. As datasets scale to tens of millions of documents, the memory footprint can easily reach hundreds of gigabytes, leading to significant operational costs in cloud environments and making deployment infeasible on resource-constrained platforms like browser runtimes or mobile applications [14].

Figure 1 visually demonstrates this storage challenge and the potential benefits of optimization techniques using a hypothetical 1536-dimension embedding as an example. A standard *float32* embedding might occupy 6 KB. Applying 8-bit quantization reduces the size by 4x to 1.5 KB by lowering the precision of each dimension. Alternatively, reducing the dimensionality (e.g. keeping only the most significant dimensions via PCA) could achieve a similar 4x reduction to 1.5 KB while maintaining *float32* precision for the remaining dimensions. Combining both techniques can yield significantly greater compression, potentially reducing the size by 16x or more. This inherent trade-off between embedding fidelity (linked to dimensionality and precision) and storage/computational cost forms the core problem addressed in this paper.

Mitigating these storage costs without excessively compromising retrieval quality motivates the exploration of efficient compression techniques. Therefore, this paper investigates the impact of various quantization data types (including standard formats like *float16* and *int8*, aggressive *binary* quantization, and low-bit floating-point formats such as *float8*) and PCA dimensionality reduction, both individually and in combination. The following section details the methodology used to evaluate the performance trade-offs of these approaches.

4 Methodology

To systematically evaluate the impact of quantization and dimensionality reduction on retrieval performance within RAG systems, we designed a comprehensive experimental plan. This section details the datasets, models, techniques, tools, and metrics employed.

4.1 Experimental Setup and Techniques

Embeddings were generated using two distinct, publicly available models selected for their strong performance and differing output dimensionalities: **BAAI/bge-small-en-v1.5** (384 dimensions) [19] and **Nomic/nomic-embed-text-v1.5** (768 dimensions) [10]. Utilizing models with different vector sizes allows for assessing how initial dimensionality influences the impact of subsequent compression techniques.

Our investigation focused on two primary optimization strategies—quantization and dimensionality reduction—applied both individually and in combination.

Quantization techniques were evaluated against the baseline *float32* format [6]. The tested lower-precision alternatives included:

- Standard reduced-precision floating-point types: *float16* and *bfloat16* [9].
- Scalar types: *int8* (unsigned 8-bit integer) and *binary* (1-bit).
- Novel low-bit floating-point types: *float8* variants (*e5m2* and *e4m3* [15]) and *float4*, utilizing implementations from the Google ml_dtypes library.

The *float8* variants, *e5m2* and *e4m3*, differ in their allocation of bits between the exponent (5 and 4 bits, respectively) and the mantissa (2 and 3 bits, respectively), providing distinct trade-offs between numerical range and precision.

Dimensionality Reduction was performed using PCA. We employed the scikit-learn library [11] implementation with default settings, training PCA models on the *MLQuestions* dataset, a large-scale dataset of question-passage pairs widely used for training and evaluating information retrieval models. We evaluated performance at several reduction levels, retaining principal components that explained cumulative variance ranging from 90% down to 25% of the original dimensions.

Combined Optimization involved applying each quantization type to the vectors resulting from each level of PCA dimensionality reduction. This allowed for analyzing the synergistic effects and performance trade-offs when both optimization strategies are used together.

4.2 Evaluation Procedure and Metrics

The evaluation workflow began by generating baseline *float32* embeddings for all documents and queries within the MTEB Retrieval benchmark datasets [5] using both selected embedding models. This benchmark is the standard for evaluating embedding models on retrieval tasks, providing a robust measure of performance. For each experimental configuration (a specific combination of embedding model, quantization type, and PCA reduction level), the corresponding transformations were applied to these baseline embeddings. Retrieval was then performed using these transformed document and query embeddings, calculating cosine similarity to rank documents against each query.

Retrieval quality was assessed using **nDCG@10** (Normalized Discounted Cumulative Gain at 10), the standard metric for the MTEB Retrieval leaderboard [1]. This metric evaluates the ranking quality of the top 10 results by considering both the relevance (rel_i) of each result and its position (i) in the list. It is calculated as:

$$nDCG@10 = \frac{DCG@10}{IDCG@10} = \frac{\sum_{i=1}^{10} \frac{rel_i}{\log_2(i+1)}}{IDCG@10} \quad (1)$$

where $IDCG@10$ (Ideal Discounted Cumulative Gain at 10) is the maximum possible $DCG@10$ score achievable with a perfect ranking, serving as a normalization factor; i denotes the rank position of a document (from 1 to 10); rel_i represents the graded relevance score of the document at position i; and $\log_2(i+1)$ is the logarithmic discount factor that assigns lower weight to relevant documents found further down the list.

The DCG component, through this logarithmic discount, assigns decreasing weight to results further down the list, penalizing relevant documents that are ranked lower. Normalization by the Ideal DCG (IDCG) ensures the final nDCG@10 score falls between 0 and 1, where 1 indicates a perfect ranking. This metric is particularly suitable for evaluating retrieval systems as it emphasizes the importance of retrieving the most relevant documents within the top positions.

Performance for each experimental configuration was measured as the percentage change relative to the nDCG@10 score achieved by the corresponding *float32* baseline on the same dataset and embedding model.

5 Results

This section presents the experimental results evaluating the impact of various quantization techniques and dimensionality reduction on the retrieval performance of embeddings within a RAG context. Performance is measured using nDCG@10 on the MTEB Retrieval benchmark [5], reported as the percentage change relative to the *float32* baseline performance for each respective embedding model.

5.1 Impact of Quantization on Retrieval Performance

We first evaluated the effect of applying different quantization techniques alone, without dimensionality reduction. The results demonstrate distinct trade-offs between storage reduction and performance degradation across data types.

Figure 2 shows that standard 16-bit floating-point formats (*float16*, *bfloat16*) consistently had minimal performance loss (typically 0.5%) compared to the *float32* baseline, while achieving a 2x reduction in storage size. The novel 8-bit floating-point formats (*float8 e5m2*, *float8 e4m3*) offered an even better compromise, providing a 4x storage reduction with similarly negligible performance degradation (often 0.3%). This highlights the efficiency of reduced-precision floating-point representations for embedding storage.

In contrast, scalar quantization formats exhibited more significant performance impacts. *int8* quantization, despite also offering a 4x storage reduction, resulted in a considerably higher performance drop (around 1.5–3.5% depending on the model) compared to *float8* formats. This difference is significant, particularly because *int8* requires an additional calibration step, unlike *float8*, which can be converted directly. Meanwhile, *binary* quantization, which offers the highest compression (32×), resulted in the most severe performance degradation with losses ranging from 7% to over 11%.

Comparing the two embedding models, the higher-dimensional **nomic-embed-text-v1.5** generally showed slightly better results with quantization, particularly for the more aggressive *binary* format, compared to the lower-dimensional **bge-small-en-v1.5**. This suggests that the information redundancy in higher-dimensional vectors may offer some buffer against precision loss.

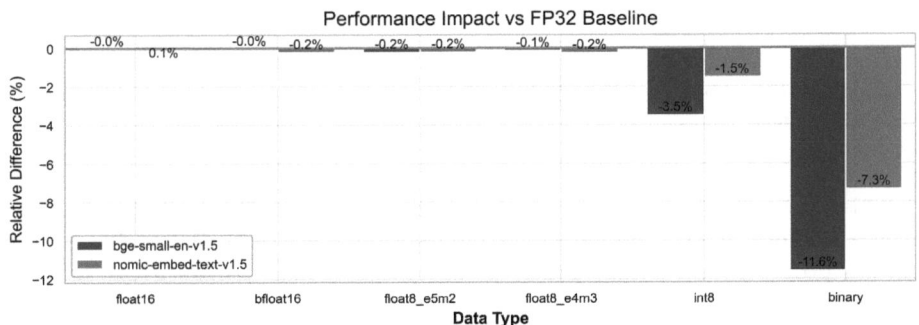

Fig. 2. Impact of quantization on retrieval performance (nDCG@10 relative to float32 baseline) for bge-small-en-v1.5 and nomic-embed-text-v1.5 across different data types.

5.2 Impact of Dimensionality Reduction (PCA) on Retrieval Performance

Next, we analyzed the effect of applying PCA dimensionality reduction alone, using *float32* precision for the reduced vectors. As illustrated by Fig. 3, retrieval performance generally decreased as the number of dimensions retained was reduced (from 90% down to 25% of original dimensions).

The impact was significantly more pronounced for the lower-dimensional **bge-small-en-v1.5** model. For instance, reducing dimensions by 75% (equivalent to a 4x size reduction) resulted in a performance loss of approximately 10% for this model, whereas the higher-dimensional **nomic-embed-text-v1.5** model experienced only around a 3.8% loss for the same relative reduction. This confirms that lower-dimensional embeddings are more sensitive to information loss from dimensionality reduction.

Notably, for equivalent storage reduction factors (e.g., 4x), quantization techniques like *float8* generally resulted in significantly less performance degradation than applying PCA alone to *float32* vectors. For example, the 0.2% loss with *float8* (4x reduction) is far superior to the 3.8%-10% loss observed with PCA retaining 25% of dimensions (also a 4x reduction).

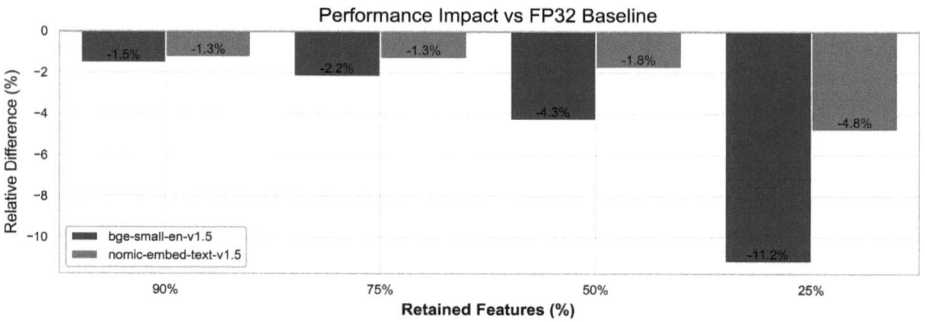

Fig. 3. Impact of PCA dimensionality reduction on retrieval performance (nDCG@10 relative to the uncompressed float32 baseline) for bge-small-en-v1.5 and nomic-embed-text-v1.5 models.

This raises the question of whether simply choosing the best quantization format is sufficient, or if dimensionality reduction offers distinct benefits. Quantization primarily affects the precision of each dimension, while PCA removes dimensions entirely based on variance. These represent different types of information loss. It is plausible that combining moderate levels of both techniques could yield a better performance-compression trade-off than applying either technique to an extreme degree individually. This motivates a closer examination of their combined effects.

5.3 Combined Effects of Quantization and PCA

The most interesting results emerge when combining quantization and PCA dimensionality reduction. In this approach, we apply each quantization type to vectors that have already been reduced in dimension via PCA.

A key observation is the differing robustness of data types to combined compression. Figure 4, depicting results for the **nomic-embed-text-v1.5** model, shows that reduced-precision floating-point formats (*float16*, *bfloat16*, *float8*) demonstrated remarkable resilience, maintaining relatively stable performance even with significant dimensionality reduction applied. In contrast, scalar formats (*int8*, *binary*) exhibited much steeper performance degradation as dimensionality was reduced, indicating lower tolerance to the combined information loss from both precision and dimension reduction. Trends for the bge-small-en-v1.5 model were qualitatively very similar, exhibiting the same relative behavior between data types, hence only one model's results are shown for clarity.

This interaction allows for fine-grained control over the storage-performance trade-off. For instance, applying *float8* quantization while retaining 50% of dimensions via PCA (an overall 8x storage reduction compared to baseline *float32*) yielded performance comparable to using *int8* quantization alone (a 4x reduction). This suggests that for achieving higher compression ratios (e.g., 8x or more), combining a robust format like *float8* with moderate PCA can be more effective than resorting directly to more aggressive quantization like *binary*.

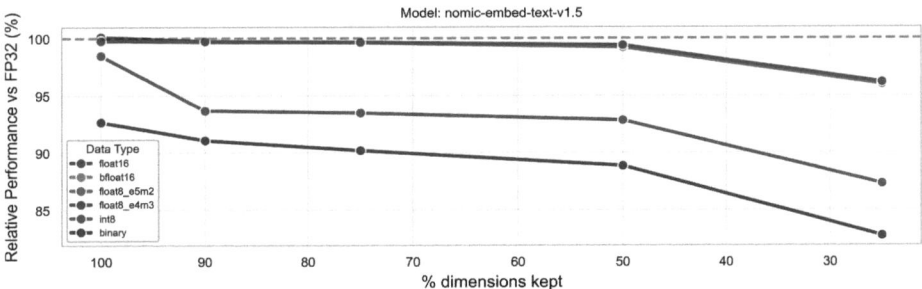

Fig. 4. Relative retrieval performance (nDCG@10 vs. float32 baseline) when combining quantization and PCA dimensionality reduction for (a) bge-small-en-v1.5 and (b) nomic-embed-text-v1.5 models. Lines show performance trends for different quantization types as the percentage of dimensions retained via PCA decreases.

6 Conclusions

This work investigated the impact of quantization and dimensionality reduction techniques on the storage efficiency and retrieval performance of embeddings in RAG systems. Our systematic evaluation yields several key conclusions regarding optimal compression strategies:

- Reduced-precision floating-point formats, particularly *float8*, offer an excellent trade-off between storage reduction and performance preservation, incurring minimal impact on nDCG@10. This significantly outperforms scalar

formats at equivalent sizes and questions the common industry practice of defaulting to *int8* or *binary* quantization.
- *float8* formats proved notably more effective than *int8* quantization. Despite occupying the same 4x compressed size, *float8* consistently demonstrated lower performance degradation and has the added advantage of not requiring a separate data calibration step.
- Strategically applying moderate PCA to vectors already quantized with robust formats like *float8* can achieve higher compression ratios while maintaining better retrieval performance compared to using more aggressive quantization methods like *binary* alone to meet strict memory constraints.
- Higher-dimensional embedding models exhibit greater resilience to both quantization and dimensionality reduction, degrading more gracefully under compression, likely due to greater information redundancy.

These findings provide a foundation for industry practitioners making decisions aimed at reducing the storage footprint required for embeddings in RAG applications. By leveraging newer floating-point formats and strategically combining compression techniques, the significant challenge of memory consumption can be effectively addressed, enabling more efficient and scalable RAG deployments without substantial performance sacrifices. Future work could explore even lower-bit floating-point formats and alternative dimensionality reduction techniques beyond PCA.

Acknowledgements. This work has been funded by the project of the Spanish Ministry of Science and Innovation grant number PID2023-153047OBI00, by the Consejería de Educación de la Junta de Castilla y León and by the Universidad de León.

References

1. MTEB Leaderboard (2025). https://huggingface.co/spaces/mteb/leaderboard
2. Brown, T., Mann, B., et al.: Language models are few-shot learners. In: Larochelle, H., Ranzato, M., Hadsell, R., Balcan, M., Lin, H. (eds.) Advances in Neural Information Processing Systems, vol. 33, pp. 1877–1901. Curran Associates, Inc. (2020). https://proceedings.neurips.cc/paper_files/paper/2020/file/1457c0d6bfcb4967418bfb8ac142f64a-Paper.pdf
3. Church, K.W.: Word2vec. Nat. Lang. Eng. **23**(1), 155–162 (2017). https://doi.org/10.1017/S1351324916000334
4. Devlin, J., Chang, M.W., et al.: BERT: pre-training of deep bidirectional transformers for language understanding. In: Burstein, J., Doran, C., Solorio, T. (eds.) Proceedings of the 2019 Conference of the North American Chapter of the Association for Computational Linguistics: Human Language Technologies, Volume 1 (Long and Short Papers), pp. 4171–4186. Association for Computational Linguistics, Minneapolis (2019). https://doi.org/10.18653/v1/N19-1423, https://aclanthology.org/N19-1423/
5. Enevoldsen, K., Chung, I., Kerboua, I., et al.: MMTEB: massive multilingual text embedding benchmark. In: The Thirteenth International Conference on Learning Representations (2025). https://openreview.net/forum?id=zl3pfz4VCV

6. IEEE: 754-2019 - IEEE standard for floating-point arithmetic (2019). https://doi.org/10.1109/IEEESTD.2019.8766229
7. Kusupati, A., Bhatt, G., et al.: Matryoshka representation learning. In: Koyejo, S., Mohamed, S., Agarwal, A., Belgrave, D., Cho, K., Oh, A. (eds.) Advances in Neural Information Processing Systems, vol. 35, pp. 30,233–30,249. Curran Associates, Inc. (2022). https://proceedings.neurips.cc/paper_files/paper/2022/file/c32319f4868da7613d78af9993100e42-Paper-Conference.pdf
8. Lewis, P., Perez, E., et al.: Retrieval-augmented generation for knowledge-intensive NLP tasks. In: Larochelle, H., Ranzato, M., Hadsell, R., Balcan, M., Lin, H. (eds.) Advances in Neural Information Processing Systems, vol. 33, pp. 9459–9474. Curran Associates, Inc. (2020). https://proceedings.neurips.cc/paper_files/paper/2020/file/6b493230205f780e1bc26945df7481e5-Paper.pdf
9. Mishra, S.M., Tiwari, A., Kumar, A.: Comparison of floating-point representations for the efficient implementation of machine learning algorithms. In: 2022 32nd International Conference Radioelektronika, pp. 1–6. IEEE (2022)
10. Nussbaum, Z., Morris, J.X., Duderstadt, B., Mulyar, A.: Nomic embed: training a reproducible long context text embedder (2024). https://arxiv.org/abs/2402.01613
11. Pedregosa, F., Varoquaux, G., et al.: Scikit-learn: machine learning in Python. J. Mach. Learn. Res. **12**, 2825–2830 (2011)
12. Perković, G., Drobnjak, A., Botički, I.: Hallucinations in LLMs: understanding and addressing challenges. In: 2024 47th MIPRO ICT and Electronics Convention (MIPRO), pp. 2084–2088 (2024). https://doi.org/10.1109/MIPRO60963.2024.10569238
13. Reimers, N., Gurevych, I.: Sentence-BERT: sentence embeddings using Siamese BERT-networks. EMNLP-IJCNLP 2019, pp. 3982–3992 (2019). https://doi.org/10.18653/V1/D19-1410, https://aclanthology.org/D19-1410/
14. Shakir, A., Aarsen, T., Lee, S.: Binary and scalar embedding quantization for significantly faster and cheaper retrieval (2024). https://huggingface.co/blog/embedding-quantization
15. Shen, H., Mellempudi, N., et al.: Efficient post-training quantization with fp8 formats. In: Gibbons, P., Pekhimenko, G., Sa, C.D. (eds.) Proceedings of Machine Learning and Systems, vol. 6, pp. 483–498 (2024). https://proceedings.mlsys.org/paper_files/paper/2024/file/dea9b4b6f55ae611c54065d6fc750755-Paper-Conference.pdf
16. Vaswani, A., Shazeer, N., et al.: Attention is all you need. In: Guyon, I., et al. (eds.) Advances in Neural Information Processing Systems, vol. 30. Curran Associates, Inc. (2017). https://proceedings.neurips.cc/paper_files/paper/2017/file/3f5ee243547dee91fbd053c1c4a845aa-Paper.pdf
17. Wang, C.H., Huang, K.Y., Yao, Y., Chen, J.C., Shuai, H.H., Cheng, W.H.: Lightweight deep learning: an overview. IEEE Consum. Electron. Mag. **13**(4), 51–64 (2024). https://doi.org/10.1109/MCE.2022.3181759
18. Wang, Y.: Single training dimension selection for word embedding with PCA. In: Inui, K., Jiang, J., Ng, V., Wan, X. (eds.) Proceedings of the 2019 EMNLP-IJCNLP, pp. 3597–3602. Association for Computational Linguistics, Hong Kong, China (2019). https://doi.org/10.18653/v1/D19-1369, https://aclanthology.org/D19-1369/
19. Xiao, S., Liu, Z., Zhang, P., Muennighoff, N.: C-pack: packaged resources to advance general Chinese embedding (2023). https://arxiv.org/abs/2309.07597

Exploratory Visualization of IoT Attacks on the NF-CSE-CIC-IDS2018 Dataset

Álvaro Villar-Val[✉], Diego Granados-Lopez, Angel Arroyo,
and Álvaro Herrero

Grupo de Inteligencia Computacional Aplicada (GICAP),
Departamento de Digitalización, Escuela Politécnica Superior, Universidad de Burgos,
Av. Cantabria s/n, 09006 Burgos, Spain
afvillar@ubu.es
https://gicap.ubu.es/main/home.shtml

Abstract. The rapid proliferation of Internet of Things devices has introduced significant security challenges, particularly due to their deployment in exposed environments and reliance on unpatched or static firmware, which enables adversaries to exploit various vulnerabilities. In response, artificial intelligence (AI) has emerged as key tools for detecting anomalous behavior and addressing evolving cyber attack threats.

This study leverages the NF-CSE-CIC-IDS2018 dataset, a streamlined variant of CSE-CIC-IDS2018 which preserves relevant security events while reducing computational overhead. The paper evaluates the impact of classical outlier-removal techniques and shows that the Grubbs test eliminates outliers that might be attacks. Furthermore, the Principal Component Analysis and t-Distributed Stochastic Neighbour Embedding visualizations are compared across different feature sets, finding that using all NF-CSE-CIC-IDS2018 attributes with t-Distributed Stochastic Neighbour Embedding yields clearer separation of major attack types. Our findings highlight the importance of using security-aware preprocessing and non-linear embeddings to preserve and reveal critical attack patterns.

Keywords: Internet of Things (IoT) · NetFlow telemetry · Intrusion detection · Dimensionality reduction · Outlier removal

1 Introduction and Related Work

The Internet of Things (IoT) has the potential to challenge conventional security assumptions, given the billions of endpoints that are deployed in exposed settings or run frozen firmware for extended periods [1]. Consequently, adversaries are able to exploit a range of vulnerabilities, including side-channel access on the device [2] and version skew between endpoints, gateways and cloud back-ends [3]. These diverse issues have driven the development of standards and EU regulatory frameworks [4].

Addressing the wide attack surface has led to the adoption of strategies, with Machine Learning (ML) being one of the most prominent in identifying anomalies in devices [5]. In cybersecurity, identifying malicious behavior early and protect system integrity. Grubbs' Test, a classical statistical method, helps detect single-point outliers in structured, normally distributed data [6]. However, outlier removal requires caution, since attacks often show higher outlierness than legitimate traffic, especially in endpoint-based features, even though attack and non-attack outlier distributions overlap significantly [7]. The capacity of AI to process substantial quantities of data facilitates expedited and precise threat detection [8], thereby surpassing conventional methodologies that frequently rely on rule-based systems, which may prove ineffective in addressing novel threats [9].

Achieving effective implementation of AI in the domain of attack detection requires training AI with a substantial and diverse dataset, encompassing a wide range of attack types. A diverse dataset exposes the model to a variety of examples, allowing it to learn a wider range of patterns and features, improving its generalization ability and prediction accuracy [10].

Publicly available datasets such as UNSW-NB15 [11], BoT-IoT [12], ToN-IoT [13], and CSE-CIC-IDS2018 [14] are commonly employed for evaluating AI-based approaches in IoT and network security research. Each one comprises a large volume of network traffic and diverse attack scenarios. Sarhan et al. [15] recast them into the same router-exportable flow attributes, releasing five structured and organized resources. The unification of features, reduction in collection cost, and circumvention of packet-level privacy issues enable researchers to train and fairly compare intrusion-detection models based on ML. This facilitates the fusion of traces to emulate diverse IoT deployments. Ultimately, this enables the testing of whether a detector learned in one environment will recognise attacks in another. This is a crucial step towards deployable IoT cybersecurity [15].

The NF-CSE-CIC-IDS2018 is the variation of the CSE-CIC-IDS2018 dataset by [15] and will be utilised in this study, in which the process of selecting, categorizing, and normalizing variables was based on the flow records generated by nProbe [16]; this tool extracts data directly from real network traffic, producing flows that include key properties such as IP addresses, ports, protocols, timestamps, and byte counts. NF-CSE-CIC-IDS2018 retains the security events from CIC-IDS2018 but employs a reduced set of 12 basic NetFlow attributes, thus facilitating its use for the evaluation of intrusion detection systems that require less computational resources. Furthermore, it enables the comparison of results with other datasets that have been converted to the same format.

Given the high dimensionality of the cybersecurity datasets UNSW-NB15 [11], BoT-IoT [12], ToN-IoT [13], and CSE-CIC-IDS2018 [14], visualization techniques such as Principal Component Analysis (PCA) [17], Uniform Manifold Approximation and Projection [18], autoencoders [19] and t-Distributed Stochastic Neighbor Embedding (t-SNE) [20] are effective [21,22]. These techniques transform the original feature space into two or three dimensions for visual human's inspection. t-SNE proved particularly effective in the UNSW-NB15 datasetcite [21], offering enhanced visualization in 2D space. Furthermore, their findings indicated that 3D visualization did not yield any substantial advantage in terms of interpretability, highlighting the practicality of 2D representations for anomaly detection tasks. PCA is recommended as an initial method to explore data structure. If no clear patterns of clusters emerge, the data may be complex or not linearly separable. In such cases, nonlinear, local techniques like t-SNE, which handles many parameters to identify clusters and preserve local relationships, are more suitable, especially for large datasets.

This paper is structured as follows. Section 2 presents the techniques and methodologies employed in the study. Section 3 describes the selected case study. Section 4 outlines the experiments conducted, the results obtained and discusses the visualization of the data and the insights derived. Finally, Sect. 5 concludes with the main findings and outlines directions for future research.

2 Techniques Applied

The following section delineates the techniques which are employed in the course of conducting the research for this paper.

2.1 Outlier Detection and Removal

Before applying dimensionality reduction, it is recommended to detect and remove outliers [22], points that depart sharply from the dataset's overall pattern [23]. In network-traffic terms, these are packets whose field values are unusually high or low and rarely reflect normal behavior. If left in, such outliers can distort statistics, skew graph scales, and twist principal-component directions [24]. These packets may contain streams with values that are either exceptionally large or exceptionally small in specific fields. The Grubbs test G is a univariate [25], statistical test designed to detect a single outlier in a data set assumed to be from a normal distribution. The next step in the process is to determine whether G exceeds a tabulated critical threshold. This is dependent upon the sample size and the significance level. If the aforementioned condition is met, then the conclusion is that the point is an outlier. This outlier can then be excluded from the analysis [26].

2.2 Dimensionality Reduction

Dimensionality Reduction [27] (DR) is defined as the process of transforming high-dimensional data into a lower-dimensional space while preserving, as far as possible, the structure of the original information. The objective of this study is to obtain two-dimensional visualizations that depict the separation between benign traffic and various types of attacks. Therefore, two techniques are employed: Principal Component Analysis (PCA) and t-Distributed Stochastic Neighbor Embedding (t-SNE).

Principal Component Analysis (PCA). is a classic linear technique for reducing dimensionality. It finds orthogonal linear combinations (eigenvectors of the covariance matrix) that capture the greatest variance [17]. By projecting data onto these components, typically keeping the first two, it retains as much information (variance) as possible while discarding the rest. Eigenvalues show how much variance each component explains. To perform this decomposition, the use of the `Covariance_eigh` solver computes the exact eigenvalue decomposition of the covariance matrix using the `eigh` algorithm. This solver is particularly efficient when the number of samples is larger than the number of features [28]. PCA is unsupervised, using no class labels, so any separation in the resulting plane reflects inherent differences in the traffic features [29].

T-Distributed Stochastic Neighbor Embedding (t-SNE). is a non-linear dimensionality reduction technique. In contrast to PCA, t-SNE does not depend on global variance, but rather prioritizes the preservation of local relationships. It attempts to project two-dimensional data in such a manner that points that are proximate in the original space remain so in the visualization. The approach under discussion involves the conversion of high-dimensional distances to neighborhood probabilities, followed by the identification of a low-dimensional distribution of points whose distribution of distances emulates the original, with the objective of minimising a Kullback-Leibler type loss; this metric intent is to minimizes the divergence $D_{\mathrm{KL}}(P \parallel Q) = \sum_x P(x) \log(P(x)/Q(x))$ between a target distribution P and a model distribution Q. Because $D_{\mathrm{KL}} \geq 0$ and is asymmetric, reducing it—often via cross-entropy—drives Q to replicate P; The model applies a Student's t-distribution in the embedded space, thereby permitting large distances.

In essence, t-SNE is capable of identifying clusters with greater efficacy; it has a propensity to amalgamate analogous points, thereby forming compact groups, while concurrently ensuring that distinct groups are separated by intervening gaps.

T-SNE allows the selection of the metric that is utilized for the calculation of distances $d(p, q)$ in the original space prior to their conversion into probabilities. The testing of different metrics has been demonstrated to have the capacity to affect both visual output and computation time [20]. In the context of network flows, the following metrics are commonly employed for evaluation purposes:

1. **Euclidean distance:** standard straight-line distance in n-dimensional space.
2. **Manhattan Distance (Cityblock):** sum of absolute differences per dimension.
3. **Chebyshev distance:** maximum of the absolute differences.
4. **Cosine Distance:** looks at the similarity in the direction of the vectors.
5. **Correlation Distance:** similar to cosine but centered on the mean, evaluating similarity in patterns of linear variation.

Moreover, t-SNE tuning process involves other key parameters. These include the perplexity, defined as the average effective number of nearest neighbors; the

Table 1. NF-CSE-CIC-IDS2018 description of the variables.

Categorical Variables (8)		
variable name	Description	Type
IPV4 SRC ADDR	IPv4 source address of the flow.	*string*
IPV4 DST ADDR	IPv4 destination address of the flow.	*string*
L4 SRC PORT	Source transport port.	*int*
L4 DST PORT	Destination transport port.	*int*
PROTOCOL	Numeric identifier of the IP level protocol used.	*int*
L7 PROTO	Level 7 protocol identified, in numeric.	*int*
Label	0 = Benign, 1 = Attack.	*int*
Attack	Text with specific attack type (DoS, BruteForce, etc.).	*string*
Continuous Variables (6)		
variable name	Description	Type
TCP FLAGS	Cumulative sum of all TCP flags observed in stream.	*int*
IN BYTES	Number of incoming bytes in stream. This value represents the amount of data from the receiver's perspective.	*int*
OUT BYTES	Number of outgoing bytes in stream. It represents the amount of data sent from source host to destination.	*int*
IN PKTS	Number of incoming packets from source to destination.	*int*
OUT PKTS	Number of outgoing packets from source to destination.	*int*
FLOW DURATION MILLISECONDS	Flow duration in milliseconds, typically calculated as last packet time minus first packet time.	*int*

learning rate, which is the step size used in the t-SNE gradient descent optimization; and the early exaggeration, which is a multiplier applied to attractive forces during the initial optimization phase [30].

3 A Real Life Case Study

The NF-CSE-CIC-IDS2018 [14] dataset provides 14 features per flow that capture protocol details, flow information, and so forth. Twelve of these columns correspond to NetFlow features per network flow, and the remaining two represent class labels denoting the nature of the attack and its benignity. The feature columns are as shown in Table 1. The dataset has a total of 8,392,401 rows, of which 87.85% is classified as benign, leaving a 12.14% classified as attack. The following categories of attacks are included [14].

1. BruteForce (288,197 rows): Brute-force attack is a method that attempts to obtain access by trying numerous inputs in a short span of time.
2. Bot (15,683 rows): Traffic generated by a compromised machine, that is under remote control of the attacker. In the majority of cases, the phenomenon under discussion is characterized by the presence of automated malicious activity emanating from within the network.

3. DoS (269,421 rows): The objective of Single-Source Denial of Service (DOS) is to overload the resources of a machine or service, thereby preventing its availability to legitimate users. In the original CIC-IDS2018 [31], the following attacks were included: DoS Hulk, DoS Slowloris and DoS GoldenEye. In the present CIC-IDS2018, these are grouped simply as DoS.
4. DDoS (380,096): Distributed Denial of Service (DDoS) is a cyber-attack in which multiple coordinated distributed sources launch an attack on a target.
5. Infiltration (62,072 rows): Infiltration can be defined as the surreptitious breaching of a system or network with the objective of the theft of data, the sabotage of operations, or the dissemination of malware. The tactics employed in order to achieve this can range from simple password-guessing and phishing to sophisticated code exploits. In the CIC-IDS2018 scenario, the aforementioned situation was represented by an internal user who had gained unauthorised access to the network after opening an infected file.
6. Web Attacks (3,642 rows): Attacks on web applications encompass a range of methods, including SQL injections, command injections and malicious file uploads.

4 Experiments and Results

The techniques delineated in Sect. 2 will be employed in the analysis of the two-case study. The first case encompasses the set of continuous variables, while the second case includes both continuous and categorical variables. It is important to note that standard PCA is based on the traditional covariance matrix, which assumes continuous numerical data with significant variance. When applied to categorical variables, such covariances do not naturally exist, and as a result, directly applying PCA may yield inadequate or uninformative results [32]. Exploring the behavior of the complete dataset is of particular interest, as it enables a more comprehensive understanding of the problem. Nevertheless, caution must be exercised as categorical data can introduce bias during the learning process [33]. The first technique employed in this study involves the identification and eradication of outliers within the dataset. This process entails the filtration of data to eliminate any anomalous elements, though it should be noted that this procedure carries a certain degree of risk, as it may inadvertently result in the elimination of valuable data, such as attacks that are identified and eradicated based on their inherent nature. This procedure is applied to the data prior to and following the implementation of PCA; see Fig. 1.

In Fig. 1.a/b, a clear distinction can be observed between some of the data points, the yellow ones, and the ones located on the bottom-right part. The subset of the information in question pertains to Distributed Denial of Service (DDOS) attacks using the LOIC-UDP method. As demonstrated in the second image of Fig. 1.a/b, the elimination of outliers results in a discernible alteration of the data, thereby illustrating the efficacy of this approach in eradicating important data points. This method, as outlined in [34], underscores the potential consequences of outlier removal in the context of cybersecurity datasets,

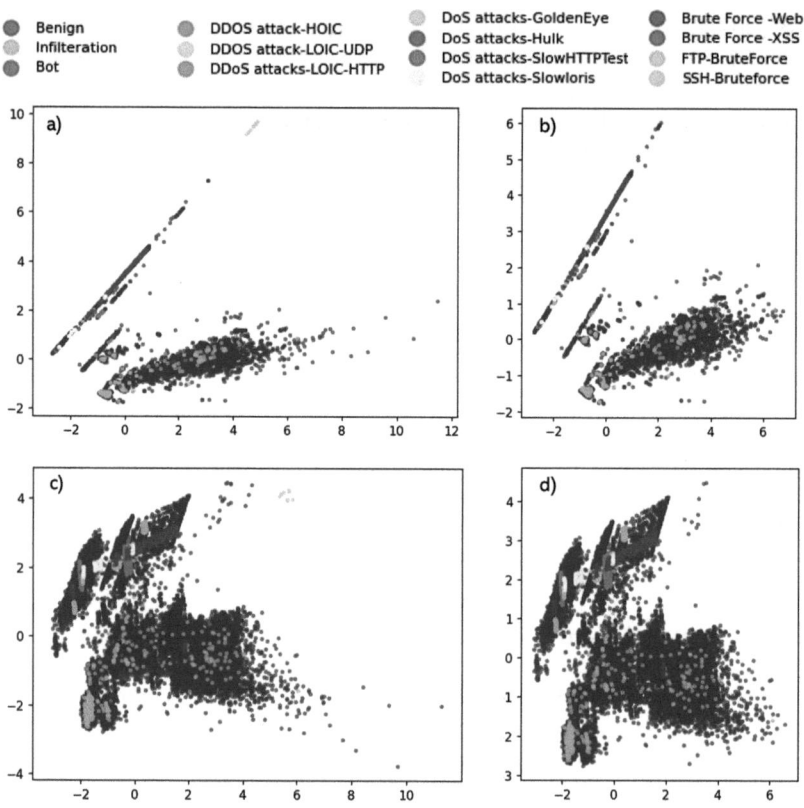

Fig. 1. PCA applied to the continuous variables(6 variables) and the complete data set (twelve variables). (a) visualization before outlier removal of the continuous variables; (b) after outlier removal of the continuous variables; (c) visualization before outlier removal of the complete data set; (d) after outlier removal of the complete data set.

emphasizing the possibility of data loss. In this particular instance, the quantity of data that has been eliminated as a result of the outlier detection and removal process amounts to 0.1275%. As illustrated in Fig. 1.a/b, PCA concentrates the majority of attacks in a single region, particularly in the case of DDoS and DOS attacks, which are predominantly concentrated in this area. It is also noteworthy that infiltrations are thoroughly intermingled with benign data. Moreover, PCA is the sole source where DDOS LOIC-UDP methods are observed to be grouped together.

In contrast, an examination of Fig. 1.c/d reveals the PCA of twelve variables and the impact of outlier removal exhibiting a comparable behaviour to the PCA of six variables. This underlines the efficacy of this method in removing significant data.The amount of percentage of data eliminated with outlier removal is 0.1275%, which is the same as in the six variable study case.

Moreover, the examination Fig. 1.a/b (six variables) versus Fig. 1.c/d (twelve variables) shows the attacks are no longer confined to a single, differentiated region and are more mixed with benign data in twelve variables, this could be because of the lack of encoding of the categorical values. However, the infiltration attacks behave similarly. It is also noteworthy that, in this process, the only attack that has been properly separated is the DDoS attack using the LOIC-UDP. This attack is later removed during outlier removal, which reduces the effectiveness of PCA in this use case.

The t-SNE technique is also applied to the two selections of data. All trainings were carried out with the parameters of the model are set as default: perplexity 30, learning rate automatic, and exaggeration 12 [30]. As illustrated in Table 2, the Kullback-Leibler type loss (KL-loss) is calculated, along with the elapsed time required to produce each result. As demonstrated in the following Table 2, the Euclidean distance demonstrates the least variability in both of the study cases when calculating the t-SNE. Conversely, the cosine metric consistently requires the most time to produce results.

Table 2. T-SNE's resource consumption (Elapsed Time in seconds) and model performance (KL-loss) for each distance metric. System configuration: CPU AMD Ryzen 7 5800X, GPU NVIDIA GEFORCE RTX 3060 Ti and 32Gb Ram.

	6 cols KL-loss	6 cols time	12 cols KL-loss	12 cols time
Euclidean	0.39	92.27	1.18	96.33
Manhattan	0.40	97.70	1.23	99.85
Chebyshev	0.42	99.25	1.22	101.36
Cosine	0.46	116.37	1.22	119.46
Correlation	0.49	113.43	1.21	119.00

Table 3. Group differentiation for each t-SNE (full dataset, Corr. means Correlation). DDOS* -Brute Force-Web, -XSS, attack-HOIC, -LOIC-UDP, -GoldenEye, Slowloris.

Attack Type	Euclidean	Manhattan	Chebyshev	Cosine	Corr.
Infiltration	No	No	No	No	No
Bot	Yes	Yes	No	Yes	Yes
DDOS*	No	No	No	No	No
SSH- Bruteforce	Yes	Yes	Yes	Yes	Yes
DDOS attacks-LOIC-HTTP	Yes	Yes	No	No	No
DoS attacks-Hulk	Yes	Yes	Yes	Yes	Yes
DoS attacks-SlowHTTPTest	Yes	Yes	Yes	Yes	Yes

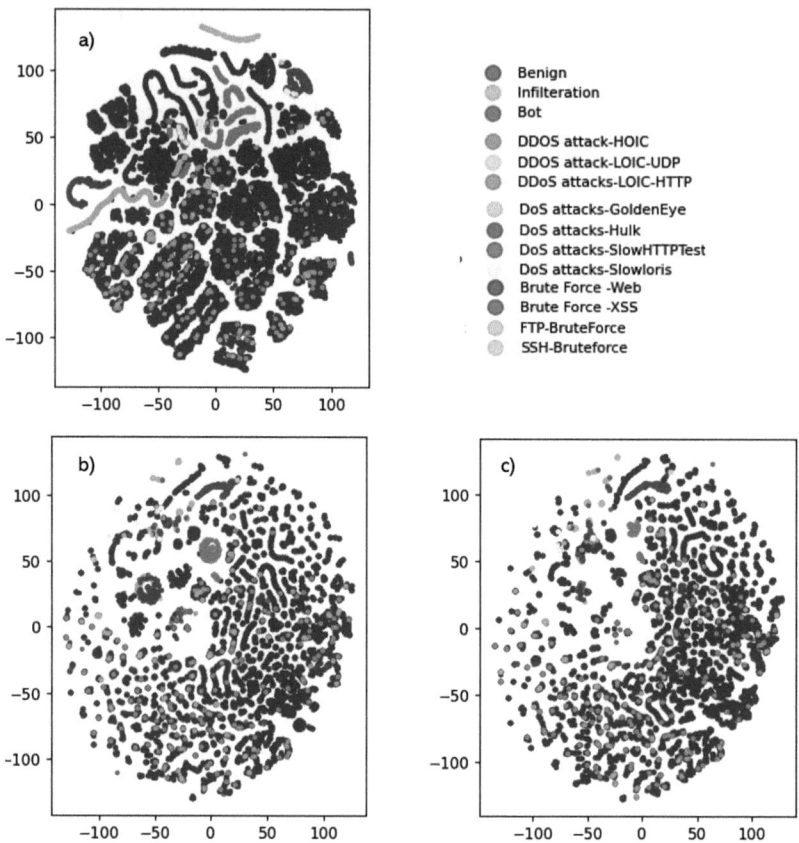

Fig. 2. t-SNE applied to the continuous variables (6 vars) and the complete dataset (12 vars). (a) complete dataset with **Euclidean** distance; (b) continuous variables with **Correlation** distance; (c) continuous variables with **Manhattan** distance.

Given the concise nature of this paper and the significant similarity among the majority of cases, it has been determined that Fig. 2.b will illustrate the most effective case of differentiating between the various types of attacks. This is because Fig. 2.b adheres to the correlation distance metric, in contrast to the least effective case depicted in Fig. 2.c, which employs the Manhattan distance metric. As is evident in both images, the majority of infiltration attacks demonstrate a similar pattern to that observed in the PCA analysis, characterized by a complete mixture with benign data. Conversely, Fig. 2.b illustrates the successful separation of some of the DOS and DDoS attacks from the benign data, thereby validating the efficacy of this method in identifying such threats. Besides, as illustrated in Fig. 2.c, the absence of proper separation among the attacks is indicative of the system's inefficiency.

In the application to the 12-variable study case, the outcomes are notably superior, resulting in the establishment of more distinctly delineated groups. Table 3 presents the results of applying various distance metrics in t-SNE, with all other parameters set to their default values. The selection criterion was based on visual inspection: a distance metric is marked as "Yes" if it enables the clear separation of the corresponding attack. This approach is considered adequate according to the criteria outlined in [35]. Given the high similarity in results across all metrics, the clearest one, Euclidean distance, has been selected for further use. By the Euclidean distance, t-SNE has yielded a substantially superior grouping outcome in comparison to that achieved by the 6-variable approach. This observation is evident in Fig. 2.a, which illustrates the successful separation of the majority of DDoS and DOS attacks, in addition to the segregation of bots from benign data. This level of performance has not been attained through the utilization of 6 variables (Fig. 2.b). Moreover, the infiltration has exhibited a consistent pattern of behavior, consistent with the results observed in previous instances. In this instance, the FTP and SSH brute-force attacks have been correctly distinguished from the benign data, yielding a notably superior outcome in comparison to that achieved by the application of six variables (Fig. 2.b).

5 Conclusion and Future Works

The analysis yielded three principal observations. First observation, outlier detection in security datasets must be applied carefully as Grubbs's test removed every DDOS LOIC-UDP instance, thereby effectively eliminating the target phenomenon. Second observation, PCA with six continuous variables distinguishes volumetric DoS/DDoS traffic but cannot separate infiltration attacks from benign activity. Moreover, PCA did not show sensitivity to categorical variables; it happens because it is based on the traditional covariance matrix. Third, t-SNE improves sensitivity by including categorical fields such as ports and protocol identifiers, being the only one that can separate bots and brute-force SSH/FTP attacks.

AI-based techniques provide a discriminative visualization that can reveal critical attack patterns of IoT devices. In future work, additional visualisation models will be implemented, including UMAP, which is known for its ability to preserve data structure, and autoencoder, which facilitates reversibility. Moreover, a deeper model optimization will be carried out, including a wider range of metrics. The NF-CSE-CIC-IDS dataset is comprised of three distinct versions, namely 14, 43 and 53. The subsequent version will undertake a study of feature selection, with a view to facilitating a more profound analysis of the original dataset feature by feature.

Acknowledgements. This publication is part of the AI4SECIoT project ("Artificial Intelligence for Securing IoT Devices"), funded by the National Cibersecurity Institute (INCIBE), derived from a collaboration agreement signed between the National Institute of Cybersecurity (INCIBE) and the University of Burgos. This initiative is carried out within the framework of the Recovery, Transformation and Resilience Plan funds, financed by the European Union (Next Generation), the project of the Government of Spain that outlines the roadmap for the modernization of the Spanish economy, the recovery of economic growth and job creation, for solid, inclusive and resilient economic reconstruction after the COVID19 crisis, and to respond to the challenges of the next decade.

References

1. Reglamento (UE) 2024/2847 https://www.boe.es/buscar/doc.php?id=DOUE-L-2024-81720. Accessed 22 May 2025
2. Devi, M., Majumder, A.: Side-channel attack in internet of things: a survey. In: Applications of Internet of Things: Proceedings of ICCCIOT 2020, pp. 213–222. Springer Singapore (2021)
3. What Are Downgrade Attacks? https://www.cyberark.com/what-is/downgrade-attacks/. Accessed 3 June 2025
4. European Cyber Security Organisation ECSO Technical Paper on Internet of Things (IoT) https://ecs-org.eu/ecso-uploads/2023/01/ECSO_WG6_IoT-Technical_paper_final.pdf. Accessed 9 June 2025
5. Mitchell, T.M.: Machine Learning. McGraw-Hill (1997)
6. Demertzis, K., Rantos, K., Magafas, L., Iliadis, L.: A cross-modal dynamic attention neural architecture to detect anomalies in data streams from smart communication environments. Appl. Sci. **13**(17), 9648 (2023)
7. Iglesias, F., Hartl, A., Zseby, T., Zimek, A.: Are network attacks outliers? a study of space representations and unsupervised algorithms. In: Joint European Conference on Machine Learning and Knowledge Discovery in Databases, pp. 159–175. Cham: Springer International Publishing (2019)
8. Buczak, A.L., Guven, E.: A survey of data mining and machine learning methods for cybersecurity intrusion detection. IEEE Commun. Surv. Tutorials **18**(2), 1153–1176 (2016). https://doi.org/10.1109/COMST.2015.2494502
9. Roshanaei, M., Khan, M.R., Sylvester, N.N.: Navigating AI cybersecurity: evolving landscape and challenges. J. Intell. Learn. Syst. Appl. **16**(3), 155–174 (2024). https://doi.org/10.4236/jilsa.2024.163010
10. Zhu, X., Vondrick, C., Fowlkes, C.C., Ramanan, D.: Do we need more training data? Int. J. Comput. Vision **119**(1), 76–92 (2015). https://doi.org/10.1007/s11263-015-0812-2
11. Moustafa, N., Slay, J.: UNSW-NB15: a comprehensive data set for network intrusion detection systems (UNSW-NB15 network data set). In: 2015 military communications and information systems conference (MilCIS), pp. 1–6. IEEE (2015)
12. Koroniotis, N., Moustafa, N., Sitnikova, E., Turnbull, B.: Towards the development of realistic botnet dataset in the internet of things for network forensic analytics: Bot-IoT dataset. Futur. Gener. Comput. Syst. **100**, 779–796 (2019)
13. Alsaedi, A., Moustafa, N., Tari, Z., Mahmood, A., Anwar, A.: TON_IoT telemetry dataset: A new generation dataset of IoT and IIoT for data-driven intrusion detection systems. IEEE Access **8**, 165130–165150 (2020)
14. Sharafaldin, I., Lashkari, A.H., Ghorbani, A.A.: Toward generating a new intrusion detection dataset and intrusion traffic characterization. ICISSp **1**(2018), 108–116 (2018)

15. Sarhan, M., Layeghy, S., Moustafa, N., Portmann, M.: NetFlow datasets for machine learning-based network intrusion detection systems. In: Deze, Z., Huang, H., Hou, R., Rho, S., Chilamkurti, N. (eds.) BDTA/WiCON -2020. LNICSSITE, vol. 371, pp. 117–135. Springer, Cham (2021). https://doi.org/10.1007/978-3-030-72802-1_9
16. https://www.ntop.org/guides/nprobe/cli_options.html. Accessed 7 July 2025
17. Salo, F., Nassif, A.B., Essex, A.: Dimensionality reduction with IG-PCA and ensemble classifier for network intrusion detection. Comput. Netw. **148**, 164–175 (2019)
18. Alqurashi, F., Ahmad, I.: A data-driven multi-perspective approach to cybersecurity knowledge discovery through topic modelling. Alex. Eng. J. **107**, 374–389 (2024)
19. Yang, Z.: A systematic literature review of methods and datasets for anomaly-based network intrusion detection. Comput. Secur. **116**, 102675 (2022)
20. Ozgode Yigin, B., Saygili, G.: Effect of distance measures on confidences of t-SNE embeddings and its implications on clustering for scRNA-seq data. Sci. Rep. **13**(1), 6567 (2023)
21. Zoghi, Z., Serpen, G.: UNSW-NB15 computer security dataset: analysis through visualization. Secur. Priv. **7**(1), e331 (2024)
22. Gondhalekar, R., Chattamvelli, R.: A comprehensive review of dimensionality reduction techniques for real-time network intrusion detection with applications in cybersecurity. Def. Sci. J. **74**(2), 246–255 (2024)
23. Hawkins, D.M.: Identification of outliers, vol. 11. Chapman and Hall, London (1980)
24. Molina-Coronado, B., Mori, U., Mendiburu, A., Miguel-Alonso, J.: Survey of network intrusion detection methods from the perspective of the knowledge discovery in databases process. IEEE Trans. Netw. Serv. Manage. **17**(4), 2451–2479 (2020). https://doi.org/10.1109/TNSM.2020.3016246
25. Grubbs, F.E.: Sample criteria for testing outlying observations. Ann. Math. Stat. **21**(1), 27–58 (1950)
26. Tietjen, G.L., Moore, R.H.: Some Grubbs-type statistics for the detection of several outliers. Technometrics **14**(3), 583–597 (1972)
27. Jia, W., Sun, M., Lian, J., Hou, S.: Feature dimensionality reduction: a review. Complex Intell. Syst. (1), 1–31 (2022). https://doi.org/10.1007/s40747-021-00637-x
28. Scikit learn PCA documentation. https://scikit-learn.org/stable/modules/generated/sklearn.decomposition.PCA.html. Accessed 7 July 2025
29. Jolliffe, I.T., Cadima, J.: Principal component analysis: a review and recent developments. Phil. Trans. R. Soc. A **374**(2065), 20150202 (2016). https://doi.org/10.1098/rsta.2015.0202
30. Scikit learn t-SNE documentation. https://scikit-learn.org/stable/modules/generated/sklearn.manifold.TSNE.html. Accessed 7 June 2025
31. A Realistic Cyber Defense Dataset (CSE-CIC-IDS2018). https://registry.opendata.aws/cse-cic-ids2018. Accessed 14 April 2025
32. Niitsuma, H., Okada, T.: Covariance and PCA for categorical variables. In: Pacific-Asia Conference on Knowledge Discovery and Data Mining, pp. 523–528. Berlin, Heidelberg: Springer Berlin Heidelberg (2005)
33. Wu, L.: Eg-conmix: an intrusion detection method based on graph contrastive learning. In: China National Conference on Big Data and Social Computing, pp. 19–34. Singapore: Springer Nature Singapore (2024)

34. Iglesias, F., Hartl, A., Zseby, T., Zimek, A.: Are network attacks outliers? a study of space representations and unsupervised algorithms. In: Joint European Conference on Machine Learning and Knowledge Discovery in Databases, pp. 159–175. Cham: Springer International Publishing (2019)
35. Anscombe, F.J.: Graphs in statistical analysis. Am. Stat. **27**(1), 17–21 (1973)

Data Mining and Decision Support Systems

A Microservice System Architecture for Receiving ETL System Patterns

Rui Monteiro[1], Bruno Oliveira[2], and Orlando Belo[1]

[1] ALGORITMI Research Centre/LASI, University of Minho, 4710-059 Braga, Portugal
pg50739@alunos.uminho.pt, obelo@di.uminho.pt
[2] CIICESI, School of Management and Technology, Porto Polytechnic, Felgueiras, Portugal
bmo@estg.ipp.pt

Abstract. The use of a service-oriented approach in ETL (Extract-Transform-Load) systems implementation is potentially very beneficial, as it allows transforming traditional ETL tasks into services, having simple and well-structured functionalities that can be reused according to the needs of the tasks and the data they handle. Furthermore, service-based approaches simplify the work of designing and implementing any ETL system that needs to be customized, as it provides a well-established, flexible and scalable infrastructure, highly modular, allowing reusing and simplify restructuring existing services in the implementation of new ETL components. In pattern based ETL systems, the use of service-based architecture allows mapping in a very natural way ETL patterns as services and orchestrate them easily using native management services. In this paper, we present, describe and discuss how we made pattern-service mapping and implemented a service-based ETL system in a concrete application domain, highlighting how ETL patterns can be materialized using a microservice architecture.

Keywords: Business Intelligence · Data Warehousing · ETL Systems · Service Oriented Architectures · ETL Patterns · ETL Patterns as Services · Microservices

1 Introduction

The concept of data warehouse is not new. Although its roots grounded practically two decades ago, it was in 1990 that its emergence really happened. The concept was first defined by Bill Inmon, as representing "A subject-oriented, integrated, time-variant, and non-volatile collection of data in support of management's decision-making process" [1]. This is a concept that persists today, both in the scientific community and in the technical and business community. From that moment on, the foundations of data warehousing systems began to be built effectively. A few years later, in 1996, Ralph Kimball [2] reinforced these foundations in a very concrete and effective way, introducing new models and techniques in the development of data warehousing systems and in the way we could populate its data structures: the data warehouses.

The existence of a data warehouse in an organization requires the implementation of several specific systems, many of them related to the population of its data structures [3]. Data warehousing populating systems, commonly referred to as ETL (Extract-Transform-Load) systems, are used by organizations to collect and organize specific sets of data, highly subject oriented, often heterogeneous and multifaceted in nature, which are especially collected to meet predefined decision requirements for supporting decision-making processes [4]. In any populating system, specific tools are used, aimed at carrying out data extraction, transformation or integration tasks. In practice, such tools allow the definition and orchestration of software components that apply and execute computational patterns that can be applied over a very diverse set of ETL tasks – e.g. data gathering, change data capture, data scrambling, or intensive loading [5]. In most cases, ETL systems are monolithic and complex, involving the setup and execution of a wide variety of tasks in a complex process pipelining. It is known that this type of organization raises serious problems during system's design and implementation process, and, subsequently, in its maintenance and operational evolution [6]. Many of these problems are caused by the intricate workflow of ETL processes and by the implementation model adopted, often rigid and not very modular. However, if we decide for a service-oriented approach in the implementation of an ETL system, we can use small autonomous software components, capable of executing small ETL tasks independently, when integrated into an architecture that hosts and run them in a cohesive ecosystem [7]. This promotes communication between components (services) and ensures they run as if they are a single system [8], ensuring system independence in technological terms, since each service can be built over the most appropriate technology, and providing adequate support to the implementation and execution of the task for which it is responsible [9]. The use of patterns is a regular technique in software design and development. Software patterns allow for creating reusable solutions to recurring problems. They can also be used for implementing ETL tasks requiring the most used data processing components and data structures, contributing to reduce the resources involved with ETL systems [10]. Thus, Oliveira et al. (2019) [7] suggested identifying the most frequently used ETL tasks and developing custom software patterns – an evolution to what was proposed by Vassiliadis et al. [11]. However, implementing ETL systems using patterns is not a standard practice. When it happens, it usually follows a monolithic architectural model, in which patterns are integrated as a part of a global system. Despite its modularity, which ensures pattern independence, it does not guarantee pattern autonomy.

In this paper we present and discuss the development of a microservice system designed for hosting ETL processes integrating ETL patterns as services and ensuring their orchestration according to the directives established for populating a specific data warehouse. Following the approach presented in [12], we designed and developed a set of ETL job pipelines using Docker containers to encapsulate ETL patterns and support their orchestration (pipelines). This approach allowed to obtain some important advantages in the process of implementing (and deploying) an ETL system, particularly in terms of technological independence, since each service can use the most appropriate technology in its implementation and in the execution of the tasks for which it is responsible, of sizing of the system, allowing the implementation of a scalable system so that there is no need to change the size of all components when another is affected, and of reusing components, which allows the reuse of services already implemented to deal with similar processes. The remaining part of this paper is organized as follows. Section 2 approaches the use of service-based systems in the implementation of ETL systems. Section 3 presents the system developed, giving particular attention to the ETL pattern implementation and their orchestration in a microservice infrastructure. Finally, Sect. 4 presents some conclusions and future work.

2 Service Oriented ETL Systems

Sabtu et al. [13] argued that a traditional ETL system cannot currently fulfil its role in an era of (near-)real-time data. These authors argue that ETL systems need to evolve to cope with new data management environments, using characteristics such as high availability, low latency and horizontal scalability. The increasing need to use large volumes of data as part of the analytical process ends up making the process of developing traditional ETL systems not scalable [14]. Zode [15] discussed the evolution of customized and manually developed ETL systems for tool-based approaches and specific use cases. Traditional "hand-coded" ETL systems face several issues, which impact their own efficiency, maintainability, and overall effectiveness. As software has become increasingly complex, development approaches have also had to evolve and adjust to the requirements that have been systematically imposed by new computational models used in modern applications. Currently, it is consensual that the effects of such an evolutionary process can be mitigated with the use of approaches that are based on flexible, scalable and modular architectures [16]. Recently, several systems, considered complex, have been migrated from monolithic architectures to collections of services, usually large, or to collections of small independent but interconnected services, acting together in the fulfilment of a single work. This type of approach allows the development of applications in a fast and sustained way, highly modular and with great robustness and fault tolerance [17].

The use of a service-oriented approach in the implementation of ETL systems, which is intuitive and practical to use, is potentially advantageous in the development and implementation of a data warehouse system. The use of microservices makes it possible to transform traditional ETL operations into simplified services that can be reused according to the inherent needs of each type of data to be used by the populating system and allows the isolation of errors. In addition, this type of approach also ensures a reduction in the workload qualified for the implementation of an ETL system, which must be customized to the needs of current analytical systems. This is possible, because it allows the system implementers to use an established infrastructural base for this implementation, requiring only the creation of additional services or the customization of existing services, to meet the requirements of the stand system. According to Ismail et al. [18], traditional approaches used in the development of ETL systems prove to be inadequate when faced with the processing of large volumes of data, with great variety and generated quite quickly. However, these characteristics can be addressed with natural scalability on a service-based architecture, using service replication and hybrid approaches.

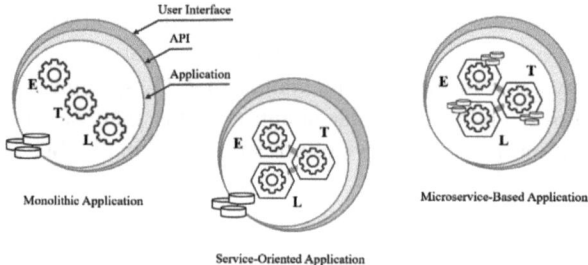

Fig. 1. Monolithic, service-oriented and microservice-based applications.

The demand for a service-oriented approach to the development of ETL systems is something that is not new [19–22]. Recently, approaches using microservice-based architectures (Fig. 1) for database systems have also been explored [23]. This architecture emerged from service-oriented architectures to address the latest needs of organizations, welcoming a combination of several good development practices from different communities. Microservices [9] are defined as small autonomous services that work together and have as their sole responsibility the implementation of a single functional requirement, non-functional or both [24]. This architecture can be seen as a new architectural paradigm for applications, which offers a lot of benefits, for example in migration processes from traditional infrastructures to cloud computing platforms, with those that are used by companies such as Microsoft, Amazon or IBM [25]. Newman [9] argued that the alternative style of microservice architectures is beneficial when combined with modern development practices. In a microservice architecture, as services are simplified, the number of microservices increases, which increases the complexity of the architecture, being usually managed through more sophisticated strategies based on automation tools and specific processes. These tools can be container-based. In their orchestration process, using Docker or Kubernetes, they benefit in terms of scalability on demand and greater reliability given the use of containers [26].

Nadareishvili et al. [27] considered that to establish and maintain control and management of a microservice system is more laborious than in other architectural style system. Therefore, it is necessary to understand whether the use of microservices will be beneficial or not. For many organizations, this cost is justified through greater resilience and, consequently, better adaptability to change. The migration from a monolithic system to a microservices-based system will present some technical difficulties given the complexity of performing the decoupling of a monolithic application. However, if we promote and carry out a development process of a pattern-based ETL system, from its preliminary design phase, its materialization in a microservice based architecture will be simpler and easier to achieve, regardless of the volume, diversity or velocity of the data required to populate a data warehouse.

3 ETL System Patterns as Microservices

3.1 A Service Oriented Approach

In service-oriented architecture, the composition of services is based on the notion of subsystems that represent regular procedures applied to the implementation of ETL systems. In [6], a prototype of a service-oriented ETL system was presented, a proof of concept for the development of ETL systems based on standard task (patterns), considering the specificities of service-oriented architectures. In this work, the main tasks of extraction, transformation, and loading were broken down into various detailed tasks (patterns) to satisfy specific requirements of ETL systems. Thus, each ETL pattern materialized a task that usually is present in a conventional ETL process. – e.g., changing data capture, replacing natural keys by artificial keys, updating dimension tables, or enhancing data quality.

In this work, we developed a similar approach, using microservices as a privileged means of materializing and orchestrating ETL patterns. Hafyani et al. [8], for example, revealed some of the advantages of doing this when they studied and developed a system to implement a data pipeline of an ETL system using microservice architecture. In this work, Apache Kafka was used as an orchestrator of microservices and as an essential means of communication between them. Apache Kafka can manage data flow between different microservices and enables its processing in a sequential and incremental way, offering message publishing and subscription functionalities [28]. We integrated the Apache Kafka solution with Docker Compose to ensure compatibility and efficiency in an ETL process, converting an ETL process description model to an Apache Kafka-based model. Soltanmohammadi and Hikmet [12] investigated the implementation of efficient ETL systems in clinical applications using a similar approach. This study sought to create and use pipelines for ETL processes integrating Docker containers and PySpark. These authors refer to the pivotal role that Docker and its containers have in terms of system scalability, efficiency and reproduction of the results obtained in the ETL process they implemented. Using Docker technology gives us some advantages. Unlike virtualization, in which it is necessary to use an operating system for each structure, Docker containers are blocks of applications divided by a server. Each container acts as an independent building block of an application and represents the executable instances of a specific image, which makes it easy to build and implement a distributed microservices architecture, with continuous integration and pipelining tools for delivery. Docker works as an operating system for containers, providing basic commands to create images or start or stop their execution [29]. To minimize the difficulties of the initial Kafka configuration, Docker images for Apache Kafka and Apache Zookeeper were used to ensure easy use in different environments. Apache Zookeeper functions as a distributed coordination server for Kafka brokers, doing the task of determining the leaders for each topic and partition, through elections, and storing settings and permissions for each topic. Its use is a prerequisite when using Apache Kafka, which is why it was used in this project [30]. Thus, to configure the containers for both technologies, a YAML file was used for Docker Compose configuration. This tool makes it possible to define multi-container applications, which facilitates the implementation of the system and ensures that services work with each other, without friction, and provide simplified orchestration and coordination. Docker provides an internal virtual network to support communication between the various containers. However, we decided not to use a specific network for certain services, but only the internal Docker network ("generic_etl_platform_default") to ensure communication between the different services of the system.

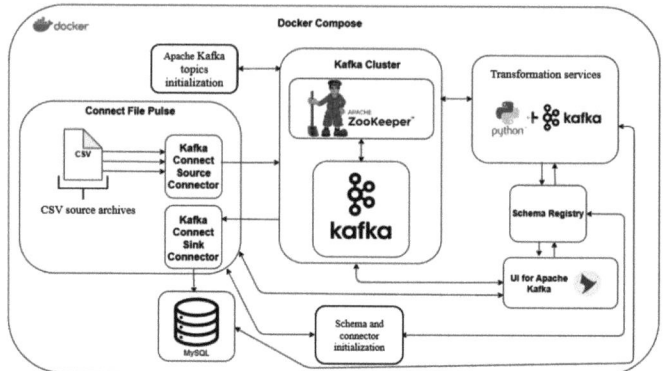

Fig. 2. An overview of the system architecture.

In Fig. 2 we can see the most relevant internal interactions between containers, as well as their general structure and organization and data flow. The services we deployed, managed and orchestrated by Docker Compose, were:

- Kafka, the Apache Kafka server of the system, which is based on the image of "confluentinc/cp-kafka:7.5.0" obtained from Docker Hub. This service defines important configurations such as the endpoint, which makes requests within the Docker network ("kafka:29092"), the port "localhost:9092" for communications outside the internal Docker network.
- Zookeeper, which is the central distributed coordination and synchronization service. This container is based on the "confluentinc/cp-zookeeper:7.5.0" image obtained from Docker Hub and its configuration environment exposes the "zookeeper:2181" port for communications between containers over the internal Docker network.
- MySQL, to host a MySQL relational database server, which is made available from its "mysql:8.3.0" image made available in Docker Hub.
- kafka-ui, which is a container created to assist system evaluation and result verification. This container manages and monitors multiple clusters in one place, visualizes Apache Kafka performance metrics, and manages messages – json, txt or Avro.
- init-kafka, which is a container created from a homonymous image configured through Dockerfile, using a script to ensure the correct creation of the Kafka topic "Dados_CSV_Topic". It is used as an entry point for data extracted from CSV files.
- schema-registry, which is a service based on the "confluentinc/cp-schema-registry:7.5.0" image obtained from Docker Hub. This service provides a centralized repository for managing schemas to be used for data serialization within the Kafka network.

- init-connectors, a service that has a Dockerfile in its context directory ("/init-connectors") defined in the "docker-compose.yml" file. The Dockerfile is used at the time-of-service startup to perform the configuration of the container.
- schemas of the Schema Registry, which depends on the "kafka", "connect-file-pulse" and "schema-registry" services, and waits for a "healthcheck" process done by Docker Compose.
- transform-service, which is the transformation service that uses the Dockerfile to create the custom Docker image, which is based on the "python:3.9-slim" image.
- Preprocessing-service, which is a pre-processing service, an extension of the "transformservice" service, which is responsible for performing the initial parsing of the data obtained in the messages that function as system input.
- Lookup-service, which is a service that has its Docker image created thanks to a Dockerfile, like the transform-service. In conjunction with the previous two services, this service is responsible for implementing the "Lookup" ETL pattern.
- rest-proxy, a service that is built on top of the official Confluent image of the Kafka REST Proxy, provided by Docker Hub ("confluentinc/cp-kafka-rest:latest"). This service acts as an interface to support interaction with the Kafka cluster, via HTTP, and allows the production and consumption of messages via RESTful calls.

To start-up the system requires almost no intervention from the system's end user. To start the system, it is only necessary to launch the services through a system console, using the command "docker-compose up -d --build", in the directory where the "docker-compose.yml" file is located. Then, the process runs autonomously, creating all Docker images from Dockerfiles and extracting pre-configured images from the Docker Hub. Subsequently, in other system runs, it is no longer necessary to create these services. We just need to run them through Docker Desktop or using the previously executed command, without the "--build" option.

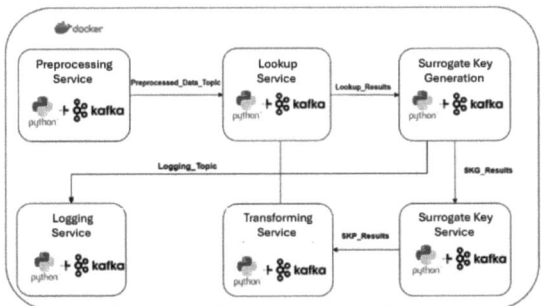

Fig. 3. The ETL pattern microservice architecture global overview.

3.2 ETL Patterns as Microservices

The implementation process was developed following a Docker service approach, using the Kafka ecosystem, aiming to autonomize the functionalities of each ETL pattern, ensuring its autonomy and allowing its reuse in other ETL Systems projects (Fig. 3). Each container seeks to be responsible for the implementation of a specific ETL pattern, rather than group several ETL patterns into the same service. Having a specific Docker container, each ETL pattern development, integration, maintenance and independence is autonomous, being not affected by other ETL patterns processes. Furthermore, we implemented a customized logging system through a Dockerfile, based on the use of a specific topic and Kafka group ("Logging_Topic" and "Logging_Service") to record any errors or warnings related to the operations performed by each ETL pattern. To ensure that data had a format that facilitates the performance of the following ETL patterns, the transform-service transformation service, initially implemented to act at the end of the data flow of the patterns, was divided into two distinct services (containers), operating at different times of the data flow. In practice, a preprocessing-service of Apache Kafka messages was defined and used, to parse the messages between ETL patterns, modifying them to follow a format suitable for system services. Finally, we implemented a transformation service, using Python. However, not all the APIs mentioned are implemented as Python libraries. Despite this, we used "confluent-kafka-python", a library that was developed by Confluent to take advantage of specific classes such as "Consumer", "Producer" and "Admin Client", or "serialization" and "schema_registry", and perform message serialization and interaction with the Apache Kafka Schema Registry. Next, we address two of the ETL patterns implemented ("Lookup" and "Surrogate Key Generator"), as well present their application and implementation within the microservices-based architecture developed.

Lookup – We implemented the ETL "Lookup" pattern in a Docker container ("LookupService"), based on a Dockerfile that builds a custom image from the "python:3.9-slim" Docker image. This pattern looks up the value of a given data element in a matching table following a given search criterion. The service of this pattern connects to Kafka Broker ("kafka:29092"), within the Docker environment, to create a new consumer for subscribing the input topic. Then, it establishes a connection to the system's database to conduct the searches it needs. In addition, a Kafka Producer is also created to ensure the continuation of the flow of data to the Kafka ecosystem, to send the messages received after processing. The data obtained by the pattern is used to get the schema of the desired data and the identifier that will be used in the search process. During the execution of this pattern, a database search is performed according to the access schema – each schema has its own lookup table –, to obtain the data corresponding to the lookup element. After this process has been conducted, an input is produced and sent in the form of a message to the registration topic ("Logging_Topic"). If it does not exist in the lookup table (Fig. 4), the pattern will forward the data obtained to the next stage of the ETL system, using the topic "Lookup_Results", after having been duly enriched with the information related to the search result in the lookup tables. If there is no lookup data for the lookup element, the system will take care of generating a new surrogate key for that element.

Surrogate Key Generator - This pattern was implemented using the Docker service "SurrogateKeyService", an instance of the Docker image "generic_etl_platform-skg-service". The generation of surrogate keys is an important task in ETL systems, as it supports most of the data reconciliation processes that take place when populating

```
{
    "schema": "olympicmedals",
    "id_natural": "USA",
    "data": {
            "NOC": "USA",
            "Gold": 36,
            "Silver": 39,
            "Bronze": 26,
            "Total": 101
    },
    "lookup_result": "Not Found"
}
```

Fig. 4. Message sent by the "Lookup" pattern to its output topic ("Lookup_Results").

a data warehouse. Surrogate keys are usually simple and easy to generate and maintain. In practice, they follow a given sequence of integers, which allows the correspondence between the natural keys of sources' data elements and the surrogate keys used in the data warehouse. This ETL pattern ("skg_processor.py") creates a Kafka consumer ("skg_service"), a Kafka producer and a database connection for hosting the new surrogate keys. The Kafka consumer uses the messages in the default service input topic ("Lookup_Results"). Messages are consumed using a specific method ("poll(1.0)"), which is executed until the service is shutdown by Docker Desktop or via the "docker stop <container>" command.

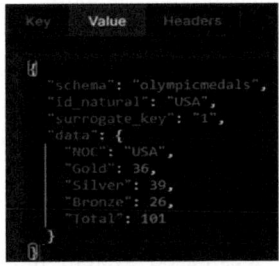

Fig. 5. Message sent by a surrogate key generator pattern to the output topic ("SKG_Results").

In Fig. 5 we can see an example of a message obtained through Kafka, in which we can see a small excerpt of the field "Value" of a Kafka message extracted from the referred topic. In this message, we can see the information regarding the search result ("lookup_result"), which contains the schema ("schema"), the natural identifier ("id_natural"), the replacement key ("surrogate_key") and the data ("data") that receives the line of the original CSV file. The "Lookup" pattern is based on the "skg-service" Docker service/container, which uses the "Lookup_result" field to determine whether the search for the replacement key had a positive result. If the result is negative, a specific method ("get_or_create_sk()") is executed, which takes as arguments the schema of the message under evaluation and its natural key.

4 Conclusions and Future Work

The use of ETL patterns revealed an interesting and powerful approach technique in ETL processes design and implementation. ETL patterns allow for creating modular, flexible and reusable solutions to recurring ETL tasks for data warehouses populating processes that shares common data processing tasks and standard operational monitoring and control. In this paper we presented and discussed the design and implementation of a microservice-based architecture for an ETL system, adopting a predefined set of ETL patterns presented in [7]. ETL patterns have been encapsulated in independent Docker services and orchestrated in a Docker Compose architecture. To ensure reliable performance and scalability in the data processing processes of the ETL system, we used Apache Kafka and Apache Zookeeper technologies, which allowed us to develop the various ETL tasks so that they could be operated in real time, in a reliable and distributed way. Compared to ETL traditional approaches, the use of microservices has the advantage of providing a highly adaptable system, which gives us great flexibility in cases where it is necessary to change ETL tasks' structure or logic, since it does not require changing the entire system's codebase, thanks to the use of microservices, in particular Docker services. Docker benefits system orchestration by reducing maintenance work, something that does not happen in more traditional approaches that are based on monolithic architectures, which involves checking established dependencies whenever a part of system is changed. Despite the advantages of adopting a microservices architecture in a data warehouse system, we have to be aware that this type of architecture brings us some disadvantages and challenges that are sometimes difficult to overcome, namely, that the operational management of this type of system (the orchestration of the various services) is usually complex, since each microservice (ETL pattern) is a separate application, requiring to be controlled, audited and maintained individually, that the number of services implemented is usually quite large, demanding the definition of a robust and effective strategy to handle any failures, and that the testing and validation of the system is more complicated than a monolithic system, given the distribution and interoperability of the services involved in the ETL process.

Although current microservices-based system implementation has revealed the potential of applying microservice technology in data warehousing populating processes, in a future review we need to review the system's structure and services to design a Kafka Connect connector having the ability to load processed and transformed messages into a data warehousing system, using the "docker-compose.yml" to ensure the portability of services (ETL patterns) between different systems and ensure the extensibility of the system, adding new services (containers) for implementing new ETL tasks or patterns. In addition, the implementation of a "SINK" connector to upload processed messages to a database in a customized way or the use of existing connectors in the Kafka Connect ecosystem to increase the flexibility and robustness of a data warehouse settlement process should also be considered.

Acknowledgements. This work has been supported by FCT – Fundação para a Ciência e Tecnologia within the R&D Unit Project Scope UID/00319/Centro ALGORITMI (ALGORITMI/UM).

References

1. Inmon, W.H.: Building the Data Warehouse. Wiley, Hoboken (1992)
2. Kimball, R., Ross, M.: The Data Warehouse Toolkit: Practical Techniques for Building Dimensional Data Warehouses. Wiley, Hoboken (1996)
3. Souissi, S., BenAyed, M.: Genus: An ETL tool treating the big data variety. In: IEEE/ACS 13th International Conference of Computer Systems and Applications (AICCSA), pp. 1–8. IEEE (2016)
4. Khan, B., Jan, S., Khan, W., Chughtai, M.: An overview of ETL techniques, tools, processes and evaluations in data warehousing. J. Big Data **6**(1–20), 2024 (2024)
5. El-Sappagh, S., Hendawi, A., El Bastawissy, A.: A proposed model for data warehouse ETL processes. J. King Saud Univ. – Comput. Inf. Sci. **23**, 91–104 (2011). https://doi.org/10.1016/J.JKSUCI.2011.05.005
6. Oliveira, O., Oliveira, O., Belo, O.: Overcoming traditional ETL systems architectural problems using a service-oriented approach. Expert Syst. J. **40**, e13442 (2023)
7. Oliveira, B., Oliveira, O., Santos, V., Belo, O.: ETL development using patterns: a service oriented approach. In: Proceedings of the 21st International Conference on Enterprise Information Systems (ICEIS 2019), vol. 1, pp. 204–210. SciTePress (2019)
8. El Hafyani, H., Abboud, M., Taher, Y.: A microservices based architecture for implementing and automating ETL data pipelines for mobile crowdsensing applications. In: Proceedings - 2021 IEEE International Conference on Big Data, Big Data 2021, pp. 5909–5911. Institute of Electrical and Electronics Engineers Inc. (2021)
9. Newman, S.: Building Microservices: Designing Fine-Grained Systems, 2nd edn. O'Reilly Media, Inc. (2015)
10. Oliveira, B., Belo, O.: An ontology for describing ETL patterns behavior. In: DATA 2016 – Proceedings of the 5th International Conference on Data Management Technologies and Applications, pp. 102–109. SciTePress (2016)
11. Vassiliadis, P., Simitsis, A., Skiadopoulos, S.: Conceptual modeling for ETL processes. In: DOLAP 2002: Proceedings of the 5th ACM International Workshop on Data Warehousing and OLAP, pp. 14–21 (2002). https://doi.org/10.1145/583890.583893
12. Soltanmohammadi, E., Hikmet, N.: Optimizing healthcare big data processing with containerized pyspark and parallel computing: a study on ETL pipeline efficiency. J. Data Anal. Inf. Process. **12**, 544–565 (2024)
13. Sabtu, A., et al.: The challenges of extract, transform and loading (ETL) system implementation for near real-time environment. In: International Conference on Research and Innovation in Information Systems, ICRIIS, pp. 1–5. IEEE Computer Society (2017)
14. Ali, S., Wrembel, R.: From conceptual design to performance optimization of ETL workflows: current state of research and open problems. VLDB J. **26** (2017). https://doi.org/10.1007/s00778-017-0477-2
15. Zode, M.: The evolution of ETL-from hand-coded ETL to tool-based ETL cognizant technology solutions ETL evolution. Technical report, Cognizant Technology Solutions (2007)
16. Valipour, M., Amirzafari, B., Maleki, K., Daneshpour, N.: A brief survey of software architecture concepts and service-oriented architecture. In: 2nd IEEE International Conference on Computer Science and Information Technology, pp. 34–38. IEEE (2009). https://doi.org/10.1109/ICCSIT.2009.5235004
17. Ponce, F., Márquez, G., Astudillo, H.: Migrating from monolithic architecture to microservices: a rapid review. In: 2019 38th International Conference of the Chilean Computer Science Society (SCCC), pp. 1–7. IEEE (2019)

18. Ismail, A., Sazali, F., Jawaddi, S., Mutalib, S.: Stream ETL framework for twitter-based sentiment analysis: leveraging big data technologies. Expert Syst. Appl. **261**, 2 (2025). https://doi.org/10.1016/j.eswa.2024.125523
19. Wang, C., Ye, Z.: An ETL services framework based on metadata. In: 2010 2nd International Workshop on Intelligent Systems and Applications, pp. 1–4. IEEE (2010)
20. Awad, M., Abdullah, M., Ali, A.: Extending ETL framework using service oriented architecture. In Procedia Comput. Sci. **3**, 110–114 (2011). https://doi.org/10.1016/j.procs.2010.12.019
21. Akkaoui, Z., Zimányi, E.: Defining etl worfklows using BPMN and BPEL. In: DOLAP 2009: Proceedings of the ACM Twelfth International Workshop on Data Warehousing and OLAP, pp. 41–48. Association for Computing Machinery (2009). https://doi.org/10.1145/1651291.1651299
22. Akkaoui, Z., Zimányi, E., Mazón, J., Trujillo, J.: A bpmn-based design and maintenance framework for etl processes. Int. J. Data Warehouse. Min. **9**, 46–72 (2013). https://doi.org/10.4018/jdwm.2013070103
23. Shakir, A., Staegemann, D., Volk, M., Jamous, N., Turowski, K.: Towards a concept for building a big data architecture with microservices. Bus. Inf. Syst. **1**, 83–94 (2021)
24. Schwartz, A.: Microservices. Inform.-Spekt. **40**(6), 590–594 (2017). https://doi.org/10.1007/s00287-017-1078-6
25. De Lauretis, L.: From monolithic architecture to microservices architecture. In: Proceedings – 2019 IEEE 30th International Symposium on Software Reliability Engineering Workshops, ISSREW 2019, pp. 93–96. Institute of Electrical and Electronics Engineers Inc. (2019). https://doi.org/10.1109/ISSREW.2019.00050
26. Gos, K., Zabierowski, W.: The comparison of microservice and monolithic architecture. In: 2020 IEEE XVI International Conference on the Perspective Technologies and Methods in MEMS Design (MEMSTECH), pp. 150–153. IEEE (2020)
27. Nadareishvili, I., Mitra, R., McLarty, M., Amundsen, M.: Microservice Architecture: Aligning Principles, Practices, and Culture. O'Reilly Media, Inc. (2016)
28. Wang, Z., et al.: Kafka and its using in high-throughput and reliable message distribution. In: Proceedings of the 8th International Conference on Intelligent Networks and Intelligent Systems, ICINIS 2015, pp. 117–120. Institute of Electrical and Electronics Engineers Inc. (2016)
29. Dongre, A.: Container technology: Docker (2023)
30. Mewada, S.: The role of the zookeeper in the kafka cluster (2023)

A Novel General Hybrid System for Data Feature Selection

Dragan Simić[1(✉)], Zorana Banković[2], José R. Villar[3], José Luis Calvo-Rolle[4], Svetislav D. Simić[1], and Svetlana Simić[5]

[1] Faculty of Technical Sciences, University of Novi Sad, Trg Dositeja Obradovića 6, 21000 Novi Sad, Serbia
`dsimic@eunet.rs, {dsimic,simicsvetislav}@uns.ac.rs`
[2] Frontiers Media SA, Paseo de Castellana 77, Madrid, Spain
[3] University of Oviedo, Campus de Llamaquique, 33005 Oviedo, Spain
`villarjose@uniovi.es`
[4] Department of Industrial Engineering, University of A Coruña, 15405 Ferrol-A Coruña, Spain
`jlcalvo@udc.es`
[5] Faculty of Medicine, University of Novi Sad, Hajduk Veljkova 1–9, 21000 Novi Sad, Serbia
`svetlana.simic@mf.uns.ac.rs`

Abstract. This paper proposes a hybrid system for feature selection, allowing the degree of importance of different features to be determined. Different feature selection techniques, specifically the following four: Univariate feature ranking for classification using chi-square tests, Rank features for classification using minimum redundancy maximum relevance, Relief-based feature selection and Constrained greedy k-means with silhouette value ranking method are employed on the three well-known datasets from UCI Machine Learning Repository: *Iris*, *Wine*, and *Ionosphere*. Subsequently, with the variables ordered from highest to lowest importance as a result of each of the four feature selection methods, an iterative clustering process is performed, agglomerating features that are used to calculate accuracy. This accuracy is employed to determine the most relevant features. The best accuracy value for *Iris* dataset is 96%, for *Wine* dataset is 80.33%, and the best accuracy for *Ionosphere* is 83.19%. Experimental results obtained with the general unsupervised hybrid clustering system proposed in this paper are absolutely comparable to other studies.

Keywords: Feature selection · Feature ranking methods · *k*-means · *k*-medoids · Fuzzy c-means

1 Introduction

Feature selection is the process of identifying and selecting the most relevant features from a dataset while discarding those that are redundant or irrelevant. It serves as a critical step in the machine learning pipeline, especially when dealing with high-dimensional datasets. By reducing the dimensionality of the data, feature selection enhances model performance, reduces computational cost, and improves interpretability [1]. The primary purpose of feature selection is to ensure that machine learning models focus on the most informative variables, leading to better generalization and predictive accuracy. Feature selection is particularly crucial in fields such as medicine, finance, manufacturing, image processing, and logistics where datasets often contain hundreds of features, many of which may not contribute significantly to the target outcome.

The objective of this paper is to present a general three-stage hybrid feature selection system. This hybrid feature selection system can be applied in various fields. Also, this general hybrid system can be used for different datasets, which have smaller or larger: (i) number of samples; (ii) number of features; and (iii) number of classes. The proposed multi-stage hybrid system is tested with three well-known datasets from UCI Machine Learning Repository: *Iris*, *Wine*, and *Ionosphere*.

This paper continues the authors' previous researches [2–6] where some of useful techniques, algorithms, automatic methods, and knowledge–based systems for feature and attribute selection are used by physicians, engineers, and managers to make better decision or diagnosis in their daily activities.

The rest of the paper is organized in the following way: Sect. 2 provides an overview of the basic idea on: (i) feature selection process; and (ii) feature extractions. Very detailed modelling of the general three-stage hybrid feature selection sys-tem, as well as applied statistical and artificial intelligence techniques, are presented in Sect. 3. The preliminary experimental results for feature selection for three well-known datasets are reported in Sect. 4. Section 5 provides conclusions and some directions for future research.

2 Feature Selection and Feature Extraction

Feature selection techniques can be applicable to any area where there is a chance of facing the dimensionality problem. However, at the beginning, it is interesting to precisely define the term *feature selection* relative to *feature extraction*. Though it seems the same, some differences do exist.

Feature selection is a type of data pre-processing task that consists of removing ir-relevant and redundant features in order to improve the predictive performance of data clustering and/or classifying methods. The dataset with the full set of features is the input to the feature selection method, which will select a subset of features. Irrele-vant features can be defined as features that are not correlated with the class variable, and removing such features will not be harmful for the predictive performance [7].

The precise meanings of a pre-processing operation and a *feature extraction* pro-cess overlap, but in general, feature extraction operation involves the reduction in dimension-ality of the pattern vector. The primary reason for such a transformation is to provide a set of measurements with more discriminatory information and less redundancy. The classifier/cluster tool depends on the information from a feature extraction device, and thus cannot normally provide that information without a completely designed feature extractor [8].

3 Modelling a General Hybrid System for Feature Selection

The proposed general hybrid system for feature selection consists of three stages. The first stage is called *Evaluation attributes*, the second stage is called *Learning stage*, and the third is called *Decision Making*; which is presented in Fig. 1.

3.1 Hybrid System for Feature Selection

(I) The first stage is realized in four steps: primary dataset is the input in the system. The first stage uses four feature ranking methods to define ranking the most important attributes - features. The applied ranking methods are: (i) *fscchi2* - Univariate feature ranking for classification using chi-square tests [9]; (ii) *fscmrmr* - Rank features for classification using minimum redundancy maximum relevance [10]; (iii) *Relief* - Relief-based feature selection [11]; and (iv) *greedy k-means* – Constrained greedy *k*-means ranking method. The outputs of *Evaluation attributes* stage are four sub-datasets, *Ranked features*, one from each ranking method, as shown in Fig. 1.

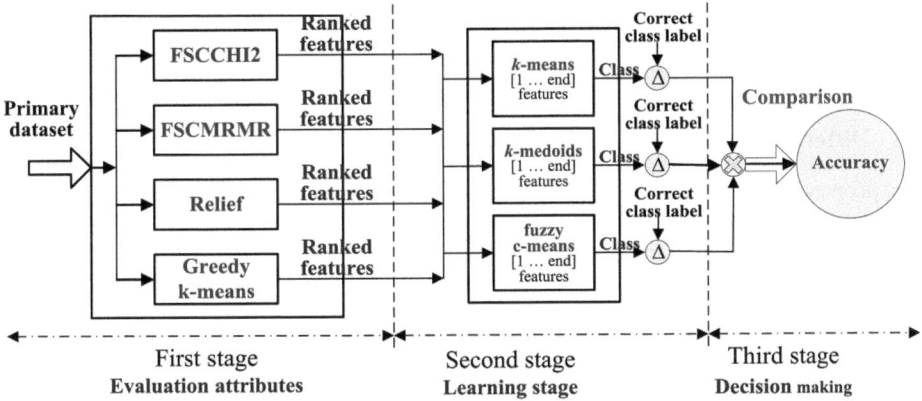

Fig. 1. A general three-stage hybrid system for feature selection

(II) Three unsupervised learning algorithms are used for data clustering in *Learning stage*. The input of this stage is four sub-datasets, called *Ranked features*. The stage consists of: (i) *k*-means clustering; (ii) *k*-medoids clustering method; and (iii) *fuzzy c-means* clustering algorithm. Each clustering algorithm tests unlabeled input data in a specific manner: first attribute; first and second [1, 2]; first and second and third [1...3]; and finally, from the first to the last attribute. The output of this stage is a large number of pairs, such as ([1...n], *Accuracy*), where higher value of accuracy presents feature collection [1...n] as important features. To assess the quality of the experimental and resulting validated clusters, semi-supervised validation is applied. The correct class label from the dataset is compared with the experimental result for the class obtained from each classifier, and *accuracy* value is calculated.

(III) The third stage aggregates and summarizes the most important groups of features in a specific manner, according to the highest value of *accuracy*, and makes decision on

Table 1. Datasets used in this study

Data source	Number of samples	Number of features	Number of classes	Class	Samples per class
Iris	150	4	3	1	50
				2	50
				3	50
Wine	178	13	3	1	59
				2	71
				3	48
Ionosphere	351	34	2	1	225
				2	126

the most important features for a specific dataset. Preliminary testing of the proposed system is completed with three well-known datasets: *Iris* [12]; *Wine* [13]; and *Ionosphere* [14]. The number of samples, features, and classes in each dataset used in this study is presented in Table 1. As shown, each dataset is balanced across classes.

3.2 Different Approaches for Evaluation Attributes

The proposed system uses four feature ranking methods for evaluating attributes in order to define the most important ones. They were selected as three traditional statistical methods and one new metaheuristic method.

Univariate Feature Ranking for Classification Using Chi-square Tests
The algorithm for Univariate feature ranking for the classification, using chi-square tests, is presented in Algorithm 1.

Algorithm 1: Univariate feature ranking algorithm for classification using chi-square tests
Begin
    Step 1:   --- *Prepare the Data*
                    Ensure that the variables are categorical
    Step 2:   --- *Convert Categories to Numbers*
                    Use encoding techniques
    Step 3:   --- *Compute Chi-Square Scores*
                    Calculate the Chi-Square statistic for each feature relative to the target variable
    Step 4:   --- *Select Top Features*
                    Choose features with the **highest Chi-Square values** as they have the strongest relationship with the target variable
End.

Rank Features Using Minimum Redundancy Maximum Relevance

The exact solution to the minimum redundancy and maximum relevance (MRMR) feature selection algorithm is the selection of k = |S| features from a set of n candidates requiring the evaluation of O(nk) candidate feature subsets [10]. Partially target function to MRMR problem, defined by arguments of the maxima (arg max), is presented in Eq. 1, which has two terms: the first term maximizes the relevance condition, whereas the second term minimizes the redundancy condition.

$$\arg \max_{i \in \Omega_s} (f(x_i, y)) - \frac{1}{|S|^2} \sum_{j \in S} g(x_i, x_j) \quad (1)$$

In Eq. 1: Ωs are indices of candidate features $\Omega - S$, x_i is ith feature in X, $f(x_i, y)$ is function that returns the relevance between a feature x_i and class labels y, S are indices of selected features, and $g(x_i, x_j)$ is a function that returns the redundancy between two features x_i and x_j.

Algorithm 2: Rank features using minimum redundancy maximum relevance		
Begin		
	Step 1:	— *Prepare the Data*
		Require: $D = <X, y>, g, f, k$
	Step 2:	— *Value Assignment*
		$S \leftarrow 0$
		add x_i = arg max f(x_j, y) to S
	Step 3:	— *For loop*
		for $t = 1 : k - 1$ **do**
		Add the feature that satisfies Eq. 1 to S
		end for
		— *End For loop*
	Step 4:	— *Select Top Features*
		Choose features with the **minimum redundancy and maximum relevance** in S
End.		

Relief-Based Feature Selection

The research paper [15] formulated the original Relief algorithm inspired by instance-based learning. As an individual evaluation filtering feature selection method, Relief calculates a proxy statistic for each feature that can be used to estimate feature 'relevance' to the target concept.

		Algorithm 3: Pseudo-code for the Relief algorithm
Begin		
	Step 1:	--- ***Prepare the Data***
		Require: for each training instance a vector of feature values and the class value
		n ← number of training instances
		a ← number of features (i.e. attributes)
		--- ***Parameter***
	Step 2:	m ← number of random training instances out of *n* used to update *W*
		initialize all feature weights W[A] ← 0.0
	Step 3:	--- ***First For loop***
		for *i* = 1 : *m* **do**
		Randomly select a 'target' instance R_i
		Find a nearest hit '*H*' and nearest miss '*M*' (instances)
	Step 4:	--- ***Second For loop***
		for A= 1 : *a* **do**
		W[*A*] = W[*A*] − diff (*A*, R_i, *H*) / m + diff (*A*, R_i, *M*) / m
		end for
		--- ***End Second For loop***
		end for
		--- ***End First For loop***
	Step 5:	--- ***Select Top Features***
		Return the vector *W* of feature scores that estimates the quality of features
End.		

As summarized by the pseudo-code in Algorithm 3, the Relief algorithm cycles through *m* random training instances (R_i). Each cycle R_i is the 'target' instance, and the feature score vector *W* is updated based on feature value differences observed between the target and neighboring instances. Therefore, in each cycle, the distance between the 'target' instance and all other instances is calculated. Relief identifies two nearest neighbor instances of the target; one with the same class, called the nearest hit (*H*) and the other with the opposite class, called the nearest miss (*M*). The last step of the cycle updates the weight of a feature *A* in *W* if the feature value differs between the target instance R_i and either the nearest hit *H* or the nearest miss *M*.

Constrained Greedy K-means Ranking Method

Feature selection is a well-known technique for supervised learning, but much less so for unsupervised learning methods, such as clustering methods. Therefore, while processing high-dimensional datasets, problems can be encountered with clustering methods.

In this short research paper, *Constrained greedy k-means* ranking algorithm is developed. It is a relatively simple greedy algorithm to perform variable selection and the main steps are presented in Algorithm 4. The algorithm has the following steps: (i) Data preparation; (ii) Selection of the maximum number of variables; (iii) Repetition and computation of Chi-Square Scores until input list is empty; and finally (iv) Variable *selected_variables*, which presents the list of the most important features.

Algorithm 4: Constrained greedy *k*-means ranking algorithm
Begin
Step 1:   --- **Prepare the Data**
list_var – list of variables; *selected_variables* - empty list
maxvars - maximum of variables you want to retain
kmin - minimum number of clusters
kmax - maximum number of clusters
Step 2:   **Repeat** from *kmin* to *kmax*
Step 3:   Record the silhouette value for every combination of variables and number of clusters using *k*-means
Step 4:   Choose the variable giving the maximum silhouette value
Step 5:   Add it to *selected_variables*
Remove it from *list_var*
Step 6:   **Until** *list_var* is empty
Step 7:   **Return** the vector *selected_variables* of most important features
End.

3.3 Applied Clustering Methods

Three implemented clustering techniques were used in the proposed system. The configuration of the clustering methods used in the development of the work is described below.

- For *k*-means clustering, the *number of centroids* was directly established after considering how many groups could be conformed and dependent on the confirmed number of classes, with 2 or 3 for applied datasets.
- For *k*-medoids clustering, the following hyper-parameters are used: *Algorithm* = Partitioning around medoid; *Method for choosing initial cluster medoid positions* = Initialization of cluster centers according to the k-means++ algorithm (*Start* = 'plus'); *Distance* = Squared Euclidean distance; *Number of iterations* = 10; and *Best_Replicate* = 1.
- For fuzzy *k*-means clustering, hyper-parameter configuration is presented: *Number of clusters*, dependent on confirmed number of classes, 2 or 3; *Maximum number of iterations* = 100; *Exponent for fuzzy partition matrix* = 2.0; *Minimum improvement in objective function* = 10^{-5}; *Method for computing distance* = "Euclidean".

4 Experimental Results and Discussion

Experimental results of the first stage, feature ranking methods and the rank of the most important attributes for three well-known datasets, *Iris*, *Wine*, and *Ionosphere*, are presented in Table 2. It can be noticed that different ranking methods deliver different experimental results. Some of the attributes are repeated in different ranking methods, though some methods include completely different attributes, as significant attributes, compared to other methods.

Table 2. The feature ranking methods and the most important attributes: fscchi2 - *Univariate feature ranking for classification using chi-square tests*; fscmrmr - *Rank features for classification using minimum redundancy maximum relevance*; Relieff - *Relief-based feature selection*; greedy k-means – *Constrained greedy k-means ranking algorithm*

Dataset	Feature ranking method	Ranking 10 attributes by importance
Iris	fscchi2	[4 3 1 2]
	fscmrmr	[4 2 3 1]
	Relieff	[4 3 1 2]
	greedy k-means	[3 4 1 2]
Wine	fscchi2	[7 13 10 12 1 11 6 2 9 4]
	fscmrmr	[7 10 4 13 2 12 1 11 9 8]
	Relieff	[13 1 4 5 7 9 3 10 11 12]
	greedy k-means	[7 10 1 13 12 6 11 9 4 8]
Ionosphere	fscchi2	[5 7 3 8 6 4 28 13 21 15]
	fscmrmr	[5 4 1 7 24 29 12 3 34 33]
	Relieff	[24 3 8 5 14 7 16 34 29 9]
	greedy k-means	[17 19 27 34 13 15 11 21 30 23]

Experimental results of the second stage, sorted by accuracy value (descending) and number of features (ascending), are presented in Table 3. All three datasets are tested with three clustering methods, *k-means*, *k-medoids*, and *fuzzy c-means*, and the accuracy values are calculated for every subset of features for each clustering method.

In *Decision making* stage, the values accuracy are compared and decisions are made for the most important features for every of three datasets. According to the *accuracy* values 96.00%, it can be concluded that the most important features for *Iris* dataset are attributes: A4 (petal width) and A3 (petal length). For *Wine* dataset, according to the accuracy value 80.33%, the most important features are: A7 (Flavanoids), A10 (Color intensity) and A1 (Alcohol). For *Ionosphere* dataset, according to the Accuracy values, around 83.19%, the most important features are: A5 (feature 5), A4 (feature 4) and A1 (feature 1), as presented in Table 3.

Table 3. The combination of the most important features for three datasets applied in k-means, k-medoids, and fuzzy c-means clustering methods and Accuracy values

Dataset	Clustering Algorithm	Features	Accuracy	Features	Accuracy
Iris	k-means	[3]	**96.00**	[4 3]	94.66
		[3]	95.33	[4 2]	92.66
		[4 2 3]	95.33	all	89.33
	k-medoids	[4]	**96.00**	[3]	94.66
		[4 3]	**96.00**	[4 2]	94.00
		[4 2 3]	**96.00**	all	88.66
	fuzzy c-means	[4]	**96.00**	[3]	93.33
		[4 3]	94.66	[4 2]	92.66
		[4 2 3]	94.00	all	89.33
Wine	k-means	[7]	**79.77**	[7 10 4 13 2]	72.47
		[7 10 1]	**79.77**	[7 10 4 13 2 12]	72.47
		[7 10]	76.96	[7 13 10 12 1 11 6]	72.47
		[7 10 1 13]	73.59	[13 1]	70.22
		[13]	72.47	[13 1 4 5 7 9]	70.22
		[7 13]	72.47	[7 10 4 13 2 12 1]	70.22
		[13 1 4]	72.47	[7 13 10 12 1 11 6 2]	70.22
		[7 10 1 13 12]	72.47	all	70.22
Wine	k-medoids	[7]	**79.77**	[13 1 4 5]	70.78
		[7 10]	78.65	[13 1 4 5 7]	70.78
		[7 10 1]	78.65	[13]	70.22
		[13 1]	72.47	[7 13]	70.22
		[13 1 4]	72.47	[7 13 10]	70.22
		[7 13 10 12]	72.47	[7 10 4 13]	70.22
		[7 10 1 13]	72.47	[7 10 4 13 2]	70.22
		[7 10 1 13 12]	72.47	[7 10 1 13 12 6]	70.22
		[7 10 4 13 2 12]	72.47	[7 10 4 13 2 12 1]	70.22
		[13 1 4 5 7 9]	72.47	[7 13 10 12 1 11 6 2]	70.22

(*continued*)

Table 3. (*continued*)

Dataset	Clustering Algorithm	Features	Accuracy	Features	Accuracy
		[7 13 10 12 1 11 6]	72.47	[7 10 4]	69.10
		[7 10 1 13 12 6 11]	72.47	all	70.78
Wine	fuzzy c-means	[7]	**80.33**	[7 10 1 13]	68.53
		[7 10 1]	**80.33**	[13 1 4 5 7 9]	68.53
		[7 10]	78.09	[7 10 4 13 2 12]	68.53
		[7 10 4]	71.34	[7 10 4 13 2 12 1]	68.53
		[13]	68.53	[7 10 1 13 12 6 11]	68.53
		[7 13]	68.53	[7 13 10 12 1 11 6]	68.53
		[13 1]	68.53	[7 13 10 12 1 11 6 2]	68.53
		[13 1 4 5 7]	68.53	all	68.53
Ionosphere	k-means	[5 7 3 8 6 4 28]	**83.47**	[24 3]	79.20
		[24 3 8 5 14 7 16]	**83.47**	[5 7]	78.91
		[5]	82.90	[5 4 1 7 24]	78.91
		[5 4]	82.90	[5 4 1 7 24 29 12]	73.50
		[5 4 1]	82.90	[24 3 8 5]	73.21
		[5 7 3]	82.62	[5 7 3 8 6 4 28 13]	72.07
		[5 7 3 8]	82.62	[17 19 27 34 13 15 11]	68.37
		[24 3 8 5 14]	82.62	[17 19 27 34 13 15]	67.52
		[24 3 8 5 14 7]	82.62	[17]	64.67
		[24 3 8 5 14 7 16 34]	81.76	[17 19 27 34 13]	64.38
		[5 4 1 7 24 29]	81.48	[24]	63.81
		[5 4 1 7]	80.34	[17 19]	63.53
		[24 3 8]	79.77	all	71.22
Ionosphere	k-medoids	[5]	**83.19**	[5 4 1 7 24]	79.20
		[5 4]	**83.19**	[5 4 1 7]	78.91

(*continued*)

Table 3. (*continued*)

Dataset	Clustering Algorithm	Features	Accuracy	Features	Accuracy
		[5 4 1]	**83.19**	[5 4 1 7 24 29 12]	71.22
		[5 7 3]	82.62	[17 19 27 34 13]	63.24
		[24 3 8 5 14]	82.62	[17 19 27 34 13 15 11]	68.66
		[5 4 1 7 24 29]	82.62	[5 7 3 8 6 4 28 13]	68.09
		[24 3 8 5 14 7 16 34]	82.33	[17 19 27 34 13 15]	67.52
		[24 3 8 5]	82.05	[17]	64.38
		[24 3 8 5 14 7]	82.05	[17 19]	63.81
		[24 3 8 5 14 7 16]	82.05	[17 19 27]	63.24
		[5 7 3 8 6 4 28]	81.76	[24]	61.82
		[5 7 3 8 6 4]	80.62	[17 19 27 34]	58.68
		[5 7]	78.91	all	70.94
Ionosphere	fuzzy c-means	[5 7 3]	**82.90**	[24 3]	76.63
		[5 4 1]	82.62	[5 4 1 7 24]	75.49
		[5]	82.33	[24 3 8 5 14 7 16]	75.49
		[5 4]	82.33	[5 7 3 8 6 4 28]	74.64
		[5 7 3 8]	81.76	[24 3 8 5 14 7 16 34]	74.64
		[24 3 8 5]	81.48	[24 3 8]	72.64
		[5 4 1 7]	80.62	[5 7 3 8 6 4 28 13]	70.94
		[24 3 8 5 14]	80.62	[17 19 27 34 13 15 11]	68.37
		[5 7 3 8 6]	80.05	[17]	64.38
		[5 7 3 8 6 4]	79.48	[17 19]	63.53
		[5 7]	78.63	[24]	58.68
		[24 3 8 5 14 7]	76.92	all	70.94

4.1 Short Discussion

Experimental results obtained with the proposed hybrid clustering system are comparable to other studies.

However, the main disadvantage of the proposed system is that correct class label has to be known. This fact significantly limits its application in real-world situations. On the other hand, its high *accuracy* value for 10 features, for datasets that have more than 10 attributes, can be a good way to expand the metrics, not to use only accuracy value,

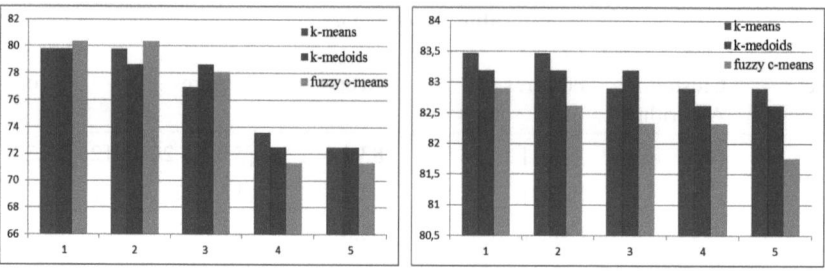

Fig. 2. The best five results per clusters for (a) *Wine* and (b) *Ionosphere* datasets

or include correlations between the attributes of the observed dataset. Figure 2 displays the best five results per clusters for (a) *Wine* and (b) *Ionosphere* datasets.

These three well-known datasets have been used numerously in different researches; therefore, we will discuss and compare our experimental results. The *Iris* dataset is used and tested more than other datasets with different classification algorithms and supervised methods, and the results are presented in [16]. On using Xgboost Classification (XgbC), accuracy values are between 81.56% and 100%, though usually it is 92.10%. On using Support Vector Classification (SVC), accuracy values are between 86.84% and 100%, though mostly it is 94.73%. On using Random Forest Classification, accuracy values are between 78.95% and 97.36%, but mostly it is 89.47%. The largest number of scientific papers and other examples that can be found in literature exclusively use A4 (petal width) and A3 (petal length) as the most important features.

The *Wine* dataset is tested with different classification algorithms and supervised methods, and the results are presented in [18]. On using XgbC, accuracy values are between 93.33% and 100%, but usually it is 97.77%. On using SVC, accuracy values are between 68.89% and 91.11%, though mostly it is 80.00%. On using RFC, accuracy value is 100%.

The *Ionosphere* dataset used is the least comparable to three observed datasets in this study. The experimental results presented in [18] demonstrate that the most important features are A3 (feature 3), A5 (feature 5), A1 (feature 1), A7 (feature 7), and A9 (feature 9), which are referred as the top 5 features in the dataset. When Gradient Boosting Decision Trees for the top 5 features on the dataset are used, the value for test accuracy is 85.40%; however, when *Linear Support Vector Machine* (LinearSVM) model is utilized, the test accuracy is 61.53%.

5 Conclusion and Future Work

The aim of this paper is to propose the novel general hybrid system for data feature selection. It combines four feature ranking methods and three clustering methods, and presents unsupervised hybrid clustering system. The proposed hybrid system is tested on three well-known datasets. Preliminary experimental results encourage further research by the authors, since the *accuracy* values are: *Iris* dataset 95%; *Wine* dataset 80%; and *Ionosphere* dataset 83%. However, the main limitation of the proposed system is that it is necessary to know the correct class label to calculate *accuracy* value. However, even if there is this large limitation, it is encouraging to state the fact that the accuracy value is high, around 70%, for datasets that have 13 and 34 attributes, and that the 10 most important features were selected.

Therefore, our future research will focus on: (i) including other metrics besides the already used accuracy; (ii) applying other methods such as: forward selection, backward elimination, or recursive elimination; and (iii) using other evolutionary techniques in order to efficiently solve feature selection for well-known datasets and real-world datasets as well.

References

1. Huang, Z., Zheng, H., Li, C., Che, C.: Application of machine learning-based k-means clustering for financial fraud detection. Acad. J. Sci. Technol. **10**(1), 33–39 (2024)
2. Michelena, Á., Díaz-Longueira, A., Novais, P., Simić, D., Fontenla-Romero, O., Calvo-Rolle, J.L.: Comparative analysis of unsupervised anomaly detection techniques for heat detection in dairy cattle. Neurocomputing **618**, 129088 (2025)
3. Simić, S., Banković, Z., Simić, D., Simić S. D.: A hybrid clustering approach for diagnosing medical diseases. In: Lecture Notes in Computer Science, vol. 10870, pp. 741–752, Springer, Cham (2018)
4. Simić, S., Villar, J.R., Calvo-Rolle, J.L., Sekulić, S.R., Simić, S.D., Simić, D.: An application of a hybrid intelligent system for diagnosing primary headaches. Int. J. Environ. Res. Public Health **18**(4), 1890 (2021)
5. Krawczyk, B., Simić, D., Simić, S., Woźniak, M.: Automatic diagnosis of primary headaches by machine learning methods. Open Med. **8**(2), 157–165 (2013)
6. Simić, S., Banković, Z., Villar, J.R., Simić, D., Simić, S.D.: A hybrid fuzzy clustering approach for diagnosing primary headache disorder. Log. J. IGPL **29**(2), 220–235 (2021)
7. Wan, C.: Hierarchical Feature Selection for Knowledge Discovery. Springer (2019)
8. Arroyo, A., Herrero, A., Tricio, V., Corchado, E.: Analysis of meteorological conditions in Spain by means of clustering techniques. Journal of Applied Logic **24**(B) 76–89 (2017)
9. Porcu, S., Floris, A., Atzori, L.: CB-FL: cluster-based federated learning applied to quality of experience modelling. In: Yétongnon, K., Dipanda, A., Gallo, L. (eds.): 16th International Conference on Signal-Image Technology & Internet-Based Systems, Dijon, 585–591 (2022)
10. El-Manzalawy, Y., Hsieh, T.Y., Shivakumar, M., Kim, D., Honavar, V.: Min-redundancy and max-relevance multi-view feature selection for predicting ovarian cancer survival using multi-omics data. BMC Med. Genomics **11**(3), 71 (2018)
11. Urbanowicza, R.J., Meeker, M., La Cava, W., Olson, R.S., Moore, J.H.: Relief-based feature selection: introduction and review. J. Biomed. Inform. **85**, 189–203 (2018)
12. Fisher, R.: Iris. UCI Machine Learning Repository (1936). https://doi.org/10.24432/C56C76
13. Aeberhard, S., Forina, M.: Wine. UCI Machine Learning Repository (1992)
14. Sigillito, V., Wing, S., Hutton, L., Baker, K.: Ionosphere. UCI Machine Learning Repository (1989)
15. Kira, K., Rendell, L.A.: The feature selection problem: traditional methods and a new algorithm. In: AAAI 1992: Proceedings of the tenth national conference on Artificial intelligent, vol. 2, pp. 129–134 (1992)
16. https://archive.ics.uci.edu/dataset/53/iris
17. http://archive.ics.uci.edu/dataset/109/wine
18. https://medium.com/data-science/classification-of-radar-returns-c79fa1ce42eb

Profiling Public Instagram Accounts with a Multimodal Vector for Hate Exposure Analysis

Asier Gonzalez-Santocildes[✉], Iker Pastor López, Marta Gorraiz-Bengoechea, and P. Garcia Bringas

Faculty of Engineering, University of Deusto,
Avda. Universidades 24, 48007 Bilbao, Spain
{gonzalez.asier,iker.pastor,m.gorraiz,pablo.garcia.bringas}@deusto.es

Abstract. This paper presents a fully automated pipeline that collects, processes, and models public Instagram data to quantify hate directed at high-profile accounts, as well as hate disseminated by them. A headless Selenium crawler gathers the fifteen most recent posts per influencer, including images, captions, up to 2,000 comments, and basic metadata, while complying with platform rate limits. A structured anonymization process ensures privacy by hashing all identifiers, and a 24-dimensional feature vector is extracted for each post to capture sentiment, engagement, visual affect, and demographic indicators. Aggregated vectors serve as profile-level representations and enable scalable session simulations that estimate user exposure to hate. Using data from 80 Spanish-speaking influencers across six topical domains, the model accurately separates content types and produces hate-intensity scores that strongly correlate with manual labels. Session-level predictions have a mean absolute error within 4% of observed values, validating the utility of the vector model for rapid, privacy-preserving sentiment estimation. All code and a partially anonymized dataset are released to support reproducibility and are publicly available in the project repository.

Keywords: Social Media Mining · Hate Speech Detection · Multimodal Profiling · Sentiment Analysis · Instagram

1 Introduction

Although more than two billion people use Instagram monthly, the platform provides no public API and only limited tools for large-scale, multimodal hate analysis. Prior studies typically focus on either image content [1,2] or text sentiment in isolation, rely on private datasets, or scrape data at API-like speeds that violate the site's terms of service. Consequently, reproducible research on hate dynamics at the profile level remains limited.

This work addresses the problem from an engineering perspective. A low-cost, ethically compliant pipeline is designed to mirrors human browsing behaviour, it extracts all publicly visible variables of interest (image, caption, comment thread, engagement, biography) and converts them into a fixed-length numerical vector bounded in [0, 1]. The vector was defined in collaboration with social-psychology researchers and covers 24 dimensions spanning polarity, subjectivity, extreme-sentiment counts, facial emotion logits, gender ratio, age, like/comment statistics and temporal slots.

With the vector in place, two complementary validations are performed based on the vector representation. First, hate-related variables are analyzed across six influencer niches, politics, news, gaming, fashion, fitness and sport and observe strong, topic-dependent regularities: news and political profiles attract the highest share of negative comments, whereas fashion remains largely positive. Second, realistic "user scrolling sessions" are simulated by sampling posts according to a topic mix; the model's predicted positivity ratios align closely with values computed from the raw data, demonstrating its suitability for rapid what-if analysis.

Our contribution is a transparent, multimodal profile-modelling method that operates solely on public data, and an empirical study that evidences its effectiveness for hate quantification and topic discrimination. Beyond its research value, the resulting toolkit can support moderators, mental-health professionals and brand-safety teams who need coarse yet reliable signals of hostility on Instagram.

2 State of the Art

Negative comments on social media have emerged as a significant concern, influencing both individual mental health and broader societal dynamics. Various studies elucidate how the internet fosters environments conducive to negativity, with implications for different demographic groups. Notably, individuals reporting lower subjective socioeconomic status exhibit a higher frequency of negative social media experiences, which can exacerbate feelings of anxiety and depression [3,4]. This association draws attention to the socioeconomic contexts that shape online interactions, revealing that disadvantaged groups may face elevated risks of negative social media exposure and its psychological repercussions.

Moreover, adolescents' interaction with social media demonstrates that they are particularly susceptible to the adverse effects of negative comments. For instance, research indicates that receiving fewer "likes" than peers induces feelings of rejection and contributes to depressive symptoms among adolescents [5]. The pressure to achieve approval in the form of likes and positive feedback can lead users to internalize negativity, degrading their self-image and emotional well-being [6]. Furthermore, virtual communication often amplifies feelings of inadequacy, as users tend to compare themselves unfavorably to others based on their social media portrayals [7].

The phenomenon of online disinhibition is another critical factor contributing to the prevalence of negativity in social media settings. Users often feel empowered to express hostile sentiments when the moral constraints common in face-to-face interactions are diminished [8]. This lack of accountability can lead to cyberbullying, with harmful comments proliferating, resulting in distress among victims [9]. Studies highlight that a significant percentage of college students reported receiving negative comments online, particularly during the COVID-19 pandemic when social interactions shifted primarily to virtual platforms [10].

Additionally, social media can foster unhealthy behaviors through exposure to negative feedback and harmful content. Users may face emotional distress and social media fatigue due to not only the negative comments they receive but also perceived overload of negative interactions [11]. Such negative social experiences can lead to a decline in social media usage or even complete withdrawal from these platforms as users seek to protect their mental health [12]. The cyclical nature of this issue illustrates how negative experiences on social media can result in decreased user engagement, compounding feelings of loneliness and alienation initially felt by victims of online negativity.

In conclusion, negative comments on social media significantly affect users' emotional states and can trigger a range of mental health challenges. This dynamic illustrates the intricate interplay between online interactions, socioeconomic factors, and psychological well-being. Future research and intervention strategies must address these factors to mitigate the risks associated with negative online experiences, especially among vulnerable populations such as adolescents and individuals with lower socioeconomic status. These challenges highlight the need for automated, scalable methods to assess and understand users' exposure to negativity in online environments.

3 Methodology

A headless SELENIUM crawler, orchestrated with `webdriver-manager`, logs in with a research account, scrolls each profile and captures the fifteen most-recent posts together with captions, full comment threads and public metadata. Random delays of 25 s and a hard quota of 20 profiles per hour keep the request rate safely below Instagram's blocking threshold, and only public endpoints are touched. All data collection complies with Instagram's terms of use [13], and the study has received ethical approval from the Research Ethics Committee of the University of Deusto.

Immediately after each download an anonymisation layer hashes usernames, avatar URLs and outbound links with SHA-256 [14]. The dataset has 200 posts and 96.000 comments from 80 Spanish-speaking influencers distributed across six topical niches: politics, gaming, fashion, fitness, sports and news.

Every raw piece of data then passes through a modular Python pipeline. *fast-Text* is employed for efficient language detection across multilingual texts. The `GoogleTrans` API [15] automatically translates non-Spanish and non-English strings into English to ensure consistency in textual analysis. Sentiment and subjectivity scores are obtained using `TextBlob` [16], a rule-based natural language processing tool that treats emojis as independent tokens to better capture emotional tone. Images are uniformly resized to 224 × 224 pixels. Facial regions are detected using `RetinaFace`, a state-of-the-art face localization model, and

DeepFace is then used to extract demographic and affective features, including seven emotion logits, gender probability, and estimated age [17].

Robustness was checked through three pilot scrapes covering 10, 20 and 40 profiles. In each run it was verified that request rates remained stable, repeated crawls produced identical JSON results and no private data were inadvertently stored. The resulting dataset serves as input for the profile-level modelling described in the next section. Figure 1 provides a visual summary of the main stages of the proposed pipeline. From data acquisition to multimodal feature extraction.

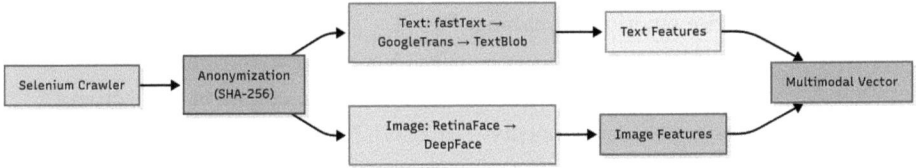

Fig. 1. Overview of the multimodal pipeline for Instagram data collection, processing, and vector calculation.

4 Data Collection and Structure

Once the processing script finishes for a given profile, it writes a comma-separated file that contains a fully anonymised vector for each of the fifteen most-recent posts. No usernames, image URLs or external links are stored; every potential identifier is replaced by a SHA-256 hash, making backward tracing impossible. In order to support topic-level analysis and future session simulations, influencers are grouped into six broad domains: *politics*, *news*, *gaming/streaming*, *fashion/lifestyle*, *fitness/food* and *sports*. All accounts were selected from public "most influential" lists published by Spanish newspapers and magazines [18].

Table 1 defines the acronyms that label each column of the generated CSV. The set mixes comment-based sentiment variables, face-level demographics and emotions, as well as simple caption features; these fields were agreed upon with the collaborating psychology team because they best capture the notion of *hate* perceived by a profile.

Table 1. Acronyms used in the post-level CSV.

Acronym	Description	Acronym	Description
PERS	People detected (yes/no)	MEN	% male faces
WOM	% female faces	ASIA	% Asian faces
INDI	% Indian faces	BLCK	% Black faces
WHIT	% White faces	EAST	% Middle-eastern faces
LATN	% Latin faces	HAPY	Happy emotion probability
ANGR	Angry emotion probability	DISG	Disgust emotion probability
FEAR	Fear emotion probability	SADD	Sadness emotion probability
SURP	Surprise emotion probability	NEUT	Neutral emotion probability
POSI	% positive comments	NEGA	% negative comments
POLA	Mean comment polarity	SUBJ	Mean comment subjectivity
MPOS	% very positive comments	MNEG	% very negative comments
TEXT	Caption present (yes/no)	UPOL	Caption polarity
USUB	Caption subjectivity		

5 Hate Metrics Across Influencers

Prior to the largescale session simulations, the hate-related features of Spanish accounts were validated, each aligned with one of the topical domains under analysis. For each influencer, six key variables were averaged over their fifteen latest posts: percentage of positive comments (POSI), percentage of negative comments (NEGA), mean polarity (POLA), mean subjectivity (SUBJ), percentage of *very* positive comments (MPOS) and percentage of *very* negative comments (MNEG). The results in Table 2 reveal clear topical contrasts: the political account attracts the highest share of negativity, whereas the fashion profile is almost unanimously praised. Gaming and streaming sit between these extremes, while the fitness creator records the most favourable sentiment of all.

These metrics fulfil a dual role. First, they reassure us that the pipeline reproduces widely held perceptions: politically charged content is more contentious than lifestyle material, and fitness posts tend to be well received. Second, the numbers provide baseline targets against which the subsequent session-level simulations (Sect. 6) can be benchmarked.

Table 2. Average hate-related metrics for five representative influencers (last 15 posts each).

Influencer	POSI	NEGA	POLA	SUBJ	MPOS	MNEG
Politics	0.72	0.28	0.60	0.54	0.12	0.05
Fashion	0.92	0.08	0.80	0.72	0.33	0.01
Gaming	0.83	0.17	0.66	0.62	0.17	0.05
Fitness	0.97	0.03	0.74	0.68	0.27	0.01
Streaming	0.84	0.16	0.65	0.63	0.14	0.05

6 Session-Level Simulation and Hate Prediction

To move beyond static profile averages, the corpus was expanded with 30 additional Spanish influencers (≈,450 posts). The final dataset comprises 120 profiles and 1 750 posts evenly split across the six aforemetioned topics: *politics*, *news*, *gaming/streaming*, *fashion/lifestyle*, *fitness/food* and *sports*. Then 20 artificial user sessions per topic were generated by randomly sampling ten posts from each topic's dataset, ten being the median burst of consecutive posts an Instagram user views in a single sitting.

For every session six hate variables were recomputed (POSI, NEGA, POLA, SUBJ, MPOS, MNEG). Table 3 reports the grand mean σ across the 20 sessions for each topic.

The pattern is consistent with the profile-level snapshot: sessions built from *politics* and *news* contain the highest concentration of negative and very-negative comments, whereas *fashion* and *fitness* remain strongly positive. Standard deviations never exceed 0.05, indicating that ten posts suffice to obtain stable topic means.

Given a user who follows topics with weights w_i ($\sum w_i = 1$), we approximate any session variable by

$$\text{var}_{\text{pred}} = \sum_{i=1}^{k} w_i \text{ var}_i,$$

where var_i is the topic mean from Table 3. For a hypothetical user whose feed is 30 % politics, 50 % news and 20 % fashion the formula predicts a positivity rate of $0.30 \cdot 0.773 + 0.50 \cdot 0.698 + 0.20 \cdot 0.919 = 0.765$ and a polarity of 0.639.

The mean absolute error across the four simulations is 0.027 for POSI and 0.016 for POLA, illustrating that a simple weighted blend of topic prototypes can already deliver useful estimates of the hostility a user is likely to encounter.

Prediction accuracy deteriorates as within-topic variance grows; highly polarized domains such as politics may require more sophisticated models. Moreover, the sessions assume independent draws, whereas real feeds are shaped by recommended loops and user actions. Extending the simulator with time-ordered sampling and feedback effects remains future work, but the current results show

Table 3. Session-level hate metrics by topic (mean ± SD over 20 sessions, 10 posts each).

(a) Comment-based metrics (I)

Topic	POSI	NEGA	POLA
News	0.698 ± 0.053	0.302 ± 0.053	0.592 ± 0.021
Politics	0.773 ± 0.034	0.227 ± 0.034	0.636 ± 0.019
Gaming/Streaming	0.871 ± 0.023	0.129 ± 0.023	0.702 ± 0.021
Fashion/Lifestyle	0.919 ± 0.023	0.081 ± 0.023	0.759 ± 0.015
Fitness/Food	0.861 ± 0.037	0.139 ± 0.037	0.713 ± 0.023
Sports	0.822 ± 0.050	0.178 ± 0.050	0.664 ± 0.025

(b) Comment-based metrics (II)

Topic	SUBJ	MPOS	MNEG
News	0.532 ± 0.033	0.103 ± 0.028	0.067 ± 0.018
Politics	0.547 ± 0.030	0.168 ± 0.034	0.054 ± 0.014
Gaming/Streaming	0.679 ± 0.030	0.243 ± 0.039	0.044 ± 0.008
Fashion/Lifestyle	0.753 ± 0.020	0.329 ± 0.027	0.027 ± 0.008
Fitness/Food	0.705 ± 0.034	0.262 ± 0.049	0.034 ± 0.013
Sports	0.574 ± 0.023	0.176 ± 0.049	0.058 ± 0.026

Table 4. Predicted vs. simulated sentiment for the mixed-topic user (30 % politics, 50 % news, 20 % fashion).

Run	POSI	POLA
Simulation 1	0.749	0.645
Simulation 2	0.764	0.647
Simulation 3	0.717	0.626
Simulation 4	0.813	0.610
Predicted	**0.765**	**0.639**

that even a first-order mixture model provides actionable, privacy-preserving estimates of session-level hate exposure.

From an architectural perspective, the system can also be understood as a hybrid intelligent approach. Although it does not rely on a monolithic end-to-end learning model, it integrates multiple intelligent components within a modular structure. Specifically, rule-based natural language processing (via `TextBlob`), pretrained deep learning models for face detection and emotion inference (via `RetinaFace` and `DeepFace`), and structured feature aggregation are combined to construct an interpretable, multimodal vector. This integration of linguistic, visual, and behavioral features supports reasoning over heterogeneous data sources and enables automated analysis of user exposure to hate. The approach thus satisfies the criteria for a hybrid intelligent system by combining diverse AI techniques into a coherent, modular decision-support pipeline.

7 Discussion

The empirical results confirm three broad tendencies of the Spanish-language Instagram sphere under study. First, hate-related variables differ systematically across topical niches. Profiles and sessions centred on *politics* or *news* exhibit the highest fraction of negative and very-negative comments (NEGA, MNEG), whereas *fashion/lifestyle* and *fitness* attract overwhelmingly positive feedback (Table 3). This aligns with offline perceptions of controversy in political discourse and the comparatively aspirational tone of fashion content, suggesting that our multimodal vector captures socially meaningful signals without relying on private data.

Second, the topic means are remarkably stable. Standard deviations below 0.05 for every hate variable indicate that ten posts already suffice to approximate a user's immediate exposure (See in related dataset [19]). Such low variance legitimizes the linear predictor equation (Eq. 1, Table 4): even though it ignores post order and recommender dynamics, its mean absolute error stays very low for both positivity and polarity. For real-time dashboards, where computational budget and privacy constraints prohibit heavyweight models, this simplicity is a feature rather than a limitation.

Third, the image-side descriptors (gender ratio, dominant emotion, dominant race) add contextual information yet exhibit larger within-topic variance than the text-side metrics. In practice the visual channels proved most useful as independent variables for qualitative analysis (e.g. confirming male over-representation in sports sessions) rather than as direct inputs to the hate estimator. Future work could explore fine-tuned vision transformers or contrastive-language pre-training to tighten these distributions.

Although the system performs reliably on datasets including hundreds of profiles and thousands of posts, its scalability to larger corpora remains an important consideration. The current implementation operates sequentially, but could be parallelized across multiple machines to enable faster scraping and feature extraction. Additionally, containerization and cloud deployment would facilitate horizontal scaling and make the pipeline suitable for real-time monitoring or large-scale social media audits.

Several limitations should be considered when interpreting the findings. The dataset contains 1 650 posts from 120 public accounts-large enough for exploratory modeling but small relative to Instagram's scale. All influencers are Spanish-speaking and operate in Western cultural contexts; hate norms vary worldwide, so cross-cultural validation is required before generalizing. Moreover, the crawler purposefully mimics conservative human-like browsing rates and therefore misses Instagram stories, live streams and recommendations that a real user might see.

Finally, ethical constraints influenced every design choice. Usernames, image URLs and outbound links are SHA-256 hashes; EXIF tags are stripped; comments are stored in plain text *only* until the sentiment pipeline finishes, after which they are discarded. This workflow fulfils GDPR's *data-minimisation* principle while still supporting reproducible research.

8 Conclusions

This paper presented a fully automated, end-to-end pipeline for large-scale analysis of public Instagram profiles. The system operates at human-like browsing speeds, applies a strict anonymisation layer to all collected data, and converts each post into a 24-dimensional multimodal vector that captures sentiment, visual affect, demographics, and engagement signals. These vectors are then aggregated into topic-level prototypes, enabling scalable and privacy-preserving simulations of user sessions across different influencer niches.

The proposed framework demonstrates practical utility in contexts where timely and privacy-conscious estimation of online sentiment is required. Its compact architecture and exclusive reliance on publicly available data facilitate integration into systems for content moderation, reputational monitoring, and digital well-being assessment. By offering interpretable indicators of affective trends at the profile level, the model provides actionable insights while remaining compliant with ethical and legal constraints on data use.

From a methodological perspective, the system can be extended through more different modeling techniques and additional input signals. In particular, supervised learning approaches could address domains with high intra-topic variance [20]. Furthermore, augmenting session simulations with temporal dependencies, platform recommendation dynamics, or structured metadata such as hashtags and reply threads may enhance the results.

The study further underscores the viability of conducting scalable social media research without compromising individual privacy. The combination of strong anonymity, modular implementation, and publicly released code and datasets supports reproducibility and adaptability to other linguistic or cultural contexts. As concerns grow regarding opaque data practices in commercial AI systems, this work contributes a transparent and responsible alternative for analyzing affective patterns in online discourse at scale.

Acknowledgments. Funding for this study was provided by the Directorate General for the Regulation of Gambling (ref.: SUBV24/00009). The funders had no role in the study design, collection, analysis or interpretation of the data, writing the manuscript, or the decision to submit the paper for publication.

References

1. Rogers, R.A.: Visual media analysis for Instagram and other online platforms. Big Data Soc. **8** (2021)

2. Alwan, W.H., Fazl-Ersi, E., Vahedian, A.: Identifying influential users on Instagram through visual content analysis. IEEE Access **8**, 169 594–169 603 (2020)
3. Skogen, J., et al.: Lower subjective socioeconomic status is associated with increased risk of reporting negative experiences on social media. findings from the "lifeonsome"-study. Front. Public Health **10**, 873463 (2022)
4. Escobar-Viera, C., et al.: Association between LGB sexual orientation and depression mediated by negative social media experiences: national survey study of us young adults. Jmir Ment. Health **7**, e23520 (2020)
5. Lee, J., et al.: Getting fewer "likes" than others on social media elicits emotional distress among victimized adolescents. Child Dev. **91**, 1346–1361 (2020)
6. Braghieri, M., et al.: Social media and mental health. Am. Econ. Rev. **112**, 1–31 (2022)
7. Skogen, J., et al.: Through the looking glass of social media. focus on self-presentation and association with mental health and quality of life. A cross-sectional survey-based study. Int. J. Environ. Res. Public Health **18**, 63319 (2021)
8. Ai, K., et al.: An experimental online study on the impact of negative social media comments on anxiety and mood (2025)
9. Muthi'Ah, A., et al.: Indonesian cyberbullying issues: the impoliteness in communication. Int. J. Educ. Lang. Religion **4**(2), 45–55 (2022)
10. Michikyan, M., et al.: Social connectedness and negative emotion modulation: social media use for coping among college students during the COVID-19 pandemic. Emerg. Adulthood **11**, 184–194 (2023)
11. Fu, Y., Li, J.: Understanding social media discontinuance from social cognitive perspective: evidence from Facebook users. J. Inf. Sci. **46**(1), 20–32 (2020)
12. Gan, S., et al.: Understanding social media discontinuance behavior in china: a perspective of social cognitive theory. Inf. Technol. People **36**(12), 256–274 (2023)
13. Instagram. Instagram terms of use (2024). https://help.instagram.com/581066165581870. Accessed 15 May 2025
14. Gilbert, H., Handschuh, H.: Security analysis of SHA-256 and sisters, pp. 175–193 (2003)
15. Google and Contributors. Google translate API for python (2024). https://pypi.org/project/googletrans/. Accessed 15 May 2025
16. Loria, S.: textblob documentation. Release 0.15, vol. 2 (2018)
17. Serengil, S., Ozpinar, A.: A benchmark of facial recognition pipelines and co-usability performances of modules. J. Inf. Technol. **17**(2), 95–107 (2024). https://dergipark.org.tr/en/pub/gazibtd/issue/84331/1399077
18. de Oliva, F.M.: The 50 most influential spanish influencers in 2024 (2024). https://fundacionmarquesdeoliva.com/estudio-de-los-500-espanoles-mas-influyentes-de-2024/influencers/. Accessed 15 May 2025
19. Gonzalez-Santocildes, A.: Multimodal hate profiling on Instagram (2025). https://github.com/AsierGonz/Multimodal-Hate-Profiling-Instagram. Accessed 15 May 2025
20. LeCun, Y., Bengio, Y., Hinton, G.: Deep learning. Nature **521**(7553), 436–444 (2015)

Symbolic Regressor: An Interpretability Tool for Non-intrusive Load Monitoring

Danel Rey-Arnal[1,2(✉)], Pablo G. Bringas[2], and Ibai Laña[1,2]

[1] Tecnalia Research and Innovation, Astondo Bidea, Edificio 700, 48160 Derio, Biscay, Spain
{danel.rey,ibai.lana}@tecnalia.com

[2] University of Deusto, Unibertsitate Etorb. 24, Deusto, 48007 Bilbao, Biscay, Spain
pablo.garcia.bringas@deusto.es

https://www.tecnalia.com/ , https://www.deusto.es/es/inicio

Abstract. Multiple sources of worries such as economic constraints and the dangers of climate change have moved society towards the process of optimizing the use of their electricity. However this approach towards energy consumption has become a source of uncertainty and worry as load monitoring becomes the norm. In order to overcome the privacy concerns techniques on Non-Intrusive Load Monitoring have been in development since the 1980s. In the field of load disaggregation applications of NILM there is constant reference to three topics to be improved on, results, interpretability and responsiveness. This paper investigates the role symbolic regression tools in the field of NILM, both as a singular tool of disaggregation and as a support instrument of deep learning models more common in the literature, such as LSTM, to improve on their prediction capabilities and adding a layer of interpretability to the results. The experimentation of this document offer two different solutions with various degrees of success depending on the proposed scenario although with quantifiable improvement over the established baseline.

Keywords: NILM · LSTM · Symbolic Regression · load disaggregation

1 Introduction

There are over 3,500 energy communities in the European Union alone [3], all of which share a common need: a solid and robust electrical infrastructure. Optimizing the electrical grid is closely tied to Demand-Side Management (DSM), which typically relies on intrusive, device-level metering. While accurate, this approach is neither scalable nor cost-effective [18]. Given these limitations, as well as privacy concerns, non-intrusive techniques have become essential, falling under the umbrella of Non-Intrusive Load Monitoring (NILM) [8].

NILM enables detailed energy consumption analysis from a single measurement point, making it widely adopted, especially in empowering users to monitor and manage their own energy use [25]. A core component of NILM is the identification of unique *load signatures* for each appliance, allowing for accurate device classification based on power consumption patterns. These signatures form the basis for categorizing appliances, improving disaggregation accuracy and enhancing DSM efficiency [1].

This paper proposes a NILM solution that combines the predictive power of Long Short-Term Memory (LSTM) networks with the interpretability of symbolic regression. The aim is to achieve state-of-the-art accuracy while addressing the lack of transparency in deep learning models from a user's perspective. The paper is structured as follows: related work, materials and methods, experiments and results, and conclusions, addressing the following research questions:

RQ1 What are the challenges of building a NILM testing baseline?
RQ2 What is the optimal way to obtain both interpretability and accuracy?
RQ3 What challenges arise from the presented solution?

2 Related Work

There is a wide variety of approaches within the NILM literature. Early research focused on Hidden Markov Models (HMM) [13], though they have gradually lost popularity as their performance is outperformed by factorial HMMs (FHMM) [24] and other alternatives. This decline is largely due to HMMs' difficulty in modeling load patterns involving multiple appliances. Optimization and evolutionary algorithms, such as genetic algorithms [5], evolutionary strategies [16], and clustering techniques [7], provided viable solutions. However, the dense nature of consumption patterns often led to slow and impractical results.

To improve both accuracy and actionability, NILM has increasingly adopted deep learning methods, including convolutional neural networks [21], autoencoders [6], and various LSTM architectures [9,22]. While these methods significantly enhance accuracy, as noted in [20], their black-box nature has raised concerns about interpretability and trust in the results. In response, there is a growing trend toward explainable NILM solutions, such as eXplainable AI (XAI) approaches [15] and interpretable frameworks [2]. This work follows the approach of integrating a symbolic regression module into an existing solution—replacing a constrained satisfaction problem with an attention-based LSTM—to improve accuracy while maintaining interpretability.

3 Materials and Methods

3.1 The Baseline

This work uses the attention based LSTM presented in [14] as a baseline for its experiments. LSTM are a variation of recurrent neural network (RNN) aimed at mitigating the vanishing gradient problem commonly encountered by traditional RNNs via the use cells with memory functions to selectively control the input of information [4]. In the referenced work the parameters of the LSTM are the following: he number of attention units (F) is set to 16, the number of attention heads (K) is set to 4, and linear as the activation function, and the two LSTM layers are set differently at 128 and 256. While its architecture consists of an initial convolutional layer with a ReLU activation function followed by the two bidirectional LSTM layers, the attention mechanisms, and dense layers in the end. The attention mechanism is described as a Permute layer to swap the data in dimensions 2 and 3. Then, the weights of the features in each timestep are then calculated. These are multiplied with the input to obtain the weighted sequence.

3.2 Dataset

This paper uses the UK-DALE dataset for its experiments [10]. The UK Domestic Appliance-Level Electricity dataset provides detailed power consumption data collected from five residential buildings in the United Kingdom over a two-year period, from 2013 to 2015. This dataset includes over 10 types of household appliances, offering a diverse range of appliance-level data for energy disaggregation research.

The dataset has been processed in order to satisfy the needs established by the baseline model. From the UK-DALE dataset the data of house 1 has been used and the selected appliances to disaggregate have been fridge, dishwasher and microwave. To ensure a robust and reliable evaluation, we focused on appliances for which our replication of the baseline model showed consistent performance. This approach allows for a more accurate and fair comparison with existing methods. While other appliances were considered, the variability in their behavior across different experimental runs made them less suitable for this particular study. The format for the inputs of the models has been designed according to the baseline work, each input is a sliding window of n time steps and each value corresponds to the Watts of the aggregated signal in the timestamp, the models output the Watts of the isolated appliance, temporally aligned according to the input sequence.

As no specific time windows or data periods were established during the baseline replication process, we devised a method to reduce the data while preserving a feature-rich model through the use of transition state analysis. By converting the raw UNIX timestamps into datetime objects and aligning the data across all appliances to ensure temporal consistency. Next, the data is resampled to one minute intervals to reduce the overall size while preserving the essential consumption patterns. A critical part of the preprocessing involves selecting the best 9-day interval for each appliance, ensuring that there is sufficient appliance activity-specifically, a minimum of two appliance state transitions per day in each of the training, validation, and test subsets. This ensures that the model is trained and evaluated on meaningful and representative data. This allowed us to identify time intervals where the expected power consumption is non-zero, ensuring that the model is trained and evaluated on meaningful, active usage patterns rather than idle or zero-consumption periods. The choice of 9 days was made to balance computational feasibility with the need for a sufficient number of appliance state transitions to train a robust model. While longer timeframes may provide more data, they also increase computational costs and the risk of overfitting, especially when the appliance is in an idle state for extended periods. Conversely, 9 days represent a reasonable compromise between data richness and computational efficiency, as the model receives a whole week of behavior for training, plus equal amounts of data for testing and validating.

3.3 Symbolic Regression

The objective via symbolic regression is the optimization not only of the predictions that come from the selected dataset. This technique seeks to understand both the model structure and its parameters, for the user this means that output wise the program will yield a series of prediction values and a mathematical expression that links the dataset to those predictions. As long as it fits properly in the trained model this mathematical expression is reusable for future data entries which can also reduce inference time [12].

As in symbolic regression the solution space not only explores data but also the combination of mathematical operators that combine to form the solution, it can become resource intensive, thus hyperparameter finetuning and techniques such as early stopping and result clipping have to be considered early into the problems design [17]. In this experiment the following hyperparameters have been selected after a hyperparameter tunning proccess: The operators to create the formulas are all the binary (+, -, *, /)and unary: (sin, cos, exp, log) operators in the PYSR python library, with 120 iterations with populations of size 20 and 25 as the *maxsize* which shows the number of formulas created by each iteration.

3.4 Model Ensemble

Model ensembling refers to the use of multiple models for the same task to improve the predictive capabilities of the selected models and make use of their particularities. In this experiment we make use of model ensembling to improve the predictions obtained via the LSTM and the interpretability of SR [19]. The ensembling technique used in this paper is stacking, training a model to combine the predictions of several other learning algorithms. Stacking performance is expected to be better than any single one of the trained models [23], on the other hand the usage of multiple models supposes more computational effort due to the addition of suplementary models. Gradient Boosting (GB) is a tree-based method that can capture nonlinear relationships between the predictions of the base regressor and the LSTM. This allows the metamodel to learn more complex combinations, such as relying more on the base regressor when the LSTM predictions are low, but less when they are high. GB builds an ensemble of decision trees iteratively, with each tree correcting the errors of the previous ones. This makes the model more robust to noisy or erroneous predictions of the base models. Via GB we can capture interactions between the predictions of the base regressor and the LSTM and adjust the predictions nonlinearly. Model ensembling allows overfitting to be controlled which helps avoid scenarios where predicting constantly 0 would yield a mostly satisfactory result by the means of total samples on 0 W.

3.5 Metrics

For this experiment, the selected metrics are Mean Absolute Error (MAE) 1 and Root Mean Squared Error (RMSE) 2. First, MAE was chosen because it is the only metric for which reliable comparisons could be made; uncertainty in the experimental process has led to a lack of replicability for alternative evaluation methods. Second, MAE offers clear advantages in load disaggregation. As a linear metric, it treats all errors equally, regardless of their magnitude, and is directly interpretable in watts. Additionally, it does not disproportionately penalize large errors, which is important in load disaggregation where both small and large errors contribute to accurate pattern recognition.

$$\text{MAE} = \sum_{i=1}^{n} \frac{|y_i - \hat{y}_i|}{n} \qquad (1)$$

From the perspective of the electrical grid, however, the ability to detect and correct large errors is particularly significant. This is where RMSE becomes more relevant, as it places greater emphasis on larger discrepancies, making it a more sensitive measure for evaluating model performance in critical load estimation.

$$\text{RMSE} = \sqrt{\frac{1}{n}\sum_{i=1}^{n}(y_i - \hat{y}_i)^2} \qquad (2)$$

4 Experiments and Results

The experiment has followed the steps defined in Fig. 1, firstly an attention based LSTM has been trained following the architecture established previously. This model outputs a series of values y_{lstm}, these are the predictions the LSTM produces. In the first iterative process we use these predictions as an input for a symbolic regressor in order to improve the accuracy while obtaining an interpretable equation that explains how the predictions obtained from the LSTM interact with the real data and the expected consumption values. In this version of the experiment our model outputs a series of values $y_{srEnhanced}$ from a combination of mathematical operators where x_{true} and y_{lstm} interact in a mathematical formulation. This approach has output the following as the best formulas for each appliance, fridge:

$$y = (-1002.56433 \,/\, (x0 + -108.05412)) + 83.90209 \qquad (3)$$

dishwasher:

$$y = exp(exp(sin(exp(sin(log(x0) \,/\, 0.50007534))) \,/\, 0.49718726)) \qquad (4)$$

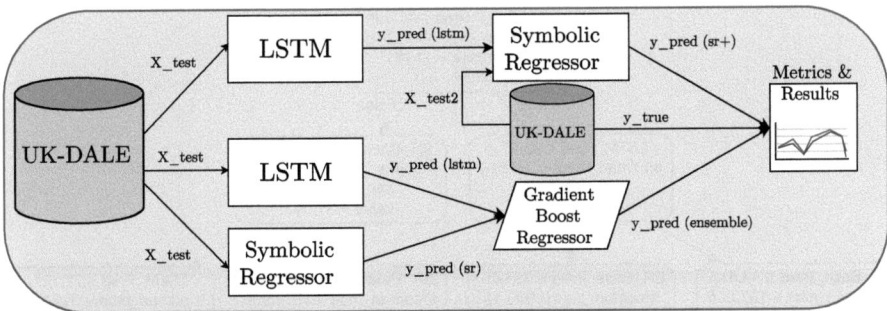

Fig. 1. Experimental processes followed, an enhancement of symbolic regression via LSTM outputs and a stacking ensembling of an LSTM and a symbolic regressor via GBR.

microwave:
$$y = exp(exp(sin(log(x0 * x0)) + 0.94749177)) \qquad (5)$$

where y is the predicted Wattage and $x0$ the predicted output of the LSTM. In order to certify that both models contribute to the prediction the second approach was devised. In this version, the LSTM is train exactly as before, while the symbolic regression is trained using only x_{true} to obtain the predictions y_{sr}, this approach has output the following formulas: fridge:

$$y = log(x0) * 8.82591 \qquad (6)$$

dishwasher:
$$y = exp(sin(x0 \:/\: -594.5249) * 7.26167) \qquad (7)$$

microwave:
$$y = x0 * 0.13723376. \qquad (8)$$

Then, the output of both models are stacked via a metamodel, GBR, in order to improve the accuracy of the models. While this application obscures the involvement of the symbolic regressor, as well as the interpretability from the equation it outputs, GBR has been selected as a metamodel not only for its efficiency but also, as an interpretable model the results can be traced back [11].

These results are, nonetheless, less interpretable than symbolic regressor but more interpretable than LSTM models. The trees generated by GBR are small (max_depth = 3), but there are multiple (n_estimators = 100). Each tree adjusts the residuals of the previous model, so they do not directly predict energy consumption, but corrections to the cumulative predictions. The features (y_{sr} and Ly_{lstm}) indicate how the metamodel combines the predictions of the SR Base and LSTM. Viewing all trees may be impractical due to the number of files generated. The interpretability of the GBR is limited because the final model is an ensemble, not a single tree. However, inspecting some trees can give clues about how the model makes decisions as seen in Fig. 2.

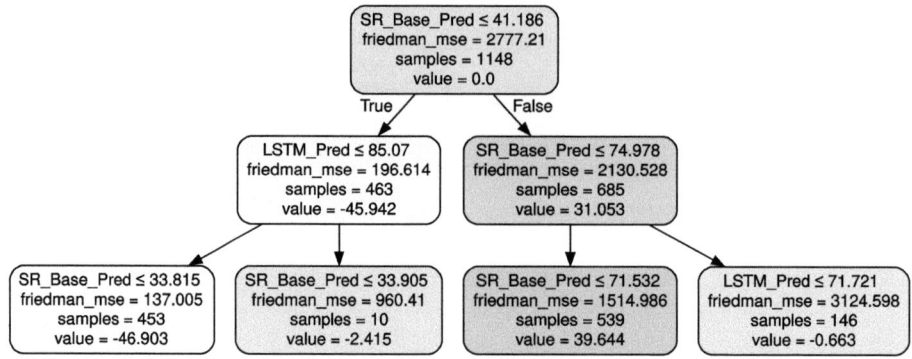

Fig. 2. First tree in the GBR for appliance: fridge (pruned for comprehension).

4.1 Results

The results for each model and appliance can be seen in Table 1. These results are the average of ten iterations per model and the standard deviation for each one has been stored in

There are two key conclusions to take from them. The second approach, the ensembling method, not only increases the interpretability of the results of the LSTM thanks to the addition of the SR and decision trees, it also offers better accuracy than the baseline for all appliances. Notably, in the fridge experiment there is a 50.79% improvement, while dishwasher and microwave offer a 37.80% y 29.58% improvement respectively. Notably, in the results of dishwasher the LSTM enhanced symbolic regressor is the most effective model, this can be attributed to domain specific knowledge as dishwashers have more clearly defined consumption patterns compared to fridges and microwaves. This makes the ability to capture temporal data of LSTM, perform better while the involvement of the symbolic regressor via ensemble methods may lose on that temporal analysis. From the analysis of the RMSE we can also understand that our model has obtained the ability to capture consumption patterns relatively well (comparing the MAE of the baseline with our approaches) however, it suffers when trying to predict consumption peaks, such as on/off events (Table 2).

This is illustrated on Fig. 3 where from the sample 400 until the end of the samples the appliance is opened and close repeatedly on a short period of time which the models have a harder time predicting over repeating patterns.

In Table 3 we compile the results of training a different house on the data of house 1 in order to evaluate the transferability of the appliance behavior with the standard deviation in Table 4. Notably, both fridge and microwave report better results than the original house 1 predictions in models LSTM enhanced SR and the ensemble method. This outcome is due to the erratic behavior seen in samples 400–500 of Fig. 3 while the test data of house 2 shows a more clearly defined behavior pattern, as reported in Fig. 4.

Table 1. Results for all the appliances across the different models, where bold text represents the best results.

Model	Fridge		Dishwasher		Microwave	
	MAE	RMSE	MAE	RMSE	MAE	RMSE
$LSTM_{att}$ (baseline)	36.37	–	36.6	–	25.36	–
$LSTM_{att}$ (this work)	29.637	43.498	23.762	202.598	27.826	190.445
Symbolic Regression	38.904	46.636	29.232	180.395	34.347	153.404
$LSTM_{att}$ enhanced SR	30.684	40.559	**19.287**	**119.263**	38.798	141.340
$LSTM_{att}$ SR ensemble	**17.896**	**35.157**	22.762	202.483	**17.858**	**102.241**

Table 2. Standard deviation for the results of Table 1

Model	Fridge		Dishwasher		Microwave	
	MAE	RMSE	MAE	RMSE	MAE	RMSE
$LSTM_{att}$	0.8058	0.2428	1.165	1.1028	0.6477	1.3204
Symbolic Regression	0.0003	0.0001	15.7757	7.2108	11.1086	10.1643
$LSTM_{att}$ enhanced SR	1.2031	0.6513	4.1703	22.9152	6.9944	6.9100
$LSTM_{att}$ SR ensemble	0.0012	0.0021	6.4938	15.1795	8.5152	8.9843

The results reported in the Dishwasher appliance show that not all appliances offer the same transferability capabilities as both the particularities of the appliance model and the behavior of the residents influence the results.

The error analysis of both houses 1 and 2 show that optimization methods such as SR and ensembling reduce the variability of the results, which suggests our hyperparameter configuration for these methods nears convergence while the methods more reliant on the LSTM results may be further improved with a configuration dissimilar to the baseline. Finally, the discrepancy between the low MAE and the high RMSE shown in Microwave suggests that low usage appliances, with lower consumption spikes may be harder to predict due to the model learning constant 0 W consumption.

Table 3. Results for house 2 predictions trained on house 1 data, where bold text represents the best results.

Model	Fridge		Dishwasher		Microwave	
	MAE	RMSE	MAE	RMSE	MAE	RMSE
$LSTM_{att}$	41.4268	51.5049	48.4085	300.3288	16.4341	134.8098
Symbolic Regression	35.8166	42.0968	63.6257	260.7981	47.0964	203.8352
$LSTM_{att}$ enhanced SR	18.6737	27.4935	**33.8938**	**124.0790**	15.2585	79.2508
$LSTM_{att}$ SR ensemble	**6.5278**	**18.16**	47.6110	300.1752	**3.6727**	**38.4454**

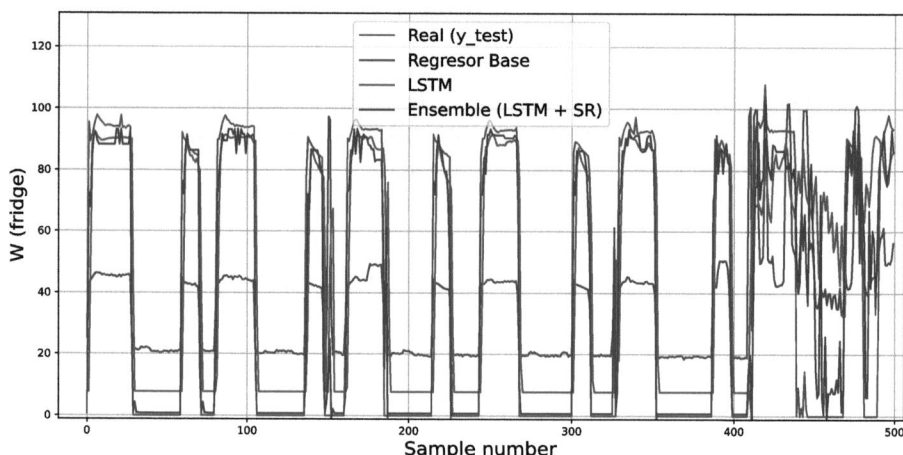

Fig. 3. The results of the diverse models used during the experiments for the appliance: fridge.

Table 4. Error analysis for Table 3

Model	Fridge		Dishwasher		Microwave	
	MAE	RMSE	MAE	RMSE	MAE	RMSE
$LSTM_{att}$	5.2041	2.9163	4.1358	5.4156	1.9703	3.7999
Symbolic Regression	0.0042	0.0027	6.1877	18.5628	9.2724	8.3123
$LSTM_{att}$ enhanced SR	3.8119	2.4024	12.8303	19.5696	0.8832	3.1368
$LSTM_{att}$ SR ensemble	0.0011	0.0006	6.6154	16.4975	8.6263	9.0041

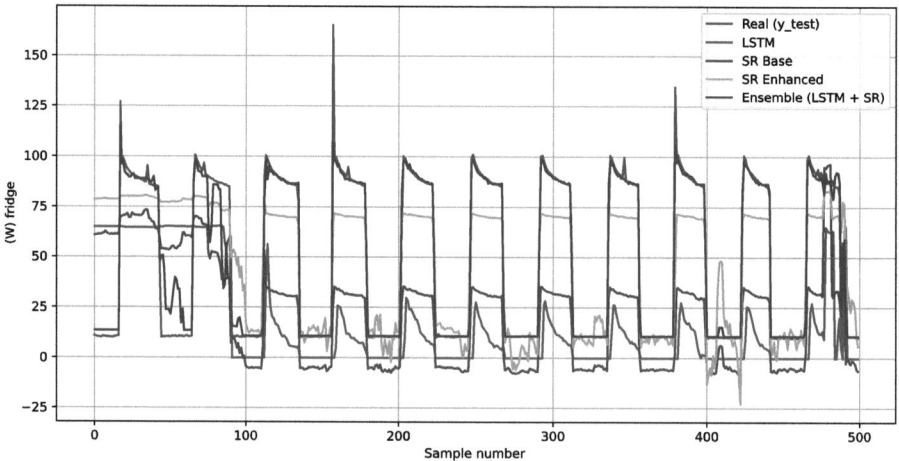

Fig. 4. The results of the appliance fridge as trained in house 1 data and tested in house 2.

5 Conclusion

In this study, we propose two novel approaches to NILM by integrating symbolic regression with LSTM networks, applied to the fridge, dishwasher, and microwave appliances in the UK-DALE House 1 dataset. The first approach enhances a symbolic regressor by incorporating LSTM predictions as an additional feature, achieving performance comparable to the baseline LSTM model. This method not only maintains accuracy but also introduces a layer of interpretability through the generation of explicit mathematical expressions, demonstrating that interpretability does not necessarily come at the cost of performance.

The second approach introduces an ensemble model that combines the symbolic regressor and LSTM using a GBR metamodel. This ensemble consistently outperforms the baseline LSTM while preserving interpretability, highlighting the potential of hybrid symbolic-temporal models to deliver more robust and transparent solutions for NILM. These results suggest that such combinations can support practical applications in energy management and sustainability by offering both accuracy and insight into energy consumption patterns.

To further assess the generalizability of the proposed models, we tested their transferability by applying them to House 2 of the same dataset. The models demonstrated strong pattern recognition capabilities, indicating promising potential for cross-household applicability. However results such as the reported in appliance dishwasher show that not all appliances have the same transferability capabilities, both appliance model consumption and human behavior are future factors to take into account.

Looking ahead, future research should focus on enhancing the interpretability and scalability of the proposed models. This could involve exploring more complex symbolic operators and integrating domain-specific knowledge to refine the generated expressions.

Furthermore, the study could be extended to larger and more diverse datasets, enabling a more thorough evaluation of model generalization across different households and usage patterns. It is also worth noting that, in pursuit of interpretability and accuracy, we have prioritized model performance over time-responsiveness, a critical factor in real-time NILM applications. Ensembling multiple models, while beneficial for accuracy, can degrade responsiveness, a trade-off that requires further investigation, while our experiment can be run in aproximately an hour in our resources, different NILM approaches may require shorter actionability.

Acknowledgments. The authors would like to thank the Basque Government for its funding support through the BIKAINTEK PhD support program (grant no. 014-B2/2022).

CRediT author statement. CRediT: Danel Rey-Arnal: Conceptualization, Data curation, Formal Analysis, Investigation, Methodology, Resources, Software, Visualization, Writing original draft; Pablo G. Bringas: Funding acquisition, Project administration, Supervision, Validation; Ibai Laña: Project administration, Supervision, Validation, Writing review & editing.

References

1. Angelis, G.F., Timplalexis, C., Krinidis, S., Ioannidis, D., Tzovaras, D.: Nilm applications: literature review of learning approaches, recent developments and challenges. Energy Build. **261**, 111951 (2022)
2. Batic, D., Stankovic, V., Stankovic, L.: Toward transparent load disaggregation-a framework for quantitative evaluation of explainability using explainable AI. IEEE Trans. Consum. Electron. **70**(1), 4345–4356 (2023)
3. Bauwens, T., et al.: Conceptualizing community in energy systems: a systematic review of 183 definitions. Renew. Sustain. Energy Rev. **156**, 111999 (2022)
4. Brattoli, B., Buchler, U., Wahl, A.S., Schwab, M.E., Ommer, B.: Lstm self-supervision for detailed behavior analysis. In: Proceedings of the IEEE Conference on Computer Vision and Pattern Recognition, pp. 6466–6475 (2017)
5. Chang, H.H., Chien, P.C., Lin, L.S., Chen, N.: Feature extraction of non-intrusive load-monitoring system using genetic algorithm in smart meters. In: 2011 IEEE 8th International Conference on e-Business Engineering, pp. 299–304. IEEE (2011)
6. Chen, H., Wang, Y.H., Fan, C.H.: A convolutional autoencoder-based approach with batch normalization for energy disaggregation. J. Supercomput. **77**(3), 2961–2978 (2021)
7. Etezadifar, M., Karimi, H., Mahseredjian, J.: Non-intrusive load monitoring: comparative analysis of transient state clustering methods. Electr. Power Syst. Res. **223**, 109644 (2023)
8. Hart, G.W.: Nonintrusive appliance load monitoring. Proc. IEEE **80**(12), 1870–1891 (1992)
9. Hwang, H., Kang, S.: Nonintrusive load monitoring using an lstm with feedback structure. IEEE Trans. Instrum. Meas. **71**, 1–11 (2022)
10. Kelly, J., Knottenbelt, W.: The UK-dale dataset, domestic appliance-level electricity demand and whole-house demand from five UK homes. Sci. Data **2**(1), 1–14 (2015)
11. Konstantinov, A.V., Utkin, L.V.: Interpretable machine learning with an ensemble of gradient boosting machines. Knowl.-Based Syst. **222**, 106993 (2021)
12. Kubalík, J., Derner, E., Žegklitz, J., Babuška, R.: Symbolic regression methods for reinforcement learning. IEEE Access **9**, 139697–139711 (2021)
13. Kumar, P., Abhyankar, A.R.: A time efficient factorial hidden markov model-based approach for non-intrusive load monitoring. IEEE Trans. Smart Grid **14**(5), 3627–3639 (2023)
14. Liu, Q., et al.: Improving wireless indoor non-intrusive load disaggregation using attention-based deep learning networks. Phys. Commun. **51**, 101584 (2022)
15. Machlev, R., Malka, A., Perl, M., Levron, Y., Belikov, J.: Explaining the decisions of deep learning models for load disaggregation (nilm) based on xai. In: 2022 IEEE Power & Energy Society General Meeting (PESGM), pp. 1–5. IEEE (2022)
16. Machlev, R., Belikov, J., Beck, Y., Levron, Y.: Mo-nilm: a multi-objective evolutionary algorithm for nilm classification. Energy Build. **199**, 134–144 (2019)
17. Mežnar, S., Džeroski, S., Todorovski, L.: Efficient generator of mathematical expressions for symbolic regression. Mach. Learn. **112**(11), 4563–4596 (2023)

18. Nasir, T., et al.: Recent challenges and methodologies in smart grid demand side management: state-of-the-art literature review. Math. Prob. Eng. **2021**(1), 5821301 (2021)
19. Ozay, M., Vural, F.T.Y.: A new fuzzy stacked generalization technique and analysis of its performance. arXiv preprint arXiv:1204.0171 (2012)
20. Rafiq, H., Manandhar, P., Rodriguez-Ubinas, E., Qureshi, O.A., Palpanas, T.: A review of current methods and challenges of advanced deep learning-based non-intrusive load monitoring (nilm) in residential context. Energy Build. **305**, 113890 (2024)
21. Silva Nolasco, L., Lazzaretti, A.E., Mulinari, B.M.: Deepdfml-nilm: a new cnn-based architecture for detection, feature extraction and multi-label classification in nilm signals. IEEE Sens. J. **22**(1), 501–509 (2021)
22. Verma, S., Singh, S., Majumdar, A.: Multi-label lstm autoencoder for non-intrusive appliance load monitoring. Electr. Power Syst. Res. **199**, 107414 (2021)
23. Wolpert, D.H.: Stacked generalization. Neural Netw. **5**(2), 241–259 (1992)
24. Yang, F., et al.: Fhmm based industrial load disaggregation. In: 2021 6th Asia Conference on Power and Electrical Engineering (ACPEE), pp. 330–334. IEEE (2021)
25. Zhuang, M., Shahidehpour, M., Li, Z.: An overview of non-intrusive load monitoring: approaches, business applications, and challenges. In: 2018 International Conference on Power System Technology (POWERCON), pp. 4291–4299. IEEE (2018)

IoT Device Fingerprinting: Optimized with Data Diversity and Feature Selection for Computational Efficiency

Chan Yeng Hui and Tan Saw Chin(✉)

Faculty of Computing and Informatics, Multimedia University, 63100 Cyberjaya, Selangor, Malaysia
sctan1@mmu.edu.my

Abstract. With the widespread adoption of IoT, IoT device fingerprinting is crucial for strengthening security and management in IoT ecosystems. Existing approaches often rely on predefined network protocols or simple correlation, lacking machine learning-based feature selection, which may overlook complex feature relationships and dependencies. Additionally, training and testing times are rarely reported, making it difficult to evaluate and compare different fingerprinting approaches. Furthermore, implementations are typically conducted on a single dataset composed of the same network of IoT devices, limiting generalization evaluation. This study aims to demonstrate the effectiveness of machine learning-based approaches, accompanied by feature selection techniques, in IoT device fingerprinting. It seeks to evaluate multiple fingerprinting approaches with a focus on performance and computational efficiency across various datasets. The proposed framework TreePrint employs various ensemble classifiers implemented on two public datasets. Three feature selection methods: Recursive Feature Elimination (RFE), Mutual Information (MI), and Principal Component Analysis (PCA) are employed. The MI-selected feature set significantly reduced training time by 38.1% without compromising accuracy. RFE improved test accuracy from 88.88% to 90.12%. These results underscore the effectiveness of machine learning-based feature selection in enhancing both performance and computational efficiency for IoT fingerprinting. Furthermore, TreePrint demonstrates strong generalization, consistently exceeding 90% accuracy on two datasets.

Keywords: IoT Fingerprinting · Feature Selection · Machine Learning

1 Introduction

IoT is a network of interconnected devices that collects stimuli from the physical environment, then communicates and exchanges data over the internet [1]. Software-Defined Networking (SDN) is an architecture that separates the control plane from the data forwarding plane, using an SDN controller for centralized management. IoT-SDN integrates these two technologies by leveraging SDN's centralized control and programmability to manage resource allocation of IoT networks [2]. This integration calls for the need for device recognition in the network as a precaution for security risk. Device fingerprinting identifies IoT devices using specific characteristics based on network interactions.

Existing works on IoT device fingerprinting using machine learning algorithms have demonstrated significant progress in accuracy and efficiency. Frameworks such as DevTag [3] and IoT Sentinel [4] highlight advancements in classification accuracy, achieving up to 99.3% for device type and 81.5% for exact devices, respectively. Computational time varies, with optimal prediction times ranging from 157.7 ms for [4] to 5.91 s per 1000 packets for [3]. However, many studies primarily rely on single datasets and often overlook the use of feature selection methods.

Feature selection is crucial for IoT device fingerprinting as it serves two primary purposes. Firstly, it helps reduce the training time of machine learning models without compromising the model's accuracy [5]. Secondly, feature selection aids in identifying attributes that are most representative of each device category or type [5].

In this article, a comprehensive framework for IoT device fingerprinting is demonstrated, highlighting two key contributions. Firstly, the framework utilizes ensemble method for IoT device fingerprinting while incorporating feature selection techniques to enhance classification accuracy and efficiency. RFE, MI, and PCA are used alongside bagging and boosting classification models. Secondly, the framework is applied to UNSW [6] and IoT Sentinel [4] datasets to validate its generalization ability. The datasets encompass packet information in passively collected traffic traces. Evaluation is conducted using metrics such as accuracy, precision, recall, F1-score, training time, and prediction time.

The article is organized into 5 sections. Section 1 introduces the research topic. Section 2 provides an overview of existing fingerprinting approaches for IoT devices. Section 3 outlines the proposed framework for fingerprinting IoT devices. Section 4 presents the implementation outcome and discussions. Finally, Sect. 5 concludes the article, summarizing the framework's findings and contributions.

2 Related Works

Wan et al. [3] demonstrates the use of deep learning models, for identifying IoT devices. The study employs multilabel classification using CNN, DPCNN, RNN, RCNN, and attention-based bidirectional LSTM, leveraging packet information to classify device category, vendor, and type. The classification models demonstrated strong performance, achieving 98.3% precision, recall, and F1-score for device category, 97.8%–97.9% for vendor classification, and 99.2%–99.34% for device type classification. The prediction time for 1000 packets was reported as 5.97 s.

Miettinen et al. [4] employs one-vs-all classification using multiple binary RF classifiers to identify device categories based on passively observed network traffic. The dataset was acquired by the authors, consisting of packets from smart home devices during the setup phase. In [4], overall accuracy of 81.5% is reported, with individual device performance ranging from 1.0 (best) to 0.5 (worst). Time taken for a single classification was 157.7 ms. ML-based feature selection is absent. [4] relies on WiFi association protocols as features.

Msadek et al. [7] adopts multiclass classification using RF, ET, KNN, AB and SVM to identify device categories based on packet information. The classification models were evaluated using accuracy, miscalculation rate, precision, recall, and F1-score. AdaBoost achieved the highest accuracy (95.5%), while SVM had the lowest (39%). RF had the longest training time (90 s), and KNN the shortest (0.7 s).

Bhattacharyya et al. [5] employs multiclass classification using RF, DT, KNN, AB and XGB to identify distinct device from one open-access dataset. Two feature sets are proposed by the author, where the features are selected based on correlation with ARP and IP protocols using a threshold of 0.03. The classification models were evaluated using accuracy, precision, recall, and F1-score. The proposed IPAssess features with RF achieved 78.3% accuracy and a 67.9% F1-score. The prediction time ranged from 0.2 s for NB to 69 s for KNN.

Sobot et al. [8] applied both ML and DL models for fingerprinting using two self-collected datasets: 3GPP NB-IoT and IEEE 802.11n. For IEEE 802.11n, the study used two extraction algorithms with RF, RNN, LSTM, RESNEXT, and SKNET to identify devices from raw CSI values. The 3GPP NB-IoT dataset leveraged NB, LR, DT, KNN, SVM, RF, and GBM models to classify devices based on radio measurements. SKNET achieved the highest accuracy (99.47%) on IEEE 802.11n, while GBM performed best on 3GPP NB-IoT with 99.19% accuracy and 98.77% F-measure. Prediction throughput was highest for RF with WEASEL (481.82 predictions/s on IEEE 802.11n) and LR (363.09 predictions/s on 3GPP NB-IoT).

Alharbi et al. [9] utilized XGB to identify IoT device types based on WiFi data captured externally without direct access. The dataset was self-collected. The model was assessed using accuracy, precision, recall, and F1-score, achieving a strong 95% accuracy.

Greis et al. [10] proposed a modified CNN and LSTM model to classify IoT device types based on raw network traffic data. The study leveraged a publicly available dataset for implementation. CNN achieved 98.2% accuracy, 98.5% precision, and 98.3% recall, while LSTM reached 97.1% accuracy, 96.3% precision, and 97.2% recall. The prediction time per device was 0.2 ms for CNN and 0.67 ms for LSTM, demonstrating strong performance.

IoTDevID is proposed in [11] which applies multiclass classification with DT, GBM, KNN, NB, RF and SVM to classify IoT device types based on packet information. The study incorporated an aggregation algorithm to refine classification results. The framework utilizes two publicly available datasets, with one used for training and both used for testing. Feature selection was performed using importance voting approach, which merge the ranking or scoring of six feature selection algorithms. DT achieved 94.1% accuracy and 93.5% F1-score on the UNSW dataset, but performance was lower on IoT Sentinel (83.3% accuracy, 86.1% F1-score). Prediction time varied, with DT requiring 0.128 s training, 0.008 s testing on IoT Sentinel, while UNSW testing took 0.022 s. In [11], training was conducted solely on the IoT Sentinel dataset, with performance remaining below 90% on this dataset.

Maiti et al. [12] leveraged CART, RF and SVM to classify IoT device types from encrypted WiFi traffic data collected using COTS radio without decryption. The dataset consists of three sets of encrypted WiFi traffic, all collected by the authors of [12] from the same IoT devices across three scenarios. RF achieved 98% accuracy, 98% precision, 97% recall, and 97% F-score. Feature selection retained features with correlation > 0.5, removing redundancies with high variance inflation factor. Although three datasets were used, they originated from the same set of devices, varying only by timing and environmental condition.

ProfilIoT in [13] used network traffic data to distinguish between IoT and non-IoT devices, as well as identify specific IoT devices. The framework combined a one-vs-rest approach with custom algorithms, employing GBM, RF, and XGB as binary classifiers. The dataset consisted of self-collected network traffic data, with TCP packets converted into sessions to extract behavioral fingerprints. Accuracy of 99.281% is reported in [13], indicating strong performance. The summary of related works is as shown in Table 1.

Table 1. Summary of Related Works.

Ref	Focus	Technique Used	Results Obtained	Dataset	Challenges
[3]	Fingerprinting devices using packet-level features via deep learning model	CNN, DPCNN, RNN, RCNN, LSTM	Precision: 99.2% Recall: 99.34% F1: 99.3%	1 self-collected dataset	No ML-based feature selection Implemented on 1 dataset
[4]	Fingerprinting IoT devices via passively observed network traffic during setup phase	One-vs-all classification with RF	Accuracy 0.815	1 self-collected dataset	No ML-based feature selection No training time Implemented on 1 dataset
[7]	Fingerprinting IoT devices using packet-level features via multiclass classification	RF, ET, KNN, AB, SVM	Accuracy: Best: AB 95.5% Worst: SVM 39%	1 public dataset.	No ML-based feature selection No prediction time Implemented on 1 dataset
[5]	Fingerprinting IoT devices using multiple feature sets of 1 dataset	RF, DT, KNN, AB, XGB.	Accuracy: 78.3% F1: 67.9%	1 public dataset	No training time Implemented on 1 dataset
[8]	Fingerprinting IoT devices using physical layer features	RF, RNN, LSTM, RESNEXT, SKNET, NB, LR, DT, KNN, SVM, RF, GBM	Accuracy, F-measures IEEE 802.11n: 99.47% 3GPP NB-IoT: 99.19%, 98.77%	2 self-collected datasets	No ML-based feature selection No training time
[9]	Fingerprinting IoT devices using externally sniffed WiFi data	XGB.	Accuracy: 95%	1 self-collected dataset	No feature selection No computation time

(*continued*)

Table 1. (*continued*)

Ref	Focus	Technique Used	Results Obtained	Dataset	Challenges
[10]	Fingerprinting IoT devices using raw network traffic data	Modified CNN and LSTM	Accuracy: 98.2% Precision: 98.5% Recall: 98.3%	1 public dataset	No feature selection No training time
[11]	Addressing the transfer problem in IoT fingerprinting using packet header and payload features	DT, GBM, KNN, NB, RF, SVM, Importance voting-based feature selection	Accuracy, F1-score UNSW: 94.1%, 93.5% IoT Sentinel: 83.3%, 86.1%	2 public datasets	Trained only on 1 dataset Performance < 90% for 1 dataset
[12]	Fingerprinting IoT devices using encrypted WiFi traffic without decryption	CART, RF, SVM, Pearson correlation-based feature selection.	Accuracy: 98% Precision: 98% Recall: 97% F1: 97%	3 self-collected datasets	No computation time
[13]	Classifying IoT vs. non-IoT devices, then identifying specific IoT devices using network traffic data	GBM, RF, XGB combined with a custom algorithm	Accuracy: 99.281%	1 self-collected dataset	No feature selection No computation time Implemented on 1 dataset

Deployment strategies for IoT device fingerprinting framework are also studied. Fingerprinting module by Zhou et al. [14] is physically connected to a mirrored port on an Ethernet switch which facilitates the both active and passive monitoring of the IoT network. The SRAM-AEN architecture [15] implements a trusted verifier model where the verifier (a network administrator's laptop) communicates directly with different IoT devices using serial or USB connections which enables periodic trace data collection from device's memory during runtime. In contrast, instead of a single fingerprinting module in a central device or location, each gateway captures traffic from connected devices and preprocesses the traffic data locally for device fingerprinting in the FICDF framework [16]. Encrypted model predictions are transmitted to a central server instead of raw traffic data which guarantees privacy in large-scale IoT environment.

3 TreePrint Framework

The flowchart in Fig. 1 illustrates the structure of TreePrint, which consists of five subsections. The first section, data extraction, involves extracting network traffic data from PCAP files. The second section, data preprocessing, prepares the data for model input. The third section focuses on feature selection. The fourth section covers hyperparameter tuning, model training and testing. Finally, the performance evaluation section assesses the framework.

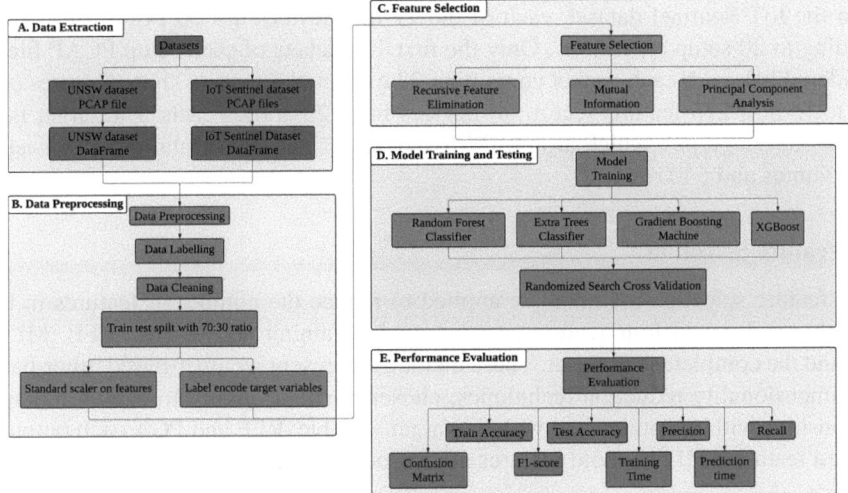

Fig. 1. Flowchart of TreePrint.

3.1 Data Extraction

The two datasets used in this implementation consist of traffic data in packets sent by various IoT devices, collected via passive traffic monitoring. Packet data are useful for IoT device fingerprinting as they contain unique information such as IP addresses, ports, and protocols for differentiating IoT devices or device categories.

UNSW dataset [6] used in this implementation consist of packet information of 29 IoT devices collected during the normal operation of the devices, stored in PCAP file. The target of this dataset is the 6 device categories. IoT Sentinel dataset [4] includes packet data from 27 IoT devices, captured during the setup phase, repeated 20 times. The target of this dataset is the 27 IoT devices.

3.2 Data Preprocessing

In both datasets, data are extracted from the PCAP files using scapy and converted into DataFrame. Duplicates and null values are checked and handled. All features are scaled using a standard scaler and the target variable is label encoded. Datasets are subjected to train test split of ratio 70:30 before feature selection.

The UNSW dataset has 802581 rows initially. There are 21 features extracted including protocols and port information. Port usages are categorized into ranges, distinguishing well-known ports and other ranges representing collections of protocols. Range 1 is from port number 0 to 1023, range 2 is from port number 1024 to 49151, range 3 is from port number 49152 to 65535. To address the class imbalance problem, 2 extreme minority classes are dropped. 60000 rows are sampled from the remaining 4 categories: Hubs, Cameras, Electronics and Switches and Triggers.

In the IoT Sentinel dataset, each of the 27 IoT devices has 20 PCAP files, corresponding to 20 setup repetitions. Only the first 12 packets of each setup PCAP file are considered [4], with each packet containing 23 extracted features. These features combine to form a 276-feature vector, all devices have 20 entries each. The target is the column 'device_type', which are the 27 IoT devices. The final DataFrame consists of 277 columns and 540 rows.

3.3 Feature Selection

Three feature selection methods are applied to reduce the number of features in both datasets, resulting in four feature sets for model training and testing: RFE, MI and PCA and the complete feature set. These methods represent wrapper-based, filter-based, and dimensionality reduction techniques, chosen for their ability to capture complex relationships within features and with the target variable. RFE and PCA each output 10 selected features, MI threshold features at 75th percentile.

3.4 Model Training and Testing

RF, ET, GBM and XGB are employed to train and test two datasets, each with four distinct feature sets. Bagging methods (RF and ET) aggregates multiple DT trained on randomized traffic features, while boosting methods (GBM and XGB) refine device classification errors sequentially during training, both approaches effectively reduce overfitting and improve precision.

The key parameters for these classifiers are the number of decision trees and the maximum depth of each tree, effectively controlling the number of splits. These parameters navigate the trade-off between accuracy and overfitting. In addition to, the learning rate and the subsample size parameters are also tuned for the boosting models. Randomized Search Cross-Validation with 10-fold cross-validation is introduced for hyperparameter tuning.

3.5 Performance Evaluation

Four performance metrics are used to evaluate and compare the 4 models implemented, which are accuracy, precision, recall, and F1 score. Both the training and testing accuracy are recorded to identify both training efficacy and performance on unseen data. Moreover, training time and prediction time are also recorded to assess the computational overhead. The performance of the models implemented across 4 sets of input features of each UNSW and IoT Sentinel dataset respectively will be compared and analyzed.

4 Results and Discussions

In this section, TreePrint is implemented, and its performance is collected and analyzed. The framework is implemented using Python 3.11.7 and Jupyter Lab as the development environment. The hardware setup features an AMD Ryzen 7 6800H CPU, NVIDIA GeForce RTX 3060 GPU, and 16 GB RAM. The performance of TreePrint on UNSW dataset and IoT Sentinel dataset are shown in Table 2 and 3.

Table 2. UNSW dataset results.

FS	FP	Train Accuracy	Test Accuracy	Precision	Recall	F1-score	Training Time/s	Prediction time/s
W/o	RF	0.93118	0.92901	0.93101	0.92910	0.92941	120.12728	0.53652
	ET	0.93123	0.92900	0.93100	0.92900	0.92940	101.38478	0.58326
	GBM	0.92917	0.92903	0.93106	0.92903	0.92935	4786.40523	1.42617
	XGB	0.92309	0.92360	0.92588	0.92360	0.92397	337.29574	0.13843
MI	RF	0.93088	0.92829	0.93068	0.92829	0.92877	93.20953	0.49993
	ET	0.93092	0.92826	0.93067	0.92826	0.92875	62.72434	0.56405
	GBM	0.92877	0.92863	0.93091	0.92863	0.92902	3133.51253	1.39896
	XGB	0.92247	0.92275	0.92529	0.92275	0.92313	263.93917	0.12324
PCA	RF	0.93120	0.92899	0.93099	0.92899	0.92938	168.64194	0.48846
	ET	0.93123	0.92894	0.93095	0.92894	0.92934	88.52994	0.43247
	GBM	0.92971	0.92969	0.93158	0.92969	0.93002	5982.45929	0.93012
	XGB	0.92515	0.92525	0.92700	0.92525	0.92557	321.26450	0.12089
RFE	RF	0.93118	0.92901	0.93101	0.92910	0.92941	106.62103	0.51008
	ET	0.93123	0.92899	0.93099	0.92899	0.92938	80.61407	0.55038
	GB	0.92906	0.92911	0.93098	0.92911	0.92942	3881.25557	1.29675
	XGB	0.92309	0.92363	0.92588	0.92363	0.92398	281.15910	0.12755

4.1 UNSW Dataset

In the UNSW dataset, the training and test accuracies remained consistently high across all feature sets and models, with training accuracies around 93% and testing accuracies around 92%. There are minimal differences between training and testing results, indicating the model performed well on both training data and unseen data.

GBM achieved the best accuracy across all feature sets, but the computational cost is significantly higher, indicating its inefficacy. RF with RFE-selected features achieved the same performance with the complete feature set, but with a training time reduction of 11.2% from 120.12728 s to 106.62103 s. Alternatively, ET with MI-selected features is observed to have a slight reduction in test accuracy of 92.826% as compared to 92.9% returned by the complete feature set. However, ET with MI demonstrated a significant decrease in training time of 38.1% and a slight decrease in prediction time from 0.58326 s to 0.56405 s. These suggest that while RFE provided marginally better classification performance, MI offered substantial improvements in computational efficiency.

4.2 IoT Sentinel Dataset

For the IoT Sentinel dataset, training accuracy across all models remained consistently high, ranging from 0.92 to 0.98. However, the lower test accuracy suggests a possible overfitting issue.

Table 3. IoT Sentinel dataset results.

FS	FP	Train Accuracy	Test Accuracy	Precision	Recall	F1-score	Training Time/s	Prediction time/s
W/o	RF	0.98677	0.88888	0.89528	0.88889	0.88476	3.21779	0.00808
	ET	0.93651	0.83951	0.85635	0.83951	0.83775	2.13076	0.00773
	GBM	0.98677	0.87037	0.88752	0.87037	0.86733	491.54000	0.01390
	XGB	0.98677	0.87037	0.88310	0.87037	0.86741	35.01212	0.00544
MI	RF	0.98413	0.89506	0.90631	0.89506	0.89208	2.90128	0.00725
	ET	0.95503	0.88272	0.89691	0.88272	0.88437	2.02254	0.00511
	GBM	0.98677	0.87654	0.89104	0.87654	0.87488	252.04881	0.00925
	XGB	0.98677	0.87037	0.88126	0.87037	0.86782	18.52996	0.00817
PCA	RF	0.98148	0.80247	0.82663	0.80247	0.79463	3.36591	0.00623
	ET	0.98677	0.80247	0.81451	0.80247	0.79244	1.90604	0.00646
	GBM	0.98677	0.75926	0.77099	0.75926	0.75027	200.80229	0.00804
	XGB	0.98677	0.79012	0.82138	0.79012	0.78057	24.26810	0.00570
RFE	RF	0.96825	0.90123	0.91036	0.90124	0.89841	2.93048	0.00716
	ET	0.92857	0.86420	0.89305	0.86420	0.86208	1.90940	0.00655
	GBM	0.98413	0.90741	0.91881	0.90741	0.90610	155.94756	0.00860
	XGB	0.98413	0.91358	0.92394	0.91358	0.91220	12.29374	0.00501

MI and RFE improved performance in all models constantly. Among the tested models, XGB with RFE produced exceptional results with 91.358% accuracy, 92.394% precision, 91.358% recall and 91.220% F1-score, followed closely by RF with RFE with metrics 90.123%, 91.036%, 90.124% and 89.841% in the same order. Despite the marginally superior performance by XGB, its training time is 3.195 times more than that of RF.

4.3 Further Analysis

The confusion matrixes of the top performing models are demonstrated. In the RF with RFE models, all four classes exhibited strong performance, as seen in the distinct diagonal line on the confusion matrix plot in Fig. 2. However, there are variations in performance across different device categories. Notably, Class 2 (Hubs) experiences the highest misclassification rate, frequently being identified as Class 0 (Cameras). This suggests that devices in the Camera and Hub categories may exhibit similar communication patterns in traffic data, making it challenging for the classifiers to differentiate between them. Conversely, Class 3 (Switches and Triggers) consistently achieves the highest performance across all tested models.

For the IoT Sentinel dataset, using the RFE feature set on RF, Class 8 (D-Link Water Sensor) has the highest misclassification rate as shown in Fig. 3. Out of six instances,

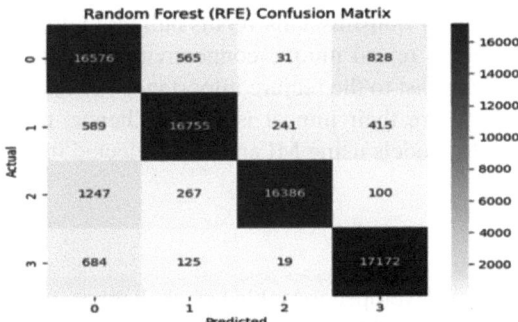

Fig. 2. Confusion Matrix of RF with RFE on UNSW dataset.

only two are correctly classified, while three are misclassified as Class 6 (D-Link Siren). These two devices may exhibit similar network behavior, particularly in the protocols they use, likely influenced by their functionality and brand.

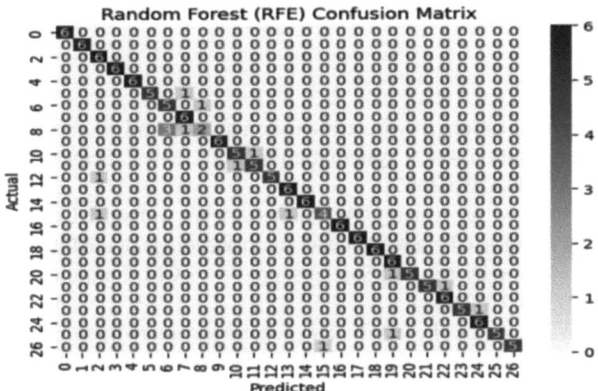

Fig. 3. Confusion Matrix of RF with RFE on IoT Sentinel dataset

Subsequently, the most discriminative features for classification are also explored. In the UNSW dataset, source and destination port ranges, packet size, and HTTPS presence features consistently ranked highest in importance. Devices performing specific functions often operate within defined port ranges, while packet size and HTTPS usage capture distinctive behavioral signatures relevant to fingerprinting. The consistent high ranking of these features by MI and RFE infers why models trained with these feature subsets achieved performance comparable to models implemented with full features set, but with significantly faster training times due to far fewer features.

In the IoT Sentinel dataset, where each row captures 23 features from the first 12 packets of a device's setup phase, Mutual Information and RFE consistently ranked packet size and destination IP address features among the most important. This suggests that these features reflect distinct device behaviors. Packet size can indicate functional roles, such as compact sensor transmissions versus bulkier multimedia exchanges. Destination IP address counters reveal unique connectivity patterns during initialization. Their significance is in contrast to the feature importance rankings from models trained on the full feature set, where their impact is diluted, hence, the lower classification performance compared to models using MI and RFE selected feature subsets.

5 Conclusion

In this study, TreePrint was developed to tackle key challenges in IoT device fingerprinting using machine learning-based feature selection across diverse datasets. By integrating RFE, MI, and PCA with bagging and boosting classifiers, the framework achieved effective classification of device category and type. Notably, ET with MI on the UNSW dataset reduced training time by 38.1% while sustaining 92.8% accuracy, and RFE with RF improved test accuracy from 88.88% to 90.12% on the IoT Sentinel dataset with reduced computation time. These results confirm that TreePrint balances performance and efficiency, revealing that targeted feature selection enables scalable, high-accuracy device identification for dynamic IoT environments.

References

1. Majid, M., et al.: Applications of wireless sensor networks and internet of things frameworks in the industry Revolution 4.0: a systematic literature review. Sensors **22**(6), 2087 (2022). https://doi.org/10.3390/s22062087
2. Tayyaba, S.K., Shah, M.A., Khan, O.A., Ahmed, A.W.: Software Defined Network (SDN) based Internet of Things (IoT): a road ahead. In: Proceedings of the International Conference on Future Networks and Distributed Systems, pp. 1–8. ACM, Cambridge (2017). https://doi.org/10.1145/3102304.3102319
3. Wan, S., Li, Q., Wang, H., Li, H., Sun, L.: DevTag: a benchmark for fingerprinting IoT devices. IEEE Internet Things J. **10**(7), 6388–6399 (2023). https://doi.org/10.1109/JIOT.2022.3225580
4. Miettinen, M., Marchal, S., Hafeez, I., Asokan, N., Sadeghi, A.-R., Tarkoma, S.: IoT SENTINEL: automated device-type identification for security enforcement in IoT. In: 2017 IEEE 37th International Conference on Distributed Computing Systems (ICDCS), pp. 2177–2184. IEEE, Atlanta (2017). https://doi.org/10.1109/ICDCS.2017.283
5. Bhattacharyya, S., Ganeriwala, P., Nandanwar, S., Muthalagu, R., Gupta, A.: IPAssess: a protocol-based fingerprinting model for device identification in the IoT (2021). https://doi.org/10.36227/techrxiv.16815232.v1
6. Sivanathan, A., et al.: Classifying IoT devices in smart environments using network traffic characteristics. IEEE Trans. Mob. Comput. **18**(8), 1745–1759 (2019). https://doi.org/10.1109/TMC.2018.2866249
7. Msadek, N., Soua, R., Engel, T.: IoT device fingerprinting: machine learning based encrypted traffic analysis. In: 2019 IEEE Wireless Communications and Networking Conference (WCNC), pp. 1–8. IEEE, Marrakesh (2019). https://doi.org/10.1109/WCNC.2019.8885429
8. Sobot, S., Ninkovic, V., Vukobratovic, D., Pavlovic, M., Radovanovic, M.: Machine learning methods for device identification using wireless fingerprinting. In: 2022 International Balkan Conference on Communications and Networking (BalkanCom), pp. 183–188. IEEE, Sarajevo (2022). https://doi.org/10.1109/BalkanCom55633.2022.9900723

9. Alharbi, I.A., Almalki, A.J., Alyami, M., Zou, C., Solihin, Y.: Profiling attack on WiFi-based IoT devices using an eavesdropping of an encrypted data frames. Adv. Sci. Technol. Eng. Syst. J. **7**(6), 49–57 (2022). https://doi.org/10.25046/aj070606
10. Greis, J., Yushchenko, A., Vogel, D., Meier, M., Steinhage, V.: Automated Identification of Vulnerable Devices in Networks using Traffic Data and Deep Learning (2021). https://doi.org/10.48550/ARXIV.2102.08199
11. Kostas, K., Just, M., Lones, M.A.: IoTDevID: a behavior-based device identification method for the IoT (2021). https://doi.org/10.48550/ARXIV.2102.08866
12. Maiti, R.R., Siby, S., Sridharan, R., Tippenhauer, N.O.: Link-layer device type classification on encrypted wireless traffic with COTS radios. In: Foley, S.N., Gollmann, D., Snekkenes, E. (eds.) Computer Security – ESORICS 2017. Lecture Notes in Computer Science, vol. 10493, pp. 247–264. Springer, Cham (2017). https://doi.org/10.1007/978-3-319-66399-9_14
13. Meidan, Y., et al.: ProfilIoT: a machine learning approach for IoT device identification based on network traffic analysis. In: Proceedings of the Symposium on Applied Computing, pp. 506–509. ACM, Marrakech (2017). https://doi.org/10.1145/3019612.3019878
14. Zhou, F., Qu, H., Liu, H., Liu, H., Li, B.: Fingerprinting IIoT devices through machine learning techniques. J. Signal Process. Syst. **93**(7), 779–794 (2021). https://doi.org/10.1007/s11265-021-01656-0
15. Kohli, V., Aman, M.N., Sikdar, B.: An intelligent fingerprinting technique for low-power embedded IoT devices. IEEE Trans. Artif. Intell. **5**(9), 4519–4534 (2024). https://doi.org/10.1109/tai.2024.3386498
16. Shengli, D., Han, D.J., Brimton, C.G., Keerthi, D.: FICDF: a federated incremental learning framework for IoT device fingerprinting, Seoul, Republic of Korea. pp. 337–344 (2024). https://ieeexplore.ieee.org/document/10778386

Improvement of Multi-Label Self-Adjusting Memory kNN Classifier for Sparse and Class-Imbalanced Data Streams

Thinzar Tun(✉) and Yuichi Goto

Department of Information and Computer Sciences, Saitama University, Saitama 338-8570, Japan
thinzar.t.677@ms.saitama-u.ac.jp, gotoh@mail.saitama-u.ac.jp

Abstract. In the multi-label data stream classification, concept drift and class-imbalanced are significant issues. Handling sparse data streams is also a considerable issue in it. Although the multi-label self-adjusting memory punitive kNN algorithm (MLSAMPkNN) proposed by Roseberry et al. is a hopeful framework for multi-label data stream classification, it has some limitations. Its punitive model removes data too quickly. Additionally, its performance with sparse and class-imbalanced data streams is not sufficient. Although we improved the its punitive model, the other limitations are remained unsolved. This paper proposes an algorithm for a multi-label self-adjusting memory kNN classifier that addresses not only drifting data streams but also sparse and class-imbalanced data streams. We changed the distance system and voting system of MLSAMPkNN to handle sparse and class-imbalanced data streams. Our experimental results demonstrate that our proposed algorithms consistently outperform other comparative models involving drifting, sparse, and class-imbalanced data streams.

Keywords: multi-label data stream classification · multi-label kNN classifier · concept drift · class-imbalanced data · sparse data

1 Introduction

The data streams are ordered sequences of instances that can be read only once or a few times because of its computing and storage capabilities [14]. Multi-label data stream classification is one of the supervised machine learning problems in which each data stream is classified into one or more predefined sets of labels. It has various applications, including online multimedia (such as movies and music), online news, and forum categorization [20]. Its classifiers can be classified into three categories: problem transformation, algorithm adaptation, and ensemble classifiers [20]. The problem transformation transforms a multi-label classification problem into a simpler single-label or multi-class classification problem . The algorithm adaptation adjusts an existing algorithm to a multi-label classification problem. The ensemble classifier combines several multi-label classifiers into a single classifier.

The k-nearest neighbor (kNN) approach is one of the expected approaches of multi-label data stream classification including concept drifts. The concept drift is the distribution of data changing over time and may lead to a degradation of prediction performance of classifiers. There are four categories of concept drift: abrupt/sudden drift, gradual drift, incremental drift, and recurring drift [4]. Most conventional methods in multi-label data stream classification concentrate on a single type of concept drift, although real-time data stream mining can involve different types of concept drift, including single or mixed types [15]. kNN is one of the famous algorithms of algorithm adaptation. It does not require an explicit training phase, making it adaptable to dynamic data streams. New instances can be added to the dataset without retraining, making it efficient for multi-label stream classification. The kNN is expected to deal with concept drifts [18].

The multi-label self-adjusting memory punitive kNN algorithm (MLSAMP-kNN) proposed by Roseberry et al. [13] is a hopeful candidate for multi-label data stream classification. Its punitive model removes data too quickly although it dynamically removes ineffective data from the current dataset. Additionally, its performance of MLSAMPkNN with sparse and class-imbalanced data streams is not sufficient [3]. Class imbalance is that some labels appear more frequently than others, and the ratio of positive and negative examples of a label may be imbalanced. Sparse data streams refer to the data stream representation where most values are zero or missing, but only a small fraction of the entries are non-zero or available. Thus, we improved the punitive model of MLSAMPkNN by changing its threshold [16]. Although the performance of the proposed algorithm for concept drift was improved, the other limitations remain unsolved.

This paper proposes an algorithm for a multi-label self-adjusting memory kNN classifier that addresses not only drifting data streams but also sparse and class-imbalanced data streams. First, we changed the distance system of MLSAMPkNN from Euclidean distance to Cosine distance to handle sparse data streams. The distance system is used to decide the nearest neighbors of a target instance in kNN algorithm. Second, we introduced the weighted voting system, rather than the majority voting system used in MLSAMPkNN, to handle class-imbalanced data streams. The voting system is used to determine the predictive labels of a target instance from the labels of its nearest neighbors. The paper also shows the effectiveness of our proposed algorithms through comparative studies. As a result, our proposed algorithm can handle drifting, sparse, and class-imbalanced data streams well, rather than previous kNN-based algorithms.

2 Related Work

2.1 MLSAMPkNN

The multi-label self-adjusting memory punitive kNN algorithm (MLSAMPkNN) [13] is the most effective algorithm among kNN-based algorithms in multi-label data stream classification. Losing et al. [7,8] proposed SAM-kNN. It is a simple kNN algorithm with the short and long-term memory of self-adjusting memory to handle heterogeneous types of concept drift. Short-term memory is used for the most recent and frequent instances, and long-term memory is used to maintain recurrent and infrequent instances. Rosberry et al. [12] proposed MLSAMkNN, upgraded and maintained with the same methods of SAM-kNN for drifting data streams. They also proposed [13] MLSAMPkNN, a multi-label kNN algorithm combined with self-adjusting memory and a punitive model for handling drifting data streams. It uses only the short term memory of the self-adjusting memory feature, unlike their previous algorithms. Zheng et al. [19] proposed SAMEP, which is an extension of MLSAMkNN by introducing a kind of punitive model. It uses both short and long-term memory of the self-adjusting memory feature. MLSAMPkNN is better than SAMEP from the viewpoint of computing resources, although they are extended algorithms of MLSAMkNN and their performance is almost the same [16].

The algorithm of MLSAMPkNN consists of three parts: determining predictive labels using kNN, self-adjusting memory, and a punitive model. Suppose $S = (s_1, s_2, \ldots, s_n)$ is a sequence of instances (n is a natural number) and an instance $s = (\mathbf{X}, \mathbf{Y}, \mathbf{Z})$ where $\mathbf{X} = (x_1, \ldots, x_m)$ (m is a natural number) is a feature vector, $\mathbf{Y} = (y_1, \ldots, y_L)$ is a vector for true labels, $\mathbf{Z} = (z_1, \ldots, z_L)$ is a vector for predictive labels, L is the number of given labels, and $y_i, z_i \in \{0, 1\}$ ($1 \leq i \leq L$). Let $s_i.Y[l]$ represents the value of l-th label in Y of an instance s_i. The role of multi-label kNN classifiers is to determine the value of $s_i.Z[l]$ ($1 \leq l \leq L$) from s_j ($1 \leq j \leq i-1$) where s_i is an incoming instance.

Determining predictive labels using kNN consists of two processes: finding the nearest neighbors of an incoming instance and calculating the predictive labels of the incoming instance. For an incoming instance s_i, the set of k-nearest neighbors NN of s_i is founded by the traditional Euclidean distance between $s \in NN$ and s_i [13]. MLSAMPkNN uses a simple majority voting to calculate the predictive labels $s_i.Z[j]$ ($1 \leq j \leq L$) [13]. The process of the majority voting is as follows. The relative frequency (rf) of the l-th label between the nearest neighbors is as below.

$$rf = \frac{1}{k} \sum_{n=1}^{k} 1 \mid s_n \in NN, s_n.Y[l] = 1 \quad (1)$$

where s_n is the n-th nearest neighbor in NN ($1 \leq n \leq k$). The value of the l-th predicted label $s_i.Z[l]$ is defined as follows.

$$s_i.Z[l] = \begin{cases} 1 & \text{if } rf \geq 0.5. \\ 0 & \text{otherwise.} \end{cases} \quad (2)$$

The self-adjusting memory is a dynamic sliding window that can adjust its size automatically and keep only current concept. The sliding window is used to keep most recent instances only when it can't keep all instances from a infinite data stream. This method is predicated on the idea that a model with fewer mistakes is produced when it processes training on internally relevant data. The detail explanation is described in paper [13].

A punitive model is to remove ineffective instances from the sliding window. Firstly, it calculates the error of neighbor instances of each incoming instance. They removed the instances suddenly from the sliding window when the error of each instance exceeded the predefined threshold, without consideration of how recently it was included in sliding window. After deciding a prediction for an incoming instance s_i, the label set of each nearest neighbor is inspected against that instance's true label vector. $s_n \in$ sliding window is a nearest neighbor of s_i. The error of s_n is E_{s_n} and is computed as below.

$$E_{s_n} = \sum_{l=1}^{L} 1 \mid s_n.Y[l] \neq s_i.Y[l] \tag{3}$$

When E_{s_n} exceeds the predefined threshold, s_n is removed from the sliding window. The predefined threshold T_{orig} is the value of the multiplication of the penalty ratio p, and the number of labels L in each dataset, and Roseberry et al. [13] used $p = 1$. If the penalty ratio value is 1, then it indicates the threshold value is dependent only on the number of labels.

$$T_{orig} = p \cdot L \tag{4}$$

MLSAMPkNN has three limitations. First, its punitive model of MLSAMP-kNN removes data too quickly because the threshold is not suitable. Second, it is difficult to calculate the distance between an incoming instance and the already existing instances in sliding window by Euclidean distance if the feature vectors of those instances are sparse. The Euclidean distance needs data standardization. It is not effective in sparse data. Finally, the majority voting may bias predictions toward the majority class and results in uncertain predictions, lower performance for the minority class in an imbalanced data stream and is less effective in data streams with high-dimensional features.

2.2 Improvement of MLSAMPkNN's Punitive Model

The current threshold of the MLSAMPkNN punitive model is small, too strict, and dependent only on the number of labels regardless of k of kNN [16]. Additionally, its punitive model punished instances too strong. The unsuitable threshold of its punitive model pushes the removal of instances too quickly from the sliding window, sometimes, especially in datasets with a small number of labels, although it can remove ineffective instances. We modified the threshold value [16], although the calculations in MLSAMPkNN's punitive model are the same except for the threshold. Suppose that k of kNN, the number of labels L in each dataset, and the adjusted number AN is 0.5. AN represents the predefined number to adjust the modified punitive equation.

$$T_{new} = L \cdot k \cdot AN \tag{5}$$

In the improvement of MLSAMPkNN's punitive model of our previous system [16], the threshold T_{new} is dependent on both the number of labels L and k of kNN.

We measured the average results of subset accuracy, accuracy, hamming score, precision, recall, and F-measure, running time, and model cost of MLSAMkNN, MLSAMPkNN, and our proposed algorithm on the 30 benchmark multi-label datasets [5]. As a result, our proposed algorithm achieved the least average time consumption and the highest average values of subset accuracy, accuracy, Hamming score, precision, recall, F-measure and lowest model cost compared to MLSAMPkNN and MLSAMkNN on all datasets [16]. However that proposed algorithm did not handle spare and class-imbalanced data stream well. We must resolve the remaining two limitations of MLSAMPkNN.

3 Proposed Algorithm

In this paper, we changed the distance system and voting system of MLSAMPkNN. First, we changed the distance system from Euclidean distance to Cosine distance to handle sparse data streams. Second, we changed from majority voting system to the weighted voting system to handle class-imbalanced data streams.

Cosine distance is a metric that is popular in machine learning environment. It is mostly used in sparse nature application such as text mining [17], star categorization [10], image classification [11]. Sparse data stream is a challenging issue in multi-label data stream classification. There is less attention on the sparse data streams issue. The current distance measuring method of MLSAMPkNN cannot adapt sparse data stream well. At present, Cosine distance has not been introduced to address the issue of sparse data streams in the multi-label data stream classification. It is derived from Cosine similarity. It measures the degree of the cosine angle to find similarities between instances. In general, It is applied when the orientation of the vector is important and not their magnitudes. The values of the cosine angles search for finding similarities between the vectors. If the cosine angle value is 1, then the data points are aligned in the same direction, and indicating that they are similar. Cosine distance is computed by subtracting the Cosine similarity coefficient from one [10]. The smaller the value of the Cosine distance between two vectors, the higher the similarity between the two vectors [1] . Cosine distance $C[s_i][s_j]$ between an incoming instance s_i and instances s_j in the sliding window is defined as follows where $s_i.X[f]$ and $s_j.X[f]$ are f-th feature of instances s_i and s_j.

$$C[s_i][s_j] = 1 - \frac{\sum_{f=1}^{n}(s_i.X[f]) * (s_j.X[f])}{\sqrt{\sum_{f=1}^{n}(s_i.X[f])^2} * \sqrt{\sum_{f=1}^{n}(s_j.X[f])^2}} \qquad (6)$$

The weighted voting system is adapted to achieve better prediction results compared to the simple majority voting of kNN. kNN with weighted voting is used in frequently class-imbalanced domain such as credit scoring, recommendation systems, natural language processing, medical diagnosis, healthcare prediction, and anomaly and outlier detection in machine learning. [2,6,20]. It is an enhancement over the standard kNN, where neighbors contribute to classification or regression based on their similarity distance to the query point [6]. Closer neighbors have more influence than farther ones. This fact can improve in the adaption of concept drifts in drifting data streams. For an incoming instance s_i, the set of k-nearest neighbors NN is founded. For each nearest neighbor $s_n \in NN$, the weight of each nearest neighbor s_n is calculated. W is defined as follows where $C[s_i][s_n]$ is the Cosine distance between s_i and s_n.

$$s_n.W = \frac{1}{(C[s_i][s_n])^2} \qquad (7)$$

The l-th predicted label $s_i.Z[l]$ of s_i is defined as follows.

$$s_i.Z[l] = \begin{cases} 1 & \text{if } P \geq N \\ 0 & \text{otherwise.} \end{cases} \qquad (8)$$

P and N are defined as follows.

$$P = \sum_{n=1}^{k} s_n.W \mid s_n \in NN, s_n.Y[l] = 1 \qquad (9)$$

$$N = \sum_{n=1}^{k} s_n.W \mid s_n \in NN, s_n.Y[l] = 0 \qquad (10)$$

4 Experiments

4.1 Method

The experiments were carried out on Intel (R) Core (TM) i7-12700 (12 cores) Windows 11 Pro PC with 32 GB of memory. These were employed on Massive Online Analysis (MOA) [9] with Java. MOA is a software platform designed to implement algorithms and run experiments related to online learning from evolving data streams. To show the effectiveness of our new proposed algorithms, we compared the results of our new proposed algorithms with the latest outperformed kNN-based algorithms MLSAMkNN [12], MLSAMPkNN [13], and our previous algorithm [16] under seven evaluation metrics: accuracy, subset accuracy, Hamming score, precision, recall, F-measure, running time, and model cost of the algorithms. Their calculation methods are explained in the paper [13]. Subset accuracy and F-measure is the most important metrics in multi-label data stream classification because subset accuracy is the strictest metric that measures in the exact match between predicted and true label sets and F-measure balances precision and recall for partial correctness and handling class-imbalanced. The 30 real-world benchmark datasets [5], including nine highly imbalanced datasets and nine highly sparse datasets, were used for our comparative study.

Table 1. The information of the 30 benchmark multi-label datasets

Dataset	Domain	Instances	Attr.	Labels	Cardinal.	D-Density	MeanIR
Birds	Audio	645	260	19	1.01	0.058	5.41
Bookmarks	Text	87,856	2,150	208	2.03	0.054	12.31
CAL500	Music	502	68	174	26.04	0.388	20.58
Corel16k	Image	13,766	500	153	2.86	0.017	34.16
Corel5k	Image	5,000	499	374	3.52	0.014	189.57
Emotions	Music	593	72	6	1.87	0.944	1.48
Enron	Text	1,702	1,001	53	4.27	0.083	73.95
Eukyaryote	Biology	7,766	440	22	1.15	0.542	45.01
Eurlex	Text	19,348	5,000	201	2.21	0.046	536.98
Flags	Image	194	19	7	3.39	0.461	2.25
Genbase	Biology	662	1,186	27	1.25	0.979	37.31
Gnegative	Biology	1,392	440	8	1.05	0.503	18.45
Human	Biology	3,106	440	14	1.19	0.579	15.29
Imdb	Text	120,919	1001	28	1.00	0.021	25.12
Langlog	Text	1,460	1004	75	15.94	0.174	39.27
Mediamill	Video	43,907	120	101	4.38	0.563	256.4
Medical	Text	978	1,449	45	1.25	0.01	89.50
Nuswide	Image	269,648	501	81	1.87	0.398	95.12
Ohsumed	Text	13,929	1002	23	0.81	0.04	7.87
Plant	Biology	978	440	12	1.08	0.525	6.69
Reuters	Text	6,000	500	103	0.11	0.832	54.08
Scene	Image	2,407	294	6	1.07	0.972	1.25
Stackex	Text	1,675	585	227	2.41	0.025	85.79
Tmc2007	Text	28,596	500	22	2.22	0.047	17.13
VirusGo	Biology	207	749	6	1.22	0.017	4.04
Water-Qual	Chemistry	1,060	16	14	5.07	0.674	1.77
Yahoo-Com	Text	124,444	34,096	33	1.51	0.004	176.69
Yahoo-Soc	Text	14,512	31,802	27	1.67	0.006	302.07
Yeast	Biology	2,417	103	14	4.24	0.917	7.20
Yelp	Text	10,806	671	5	1.64	0.054	2.88

Imbalanced datasets are underlined and sparse datasets are italicized.

All algorithms are measured under the same criteria: the minimum window size is 50, the maximum window size is 1,000, penalty ratio is 1, k of kNN classifiers is 3, and the adjusted number is 0.5. The value of the adjusted number was defined through experiments in our previous work [16]. For drifting data streams with concept drift, drifting RandomTree generator (10 attributes, 10 class labels, and 100,000 instances) of MOA is used. To test in a sparse data stream environment, we added a sparse parameter to the generator, using a sparsity value of 0.7 under mixed-type drifts on seven evaluation metrics. Table 1 displays the information of the 30 multi-label datasets. Cardinality presents the average number of labels correlated with each instance. Dataset density (D-density) is measured by the ratio of non-zero values in the dataset relative to the total number of possible values. Datasets with low density tend to be sparse. MeanIR represents the imbalance ratio of datasets. The datasets were sourced from the KDIS multi-label dataset repository [5].

4.2 Results

This section demonstrate the effectiveness of our new proposed algorithms in comparison to MLSAMkNN, MLSAMPkNN, our previous algorithm [16] for drifting, sparse, and class-imbalanced data streams. Table 2 shows the average results of seven metrics: subset accuracy, accuracy, Hamming score, precision, recall, F-measure, and running time of comparative algorithms on the 30 benchmark multi-label datasets. In Table 2, our new proposed algorithms (our previous algorithm [16] with the weighted voting (WV) and the Cosine distance (CD), PM^++WV+CD for short) gives the highest average results of subset accuracy, accuracy, Hamming score, precision, recall, and F-measure over previous algorithms except running time (R-time) on all the datasets. In terms of running time, our previous algorithm (PM^+) is the most time-efficient. In terms of model cost (RAM-H) [16], all algorithms share the exact low model cost of 1.07, except MLSAMkNN, which uses 1.87, suggesting efficient resource utilization across most methods. The model cost of an algorithm is calculated by multiplying the memory usage (in gigabytes) of its algorithm by the total training time

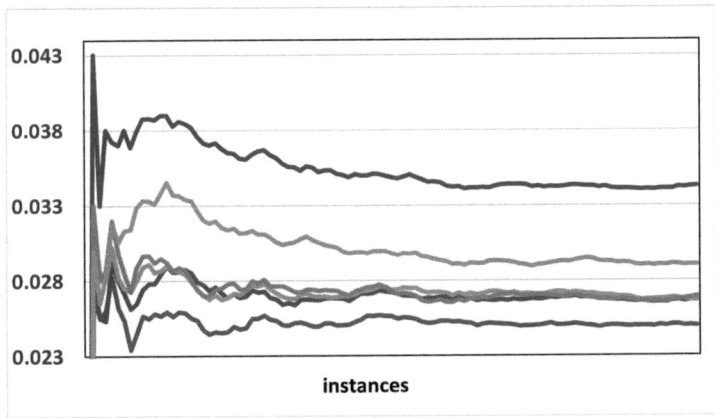

Fig. 1. Mixed Drifts: Subset Accuracy on Random Tree (blue: MLSAMkNN, red: MLSAMPkNN, green: our previous algorithm (PM^+), cyan: PM^+ with Cosine distance (CD), orange: PM^+ with weighted voting (WV), purple: PM^+ with CD and WV. (Color figure online)

Table 2. The average results of the seven metrics

Algorithms	S-Accuracy	Accuracy	Hamming	Precision	Recall	F-measure	R-time
MLSAMkNN	0.3674	0.4189	0.9262	0.4694	0.4195	0.4666	42.54
MLSAMPkNN	0.3702	0.4255	0.9272	0.4639	0.4132	0.4704	27.06
PM+	0.3749	0.4309	0.9285	0.4949	0.4230	0.4765	**24.94**
PM++WV	0.3788	0.4484	0.9231	0.5039	0.4358	0.48	29.86
PM++CD	0.389	0.4592	0.929	0.49	0.4413	0.5085	28.19
PM++WV+CD	**0.3901**	**0.4827**	**0.9297**	**0.5085**	**0.4694**	**0.5109**	34.75

Best average results are bolded.

Table 3. The average results of subset accuracy and F-measure on sparse and imbalanced datasets

Algorithms	Sparse		Imbalanced	
	S-Accuracy	F-measure	S-Accuracy	F-measure
MLSAMkNN	0.2580	0.3052	0.1942	0.3510
MLSAMPkNN	0.2537	0.3121	0.1952	0.3542
PM+	0.2637	0.3238	0.1954	0.3575
PM++WV	0.2668	0.3275	0.2008	0.3617
PM++CD	**0.2931**	**0.3946**	0.2158	0.4058
PM++WV+CD	0.2898	0.3929	**0.219**	**0.4094**

Best average results are bolded.

(in hours). All experimental results prove that PM++WV+CD algorithm is the most reliable, robust, and accurate candidate with highest performance in drifting, sparse and class-imbalanced data stream over previous studies. And it has a slightly longer running time than our efficient previous algorithm. MLSAMkNN performs poorly across all metrics and it is unsuitable in the multi-label data stream classification.

Table 3 displays the comparative average results of subset accuracy and F-measure on MLSAMkNN, MLSAMPkNN, our previous algorithm, and our proposed algorithms on nine highly sparse datasets and nine highly imbalanced datasets. Under sparse datasets, PM++CD got the highest average results and PM++WV+CD got the second highest average results over other algorithms on subset accuracy and F-measure. That proves that the Cosine distance is an effective, adaptive and suitable measuring system that can enhances its ability to handle the sparse datasets. Under imbalanced datasets, PM++WV+CD got the highest average results and PM++WV got the third highest average results over other algorithms on subset accuracy and F-measure. That proves the weighted voting system is effective in distributing class-imbalanced datasets. Table 4 displays the detailed subset accuracy results of MLSAMkNN, MLSAMPkNN, our previous algorithm, and our new proposed algorithms. PM++WV+CD (ω) got the best subset accuracy in 14 datasets, PM++CD (θ) got the best subset accu-

Table 4. Subset Accuracy of MLSAMkNN (α), MLSAMPkNN (β), our previous algorithm (δ), our proposed algorithms: with weighted voting (γ), with Cosine distance (θ), combining weighted voting and Cosine distance(ω) for 30 datasets

Dataset	Subset Accuracy					
	α	β	δ	γ	θ	ω
Birds	0.4674	0.4643	0.4612	0.4472	0.4534	**0.4689**
Bookmarks	0.2290	0.2293	0.2294	0.2371	0.2422	**0.2475**
CAL500	0.0000	0.0000	0.0000	0.0000	0.0000	0.0000
Corel16k	0.0820	0.0877	0.0835	0.0873	0.1021	**0.1040**
Corel5k	0.0314	0.0334	0.0326	0.0333	0.0388	**0.0410**
Emotions	0.2568	0.2348	0.2568	**0.2703**	0.2416	0.2331
<u>Enron</u>	0.1563	0.1470	0.1564	0.1600	**0.1946**	0.1922
Eukyaryote	0.8173	0.8178	0.8189	0.8187	0.8267	**0.8313**
<u>Eurlex</u>	0.1475	0.1479	0.1482	0.1661	0.2000	**0.2250**
Flags	0.0985	0.0622	0.0777	0.0829	**0.1036**	0.0880
Genbase	0.8790	0.8790	0.8790	0.9047	0.8790	**0.9093**
Gnegative	0.8533	**0.8677**	0.8620	0.8620	0.8627	0.8641
Human	0.7188	0.7282	0.7317	0.7314	0.7311	**0.7359**
Imdb	**0.4515**	0.4148	0.4134	0.4148	0.4302	0.4321
Langlog	0.2015	0.1988	0.2015	0.2029	0.2282	**0.2289**
<u>Mediamill</u>	0.1608	0.1608	0.1608	**0.1824**	0.1573	0.1823
Medical	0.5844	0.5875	0.5895	0.5875	**0.5927**	0.5793
<u>Nuswide</u>	0.2304	0.2308	0.2311	0.2255	**0.2364**	0.2304
Ohsumed	0.0951	0.0836	0.1344	0.1367	0.2576	**0.2580**
Plant	0.6213	0.6807	0.6970	0.6960	0.7185	**0.7216**
Reuters	1.0000	1.0000	1.0000	1.0000	1.0000	1.0000
Scene	0.8292	**0.8400**	0.8358	0.8358	0.8280	0.8288
Stackex	0.0161	0.0149	0.0137	0.0149	**0.0245**	0.0215
Tmc2007	0.3821	0.3902	0.3889	0.3889	**0.4237**	0.4227
VirusGo	0.6408	0.6505	0.6796	0.6893	**0.6942**	0.6699
Water-Qual	0.0198	0.0198	**0.0236**	0.0217	0.0236	0.0151
Yahoo-Com	0.2803	0.2713	0.2703	0.2843	**0.2883**	0.2843
Yahoo-Soc	0.1407	0.1393	0.1559	0.1531	0.2097	**0.2182**
Yeast	0.1361	0.1540	0.1515	0.1585	**0.1726**	0.1523
Yelp	0.4932	0.5693	0.5618	**0.5701**	0.5090	0.5174
Average	0.3674	0.3702	0.3749	0.3788	0.3890	**0.3901**

Imbalanced are underlined, sparse are italicized and best results are bolded.

racy in 12 datasets, and PM$^+$+WV (γ) got the best subset accuracy in 5 datasets among 30 datasets. Our algorithms achieved the highest average subset accuracy results compared to other previous algorithms. That proves that our all proposed algorithms are reliable and accurate candidates than other previous algorithms.

We also compared the experimental results of all algorithms on drifting data stream with concept drifts. In this experiment, the adjusted number is 0.3. The value was defined through experiments in our previous work [16]. We also added sparsity parameter to the generators to test on sparse data streams and use with sparsity value 0.7. Figure 1 shows the subset accuracy of MLSAMkNN, MLSAMPkNN, our previous algorithm and our proposed algorithm on mixed drifts generated by the three generators. As those experimental results, our proposed algorithms adapt to heterogeneous types of mixed concept drifts, including abrupt, gradual, and incremental drifts, promising to achieve the best rank over all previous algorithms. Our proposed algorithm not only improves the subset accuracy but also provides a robust framework for dynamic environments.

5 Concluding Remarks

In this paper, we proposed a multi-label kNN classifier that is effective and robust for drifting, sparse, and class-imbalanced data streams. The proposed algorithm is an extension of our previous algorithm [16] by changing the distance system from Euclidean distance to Cosine distance and the voting system from majority voting to weighted voting to handle sparse and class-imbalanced data streams. Cosine distance, an adaptive distance, is used to handle sparse data streams, and weighted voting system is employed to achieve accurate label prediction performance. Our proposed algorithms compared with previous multi-label kNN-based algorithms on 30 benchmark datasets and MOA generator. As reported by experimental results, our proposed algorithm outperforms the previous research works for all quality metrics. The limitation of our proposed model is that it lacks adaptive feature selection mechanisms and exploration of label correlation mechanisms. In future work, we will incorporate an online feature mechanism and a label correlation mechanism in our algorithm to improve prediction quality and reduce computational time.

References

1. Abu Alfeilat, H.A., et al.: Effects of distance measure choice on k-nearest neighbor classifier performance: a review. Big Data **7**(4), 221–248 (2019). https://doi.org/10.1089/big.2018.0175
2. Bifet, A., Gavaldà, R., Holmes, G., Pfahringer, B.: Machine Learning for Data Streams: with Practical Examples in MOA. The MIT Press, Cambridge (2017). https://doi.org/10.7551/mitpress/10654.001.0001
3. Han, M., Wu, H., Chen, Z., Li, M., Zhang, X.: A survey of multilabel classification based on supervised and semi-supervised learning. Int. J. Mach. Learn. Cybern. **14**(3), 697–724 (2023). https://doi.org/10.1007/s13042-022-01658-9
4. Iwashita, A.S., Papa, J.P.: An overview on concept drift learning. IEEE Access **7**, 1532–1547 (2019). https://doi.org/10.1109/access.2018.2886026
5. Knowledge Discovery and Intelligent Systems research group: Multi-label classification dataset repository. https://www.uco.es/kdis/mllresources/. Accessed 9 Aug 2024
6. Liu, S., Zhu, P., Qin, S.: An improved weighted KNN algorithm for imbalanced data classification. In: 2018 IEEE 4th International Conference on Computer and Communications (ICCC), pp. 1814–1819. IEEE, Chengdu (2018). https://doi.org/10.1109/compcomm.2018.8780580

7. Losing, V., Hammer, B., Wersing, H.: KNN classifier with self adjusting memory for heterogeneous concept drift. In: 2016 IEEE 16th International Conference on Data Mining (ICDM). pp. 291–300. IEEE, Barcelona (2016). https://doi.org/10.1109/icdm.2016.0040
8. Losing, V., Hammer, B., Wersing, H.: Tackling heterogeneous concept drift with the Self-Adjusting Memory (SAM). Knowl. Inf. Syst. **54**(1), 171–201 (2017). https://doi.org/10.1007/s10115-017-1137-y
9. MOA project: MOA. https://moa.cms.waikato.ac.nz/. Accessed 9 Aug 2024
10. Nayak, S., Bhat, M., Subba Reddy, N.V., Ashwath Rao, B.: Study of distance metrics on k - nearest neighbor algorithm for star categorization. In: AICECS 2021. Journal of Physics: Conference Series, vol. 2161, pp. 1–9, article no. 012004. IOP Publishing (2022). https://doi.org/10.1088/1742-6596/2161/1/012004
11. Qiao, X., Wu, H., Roy, S.K., Huang, W.: Hyperspectral image classification based on 3d sharpened cosine similarity operation. In: 2023 IEEE International Geoscience and Remote Sensing Symposium (IGARSS), pp. 7669–7672. IEEE, Pasadena (2023). https://doi.org/10.1109/igarss52108.2023.10281949
12. Roseberry, M., Cano, A.: Multi-label knn classifier with self adjusting memory for drifting data streams. In: Torgo, L., Matwin, S., Japkowicz, N., Krawczyk, B., Moniz, N., Branco, P. (eds.) Proceedings of the Second International Workshop on Learning with Imbalanced Domains: Theory and Applications. Proceedings of Machine Learning Research, vol. 94, pp. 23–37. PMLR (2018)
13. Roseberry, M., Krawczyk, B., Cano, A.: Multi-label punitive kNN with selfadjusting memory for drifting data streams. ACM Trans. Knowl. Disc. Data **13**(6), 1–31 (2019). https://doi.org/10.1145/3363573
14. Rutkowski, L., Jaworski, M., Duda, P.: Stream Data Mining: Algorithms and Their Probabilistic Properties. SBD, vol. 56. Springer, Cham (2020). https://doi.org/10.1007/978-3-030-13962-9
15. Sun, Y., Shao, H., Wang, S.: Efficient ensemble classification for multi-label data streams with concept drift. Information **10**(5), 1–14, 158 (2019). https://doi.org/10.3390/info10050158
16. Tun, T., Goto, Y.: Improvement of multi-label kNN classifier with self-adjusting memory using a punitive model for drifting data streams. In: Sombattheera, C., Weng, P., Pang, J. (eds.) Multi-Disciplinary Trends in Artificial Intelligence. MIWAI 2024. Lecture Notes in Computer Science, vol. 15432, pp. 285–297. Springer, Singapore (2025). https://doi.org/10.1007/978-981-96-0695-5_23
17. Zhang, J., Wang, F., Ma, F., Song, G.: Text similarity calculation method based on optimized cosine distance. In: 2022 International Conference on Electronic and Devices, Computational Science (ICEDCS), pp. 37–39. IEEE, Marseille (2022). https://doi.org/10.1109/icedcs57360.2022.00015
18. Zhang, P., Gao, B.J., Zhu, X., Guo, L.: Enabling fast lazy learning for data streams. In: 2011 IEEE 11th International Conference on Data Mining (ICDM), pp. 932–941. IEEE, Vancouver (2011). https://doi.org/10.1109/icdm.2011.63
19. Zheng, X., Li, P.: An efficient framework for multi-label learning in nonstationary data stream. In: 2021 IEEE International Conference on Big Knowledge (ICBK), pp. 149–156. IEEE, Auckland (2021). https://doi.org/10.1109/ickg52313.2021.00029
20. Zheng, X., Li, P., Chu, Z., Hu, X.: A survey on multi-label data stream classification. IEEE Access **8**, 1249–1275 (2020). https://doi.org/10.1109/access.2019.2962059

HYBPARSIMONY-IDT: Hybrid Parsimonious Search for Interpretable Decision Trees

Francisco Javier Martinez-de-Pison[1](✉), Alpha Pernia-Espinoza[1], and Jose Divasón[2]

[1] Scientific Computation Research Institute (SCRIUR), University of La Rioja, Logroño, Spain
fjmartin@unirioja.es, alpha.pernia@unirioja.es
[2] Department of Mathematics and Computer Science, University of La Rioja, Logroño, Spain
jose.divason@unirioja.es

Abstract. HYBPARSIMONY-IDT is a hybrid optimisation framework for learning interpretable decision trees across a wide range of tabular datasets. It combines Particle Swarm Optimisation and Genetic Algorithms with an interpretability-aware objective that integrates structural constraints and a novel metric based on rule coverage and class purity. This metric guides model selection when predictive performance is statistically indistinguishable, promoting simpler and more transparent solutions. Experimental results on 43 benchmark datasets demonstrate that the method significantly improves interpretability without compromising test accuracy. These findings highlight the potential of incorporating interpretability as a primary optimisation criterion in AutoML pipelines.

Keywords: HYB-PARSIMONY · interpretability · simulability · auto machine learning

1 Introduction

In today's data-driven landscape, many organisations—particularly in sensitive sectors such as healthcare, finance, and public policy—demand machine learning models that are not only accurate but also transparent and interpretable. This demand reflects regulatory pressures and the practical need for human-understandable decision support systems. Although many state-of-the-art solutions continue to rely on complex ensembles or deep architectures that remain opaque, recent years have seen a growing interest in explainable AI (XAI), driven by the need for transparency and trust in critical applications.

Among inherently interpretable models, decision trees (DTs) stand out for their structural simplicity and capacity to reveal the hidden knowledge extracted from data, offering a structured view of patterns and relationships that may not be immediately observable. They provide a global, symbolic representation of the decision process, making them particularly suited to scenarios where human oversight and post-hoc justification are essential. However, interpretability is not guaranteed merely by the use of trees: large, deep, or unbalanced trees can be as inscrutable as black-box models. To address this, the notion of "simulability" has emerged as a central criterion. Simulability refers to how easily a human can mentally simulate and comprehend a model's internal decision-making process. For decision trees, it implies that users can trace paths from root to leaf without external tools, an aspect typically ensured by restricting tree depth, simplifying conditions, and minimising the number of rules.

This paper introduces HYBPARSIMONY-IDT, a hybrid intelligent optimisation strategy designed to generate shallow, high-performing, and simulable decision trees. Our method combines particle swarm optimisation and genetic algorithm search, integrated with structural constraints and a novel coverage-purity interpretability metric. Building on the broader HYBPARSIMONY framework [3], HYBPARSIMONY-IDT provides a principled approach to constructing decision models that are not only efficient and accurate but also compatible with current interpretability standards in regulated domains.

The remainder of this paper is structured as follows: Sect. 2 reviews related work on interpretable decision trees. Section 3 presents the proposed methodology. Section 4 describes the experimental setup and benchmarks. Section 5 discusses the results, and Sect. 6 concludes the paper.

2 Related Work

Recent advances in interpretable machine learning have fostered the development of methods that learn decision trees while jointly optimising for accuracy and simplicity. Among the most relevant are exact or near-exact approaches that aim to balance interpretability and accuracy through different algorithmic paradigms. In this section, we review representative contributions and identify their limitations, particularly regarding generalisation, feature selection bias, and the richness of their interpretability metrics.

Demirović et al. with *MurTree* [2] formulate the construction of optimal decision trees as a dynamic programming problem, leveraging aggressive caching and pruning strategies to guarantee global optimality under structural constraints (e.g., tree depth and number of nodes). While the method is highly efficient for small to medium datasets, it relies exclusively on training error and lacks validation-based pruning or mechanisms to mitigate greedy bias in feature selection. Also, the method does not predict probabilities. *DL8.5* [1] library combines branch-and-bound optimisation with frequent itemset mining and a cache-based dynamic programming formulation. It achieves excellent computational performance, especially for binary tabular data, and supports structural constraints such as depth and support thresholds. However, the accuracy is still computed on the training set and thethe interpretability is reduced to structural proxies. *FLIT* [4] proposes a hybrid strategy where sparse oblique feature transformations are learnt together with differentiable decision trees. The resulting models are compact and performant, but lack transparency due to the use of nonaxis-aligned splits. Additionally, interpretability is not explicitly quantified during optimisation and external validation is not considered. Kohler et al. with *DPDT* [5], reinterprets tree induction as a Markov Decision Process (MDP), training a reinforcement learning (RL) agent to build decision trees by trading off performance and complexity through a reward signal. This paradigm allows the generation of Pareto-optimal trees with varying complexity. However, interpretability is measured only through average path length and models are limited to shallow depths (typically ≤ 4). Chen et al. presented *DQNDT* [6], an extension of DPDT, employs deep Q-learning to train an agent in a fully observable MDP. It formalises the accuracy-interpretability trade-off but retains a narrow view of interpretability (number of nodes) and is computationally intensive. Moreover, external validation is not part of the optimisation pipeline.

2.1 Limitations

The five reviewed methods represent significant strides in the development of interpretable decision tree models. However, they exhibit common limitations that our proposed methodology aims to address. The key improvements are as follows:

1. *Enhanced Generalisation through Cross-Validation*: While the reviewed methods primarily rely on training error for model evaluation, our approach incorporates repeated cross-validation. This technique provides a more robust estimation of model performance on unseen data, thereby reducing the risk of overfitting.
2. *Mitigation of Feature Selection Bias via Stochastic Feature Masking*: To counteract the greedy bias in early feature selection observed in methods like *MurTree* and *DL8.5*, our methodology employs stochastic feature masking during the search process. This strategy promotes a more balanced exploration of the feature space, leading to more generalisable models.
3. *Comprehensive Interpretability Metric Incorporating Rule Coverage and Class Purity*: The interpretability metrics in the reviewed methods often rely on structural proxies such as tree depth or node count. In contrast, our approach introduces a nuanced metric that combines rule coverage and class purity, offering a more meaningful assessment of model interpretability.
4. *Joint Optimisation of Accuracy and Interpretability*: Unlike methods that focus predominantly on accuracy or interpretability, our methodology simultaneously optimises both objectives. This dual optimisation ensures that the resulting models maintain high predictive performance while remaining interpretable.
5. *Scalability to High-Dimensional, Low-Sample-Size Datasets*: The reviewed methods often struggle with datasets characterised by high dimensionality and limited sample sizes. Our approach is specifically designed to handle such scenarios effectively, maintaining model performance and interpretability.

By addressing these limitations, our methodology advances the field of interpretable machine learning, offering a robust and scalable solution to construct decision trees that balance accuracy and interpretability.

3 Methodology

3.1 Overview of HYBPARSIMONY

The HYBPARSIMONY framework [3] is a hybrid evolutionary optimisation strategy that integrates Particle Swarm Optimisation (PSO) and Genetic Algorithms (GA) to simultaneously perform hyperparameter tuning and feature selection in machine learning models. This approach is particularly designed for high-dimensional, small-sample datasets, where classical optimisation strategies often fail to yield parsimonious yet accurate models.

The general workflow of HYBPARSIMONY consists of four main stages. First, a population of individuals is randomly initialised using Latin hypercube sampling; each individual encodes a candidate model defined by a subset of features and hyperparameters. Then, models are evaluated via repeated cross-validation using a performance loss (e.g., RMSE or classification error), combined with a structural complexity penalty [7]. In particular, when the predictive losses are statistically similar, the algorithm promotes models with lower complexity. This re-ranking mechanism ensures that the search process prioritises parsimonious models with high predictive accuracy. The search process follows a hybrid GA-PSO strategy: early iterations emphasise genetic operations (selection, crossover, mutation) to enhance global exploration, while later stages rely on PSO for local exploitation. Therefore, model parsimony is encouraged through explicit penalisation of complexity, and tie-breaking between equally accurate models favours simpler structures.

3.2 The HYBPARSIMONY-IDT Framework

Building on this foundation, we propose HYBPARSIMONY-IDT, a specialised adaptation of the framework for learning interpretable decision trees (IDT). While the algorithmic structure remains unchanged, the model search is now restricted to axis-aligned decision trees with bounded depth, ensuring simulability. Moreover, instead of relying on general-purpose complexity measures (e.g., number of features), the objective function incorporates a novel interpretability metric that captures both the number of rules required to explain most of the data (coverage) and their internal consistency (purity). This modification reorients the optimisation towards producing accurate yet transparent models, suitable for decision support in sensitive domains. The following subsections describe the structural constraints, the interpretability metric, and the hybrid optimisation process in greater detail.

3.3 Structural Constraint

To ensure that the resulting trees remain accessible and interpretable to human analysts, we impose explicit structural restrictions on their complexity. Specifically, we enforce a maximum depth constraint $d_{\max} \leq D^*$ (typically with $D^* = 4$), which guarantees that each path in the tree can be manually inspected by an expert, as the induced rules remain understandable and traceable due to their limited depth. This constraint also ensures compatibility with the literature on optimal depth-bounded decision trees.

3.4 Coverage—Purity Interpretability Metric

Although bounding the tree depth guarantees a minimal level of interpretability, it does not account for how the rules are distributed or how coherent they are in practice. To address this, we introduce a refined metric that captures two critical aspects of tree interpretability: the number of rules required to explain the majority of the data (coverage), and the consistency or purity of the output within each rule (purity).

The proposed interpretability metric $I(T; \tau)$ takes as input a decision tree T and a coverage threshold $\tau \in (0, 1]$, typically set to 0.90. The rationale is to quantify how many decision rules (i.e., leaf nodes) are necessary to describe at least $\tau \cdot 100\%$ of the validation data, giving higher priority to trees that concentrate most decisions into a few dominant rules.

The metric is computed as follows:

1. For each instance i in the validation set D_{val}, record the leaf index L_i assigned by tree T. If the tree is empty or has no leaves, we define $I(T; \tau) = +\infty$.
2. Compute the coverage of each leaf ℓ as the number of validation instances that fall into it:

$$\text{count}(\ell) = \#\{i \in D_{\text{val}} \mid L_i = \ell\}.$$

Sort leaves in descending order of count.

3. Let K be the minimum number of top-ranked leaves whose cumulative coverage reaches at least $\tau \cdot N$, where $N = |D_{\text{val}}|$. If no such set exists, we set $I(T; \tau) = +\infty$.
4. For each of the selected leaves $\ell \in \{\ell_1, \ldots, \ell_K\}$, we define the multiset $y_\ell = \{y_i \mid i \in D_{\text{val}}, L_i = \ell\}$, where y_i denotes the ground-truth label of instance i and L_i is the index of the leaf to which T assigns it. From this multiset, we compute the majority class proportion $\overline{y}_\ell \in [0, 1]$, representing the empirical probability of the dominant class within the leaf. For example, if leaf ℓ receives 10 validation instances, of which 7 belong to the positive class and 3 to the negative class, then $\overline{y}_\ell = \frac{7}{10} = 0.7$. This proportion is used to define a constant probabilistic prediction vector $[1 - \overline{y}_\ell, \overline{y}_\ell]$, against which the binary log-loss is computed between the true labels y_ℓ and the prediction. This value, referred to as the Constant Sub-tree Score (CSS), is denoted $\text{CSS}(\ell)$ and reflects the

internal consistency or purity of the rule represented by the leaf in terms of its ability to summarise a well-defined majority class:

$$\text{CSS}(\ell) = \log\text{-loss}(y_\ell, [1 - \overline{y}_\ell, \overline{y}_\ell]).$$

5. Compute the average purity score over the selected leaves:

$$\text{CSS} = \frac{1}{K} \sum_{k=1}^{K} \text{CSS}(\ell_k).$$

6. The final interpretability score is given by:

$$I(T; \tau) = 10^6 \cdot K + \text{CSS}.$$

This formulation ensures that trees requiring fewer rules to explain the data are ranked higher. The large multiplicative constant 10^6 enforces lexicographic priority: the number of explanatory rules K dominates the interpretability score, while CSS acts as a tie-breaker based on the internal consistency (purity) of those rules. The use of *log-loss* is justified as it penalises mixed or uncertain predictions more strongly than simple majority vote error, providing a smooth and sensitive measure of rule coherence.

3.5 Hybrid Search

The core of our methodology relies on an effective and flexible search strategy that can balance exploration and exploitation while navigating the complex space of tree configurations. To guide the search towards solutions that balance predictive performance and interpretability, we adopt a bi-objective optimisation strategy: particles are evaluated using the bi-objective $(\widehat{L}(T), I(T;\tau))$. Following lexicographic optimisation, we first minimise $\widehat{L}(T)$; ties are resolved by minimising $I(T;\tau)$. In this way, the optimisation process aims to find models that are not only accurate but also favour those that are more interpretable.

The algorithm proceeds as follows: each particle (or chromosome) encodes $\lambda = (\theta, b)$, where θ contains the depth of the tree $d_{\max} \leq D^*$, the minimum leaf size $mls_{\min}$, the minimum splitting criterion $msp_{\min}$, and pruning parameters, while $b \in \{0, 1\}^p$ is a mask of features. Then, an aggressive GA phase (replacement rate $p_c(t) = 0.8\, e^{-\gamma t}$) quickly reduces structural complexity, after which the exploitation of PSO dominates. In each generation, the population is first ranked by $\widehat{L}(T)$; individuals whose errors differ by less than a threshold $ReRank$ (e.g. 0.01 of $\widehat{L}(T)$) are subsequently reordered by the interpretability metric $I(T;\tau)$.

Table 1. Summary of results per dataset comparing interpretability-based (i) and parsimony-based (p) optimisation strategies. The reported metrics include repeated cross-validated and testing log-loss values ($5CV_i$, $5CV_p$, TST_i, TST_p), interpretability scores divided by 1e6, (i_i, i_p), tree depth (d_i, d_p), number of leaves (l_i, l_p), and number of distinct features used in the best trees (f_i, f_p). Datasets are sorted by the number of input variables (ncols). All values represent the average over 30 independent runs.

Dataset	nrows	ncols	$5CV_i$	$5CV_p$	TST_i	TST_p	i_i	i_p	d_i	d_p	l_i	l_p	f_i	f_p
Titanic	2201	4	0.538	0.539	0.551	0.552	5.3	4.8	3.9	3.8	8.3	7.7	3.0	2.9
MagicTelescope	19020	11	0.453	0.453	0.456	0.458	8.2	7.9	4.0	4.0	15.3	15.2	5.4	5.2
credit	16714	11	0.505	0.505	0.507	0.507	7.4	7.3	4.0	4.0	13.4	13.5	4.3	4.2
eeg	14980	15	0.592	0.592	0.594	0.593	7.8	7.9	4.0	4.0	13.5	13.7	6.8	6.8
compas	5278	20	0.616	0.616	0.618	0.618	11.7	11.9	4.0	4.0	14.2	14.3	2.9	2.3
Long	4477	20	0.175	0.176	0.171	0.173	6.5	6.6	4.0	3.9	10.6	10.6	2.0	2.0
law	20800	20	0.000	0.000	0.000	0.000	2.0	2.1	1.0	1.1	2.0	2.1	1.0	1.1
ringnorm	7400	21	0.504	0.505	0.523	0.523	6.4	6.4	4.0	4.0	9.4	9.6	4.4	4.2
twonorm	7400	21	0.478	0.478	0.499	0.499	11.6	12.1	4.0	4.0	16.0	15.8	5.0	4.6
jm1	10885	22	0.614	0.612	0.614	0.614	8.9	10.1	3.8	3.9	11.0	13.1	4.9	4.3
kc1	2109	22	0.542	0.540	0.553	0.555	4.7	5.8	2.9	3.2	5.6	6.9	2.8	2.7
heloc	10000	23	0.578	0.577	0.580	0.579	9.8	9.6	4.0	4.0	13.3	13.7	3.8	3.0
default	30000	24	0.567	0.568	0.566	0.567	8.7	7.9	4.0	4.0	14.5	14.0	8.5	6.9
Intersectional	10000	25	0.120	0.120	0.124	0.124	5.6	6.4	4.0	4.0	13.0	12.9	3.5	3.2
turing	10000	27	0.615	0.614	0.615	0.614	12.0	12.6	4.0	4.0	14.0	14.8	3.0	2.7
shrutime	10000	29	0.494	0.494	0.498	0.498	10.8	10.5	4.0	4.0	15.7	15.7	6.3	6.2
Contaminant	2400	31	0.420	0.422	0.441	0.445	6.7	7.0	4.0	4.0	8.8	8.9	6.4	5.9
churn	5000	34	0.386	0.386	0.386	0.393	7.5	5.6	4.0	4.0	12.1	12.2	8.7	8.4
Satellite	5100	37	0.154	0.154	0.180	0.194	3.7	2.1	3.7	3.7	6.9	7.2	4.8	4.5
mc1	9466	39	0.216	0.212	0.239	0.226	4.5	3.7	4.0	4.0	11.2	10.7	7.2	6.6
FICO	9871	40	0.570	0.568	0.571	0.568	10.7	10.6	4.0	4.0	14.0	14.8	3.8	2.5
sick	3772	53	0.137	0.134	0.149	0.145	3.3	2.3	3.2	3.3	6.9	6.9	3.7	3.4
dis	3772	55	0.286	0.278	0.313	0.316	4.6	4.5	3.5	3.7	7.6	8.5	3.6	3.8
spambase	4601	58	0.307	0.306	0.324	0.326	5.2	4.9	4.0	4.0	9.5	9.7	5.9	5.6
PhishingWebsites	11055	69	0.190	0.189	0.197	0.196	6.1	6.0	4.0	4.0	11.4	11.3	6.8	6.8
Insurance	23548	74	0.693	0.693	0.693	0.693	2.7	2.9	1.9	2.2	3.2	3.9	2.1	2.3
kr	3196	75	0.181	0.181	0.187	0.187	5.8	5.8	4.0	4.0	7.9	7.7	6.8	6.5
national	4908	81	0.002	0.002	0.002	0.002	2.0	2.1	1.0	1.2	2.0	2.2	1.0	1.1
coil2000	9822	86	0.588	0.586	0.601	0.596	8.3	10.8	3.9	4.0	11.2	13.2	8.1	7.7
ada	4562	103	0.460	0.459	0.468	0.469	6.7	5.9	4.0	4.0	10.5	10.7	4.7	4.6
sylva	14395	109	0.060	0.060	0.061	0.063	2.4	3.1	4.0	4.0	8.6	9.2	4.6	4.6
mushroom	8124	126	0.004	0.004	0.005	0.004	3.7	4.1	4.0	4.0	9.7	9.8	8.2	7.9
ECG5000	4998	141	0.076	0.075	0.097	0.097	2.1	2.2	3.9	3.9	7.3	7.5	5.6	5.5
clean2	6598	169	0.000	0.000	0.000	0.000	2.0	2.0	1.0	1.1	2.0	2.1	1.0	1.1
madeline	3140	260	0.525	0.522	0.531	0.527	10.8	11.2	4.0	4.0	14.0	14.4	6.8	6.8
jasmine	2984	281	0.435	0.436	0.447	0.453	4.7	4.9	3.8	3.7	6.3	6.2	4.5	4.3
scene	2407	305	0.320	0.317	0.334	0.332	4.0	4.8	4.0	4.0	5.1	5.5	4.1	4.5
philippine	5832	309	0.530	0.525	0.535	0.531	8.5	9.5	3.9	3.9	11.4	12.4	6.0	5.7
SpeedDating	8378	501	0.519	0.516	0.518	0.516	10.4	12.1	4.0	4.0	13.8	15.1	8.0	7.8
kdd	10108	576	0.313	0.312	0.322	0.323	6.0	6.7	4.0	4.0	12.8	12.7	9.3	8.9
shill	6321	1066	0.060	0.062	0.072	0.074	3.2	2.2	4.0	3.8	7.6	7.3	4.3	4.0
Bioresponse	3751	1777	0.529	0.527	0.544	0.544	6.3	6.5	3.5	3.4	8.9	8.5	7.9	7.1
UCI	3333	3405	0.382	0.381	0.394	0.386	7.3	6.4	4.0	4.0	11.4	11.7	6.7	6.6

4 Experiments

Due to practical limitations, a direct and fair comparison with our proposed method was not feasible for most of the state-of-the-art approaches. Specifically *DL8.5* only supports binary inputs, requiring aggressive binarisation that inflates feature dimensionality and can distort interpretability assessments. Meanwhile, *FLIT* has no public implementation, and both *DPDT* and *DQNDT* rely on reinforcement learning frameworks with high computational demands, stochastic behaviour, and no native probability estimation—further preventing their inclusion in a reproducible, metric-driven evaluation.

To evaluate the efficiency of our method[1] under the proposed interpretability metric, we conducted experiments on 43 binary classification datasets of medium size and varying dimensionality (see Table 1). We compared the performance of HYBPARSIMONY using the new interpretability function $i(T;\tau)$, with $\tau = 0.90$, against its original parsimony-based objective [7], defined as $num\_features(T) \cdot 10^9 + internal\_complexity(T)$. While the original parsimony criterion led *HYBPARSIMONY* to prioritise a balance between predictive performance and structural complexity, the new metric shifts the optimisation objective towards a trade-off between interpretability and predictive confidence.

Each configuration was assessed over 30 independent runs per dataset and metric, using different seeds to ensure robustness. Predictive performance was measured using log-loss ($\widehat{L}(T)$) under a 10 repeated 5 times cross-validation evaluation. HYBPARSIMONY, with both metrics, was run with 200 iterations, a population of 50 individuals, and a reranking rate of $ReRank = 0.01$. This setup enables an unbiased comparison of the influence of the interpretability criterion on the compactness and accuracy of the model.

In both configurations, the decision trees were restricted to a maximum depth of 4 to favour simulability. The tree induction parameters were maintained consistent across the runs: the splitting criterion was set to 'gini'; classes weights were balanced; the minimum number of samples required to split an internal ($min\_samples\_split$) varied between 2 and 20% of the dataset size; the minimum number of samples per leaf ($min\_samples\_leaf$) ranged from 1 to 20% of total samples; and the post-pruning complexity parameter (ccp_alpha) was selected within the interval [0, 1].

5 Results

Table 1 summarises the comparative performance of interpretability-driven (i) and parsimony-driven (p) optimisation strategies across multiple datasets. The reported metrics include the average log-loss under 10 repeated 5-fold cross-validation ($5CV_i$, $5CV_p$) and on a separate test set (TST_i, TST_p), the scaled interpretability scores (i_i, i_p), tree depth (d_i, d_p), number of leaves (l_i, l_p), and number of distinct features used in the best tree (f_i, f_p). The interpretability score $I(T;\tau)$ is divided by 1e6 for readability, and reflects the number of

---
[1] Code is available at https://github.com/jpison/hybparsimony-idt/.

rules required to cover at least 90% of the weighted data mass, with smaller values indicating simpler, more generalisable models. As such, i_i and i_p provide an approximate estimate of the number of decision rules needed to describe the dominant patterns in each dataset. All values represent the average over 30 independent runs.

Table 2. Comparison of interpretability-driven (i) versus parsimony-driven (p) optimisation across multiple evaluation metrics. Each row corresponds to a pair of indicators (i vs. p), showing the percentage of datasets where the i-based solution was better (**Better%**), equal (**Equal%**), or worse (**Worse%**). The p-value corresponds to a paired t-test, and the last column indicates whether the difference is statistically significant at the 0.05 level.

Pair	Better%	Equal%	Worse%	p-value	Significance
$5CV_i$ vs $5CV_p$	16.28	37.21	46.51	0.0036	True
TST_i vs TST_p	34.88	32.56	32.56	1.0000	False
i_i vs i_p	60.47	0.00	39.53	0.5179	False
d_i vs d_p	20.93	65.12	13.95	0.2917	False
l_i vs l_p	67.44	2.33	30.23	0.0037	True
f_i vs f_p	18.60	2.33	79.07	0.0000	True

Table 2 presents a comparative analysis of both optimisation strategies across multiple evaluation metrics. For each metric, the table reports the percentage of datasets where the interpretability-based solution obtained a lower value (interpreted as better), an equal value, or a higher value compared to the parsimony-based original method. This convention of "better" meaning "lower" applies uniformly to all indicators. A paired t-test was applied to each metric to assess the statistical significance of the differences, with the final column indicating whether the difference is significant at the 0.05 level.

Although Table 2 shows that the interpretability-driven approach yields a higher proportion of worse cases in terms of cross-validation error (5CV), the magnitude of these differences is generally small (as can be observed in Table 1). Moreover, when focusing on test error metrics, the differences between the two strategies become statistically insignificant, and the proportions of datasets where each approach performs better are much more balanced (34.88% vs 32.56%). This observation suggests that the use of the proposed interpretability metric, despite slightly degrading cross-validation performance, does not impair the generalisation ability of the resulting models. In practice, test errors remain comparable, indicating that the models selected through the interpretability-based strategy generalise just as effectively as those optimised for parsimony alone.

Although the interpretability-driven (i) strategy explicitly optimises the interpretability metric $I(T;\tau)$ (60.47%), there is still a substantial proportion

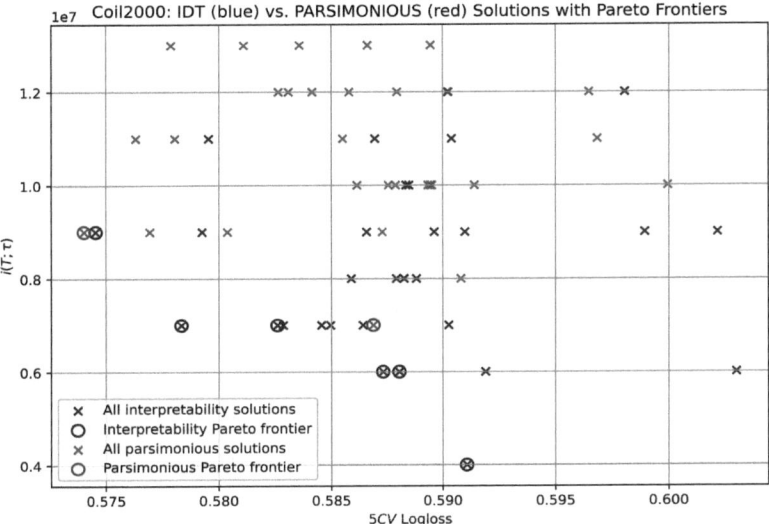

Fig. 1. Pareto frontier of interpretability ($i(T; \tau)$) vs. 5-fold CV log-loss (5CV) for all solutions generated by HYBPARSIMONY_IDT (blue) and HYBPARSIMONY (red) on the Coil2000 dataset. Each "×" marker represents the best solution from a single run. The hollow circles "o" highlight those solutions that are non-dominated in the trade-off space between interpretability and predictive accuracy-i.e., the Pareto front for each method.

of cases (39.53%) where the parsimony-driven approach yields a lower interpretability score. This suggests that the parsimony-based method is also capable of producing models with good interpretability, possibly because of its inherent preference for compact internal structures. However, the percentage of cases with improved interpretability is clearly higher when $I(T; \tau)$ is directly optimised (60.47% vs. 39.53%). Although no statistically significant differences were observed in the average tree depth, the proportion of data sets in which the interpretability-based strategy yields shallower trees is nearly twice as high (20.93% vs 13.95%), indicating a slight trend toward simpler tree structures. More notably, the proposed methodology leads to a significant reduction in the number of leaves (67.44% vs. 30.23%), which aligns with the design of the interpretability metric. This improvement comes at the cost of using a greater number of features to construct more interpretable trees (18.60% vs. 79.07%), reflecting a trade-off between structural simplicity and feature sparsity.

Figure 1 provides a particularly illustrative example of the trade-off between interpretability and predictive performance on the Coil2000 dataset. It displays the best solutions obtained by HYBPARSIMONY-IDT and the original HYBPARSIMONY method over multiple independent runs. The interpretability-driven strategy clearly produces models with substantially lower $I(T; \tau)$ scores, indicating superior interpretability. Moreover, the identification of Pareto-optimal solutions—highlighted as non-dominated points—demonstrates the value of exploring the joint space of interpretability and accuracy. This visualisation supports expert-driven model selection by presenting a diverse set of candidates, each representing an optimal trade-off between simplicity and predictive confidence.

The decision tree shown in Fig. 2 ($5CV_i = 0.59108$ and $I(T;\tau) = 4000033$) was selected from the bottom of the Pareto front obtained on the Coil2000 dataset. Although the tree comprises 7 leaves—each of which can be interpreted as a distinct decision rule—the interpretability metric $I(T;\tau)$ indicated that just 4 of these rules were sufficient to cover over 90% of the weighted data mass. Among all models satisfying this coverage criterion, the selected tree exhibits the highest average rule purity, making it a compelling solution in terms of both transparency and predictive reliability. One key advantage of using the Pareto frontier is that alternative trees can be selected to prioritise higher predictive accuracy, although if they require more rules (e.g., 6 or 7, $I(T;\tau) \approx 0.6 \cdot 1e7$ or $I(T;\tau) \approx 0.7 \cdot 1e7$ respectively) to achieve the same coverage threshold.

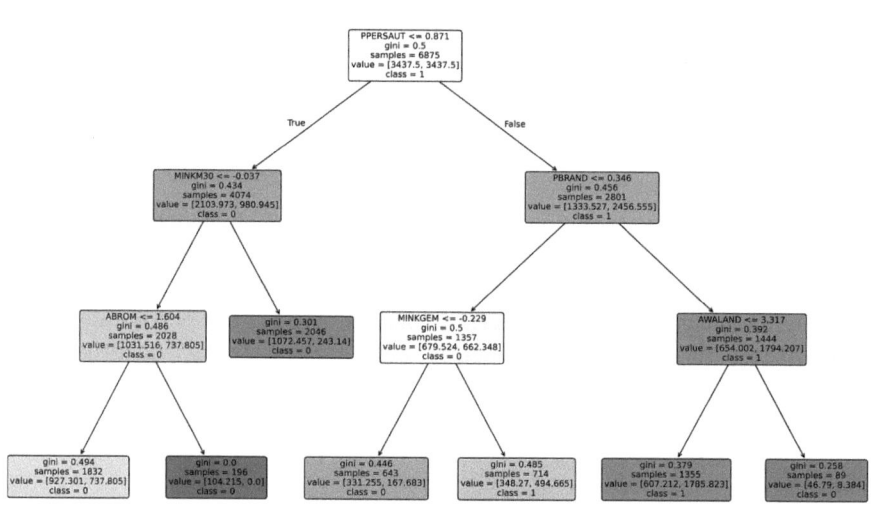

Fig. 2. Example of a decision tree extracted ($5CV_i = 0.59108$ and $I(T;\tau) = 4000033$) from the Pareto front on the Coil2000 dataset. The selected model guarantees an optimal trade-off between interpretability and predictive performance, as it belongs to the non-dominated set of solutions.

6 Conclusions

This work introduces HYBPARSIMONY-IDT, a hybrid optimisation framework for learning interpretable decision trees based on a bi-objective search strategy that balances predictive accuracy and structural simplicity. The method combines particle swarm optimisation and genetic algorithms with an interpretability-aware ranking function that integrates rule coverage and class purity. The use of a combined interpretability metric, together with the multi-objective accuracy—interpretability search, effectively guides the discovery of models that are both accurate and transparent. The framework is particularly well suited for tabular data, and the integration of stochastic feature masking fosters a more balanced exploration of the feature space.

Experimental results across a wide range of datasets demonstrate that the method produces compact and accurate models that satisfy interpretability constraints. Overall, HYBPARSIMONY-IDT offers a principled and practical approach for generating transparent and robust decision models, facilitating the deployment of trustworthy AI systems in regulated domains.

Future work will delve deeper into its contribution through ablation studies, and assess the method's scalability in high-dimensional, low-sample-size settings. Comparative evaluations against recent interpretable tree methods will also be pursued as reliable implementations become available.

Acknowledgments. The work is supported by project INICIA2023/02 funded by La Rioja Government (Spain), and by project PID2021-123219OB-I00, funded by MICIU/AE/10.13039/501100011033 and by ERDF/EU.

References

1. Aglin, G., Nijssen, S., Schaus, P.: Learning optimal decision trees using caching branch-and-bound search. In: Proceedings of the AAAI Conference on Artificial Intelligence, vol. 34, pp. 3146–3153 (2020). https://ojs.aaai.org/index.php/AAAI/article/view/5711
2. Demirović, E., et al.: Murtree: optimal decision trees via dynamic programming and search. J. Mach. Learn. Res. **23**(26), 1–47 (2022). https://jmlr.org/papers/v23/20-520.html
3. Divasón, J., Pernia-Espinoza, A., Pison, F.J.M.: Hyb-parsimony: a hybrid approach combining particle swarm optimization and genetic algorithms to find parsimonious models in high-dimensional datasets. Neurocomputing **560**, 126840 (2023). https://doi.org/10.1016/j.neucom.2023.126840
4. Good, B., Smith, A., Johnson, M.: Flit: feature learning and interpretable trees. In: Proceedings of the 40th International Conference on Machine Learning (ICML), pp. 1234–1245 (2023). https://proceedings.mlr.press/v202/good23a.html
5. Kohler, M., Zhang, W., Thompson, S.: DPDT: decision process for decision trees. In: Proceedings of the 37th AAAI Conference on Artificial Intelligence, pp. 5678–5685 (2023). https://aaai.org/Library/AAAI/aaai23contents.php

6. Li, C., Kumar, R., Lee, H.: Dqndt: deep q-networks for decision tree induction. In: Proceedings of the 30th International Conference on Neural Information Processing Systems (NeurIPS), pp. 7890–7899 (2023). https://papers.nips.cc/paper/2023/hash/abcdef1234567890abcdef1234567890-Abstract.html
7. Martinez-de Pison, F.J., Ferreiro, J., Fraile, E., Pernia-Espinoza, A.: A comparative study of six model complexity metrics to search for parsimonious models with GAparsimony R package. Neurocomputing **452**, 317–332 (2021). https://doi.org/10.1016/j.neucom.2020.02.135

Analysis of Kernel Thinning for Scalable Support Vector Machines

Blanca Cano[✉], Ángela Fernández, and José R. Dorronsoro

Universidad Autónoma de Madrid, Madrid, Spain
{blanca.cano,a.fernandez,jose.dorronsoro}@uam.es

Abstract. Kernel Support Vector Machines (KSVMs) are effective methods for nonlinear classification but face scalability challenges due to high training costs. We explore kernel thinning (KT) as a coreset selection method for KSVMs, focusing on its impact on performance, computational efficiency, and its effect and connection with support vectors. Our experiments show that KT-based models achieve comparable accuracy to full KSVMs while using significantly fewer training samples and iterations. Notably, the KT coresets do not strongly overlap with traditional support vectors, suggesting a distinct yet effective representation. We also demonstrate that KT enables fast, reliable hyperparameter tuning, making it a practical approach for scalable SVM kernel learning.

Keywords: Kernel Thinning · Support Vector · Machines Classification

1 Introduction

Kernel methods are a powerful tool in machine learning, enabling the modeling of complex nonlinear relationships by implicitly mapping input data into high-dimensional feature spaces. Among these methods, Support Vector Machines (SVMs) [3] have shown remarkable performance in both binary and multi-class classification tasks. However, a well-known limitation of kernel-based SVMs is their high computational cost, especially during training, whose complexity typically surpasses the quadratic cost [15,19]. This drawback hinders their applicability to large-scale datasets.

To mitigate this issue, various approximation techniques have been proposed. One such method is the use of Random Fourier Features (RFF) [13,14], which approximates the kernel function through an explicit feature mapping, thus enabling the use of linear models in the transformed space. Despite its practical success, RFF does not reduce the number of training samples, so the size of the dataset remains a bottleneck in terms of memory and computational cost.

An alternative approach is the Nyström method [20], which approximates the full kernel matrix using a low-rank decomposition based on a subset of randomly selected samples. While effective, its reliance on uniform or random sampling may result in suboptimal approximations, especially in scenarios where the data distribution is highly non-uniform or structured.

Recently, a novel technique known as kernel thinning (KT) [7] has been introduced, which seeks to select a subset of training points that best approximate the original kernel function. KT can be interpreted as a principled coreset selection method [8] for kernel-based learning. Unlike random subsampling, KT aims to identify a subset that minimizes a discrepancy measure with respect to the full dataset, resulting in a more informative and compact representation.

In the context of kernel SVMs (KSVMs), the concept of an optimal subset is already embedded in the notion of support vectors—the critical data points that define the decision boundary. This observation naturally leads to the question: is there a relationship between the support vectors identified by an SVM and the coreset obtained through KT?

Beyond this conceptual question, several practical concerns arise when combining KT with KSVMs. For instance, how does the classification performance evolve as a function of the coreset size? Can KT significantly reduce the computational cost of SVM training without degrading performance? How does the optimization process (e.g., number of iterations to convergence) behave when training is performed on the full dataset versus on the coreset?

To the best of our knowledge, the integration of KT with KSVMs has not yet been fully explored in the literature. Moreover, experimental studies analyzing the trade-offs involved in this combination, particularly in terms of classification accuracy, computational efficiency, and the relationship between coresets and support vectors, remain scarce. In this work, we address these gaps by conducting a comprehensive empirical analysis on a diverse set of classification datasets:

- We evaluate how SVM balanced accuracy evolves as a function of training set size by comparing the full dataset to the KT-induced coreset. We found that reducing a dataset by half or a quarter did not significantly affect the balance accuracy of most of the studied datasets.
- We investigate which elements of the KT coreset overlap with or approximate the full set of SVM support vectors. The overlap is proportional to the reduction. However, the support vectors of the fully trained SVM are effectively approximated by those of the KT-SVM, which explains the good performance of the KT methods.
- We study computational optimization based on: (1) the convergence behavior of the SVM optimization process when trained on the full dataset versus on the coreset, in terms of the number of iterations; and (2) the efficiency of hyperparameter selection. As a result, training with KT coresets reduces sample size and the number of iterations required and additionally lowers the computational cost of grid search.

This paper is organized as follows. In Sect. 2, we introduce KSVM and kernel thinning. Then, in Sect. 3, we present the experimental section, explaining the methodology and showing the results. Finally, in Sect. 4, we conclude with a conclusion and discuss some further work.

2 Kernel SVM and Kernel Thinning

2.1 SVM

One of the most important models for supervised learning are the Kernel Support Vector Machines (KSVM) [3]. Consider a training dataset $(x_1, y_1), \ldots, (x_n, y_n)$, where $x_i \in X \subseteq \mathbb{R}^d$ represents the input data and $y_i \in \{-1, 1\}$ denotes binary class labels. For multiclass problems, a one-vs-one strategy [2] is typically employed, where a binary classifier is trained for each pair of classes and the final prediction is made via majority voting.

Let $k : X \times X \to \mathbb{R}$ be a positive definite kernel function; the predicted label for a new instance x is computed as $f(x) = \text{sign}\left(\sum_{i=1}^{n} y_i \alpha_i^* k(x_i, x) + b^*\right)$, where $\text{sign}(\cdot)$ is the sign function and the coefficients α_i^* and bias b^* are the solution to the dual optimization problem. The kernel function satisfies $k(x_i, x_j) = \phi(x_i)^T \phi(x_j)$ for some (possibly implicit) feature map ϕ. The primal problem is

$$\min_{w,b,\xi} \left\{ \frac{1}{2} w^T w + C \sum_{i=1}^{n} \xi_i \right\} \quad \text{s.t.} \quad \begin{cases} y_i(w^T \phi(x_i) + b) \geq 1 - \xi_i, \\ \xi_i \geq 0, i \in \{1, \ldots n\}. \end{cases} \quad (1)$$

But, rather than solving the primal formulation, which depends on the explicit feature map $\phi(x)$ (often unknown or infinite-dimensional), we solve the dual problem:

$$\min_{\alpha} \left\{ \frac{1}{2} \alpha^T y_i y_j k(x_i, x_j) \alpha - \sum_i \alpha_i \right\} \quad \text{s.t.} \quad \begin{cases} y^T \alpha = 0, \\ 0 \leq \alpha_i \leq C, \ i \in \{1, \ldots n\}. \end{cases} \quad (2)$$

Once this dual problem is solved, the optimal weight vector can be expressed as $w^* = \sum_{i \in SV} \alpha_i^* y_i \phi(x_i)$, where SV is the set of support vectors (those for which $\alpha_i^* > 0$). $b^* = \frac{1}{s} \sum_{j \in SV} \left(y_j - \sum_{i \in SV} \alpha_i^* y_i k(x_i, x_j) \right)$ represents the optimal bias term, where $s = |SV|$.

The dual problem (2) is commonly addressed using the Sequential Minimal Optimization (SMO) algorithm [12]. As noted by [18], SMO requires a minimum of n iterations, each with a computational complexity of $\mathcal{O}(n)$. Consequently, the overall training cost is bounded below by $\Omega(n^2)$-and often exceeds this-even when kernel evaluations are not taken into account. This makes SMO computationally impractical for large-scale datasets.

2.2 Kernel Thinning

Kernel Thinning (KT) [6,7,9] was introduced as a novel procedure for compressing a distribution P more effectively than by i.i.d. sampling or standard thinning techniques. Given a reproducing kernel k, the method compresses n points of P into an approximation with a random set of size $\frac{n}{2m}$ (where m is a prefixed integer) with comparable worst-case integration error in the associated Reproducing Kernel Hilbert Space (RKHS) [16], with an overall computational cost of $\mathcal{O}(n^2)$. Besides the base kernel k, KT also uses a so called square root kernel, defined as follows.

Algorithm 1. Kernel Thinning Return coreset of size $\lfloor n/2^m \rfloor$ with small $\mathrm{MMD}_{k^\star}$

Require: Kernels (k, k_{rt}), input points $S_n = (x_i)_{i=1}^n$, thinning parameter $m \in \mathbb{N}$, probabilities $(\delta_i)_{i=1}^{\lfloor n/2 \rfloor}$
1: $(S^{(m,\ell)})_{\ell=1}^{2^m} \leftarrow \text{KT-split}(k_{\mathrm{rt}}, S_n, m, (\delta_i)_{i=1}^{\lfloor n/2 \rfloor})$ ▷ Split S_n into 2^m candidate coresets of size $\lfloor n/2^m \rfloor$
2: $S_{\mathrm{KT}} \leftarrow \text{KT-swap}(k, S_n, (S^{(m,\ell)})_{\ell=1}^{2^m})$ ▷ Select best coreset and iteratively refine
3: **return** S_{KT}

Definition 1 (Square-root Kernel). *Let $k : \mathbb{R}^d \times \mathbb{R}^d \to \mathbb{R}$ be a symmetric, positive-definite kernel. A function $k_{\mathrm{rt}} : \mathbb{R}^d \times \mathbb{R}^d \to \mathbb{R}$ is called a square-root kernel for k if $k_{\mathrm{rt}}(x, \cdot)$ is square-integrable for all $x \in \mathbb{R}^d$, and*

$$k(x, y) = \int_{\mathbb{R}^d} k_{\mathrm{rt}}(x, z)\, k_{\mathrm{rt}}(y, z)\, dz \quad \text{for all } x, y \in \mathbb{R}^d.$$

The Square-root kernel for the Gaussian kernel $k(x,y) = \exp\left(-\frac{\|x-y\|^2}{2\sigma^2}\right)$, is $k_{rt}(x, y) = \left(\frac{2}{\pi\sigma^2}\right)^{d/4} \exp\left(-\frac{\|x-y\|^2}{\sigma^2}\right)$. KT steps are summarized in Algorithm 1 and explained in detail in [7] in Algorithms 1a and 1b. Algorithm 1a (KT-SPLIT) recursively partitions the input point sequence into 2^m candidate coresets of size approximately $n/2^m$. This is done via a randomized, online halving process using a square-root kernel k_{rt}, which encourages balance and diversity in each subset. Algorithm 1b (KT-SWAP) selects the best candidate coreset by minimizing the maximum mean discrepancy (MMD) [10,17] with respect to the full input. It then refines this coreset via a greedy swapping procedure to further reduce MMD, using the target kernel k. Together, these steps ensure that the final coreset achieves near-optimal MMD guarantees while reducing the number of points used to $\frac{n}{2^m}$.

3 Experiments

In this section, we present the experimental analysis, which aims to validate three preliminary hypotheses. The first hypothesis explores whether kernel thinning is an effective alternative for approximating a full KSVM. The second, if there is a link between the support vectors obtained from a KSVM trained on the training set and those obtained from a coreset computed via kernel thinning. The third hypothesis investigates whether kernel thinning leads to a reduction in computational cost, beyond the theoretical advantages previously discussed. To this end, we compare different KSVMs trained on either the full training dataset or a kernel thinning coreset, and analyze their balanced accuracy, number of iterations, support vectors, and predictions.

Table 1. Datasets dimensions, number of classes and classes distribution.

ID	Dataset Name	X Shape	Classes	Class Distribution
17	Breast Cancer Wisconsin (Diagnostic)	(569, 30)	2	(62.74%, 37.26%)
19	Car Evaluation	(1728, 15)	4	(22.22%, 3.99%, 70.02%, 3.76%)
27	Credit Approval	(690, 37)	2	(44.49%, 55.51%)
53	Iris	(150, 4)	3	(33.33%, 33.33%, 33.33%)
76	Nursery	(12960, 19)	5	(33.33%, 32.92%, 31.20%, 2.53%, 0.02%)
80	Optical Recognition of Handwritten Digits	(5620, 64)	10	(9.86%, 10.16%, 9.91%, 10.18%, 10.11%, 9.93%, 9.93%, 10.07%, 9.86%, 10.00%)
101	Tic-Tac-Toe Endgame	(958, 18)	2	(34.66%, 65.34%)
144	German Credit Data	(1000, 48)	2	(70.00%, 30.00%)
267	Banknote Authentication	(1372, 4)	2	(55.54%, 44.46%)
327	Phishing Websites	(11055, 30)	2	(44.31%, 55.69%)
468	Online Shoppers Purchasing Intention Dataset	(12330, 26)	2	(84.53%, 15.47%)
529	Early Stage Diabetes Risk Prediction	(520, 16)	2	(38.46%, 61.54%)
544	Estimation of Obesity Levels Based On Eating Habits and Physical Condition	(2111, 23)	7	(12.88%, 13.60%, 16.63%, 14.07%, 15.35%, 13.74%, 13.74%)
850	Raisin	(900, 7)	2	(50.00%, 50.00%)
863	Maternal Health Risk	(1014, 6)	3	(26.82%, 40.04%, 33.14%)

3.1 Datasets and Preprocessing

This study combines a diverse selection of publicly available classification datasets, covering binary and multiclass problems. We selected 15 datasets from the UCI Machine Learning Repository [5]. These datasets cover a range of shapes and complexities for comprehensive evaluation (as seen in Table 1). All datasets can be accessed via the fetch_ucirepo(id) function from the *ucimlrepo* library, where id corresponds to the dataset **ID** in Table 1. Once the dataset is downloaded, we preprocess the labels, first ensuring they are consistent. After this, the labels and categorical features are transformed using one-hot encoding. In the next step, we split it into training and test sets using a 50% stratified split, ensuring reproducibility by setting the random seed to 42. The test data is used to report the balanced accuracy results, while the training set is employed for hyperparameters tuning and training through cross-validation. Finally, data is normalized without introducing bias into the test sets.

3.2 Experimental Methodology

To evaluate the balanced accuracy, number of iterations, support vectors, and predictions of the KSVM, we begin by determining the optimal hyperparameters for each model-dataset pair. To this end, we perform a 5-fold cross-validation grid search on the training data over the following parameter space:

- γ: 10 values logarithmically spaced between 2^{-2} and 2^7, each scaled by the input dimensionality d of the dataset.
- C: 10 values logarithmically spaced between 10^{-2} and 10^5.

After identifying the optimal hyperparameters, we train the KSVM on the corresponding training data. In the case of coreset selection, each experiment is repeated 15 times to ensure robustness and account for stochastic variability of the models due to the KT coreset selection. Finally, the reported values—balanced accuracy, number of iterations, number of supports vectores—represent the mean across all repetitions, providing a reliable estimate of each model's performance. The training process for a KSVM using kernel thinning is as follows:

1. First, we select a subset X_c of samples from the training set using Algorithm 1. The parameters involved in this step are the kernel and the thinning parameter m.
   - The kernel must have a squared-kernel equivalent. Accordingly, we adopt the Gaussian kernel, with the optimal γ chosen from $\gamma \in [2^{-2}, 2^7]/d$.
   - The thinning parameter m controls the coreset size and its fidelity in approximating the kernel. We consider $m \in 1, 2, 3, 4$, yielding coreset sizes of $\frac{n}{2^m}$, where n is the original training set size.
2. Then, we train a Gaussian kernel SVM using the optimized γ, the selected subset X_c, and the regularization parameter C obtained by grid search on X_c. Additionally, we set the KSVM tolerance to 10^{-3}, for all models.

The prediction process for a new input set X consists solely of evaluating the KSVM trained on X_c.

We evaluate three distinct KSVM training strategies:

a) **KT_m**: This model involves an indivisible end-to-end pipeline consisting of first computing the coreset using kernel thinning with a fixed value of m, and secondly, training the KSVM on the resulting subset after obtaining the optimal γ, C.
b) **sub$_m$KSVM**: This model involves training a KSVM on the full training dataset, but using the hyperparameters (γ, C) previously obtained from the KT_m model.
c) **Full KSVM**: This model is trained on the full training dataset, with hyperparameters selected through a grid search performed on the full data.

All implementations are based on the SVC class from [11], which itself is built on the LIBSVM library [2]. The KT coreset selection relies on the original Python code provided by the authors [7].

3.3 Balanced Accuracy Analysis

The balanced accuracy for KSVM and the mean balanced accuracy over the 15 experiments for model KT_m is reported in Table 2, for every dataset and value of m. Additionally, the average of each column is shown below the table. Note that if a row contains a missing value, it is excluded from the average computation. Moreover, for each dataset, we compared the test predictions of KSVM and each KT_m using the Wilcoxon signed-rank test, with the Bonferroni

Table 2. Mean and standard deviation of balanced accuracy for KSVM vs KT-KSVM across datasets and varying m. Significant differences are in bold.

ID	KSVM	KT m = 1	KT m = 2	KT m = 3	KT m = 4
17	97.13	96.11 ± 1.12	95.1 ± 1.84	94.91 ± 1.88	**92.31 ± 3.38**
19	93.22	**87.14 ± 3.18**	77.1 ± 4.71	65.11 ± 6.64	51.74 ± 4.36
27	87.56	88.02 ± 0.26	86.92 ± 1.55	84.62 ± 4.12	84.07 ± 4.16
53	98.55	96.2 ± 2.59	95.53 ± 3.42	93.36 ± 4.96	**86.41 ± 4.18**
76	80.0	78.85 ± 0.36	**75.81 ± 0.61**	72.57 ± 1.48	68.53 ± 1.81
80	99.12	98.48 ± 0.18	**97.96 ± 0.2**	96.77 ± 0.28	95.3 ± 0.38
101	98.61	97.58 ± 0.82	96.71 ± 0.43	**93.66 ± 3.81**	69.75 ± 3.14
144	68.97	67.25 ± 2.37	**64.35 ± 2.9**	**61.72 ± 3.55**	58.42 ± 3.74
267	100.0	99.94 ± 0.1	99.67 ± 0.22	99.39 ± 0.45	98.58 ± 1.01
327	95.4	94.77 ± 0.23	93.56 ± 0.29	**92.52 ± 0.3**	**91.47 ± 0.6**
468	82.26	80.95 ± 0.54	79.89 ± 0.91	77.21 ± 1.54	74.5 ± 1.86
529	96.69	94.4 ± 1.39	**92.17 ± 0.87**	90.39 ± 1.45	88.18 ± 3.48
544	95.23	91.45 ± 1.11	**84.9 ± 2.17**	70.54 ± 2.91	60.8 ± 2.55
850	86.14	86.16 ± 0.76	86.26 ± 0.66	84.99 ± 1.47	**84.58 ± 2.24**
863	78.1	**68.12 ± 1.61**	**62.35 ± 2.12**	60.36 ± 4.49	56.84 ± 3.24
Mean	90.47 ± 9.47	88.36 ± 10.48	85.89 ± 11.84	82.54 ± 13.50	77.43 ± 15.46

correction applied [1,4]. The null hypothesis, i.e. the prediction distributions of the two models are equivalent, is rejected if $p \leq 0.0125$ for $\alpha = 0.05$. In this case KT_m, usually with a lower accuracy, is highlighted in bold.

First, if we focus on $m = 1$, when the training dataset is halved, we see that the results on only two of the 15 datasets (19 and 863) are significantly different. Increasing m to two also affects datasets 80, 144, 529 and 544. For $m = 3$, eight out of 13 datasets have significative differences, and for $m = 4$, all of them have significant differences. For imbalanced datasets, KT may perform worse, especially when certain combinations of m and γ do not include representatives from all classes. Nevertheless, we can conclude that, in general, using $m = 1$ or even $m = 2$ is an effective choice for reducing the size of the training dataset while maintaining balanced accuracy.

3.4 Support Vectors and Kernel Thinning KSVM

In this section we investigate the link between support vectors of KT_m and $sub_m KSVM$, and their coresets.

In Table 3, we presents the percentage of support vectors of $sub_m KSVM$ that are also included in the coreset of KT_m. In the "Average" row we show the mean of each column, excluding any missing value. The final "Estimation" row shows the percentage of data remaining after reduction based on the coreset size, computed as $\frac{100}{2^m}$.

Table 3. Percentage of support vectors of $sub_m KSVM$ that are included in the kernel thinning coreset.

m Dataset ID	1	2	3	4
17	47.71 ± 6.51	25.6 ± 7.05	10.19 ± 3.69	6.49 ± 2.77
19	46.51 ± 2.18	23.79 ± 2.03	12.04 ± 1.07	6.11 ± 1.01
27	47.83 ± 1.27	22.88 ± 1.64	11.54 ± 1.17	5.2 ± 1.24
53	46.07 ± 9.87	20.54 ± 12.66	13.81 ± 4.5	5.53 ± 4.66
76	47.29 ± 0.53	24.29 ± 0.82	12.31 ± 0.48	6.29 ± 0.43
80	49.83 ± 0.87	22.6 ± 0.67	10.57 ± 0.83	4.42 ± 0.7
101	46.67 ± 3.53	24.48 ± 3.29	12.14 ± 3.91	5.28 ± 0.89
144	47.42 ± 1.76	24.06 ± 1.04	12.48 ± 1.11	5.92 ± 0.79
267	34.97 ± 17.04	19.07 ± 11.13	10.16 ± 6.3	5.26 ± 5.72
327	42.5 ± 0.96	21.74 ± 0.91	11.47 ± 0.83	6.22 ± 0.67
468	45.43 ± 0.84	23.26 ± 0.38	12.02 ± 0.43	6.06 ± 0.21
529	35.52 ± 2.3	8.09 ± 3.54	5.1 ± 3.79	2.88 ± 2.43
544	46.92 ± 2.09	24.18 ± 1.89	12.47 ± 0.92	5.84 ± 0.66
850	44.68 ± 2.94	23.38 ± 2.29	11.88 ± 1.93	6.02 ± 1.27
863	34.42 ± 1.62	18.87 ± 1.26	10.81 ± 0.66	5.72 ± 0.62
Mean	44.25 ± 5.07	21.79 ± 4.26	11.27 ± 1.96	5.55 ± 0.91
Estimation	50.00	25.00	12.50	6.25

Interestingly, on average, the prevalence of support vectors in the coreset is slightly lower than in "Estimation" (although this falls in the interval with size the standard deviation). This suggests that the kernel thinning coreset does not preferentially include support vectors, since their presence has the same expected value as if they were selected uniformly at random without replacement. To deepen our analysis, we computed the number of support vectors used by KT_m and by $sub_m KSVM$. The results are reported in Table 4.

As shown in Table 4, KT_m consistently uses fewer support vectors than $sub_m KSVM$, as expected due to the reduced training size. However, the number of support vectors still exceeds the proportional reduction one would anticipate—for instance, being half for $m = 1$, a quarter for $m = 2$, and so on- indicating that KT_m retains key vectors to capture the underlying problem complexity despite the reduced training size.

Based on the two previous observations in this section, concerning the support representation, we examined the relationship between the support vectors of KT_m and those of the $sub_m KSVM$ using the Euclidean distance. To this end, we computed the distance from each support vector of $sub_m KSVM$ to the closest support vector in the set of support vectors of KT_m. These resulting dis-

Table 4. Number of support vectors in KT_m and $sub_m KSVM$.

ID	KT m = 1	sub m = 1	KT m = 2	sub m = 2	KT m = 3	sub m = 3	KT m = 4	sub m = 4
17	33 ± 15	52 ± 26	20 ± 9	46 ± 24	13 ± 5	45 ± 18	9 ± 2	52 ± 17
19	178 ± 25	295 ± 48	111 ± 31	301 ± 108	61 ± 14	254 ± 94	36 ± 5	263 ± 79
27	116 ± 15	192 ± 19	59 ± 11	170 ± 20	30 ± 3	149 ± 12	16 ± 3	136 ± 14
53	12 ± 3	16 ± 5	8 ± 2	12 ± 4	8 ± 2	20 ± 8	4 ± 0	30 ± 26
76	983 ± 119	1632 ± 211	596 ± 71	1555 ± 177	421 ± 56	1769 ± 427	275 ± 18	1797 ± 414
80	627 ± 66	929 ± 117	423 ± 19	980 ± 70	264 ± 13	973 ± 75	153 ± 6	943 ± 88
101	100 ± 28	114 ± 44	69 ± 9	114 ± 40	40 ± 4	74 ± 18	27 ± 3	284 ± 100
144	175 ± 20	342 ± 25	88 ± 16	331 ± 34	49 ± 9	337 ± 50	25 ± 4	311 ± 47
267	10 ± 2	11 ± 3	11 ± 6	14 ± 9	16 ± 7	21 ± 12	12 ± 6	22 ± 13
327	1027 ± 245	1587 ± 345	458 ± 50	1198 ± 93	246 ± 57	1116 ± 128	130 ± 23	1054 ± 87
468	1405 ± 60	2752 ± 93	691 ± 45	2697 ± 63	339 ± 37	2708 ± 69	169 ± 23	2694 ± 71
529	71 ± 15	94 ± 22	48 ± 9	90 ± 17	27 ± 5	94 ± 30	15 ± 2	73 ± 23
544	270 ± 11	380 ± 20	172 ± 9	381 ± 23	113 ± 4	522 ± 78	61 ± 1	576 ± 42
850	84 ± 13	162 ± 14	47 ± 10	166 ± 18	28 ± 7	171 ± 14	18 ± 5	180 ± 13
863	161 ± 21	289 ± 25	93 ± 15	301 ± 47	48 ± 9	345 ± 37	25 ± 4	336 ± 36

tances were sorted and plotted as percentiles, as shown in Fig. 1. The behavior is similar across all datasets, so only three are shown.

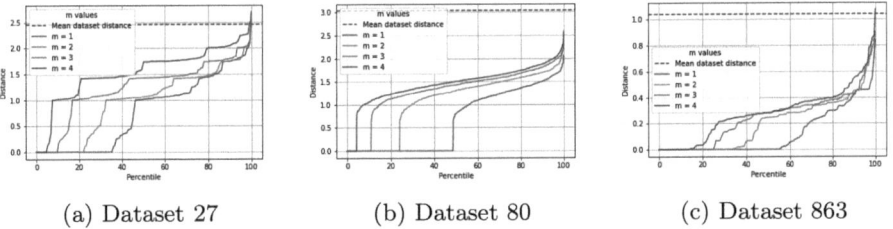

(a) Dataset 27 (b) Dataset 80 (c) Dataset 863

Fig. 1. Percentile plots of distances from sub_mKSVM to KT_m support vectors.

The plots reveal that as m increases-corresponding to a smaller coreset size- the average distance to the nearest support vector in KT_m increases. This trend is expected, as reducing the number of points increases the likelihood that selected samples lie farther from the original support vectors. Nevertheless, the distance is 0 for a sizeable amount of SVs (see Fig. 1) and all of these distances consistently remain below the overall mean pairwise distance between data points, indicated by the horizontal dashed line.

It is noteworthy that KT_m requires fewer support vectors, as it is trained on a reduced coreset. At it has a direct consequence on the number of iteration, since the number of SVs divided by two is a lower bound of the number of iteration [18]. Consequently, $sub_m KSVM$ may require fewer iterations to converge. To examine this, we analyze the average number of iterations required by each model across experiments, using a convergence tolerance of 10^{-3}. Results are reported in Table 5, where column averages exclude datasets with missing values.

Table 5. Number of iterations taken by KT_m and $sub_m KSVM$

ID	KT m = 1	sub m = 1	KT m = 2	sub m = 2	KT m = 3	sub m = 3	KT m = 4	sub m = 4
17	252 ± 224	508 ± 389	127 ± 68	997 ± 1121	58 ± 27	664 ± 723	25 ± 12	409 ± 353
19	670 ± 242	3585 ± 1790	252 ± 112	2174 ± 1396	98 ± 36	2403 ± 1618	54 ± 76	2346 ± 1546
27	204 ± 116	480 ± 393	103 ± 27	713 ± 476	68 ± 20	978 ± 497	48 ± 14	4806 ± 9932
53	13 ± 9	14 ± 7	9 ± 8	12 ± 4	11 ± 5	22 ± 8	2 ± 2	19 ± 14
76	5167 ± 562	5533 ± 953	4377 ± 1145	5558 ± 782	4230 ± 1149	5102 ± 588	3747 ± 865	5338 ± 621
80	106 ± 31	141 ± 28	93 ± 18	140 ± 5	67 ± 12	139 ± 6	45 ± 10	137 ± 7
101	3415 ± 1386	4793 ± 2457	2829 ± 623	9185 ± 3455	1097 ± 265	5297 ± 1689	98 ± 92	2439 ± 2474
144	710 ± 777	1439 ± 2010	510 ± 455	2344 ± 2298	191 ± 171	3923 ± 6779	88 ± 48	8018 ± 11040
267	1223 ± 832	1025 ± 156	476 ± 383	671 ± 333	191 ± 104	382 ± 230	106 ± 72	435 ± 238
327	2849 ± 568	4651 ± 1037	1449 ± 350	3935 ± 1219	795 ± 167	3632 ± 724	453 ± 224	3986 ± 2998
468	51525 ± 62339	126461 ± 148345	37504 ± 45378	173590 ± 136257	13334 ± 10818	163500 ± 137530	8030 ± 4934	211337 ± 212514
529	164 ± 13	231 ± 28	114 ± 12	228 ± 40	58 ± 11	234 ± 58	34 ± 6	240 ± 104
544	3407 ± 988	6815 ± 1534	1592 ± 479	6820 ± 1626	196 ± 200	2246 ± 1797	41 ± 11	1103 ± 349
850	2192 ± 2895	8676 ± 15139	1911 ± 6016	12618 ± 44669	158 ± 372	860 ± 1538	28 ± 10	361 ± 318
863	280 ± 78	703 ± 329	251 ± 248	1400 ± 1837	281 ± 379	9112 ± 28602	84 ± 78	21888 ± 39999
Mean	4812 ± 13019	11004 ± 32060	3440 ± 9506	14692 ± 44115	1389 ± 3473	13233 ± 41649	859 ± 2199	17524 ± 53905

As shown in the results, KT_m consistently requires fewer iterations than $sub_m KSVM$ for any value of m. Furthermore, the number of iterations decreases as the coreset size becomes smaller. This observation is particularly significant: kernel thinning reduces computational cost not only by lowering the number of training samples, but also by reducing the number of optimization iterations. This is especially beneficial given that each SVM iteration has a computational complexity of $\Omega(n^2)$ [18].

3.5 Hyperparameter Selection Efficiency Using KT as a Surrogate

Grid search procedures typically require evaluating a large number of candidate models, making hyperparameter tuning computationally intensive. Consequently, it is important to identify strategies that reduce this cost while maintaining reliable performance. Kernel thinning (KT_m) could serve as a fast surrogate: first identifying optimal hyperparameters on the KT coreset, and then applying those settings to train the full KSVM.

To evaluate this approach, we compare the balanced accuracy of $sub_m KSVM$ against that of the full KSVM. Table 6 presents the mean balanced accuracy across 15 runs for $sub_m KSVM$ and one run for the full KSVM, reported for each dataset and value of m. Column averages are shown below the table, excluding rows with missing values from the calculation.

For each dataset, we compared the test predictions of sub_mKSVM and the full KSVM using the Wilcoxon signed-rank test with Bonferroni correction [1,4]. The null hypothesis is rejected with $\alpha = 0.05$. Significant cases are highlighted in bold.

Table 6. Balanced accuracy of KSVM vs. sub$_m$KSVM.

ID	KSVM	sub KSVM m = 1	sub KSVM m = 2	sub KSVM m = 3	sub KSVM m = 4
17	97.13	96.16 ± 0.5	96.24 ± 0.71	96.46 ± 0.8	96.97 ± 0.76
19	93.22	92.73 ± 0.95	**91.04 ± 2.41**	**90.99 ± 1.81**	**91.76 ± 1.52**
27	87.56	87.61 ± 0.18	87.67 ± 0.23	87.67 ± 0.23	85.59 ± 3.62
53	98.55	96.74 ± 1.5	96.01 ± 1.23	96.62 ± 1.02	91.97 ± 14.9
76	80.0	80.0 ± 0.0	80.0 ± 0.01	79.28 ± 1.15	78.96 ± 1.27
80	99.12	99.06 ± 0.05	99.1 ± 0.04	99.09 ± 0.07	99.06 ± 0.09
101	98.61	97.83 ± 0.72	97.4 ± 1.02	98.27 ± 0.5	98.61 ± 0.69
144	68.97	68.16 ± 0.68	68.02 ± 1.06	68.09 ± 1.4	**67.66 ± 1.8**
267	100.0	100.0 ± 0.0	100.0 ± 0.0	100.0 ± 0.0	100.0 ± 0.0
327	95.4	95.45 ± 0.24	95.05 ± 0.32	94.62 ± 0.41	94.09 ± 0.6
468	82.26	82.03 ± 0.22	82.17 ± 0.15	82.15 ± 0.17	82.14 ± 0.16
529	96.69	96.17 ± 0.96	95.86 ± 1.08	95.86 ± 1.24	95.03 ± 1.29
544	95.23	95.25 ± 0.3	95.12 ± 0.62	91.75 ± 1.59	**90.18 ± 1.86**
850	86.14	86.24 ± 0.65	86.33 ± 0.64	86.63 ± 0.52	86.9 ± 0.41
863	78.1	76.42 ± 1.39	74.13 ± 3.48	**70.42 ± 3.02**	**70.58 ± 2.15**
Mean	90.47 ± 9.47	89.99 ± 9.54	89.61 ± 9.68	89.19 ± 10.15	88.63 ± 10.05

The results show that only in 7 out of 60 model comparisons, the full KSVM exhibits a statistically significant advantage, and 4 of those 7 correspond to a rather restrictive $m = 4$. In terms of datasets, for $m = 1$, this effect is not observed in any dataset. For $m = 2$, it is only observed in dataset 19, and for $m = 3$, it also appears in dataset 863. Notably, datasets 19 and 863 are the ones that fail for $m = 1$ with KT_m (see Table 2). These findings suggest that kernel thinning can serve as an effective surrogate for hyperparameter selection, substantially reducing the computational burden of grid search. By tuning on a significantly smaller coreset, one can retain nearly the same predictive performance while greatly decreasing the training cost of the models involved.

Considering that the computational cost of KSVM is $\Omega(n^2)$, and that kernel thinning also incurs a cost of $\mathcal{O}(n^2)$, we analyze the overall complexity of performing a grid search, where n_c is the number of regularization parameter (C) values and n_γ is the number of kernel parameter (γ) values. For the full KSVM, the total cost is $n_c n_\gamma n^2$. For KT_m, the cost becomes $n_c n_\gamma \left(\frac{n}{2^m}\right)^2 + n_\gamma n^2$, accounting for both training on the reduced dataset and the initial thinning step. KT_m is faster when $n_c n_\gamma \left(\frac{n}{2^m}\right)^2 + n_\gamma n^2 < n_c n_\gamma n^2$ and this is when $n_c > 1 + \frac{1}{2^{2m}}$. Therefore, KT_m is beneficial when $n_c \geq 2$, which is typically the case, since otherwise there would be no point in tuning the hyperparameter C.

4 Conclusions and Future Work

The experimental results provide strong empirical support for the three hypotheses under investigation. First, we demonstrated that KT can be efficiently used with KSVMs. Secondly that although KT_m and $sub_m KSVM$ achieve similar balanced accuracy across most datasets, their support vectors do not substantially overlap. This suggests that kernel thinning does not explicitly capture traditional support vector structure, yet still produces models of comparable predictive quality.

Finally, we observed that KT_m consistently reduces computational requirements—not only by reducing the dataset size, but also by lowering the number of SVM iterations. This leads to meaningful runtime improvements, particularly valuable during hyperparameter optimization. Indeed, our analysis shows that KT_m can serve as an effective surrogate for grid search: in most cases, the hyperparameters found on the coreset yielded performance nearly equivalent to that of a fully tuned KSVM.

Overall, these findings confirm that kernel thinning offers a practical and theoretically grounded strategy for scalable kernel SVM training and hyperparameter tuning, with small loss in predictive performance.

This study opens several avenues for future research. First, it would be valuable to explore how to adapt kernel thinning (KT) to imbalanced problems to ensure representative selection from all classes. In principle it is not clear how to adapt well-known techniques such as SMOTE, but simpler alternative mechanisms such as applying KT only on the larger classes and adding afterwards the small ones to the final sample could be explored to check whether this ensures short training times and good classification results. Notice also that this would not be an issue in support vector regression.

Second, our analysis shows that KT selects informative coresets and, also, that about half the KT supports vectors coincide with the support vectors of the full SVM when $m = 1$. This suggests to further explore this experimental relationship between the KT and full SVM support vector subsets, particularly when applying sub_mSVMs, as they and the full SVM share the entire sample: if their support vectors largely agree, the KT end result would be strong SVM models but with a much smaller hyperparametrization cost.

Finally, although we focused on classification tasks using Gaussian kernels, future work could extend KT to other kernel types, such as Matérn. Also, support vector regression would be a different but very important learning objective where KT could prove to be valuable.

We are currently working on these and other ideas as, in our opinion, KT can be a valuable tool to reduce SVM training times while yielding valuable models.

Acknowledgments. The authors acknowledge financial support from project PID2022-139856NB-I00 funded by MCIN/ AEI/10.13039/ 501100011033 / FEDER, UE and project, IDEA-CM (TEC-2024/COM-89) from the CAM and from the ELLIS Unit Madrid, Cátedra UAM-IIC de Ciencia de Datos y Aprendizaje Automático and FPI-UAM. The authors acknowledge computational support from the Centro de Computación Científica-Universidad Autónoma de Madrid (CCC-UAM).

References

1. Benavoli, A., Corani, G., Mangili, F.: Should we really use post-hoc tests based on mean-ranks? JMLR **17**(1), 152–161 (2016)
2. Chang, C.C., Lin, C.J.: LIBSVM: a library for support vector machines. ACM Trans. Intell. Syst. Technol. (TIST) **2**(3), 1–27 (2011)
3. Cortes, C., Vapnik, V.: Support-vector networks. Mach. Learn. **20**, 273–297 (1995)
4. Demšar, J.: Statistical comparisons of classifiers over multiple data sets. JMLR **7**, 1–30 (2006)
5. Dheeru, D., Karra Taniskidou, E.: UCI machine learning repository (2025). http://archive.ics.uci.edu/ml
6. Dwivedi, R., Mackey, L.: Generalized kernel thinning. arXiv preprint arXiv:2110.01593 (2021)
7. Dwivedi, R., Mackey, L.: Kernel thinning. JMLR **25**(152), 1–77 (2024)
8. Feldman, D.: Core-sets: updated survey. Sampling techniques for supervised or unsupervised tasks, pp. 23–44 (2020)
9. Gong, A., Choi, K., Dwivedi, R.: Supervised kernel thinning. arXiv preprint arXiv:2410.13749 (2024)
10. Gretton, A., Borgwardt, K.M., Rasch, M.J., Schölkopf, B., Smola, A.: A kernel two-sample test. J. Mach. Learn. Res. **13**(1), 723–773 (2012)
11. Pedregosa, F., Varoquaux, G., et al.: Scikit-learn: machine learning in Python. JMLR **12**, 2825–2830 (2011)
12. Platt, J.: Sequential minimal optimization: a fast algorithm for training support vector machines. Adv. Kernel Methods-Support Vector Learn. **208** (1998)
13. Rahimi, A., Recht, B.: Random features for large-scale kernel machines. In: NeurIPS, vol. 20, pp. 1177–1184 (2007)
14. Rahimi, A., Recht, B.: Weighted sums of random kitchen sinks: replacing minimization with randomization in learning. In: NeurIPS, vol. 21, pp. 1313–1320 (2008)
15. Speckhard, D., Bechtel, T., Ghiringhelli, L.M., Kuban, M., Rigamonti, S., Draxl, C.: How big is big data? Faraday Discuss. **256**, 483–502 (2025)
16. Sriperumbudur, B.K., Gretton, A., Fukumizu, K., Schölkopf, B., Lanckriet, G.R.: Hilbert space embeddings and metrics on probability measures. J. Mach. Learn. Res. **11**, 1517–1561 (2010)
17. Tolstikhin, I., Sriperumbudur, B.K., Muandet, K.: Minimax estimation of kernel mean embeddings. J. Mach. Learn. Res. **18**(86), 1–47 (2017)
18. Torres-Barrán, A., Alaíz, C.M., Dorronsoro, J.R.: Faster SVM training via conjugate SMO. Pattern Recogn. **111**, 107644 (2021)
19. Wang, M., Fu, W., He, X., Hao, S., Wu, X.: A survey on large-scale machine learning. IEEE Trans. Knowl. Data Eng. **34**(6) (2020)
20. Williams, C.K., Seeger, M.: Using the Nyström method to speed up kernel machines. In: Neural Information Processing Systems. vol. 13, pp. 682–688 (2001)

Author Index

A
Álvarez, Rubén 198
Álvarez-Crespo, Marta-María 143
Arroyo, Angel 210
Asencio-Cortés, G. 27
Aveleira-Mata, Jose 143

B
Banković, Zorana 237
Belo, Orlando 225
Benavides, Carmen 143
Botti, Vicent 64

C
Caballero-Gil, Pino 127
Calvo Calleja, Pablo 115
Calvo-Rolle, José Luis 143, 237
Cano, Blanca 309
Casteleiro-Roca, José-Luis 3
Chacón-Albero, Oriol 64
Chacón-Maldonado, A. M. 27
Chin, Tan Saw 180, 272
Chira, Camelia 79
Chiuzbăian, Rareș 91
Costa, Ana 52
Cyganek, Bogusław 39

D
Dalla-Porta Acosta, Alinne 115
De la Cal Martin, Enrique Antonio 103
Díaz Pérez, Ricardo 115
Díaz-Labrador, Anabel 3
Dicu, Mădălina 79
Díez-González, Javier 198
Divasón, Jose 296
Dorronsoro, José R. 309
Durães, Dalila 52

F
Fernández Llamas, Camino 15

Fernández, Ángela 309

G
G. Bringas, Pablo 260
Garcia Bringas, P. 250
García-Fischer, Agustín 3, 143
González Fernández, Irene 15
González, Enol García 79
González, Víctor M. 115
Gonzalez-Santocildes, Asier 250
Gorraiz-Bengoechea, Marta 250
Goto, Yuichi 284
Granados-Lopez, Diego 210
Gutiérrez, María Antonia 115

H
Herrero, Álvaro 210
Huerga-Pérez, Naamán 198
Hui, Chan Yeng 272

J
Jordán, Jaume 64
Julian, Vicente 64

K
Knapik, Mateusz 39
Kovacs, Norbert 91

L
Laña, Ibai 260
Lima-Bullones, Emilio 143
Looven, N. Martínez Van der 27

M
Măcelaru, Mara 91
Marques, Gabriel Souza 154
Martín, Francisco 15
Martinez-de-Pison, Francisco Javier 296
Michelena, Álvaro 3, 143
Mihirette, Samson 103

Moncada Martins, Fernando 115
Monteiro, Rui 225

N
Nižník, Jakub 166
Novais, Paulo 154

O
Oliveira, Bruno 225
Otero-González, Gonzalo Xoel 3

P
Pastor López, Iker 250
Peña-Narvaez, Juan Diego 15
Pernia-Espinoza, Alpha 296
Pop, Petrică C. 91

R
Rey-Arnal, Danel 260
Rodríguez Lera, Francisco J. 15
Rodriguez-Vega, Marcos 127
Rubiños, Manuel 3

S
Sánchez-Fernández, Álvaro 198
Santos, Flávio Arthur Oliveira 154

Simić, Dragan 237
Simić, Svetislav D. 237
Simić, Svetlana 237
Sobrín-Hidalgo, David 15
Sokol, Pavol 166
Souza, Maynara 154
Staňa, Richard 166

T
Tan, Qing 103
Troncoso, A. 27
Tun, Thinzar 284

U
Urdiales Sánchez, Sara 115

V
Villar, José R. 79, 115, 237
Villar-Val, Álvaro 210

W
Wen, Chin Jia 180

Z
Zanchettin, Cleber 154

MIX
Papier aus verantwortungsvollen Quellen
Paper from responsible sources
FSC® C105338

If you have any concerns about our products,
you can contact us on
ProductSafety@springernature.com

In case Publisher is established outside the EU,
the EU authorized representative is:
Springer Nature Customer Service Center GmbH
Europaplatz 3, 69115 Heidelberg, Germany

Printed by Libri Plureos GmbH
in Hamburg, Germany